A Jericho Wr

How to Write a Novel

That will sell well and satisfy your inner artist

Harry Bingham

PRAISE FOR A PREVIOUS EDITION

'**Best book on writing I have ever read**. There is a lot of drivel out there but this book's not one of them. Full of concrete, actionable advice and very well-written (as you would hope). Looking forward to reading again soon.'

– Lovely Rita, Amazon review

'**Excellent.** A full guide to writing for publication in every genre together with author examples (of how to do it and also how not to do it!!). **Extremely useful and crammed with snippets of all sorts**.'

– Intheamazone, Amazon review

'I should have read this before I started writing! Much of it I already knew but there was a lot that I didn't know. **If you are a writer and you would like to polish your craft then read this book**'.

– Jonathan Nicholas, Author

About Harry Bingham

Harry is the author of a dozen novels and several works of non-fiction. He's been published all over the world, been prize short- and long-listed, had his work adapted for TV and has won global critical acclaim. Best of all: he loves writing as much as he ever did. He's also the founder and owner of Jericho Writers.

If you want to explore Harry's fiction, your best bet is to start with *Talking to the Dead*, the first book in the Fiona Griffiths series.

A Jericho Writers Guide

How to Write a Novel

That will sell well and satisfy your inner artist

Harry Bingham

Published by Jericho Writers Publishing, 2020
www.jerichowriters.com

Copyright © Harry Bingham, 2020
The moral right of the author has been asserted.

Copyeditor: Karen Atkinson
Formatting: BB eBooks
Cover design: Kelly Finnegan

All rights reserved. No part of this publication may be reproduced, stored in a
retrieval system or transmitted, in any form or by any means without the prior
written permission of the author, nor be otherwise circulated in any form of
binding or cover other than that in which it is published and without a similar
condition being imposed on the purchaser.

TABLE OF CONTENTS

INTRODUCTION

This book will tell you how to write, but it is not a creative writing book. It will, as it happens, teach you to express yourself better than you have ever done before, better than you ever thought possible, but it is not a book about self-expression.

Self-expression, after all, is easy. You only have to please yourself. Our goal is more difficult than that, more difficult and more worthwhile. We're seeking to learn the delicate art of pleasing others – in this case, readers. Pleasing them enough that they will want to spend $4.99 on an e-book, $9.99 on a paperback, or $28.99 on a hardcover. Pleasing them enough that publishers will do the commercial mathematics and decide that your book is worth investing in. Pleasing them enough that a jaded literary agent will, on coming across your manuscript, suddenly sit more upright in her chair and leave her coffee stone-cold as she turns your pages.

These things are hard to achieve. A good literary agency in London or New York may well receive upwards of 5,000 unsolicited manuscripts a year. The agency will, most likely, take those manuscripts very seriously. After all, there will be times when that mountain of paper contains, somewhere in its bowels, a few chapters from the next J.K. Rowling, the next Dan Brown, the next Jonathan Franzen or Zadie Smith. The biggest new authors of tomorrow have a delightful habit of being unknown today, of coming from nowhere. Agencies need that new blood to survive and thrive. All agencies – or all the good ones, anyway – do their best to hunt out the talent in the torrent of submissions. A lot of time and manpower is dedicated to that hunt.

At the same time, shockingly few manuscripts make the grade. A top-quality agent may take on one manuscript in every two thousand. A younger, hungrier agent might look to take on one in a thousand, or even slightly more. It's not that these agents run any kind of quota system. If an agent happens to have taken on two new clients by the end of June, that doesn't mean they'll reject everything that comes their way from July to December. On the contrary: if a manuscript is good enough, it's good enough. An agent will take it on and be delighted to do so.

Agents are this selective for a reason. They only get paid if they make a sale, and it has become harder than ever to convince publishers to acquire new work. That's got something to do with the costs of launching a new book. These days, a budget of $75,000/£50,000 would be perfectly routine for much new fiction and mainstream non-fiction. That figures excludes the advance paid to you, the author, so the total financial risk riding on a new book is considerable. In addition, publishers know perfectly well that the majority of the books they launch will not succeed, that they will 'not meet budget expectations' in one of the standard euphemisms of the trade. And then too, recession has left the publishing landscape less hospitable than it was. Some major retailers have collapsed. Others are threatened. Sales of traditionally published fiction are falling steadily over time, and no stopping point has yet been reached.

I've spoken so far about traditional publishing, but many writers will already have concluded that they'd prefer to publish direct onto Amazon and find their readers that way. And that's great, really. (I have a long trad publication record myself, but I also self-publish and have done so very successfully. I love both routes to publication, and the rise of self-publishing has been the single best change for authors in my twenty-plus-year career.)

At the same time, the remorseless logic of the industry doesn't alter just because you choose to publish direct. Yes, self-published writers don't need the approval of a literary agent or a Big Five editor in order to get their work out there. But they do need the approval of readers. If you want to make a living from self-publishing, the single most critical determinant of your success will be: do readers like your books? If they read book #1 in a series, do they want to go on to read book #2? And then book #3? And so on. If the answers to those questions are firmly positive, everything else is just a matter of mechanics. If they're not, then no amount of marketing wizardry will ever give you the career you want.

Put bluntly, and no matter what your path to publication, your books won't sell unless they're good. Unless readers love them.

And that's what *this* book is all about. How to write books that people love.

In fact, this book aims to teach one of the hardest skills in the world, in preparation for one of the world's hardest professions. If you succeed at this game, you will have succeeded in something wonderful. For one thing, your new career will be one where you never have to work again, not because you won't have to put in long hours of graft (you'll be doing plenty of that), but because those hours will never seem like labour. They'll be work and play all in one; a way of earning money and a reliable pathway to a kind of joy, the joy of creation. And then too, being a writer has all kinds of other benefits. People will *like* your work. You'll get letters from strangers telling you how much you moved or thrilled them. You'll be respected. You'll be able to determine your own working habits and follow your preferences in a way that you never could in a more ordinary job. Being a writer may be one of the toughest jobs in the world, but it's also one of the best.

If you're the sort of person who likes to hurry on and get stuck in to things, feel free to flip forward a few pages and get stuck in. If you prefer to have everything laid out just so before you start, bear with me a moment or two longer.

First of all, you should be clear that this book is about novels (whether for children or adults) and it's about narrative non-fiction: the sort of non-fiction which tells a story. Travel, memoir, history and biography are the most obvious examples of narrative non-fiction, but a good writer may be able to bring the discipline and energy of narrative to entirely unexpected subjects. This book will deal with all those things too.

The book will not, however, deal with a whole host of other things that you may be interested in writing. It won't deal with news or feature journalism. It won't deal with screenplays for film or TV, nor with stage or radio drama. It won't teach you poetry (there's almost no market for that anyway), and it will have no especial focus on short stories (which are a fine way to practice certain skills, but which won't, in most cases, lead to any kind of durable writing career.) If you want to write poetry or short stories, you should certainly do so – but be aware that those are fields tilled more often by the creative writer than the working one.

Secondly, this book is going to teach the core skills of story-telling: story, character, prose style, and a whole host of attendant complexities. Those things are ones that few people master successfully and that you absolutely have to understand in order to succeed. But that focus also means that this book will not have space to talk about grammar and punctuation, nor will it take time off its more urgent tasks to remind you whether 'stationery' means 'pens and paper' or 'not moving'. You have to know those things – you need to be a perfectionist about them – but there are plenty of books that explain such matters perfectly well already. Nor will this book teach you about the commercial side of writing: the whole business of getting an agent, negotiating a book deal and all the rest of it.

If traditional publishing doesn't float your boat, boil your kettle, or stuff your pipe with baccy, then you probably want a good guide on self-publishing. I haven't (yet) written that book, but there are some good 'uns out there: David Gaughran, Joanna Penn, Tammi Labrecque and Nicholas Erik are all names you can trust.

Thirdly, and having just talked about a few things that this book doesn't do, let me be absolutely clear about one thing it *does* do. This book is designed for *any* novelist or narrative non-fiction author, no matter what their genre or interest. If you want to write high-end literary fiction, this book will accommodate your interests. But we're not snobbish. This book will be delighted to hold your hand and keep you company, no matter whether you write children's fiction, or crime thrillers, or young adult fantasy, or genre romance, or sci-fi, or paranormal romance, or any other genre whatsoever. Because the skills required for these different genres vary, I'll be very clear about what does and doesn't matter to you, given the particular ambitions you have. I will, very often, talk about 'novels' rather than 'novels and all narrative non-fiction works', simply because that latter phrase is too long and awkward to have clanking around us all through the book. Nevertheless, pretty much everything in here applies to pretty much everyone reading it. Where it's important to separate between fiction and non-fiction, or between genre fiction and literary fiction, I'll make those distinctions clear.

Next, you will want to know a little more about me. I'm a writer myself. I've written eleven novels, with more on the way. My work has ranged from crime fiction – my current area of interest – through to historical romance. My fiction isn't literary, but it stands at the fancier end of commercial: the sort of thing that intelligent people could read on the beach without having to hide the cover in embarrassment. I've also written four works of non-fiction, have edited an anthology of short stories, and have ghosted some things that I can't tell you about without biting down on my ever-handy cyanide pill.

If you have a question about how successful I am (and please don't pretend that the thought hasn't crossed your mind; we've got a few hundred pages to get through together, so we may as well be honest), it all depends on what you mean. I've always received generous advances from first-class publishers. My work has featured on bestseller lists. I've never won a literary prize, but I have been short- or long-listed for a couple of important ones. My work has been very warmly reviewed in pretty much every major newspaper in the US and the UK. My work has always sold in Britain and Commonwealth countries, but I've also had book deals in the US, Germany, France, Italy, Spain, China, Japan, and a whole raft of smaller countries besides. My career as an author has flourished.

At the same time, I've never been the kind of bestselling author whose name has become an international brand, nor am I the kind of minimally selling author who is nevertheless revered for his prose style or adulated for his dissection of post-Cartesian *ennui*. Rather, if I have authority in this field, it's for another reason. I run a company called Jericho Writers, which works intensively with new writers. We offer feedback on draft manuscripts. We run courses. We host events. We arrange mentoring. We do a great deal else besides.

What's more: we get people published. Hundreds of them. Some have ended up getting big international book deals with major global publishers. Others have been million-selling indie successes. Others have had tiny deals with small but passionate publishers and have more than met their publishing goals as a result.

And because so many writers come to us saying, in effect, 'I know this manuscript isn't yet right, but I don't know how to fix it,' we've had to become experts in answering that exact question. What's wrong with this story? Why doesn't this character feel lifelike and compelling? What's wrong with this sentence? Why does this dialogue feel heavy, rather than wooden?

Those questions have *precise* answers. They are technical questions with technical solutions. So no, I can't give you a miraculously good idea or turn you, overnight, into some kind of writing genius. But I can – and will – teach you completely reproducible techniques for making your writing better. That's the purpose of Jericho Writers. It's also the purpose of this book. Thousands and thousands of writers have improved their work by using the tools we're about to explore. There is no reason on earth why you shouldn't be able to join their number. I'm sure you will.

Needless to say, you should use this book just as you like. If you're wrestling with prose style, then skip forward to the bits that deal with prose, but make sure you come back to read everything else too. One of the hardest, and most satisfying, features of writing is the way that everything interrelates. If your prose style lets you down, then your characterisation will be impoverished. It can't not be. If your characters are weak, your plot will feel a little mechanical. If your plot is mechanical, your book's sense of place and time will feel stagey and unconvincing. And so on.

Furthermore, this book won't be a single-read affair. If you're at an early stage in your writing journey, some parts of this book will strike you as illuminating and essential. If you come back to them later, those parts will seem obvious, while other passages will seem to glow with meaning. And this, with luck, is a journey that will never end. Securing your first book deal doesn't mean you're now a qualified writer; it just means you get paid to continue your apprenticeship. I've been in that happy position for twenty years now. With luck and a following wind, I hope to continue the same way for many years yet. I wish the same blessing for you. Good luck.

Harry Bingham
Jericho Writers

Part One

Planning

Writing a novel is like driving a car at night. You can only see as far as your headlights, but you can make the whole trip that way.

– E. L. Doctorow

Close the door. Write with no one looking over your shoulder. Don't try to figure out what other people want to hear from you; figure out what you have to say. It's the one and only thing you have to offer.

– Barbara Kingsolver

It's none of their business that you have to learn to write. Let them think you were born that way.

– Ernest Hemingway

A blank piece of paper is God's way of telling us how hard it is to be God.

– Sidney Sheldon

'I don't see much sense in that,' said Rabbit. 'No,' said Pooh humbly, 'there isn't. But there was going to be when I began it. It's just that something happened to it along the way.'

– Winnie the Pooh (A. A. Milne)

What is Your Market?

Writing books is a scary business in a number of ways, but one of the scariest bits of the entire game is this: it's easy – commonplace, in fact – to make a complete mess of the entire project before you have written your first word. You can misjudge the market. You can foul up your plot. You can have a hopelessly insufficient knowledge of your characters, or the world in which they find themselves. If you get these things badly wrong from the outset, you're like a polar explorer boldly setting forth into the arctic cold with a compass that reads thirty degrees off true. No doubt you'll feel like a real novelist as you tap away. Your manuscript will grow. Your word count will slowly creep up towards something respectable. Yet your destination won't be a flutter of flags as you arrive at the Pole; it'll be some wasteland of crevasses and creaking floes, possibly hundreds of miles away from where you needed to be.

Writers, like polar explorers, can in principle put right any mistake. You can always heave yourself back onto your dog sled, correct your course, and start again, but the labour involved may well be similar to writing your novel from scratch. Based on the first-time manuscripts that have come my way, I'd say that at least half of them have problems of this sort. In plenty of cases, indeed, the very concept of the project is so flawed that the best advice to the writer is to discard the whole idea and start again with a blank drawing board.

So, planning matters. At the same time, it's possible to get locked into a kind of authorial *rigor mortis*. Some writers get so worried that their initial direction finding may be askew that they spend countless months on research, on writing courses, on note-taking, on character development and on all the rest of it – to the extent that they almost forget the need to *write* the darn thing. And naturally, any form of expressive writing needs fluidity. It's just not possible to plan your book out completely. For one thing, it's hard to squash all your inventiveness into the three-month period you've allotted. For another, the process of writing will reveal more to you about your characters and your story, and you need to give yourself room to respond to these insights.

The seat of your trousers

There is no one single way to approach these issues. I know one (very good) author who wrote so many notes when researching her first novel that the notes ended up being longer than the book itself. I also know an excellent author (one of whose books was heavily promoted on TV and which sold a huge number of copies as a result) who takes precisely the opposite approach. She likes to research a period, get interested in some aspect of it, and then just start writing. She barely knows her characters and knows nothing of the story; she simply throws the door open and waits to see what will come along. There are any number of commercially successful authors who work in a similar way. When Lee Child sits down to write a new chapter, he has no idea, yet, what's going to happen.

So, there are different routes you can take, but most new writers who take one of these more extreme routes will have cause to regret it. If you are an extreme note-taker, ask yourself honestly whether your book needs more research or whether you are simply procrastinating. It may well be that you are afraid of starting, which is a perfectly understandable fear and one to be cured in one way and one way only: by getting stuck in. As Kingsley Amis famously put it, 'The art of writing is the art of applying the seat of one's trousers to the seat of one's chair'. There's a little more to it than that, maybe, but it's still Lesson One; the only rule that tolerates no exceptions.

Equally, if you're attracted to the vigour and boldness of the 'just get started' approach, ask yourself whether you might be, in fact, afraid of the disciplines of planning; whether you are afraid of them because they're precisely what you most need. It's possible that, without planning anything out, you will write a wonderful novel, appear on TV and sell a zillion copies – but statistically speaking, you are vastly more likely to end up with an unsaleable manuscript, full of flaws which were entirely predictable from the outset.

Chasing Kay Scarpetta

Let's assume, then, that you're sold on the idea of planning things out to some (non-obsessive) extent. Where should you start? You start, inevitably, where you hope to finish: in a bookshop, whether physical or online. A bookshop isn't simply a repository of all the world's greatest fiction and non-fiction; it's a market-place and a catwalk too.

You need that bookshop for every possible reason. No decent writer is ignorant of classic literature, nor has any decent writer failed to read a good old slab of fiction in translation and more recent classics as well. What's more, I'd say that capable writers tend to ignore boundaries. In any given year, I'll certainly read literary fiction (my main diet) and crime fiction (the area I write in), but I'll also nibble away at some sci-fi, some chick lit, maybe some fantasy, possibly some young adult, definitely some poetry, and most likely a few classics that have somehow passed me by. I read more fiction by British, Irish and American authors than anything else, but I'm seldom that far from a weird French novel or a neglected Iranian classic. I'm not too programmatic about any of this. I take care to read enough crime fiction, but aside from that I allow my taste and fancy to wander wherever it happens to take me. That neglected Iranian classic may well end up hurled into a corner of a room after fifty pages or so (I'm not, by any means, someone who finishes every book I start), but I've probably learned something along the way. If you think that my reading taste seems a bit highbrow for the kind of thing you're seeking to write – well, I'm not so sure. Stephen King's *On Writing* is an interesting book, not least for the list of reading matter included at the back. He's a popular author in what he *writes*. He's an eclectic and ambitious author in what he *reads*. If you think you'll achieve the first without bothering with the second, you may just find you're wrong.

But this chapter is not here to give you a homily on the importance of reading more broadly. Rather, it's here to tell you to read more wisely, more commercially. Let's say, for example, that you intend to write crime fiction. Perhaps you happen to have a soft spot for the British crime fiction of the 'Golden Age'. You love Agatha Christie, Dorothy L. Sayers, Margery Allingham, Bulldog Drummond, *The Saint* and all the rest of it – so you want to do something similar. Something with a modern setting, perhaps, but nevertheless a novel that brews up the same attractive blend of country houses, shared social values, amateur sleuths, decent but bumbling policemen, and a good splash of upper-class living. So you do. You write that book. It boasts strong characters, warm prose and a deft, if contrived, plot. (The contrivances are part of the feel.) You may well achieve a manuscript that perfectly accomplishes its goals.

And it will never sell. Perhaps, in truth, if the book was good enough, you might find a second-tier publisher to take it off you for a very small advance. You might even, with a little luck, lure a big publisher into launching the book at the cosy crime market, where you can perhaps aim to sell 5 or 10,000 paperbacks tops, with little hope of cracking any overseas market. But you'll never make a living from writing – and indeed, because agents know the way the dice are likely to fall, you'll have the greatest difficulty in achieving even this success, because it won't be worth most agents' while to help you there.

Why is this? It's because you're writing for the market as it was seventy years ago, not as it is today. Modern crime writers have to respond to the Dashiell Hammett/Raymond Chandler revolution of the 1940s. They have to deal with an audience that has learned forensics from Patricia Cornwell, seen policing from the viewpoint of Michael Connelly, encountered feminism from Sara Paretsky, learned place from Ian Rankin, studied mood and light with the Scandinavians, and that expects books, like Hollywood, to deliver thrills as well as mysteries.

You can't even model your work after current bestsellers. Take the forensics-driven novels of Patricia Cornwell as an example. She's still an active writer, and her work still routinely tops bestseller lists on both sides of the Atlantic. But if you write like her, your book won't sell. That may seem crazy. She's a smash-hit, number one, multimillionaire bestseller. If you write like her, how can you not do well? At another level, though – that of commercial reality, in fact – it makes perfect sense. If people want to read Patricia Cornwell, they will read Patricia Cornwell. Following her exhilarating decision to put forensics at the heart of the crime novel, others have followed suit, notably Kathy Reichs and the CSI TV series. There is now a huge forensics-led crime literature, dominated by the names that created it. If, more than two decades after Kay Scarpetta first emerged, you are seeking to chase an identical audience, you're twenty years out of date.

Instead, you need to learn the market. You need to feel out its leading edge. You certainly need to know the big names in the market you want to write for. In crime fiction, for example, no writer can afford not to read Patricia Cornwell, because she's created such a large chunk of the contemporary crime vocabulary. But that's the historical part of your research. The current part is this: *you need to buy and read debut novels issued by major publishers in the last two or three years.* You need to pay particular attention to the novels that have done unusually well (won prizes, been acclaimed, sold lots of copies), because these are the novels that publishers themselves will use as their lodestars. The recency of the novels matters acutely, because that's your guarantee of contemporaneity. The fact that they are debut novels (or perhaps second novels) also matters, because it proves that the work is being published for the qualities of the work itself, not because of the author's name, fame, or past achievements. That a major publisher has its name on the book also matters, because it's likely to indicate that a good sum of money has been paid for it. It's a probable indication that the market considered that book by that author to be 'hot'.

It's not enough just to read these books. You also have to know what to do with them. You aren't reading because you want to replicate them, but you need to understand literature as being in a kind of long-running conversation with itself. You need to understand what feels current, what feels settled, what feels disputed, what holes and voids and gaps may be opening up. Needless to say, you need to understand this conversation as it applies to your particular genre, whatever that is, but no genre exists in complete isolation from the rest (though sci-fi and fantasy gets closer than most). If you read narrowly, you're likely to miss an important part of the developing conversation. That also means that if you are intending to write fiction, you need to read non-fiction too, and vice versa. Dava Sobel's *Longitude*, for example, spoke as much to the historical fiction market as it did to the market for historical biography. The market for travel books is reshaped almost as emphatically by le Carré's *The Constant Gardener* as by such things as *Eat, Pray, Love*. And the success of *Eat, Pray, Love* in turn propelled its author, Elizabeth Gilbert into a very successful fiction-writing career. Same coin, different sides.

Reading the market well is an extraordinarily difficult art. It is also an extraordinarily important one. It's both the most elusive and the most vital skill that any writer can have. Remember that you're at a huge disadvantage in this area. Every agent and every publisher is constantly in the market, buying, selling, talking, comparing. These people aren't mostly reading the books that are on the bookshelves now. They're reading the books that will be on the bookshelves in eighteen months' time. They'll know exactly which books are most hotly contested at auction. They'll know which books almost didn't sell at all. They'll know the advances and the sales stats. When a book does unusually well or flops unusually badly, the trade will grope towards a consensus understanding of the outcome and alter its buying habits accordingly.

Reading this, most writers will take the only logical approach: they will instantly seek a romantic liaison with a talkative literary agent or gossipy commissioning editor. That's a good strategy, and one I commend unreservedly. If, however, you're unlucky enough to be happily married, you'll simply need to rub along as best you can. That means reading a lot, reading widely, and staying current.

Looking inward

These strictures might sound as if they're talking about something external, but they're not really. They're talking about you. Most books that fail at the very first hurdle – that of concept – are more than anything else failures of honesty. You need to approach your own ideas with radical honesty. Is your idea for a book *really* founded on a good idea? Or do you simply have a personal attachment to it – are you attached to it simply because it was the first idea that came to you? In very many cases, it's the latter.

In my case, I wrote the first idea that came to me. It wasn't a bad idea. (The book was about three brothers racing to make a million pounds in order to win a huge inheritance from their multimillionaire father.) I executed the idea well and the book sold strongly, first to publishers, then to readers. Yet the tone was old-fashioned. Publishers compared me to Jeffrey Archer and Sidney Sheldon, which felt like a compliment, except that those authors had their best years a long way behind them. In seeking to establish my name with readers, my publisher simply wasn't able to situate me in any contemporary-feeling niche. My agent at the time liked to comment brightly, 'Harry, you're so unfashionable – it's a good thing. It means the wheel must be about to come full circle'. But no matter how the good people in marketing and cover-design twisted and turned, they never found a way to establish me. Taken in isolation, my books were fine, but I had misjudged the market and, short of completely reinventing myself, my sales would never match my ambitions, nor those of my publisher. I've chosen, therefore, to reinvent myself. I wrote a series of non-fiction books, then came back to fiction with a series unlike anything I'd written before – and which does its very best to engage with the market as it is today.

Clear-sighted honesty is desperately hard to come by. It took me maybe ten years to get close, and that wasn't the end of the learning. But one powerful tip is this: you must cultivate a positive stance towards contemporary fiction. In my role as editorial consultant, I often hear new writers say, 'There's so much rubbish published these days,' or words to that effect. No one who has ever spoken those words has got within a mile of publication. That's not to say all new books are good. They aren't, and there has never been a moment in history when they were. But it's very rare that books are published which are incompetent *for their genre*. Dan Brown writes bad prose, but his audience doesn't care as long as the story cracks on. John Banville's narratives sometimes seem to stall completely in a flow of beautiful sentences, but his readers don't come to him for shootouts and car chases. Both authors excel at what they do. If you treat contemporary fiction as an embarrassment and a let-down, you can't hear its conversation. You won't write anything which seems timely or pertinent. You won't get published and don't deserve to.

The cynical route to failure

It's also worth being clear about one other thing. I am *not* advocating cynicism. No cynically written book has ever sold. At the Mills & Boon end of the market, perhaps, a few cynically written books are acquired, though not often even then.

You must write for the market, because if you don't, the market is unlikely to want what you produce. But you must also write with passion and conviction. You must – let's call a spade a spade – write with love. This game is so hard, so full of challenges, that you don't have a hope unless you do.

Dear Miss Austen

Most books on how to write base themselves, for understandable reasons, in a broad view of literature – a view that takes in world literature from the dawn of the novel onwards. But using examples from past eras risks deceiving writers into thinking that it's OK to write like that now. And it isn't – at least, not if you want to sell your work. So, the examples (both positive and negative) scattered throughout this book concentrate heavily on more recent work. The book focuses exclusively on authors writing in English and deals largely with well-known authors and books.

This method excludes the vast bulk of world literature, but then the vast bulk of world literature wouldn't convince most publishers to get out their cheque-books. In a recent stunt, a frustrated author sent the opening three chapters of some of Jane Austen's most celebrated work, with titles and other details slightly amended, to eighteen agents and publishers. He received eighteen rejection letters, only one of which noticed the plagiarism. The author, David Lassman, professed himself shocked: 'I was staggered. Here is one of the greatest writers that has lived, with her oeuvre securely fixed in the English canon and yet only one recipient recognized them as Austen's work'.

Yet Lassman was wrong and the publishers were right. Anyone who wants to read Jane Austen will read Jane Austen. If you want to write like her, then prepare for rejection – and read a different textbook on how to write. The rest of us can move on. We're aiming for publication.

Chapter Summary

- You will need to plan your work. Tailor the way you plan to suit your working habits but avoid extreme under- or over-preparation.
- You should read widely (across genres, across time, across geographies).
- In particular, you should read a lot of recent, successful debut fiction in your genre.
- Try to approach your ideas with radical honesty. This is hard to achieve!
- Don't be cynical about contemporary fiction, or cynical in your attitude to your own work.
- Write for today's market.

WHAT IS YOUR PLAN?

The hardest moment in developing any book is figuring out how to start. Do you start with story? With character? With place and time? Or even theme and ideas? These things interrelate so intricately that it's hard to develop one without the other – and yet you have a blank sheet in front of you and need to start somewhere.

Different authors will work these things differently. There's no single recipe and the most I can suggest is a middle-of-the-road approach for you to adjust and customise as suits your own working habit. (Though, please note, starting to write without any preparation whatsoever is not a working habit. It's a disaster.)

The recipe

On the whole, you'll do well to make notes on your story, your characters, your settings and your themes before you get as far as writing your first sentence. And because everything interrelates so intricately, your best advice is to start from everywhere at once.

Do this. Take paper (or a computer screen) and give yourself some headings. You might choose the following:

Story

Characters

Place & time

Themes

Voice

Then start to fill in what you know. Perhaps, for example, you are writing a contemporary romance between a sophisticated New Yorker guy, and a just-arrived-from-Oklahoma, awkward-but-nice girl. That doesn't feel like much of a story, so let's have the New Yorker be a Chinese-American ER doctor, and let's have the Okie girl be the victim of a hit-and-run accident. Let's give our protagonists some names (which are completely provisional at this stage). The ER doc can be John Woo Lai. The girl can be Elly someone-or-other. There's still a load we don't yet know, but even identifying the gaps can be useful, and already we can fill out our headings a little, as follows:

Story:

Elly's hit by a car. (How badly? How injured?) Blurry with shock and medication, she meets attractive doc, John Woo Lai.

They're attracted. Some problem arises (what?).

Then they get it together.

Characters:

John is calm and capable. Immigrant parents, he's fully Americanised. Culturally sophisticated. Collects original art. Reads. (What – poetry? Too pretentious? Writes short stories? Plays jazz?)

Elly – ditzy. Spent most of her life in small-town Oklahoma. Overwhelmed by NY. What attracts her to John?

Place & time:

New York, obviously. Manhattan? Too obvious? Brooklyn? Westchester? Maybe a wintry thing going on: *A Winter's Tale*? Maybe Elly is hit by a skidding car in the first hard frost of winter. Aim to have whole romance play out through a single season.

Themes:

What is this book *about*? Romance needs to find some edge.

Voice:

Is this Elly's book, or John's, or do they share 50/50? First person or third?

Notice that we haven't solved a tremendous amount yet, but it becomes easier to feel the gaps. Simply having some notes down on paper means that you can concentrate on particular issues that occur to you as they arise, without having to struggle to remember the entire edifice. Those little comments that are scattered through these notes – like: 'Some problem arises (what?)' – may not have solved anything, but they're markers for the things that will claim your attention when you return to them.

What's more, you're already a step or two ahead. Simply by creating the heading '*Place & time*', you forced yourself to think about it. OK, you may not yet have fixed your place (though Manhattan would work nicely for me), but your mind jumped from the image of a car skidding in snow right to the idea of a possible title (*A Winter's Tale*), a structure (a single-season romance), and no doubt a set of images (snowy streets, skating at the Rockefeller Center, hot coffees and mittened hands). A story that has, until now, seemed impossibly loose, impossibly generic, has suddenly acquired a little individuality. It's got a tiny little hint of edge.

And one more thing's worth noticing. The notes above are badly written – or at least, they're carelessly written. And so they should be! If you start anxiously correcting your prose at this stage, you are completely missing the point. No one but you will ever read it. If commas in the wrong place bother you enough that you can't concentrate on other more important things, by all means correct your commas. Apart from that, forget about it. These are working notes. You're going to alter them, delete and replace bits, chop and change the sequence of headings and perhaps even the headings themselves.

Let's take our story a little further. The gaps that we've identified before deserve some attention, and there'll be other things
that come to mind along the way. Our notes, once again, get a
little fuller:

Story:

Elly's hit by a car. A complex fracture of the leg. Two
sprained wrists. Nasty.

Blurry with shock and medication, she meets attractive
doc, John Woo Lai. he seems really warm. Clearly attracted to her.

Some problem arises – <u>BUT WHAT</u>?

Then they get it together.

Characters:

<u>John</u> is calm and capable. Immigrant parents, he's fully
Americanised. Culturally sophisticated. Collects original
art. Plays jazz piano.

Immigrant parents. Not Americanised. Eat strange Chinese
food (investigate!). Father maybe a Traditional Chinese
Medicine herbalist. Clash between his traditions and his
son's?

How much family is in US, how much still in China?
Or – interesting! – a close relative of John's (sister? brother? uncle?) is in the US illegally and was at the wheel of
the car that knocked down Elly. If he's caught, he'll be
deported. Is that a big enough issue? Maybe he's a Chinese
democracy activist. (Or environment?) Being sent home
risks jail, or worse.

What are John's politics? Why is his sister/brother/uncle
politically active and he's not? Or is he?

<u>Elly</u> – ditzy. Spent most of her life in small-town Okla-
homa. Overwhelmed by NY.

OK, and her dad's a cop. She's maybe dabbled a bit with policework, but anyway has loads of that stuff in her family. She got some kind of clue as to the car that knocked her down (registration? Some odd quirk about the car? A bumper sticker?). She's mad at the driver and wants to track him/her down.

John finds out that E's on the hunt. If she's successful, John's sister goes to China, and that means to prison camp.

Hey now, we've got us a romantic problem! John cuts off from Elly when he realises his attraction to her jeopardises his brother/sister/uncle's safety. He's torn both ways. *Excellent.* (need to work out the exact mechanics of this. And let's go with sister for now. Might need to change that.)

Place & time:

OK, Manhattan it is. *A Winter's Tale.* A one-season romance. Winter themes and images throughout. But also, maybe, there could be a connection between this sparkly, twinkly, *safe* New York winter and the winter that would greet the sister back in China. Cold and killing. Repressive. A winter of the heart. Do they still have labour camps there? And for women? If so, maybe the sister escaped from a Chinese prison camp or similar in winter. Maybe that escape still haunts her.

Themes:

Winter maybe gives us a theme too. New York is free but cold. China lives in a permanent winter of freedom. Need to bring this *inside* the romance, though. How to do that? At the moment, John is risking nothing except his sister's safety. But maybe John has committed a felony by protecting her? If his immigration status were less than ironclad, then maybe the romance threatens him directly?

Voice:

Hmm. First thought about this more as Elly's book, probably first person, a bit chick-litty. But it's getting darker – also tauter and more interesting – all the time. Now, though, most of the interest seems to lie on John's side, so maybe this needs to be a two-hander. Half from E's point of view, half from John's. Does the sister get a point of view? If so, does that break up the romance? Another reason, perhaps, to place John in more direct jeopardy. And what's his backstory?

Already, this is beginning to feel like the stirrings of a real novel. The simple boy-meets-girl tale was perfect, in the sense that there will never fail to be a market for romantic fiction. On the other hand, our initial ideas had absolutely nothing to commend them, nothing to distinguish them from an infinity of similar stories. Then we made one crucial jump (*A Winter's Tale*), and then another (the democracy activist sister at risk of being deported back to China). Already, this feels like a book that could potentially interest an agent and publisher.

To be clear, though, we're still not at all close to a final plan for the book. To mention just a few obvious points:

- We've done almost nothing to define John and Elly's characters. She's ditzy, he's sophisticated. That's pretty much all we have for now – and those labels feel provisional. They have an 'idea first thought of' quality to them and may need to be discarded as we develop things further.
- The idea of the democracy activist facing deportation seems like a thrilling element to insert into a potentially sugary New York romance, but the details are still very vague. Is it a sister or an uncle? What are John's politics? Is he himself going to be at risk of deportation and if so why and for what? What is his backstory? Are we going to see any of it in flashback, for example?

- Elly seems a bit inert. All the excitement and interest are coming from John's side of things. We need to find some way to bring interest to Elly's character. Maybe that will come from the ditzy/Oklahoma/cop's daughter element, but maybe it's something else completely.

- We've got no hint of the voices of Elly or John. We couldn't do at this stage: we need to know more about them as characters first.

- The title *A Winter's Tale* recalls Shakespeare's play of that name. Shakespeare's plot is completely bananas (it's the one with the stage direction 'Exit, pursued by a bear'), but it might be cute to steal some of his devices for this romance. In Shakespeare's story, for example, there's a bit where the king's lost wife appears as a statue who then comes to life. Might there be a way (plausibly, and with some comic knowingness) to make use of a similar trick towards the end of this book?

These questions aren't *problems*; they're questions. These uncertainties and hesitations are the spaces in which your creativity will grow. If you're too fast about filling them in or hold too tightly to the ideas you first came up with, you'll end up with a worse novel than you would do if you were more relaxed.

That also means that the process of developing the novel should be slow. I allowed the sketch above to develop pretty much as fast as I was typing it, but even so there are a couple of elements which could work in a real live novel. On the other hand, there are plenty of other elements (Elly as ditzy Oklahoma girl) which don't feel like they have a future at all. (Or perhaps that's an aspect which does work for you, in which case, good: you just need to develop it.) If you allow yourself to *feel* the inadequacies and holes in your outline plan, your brain will be thinking about those things as you walk the dogs, do the shopping, or whatever else fills your day. Naturally you'll need to let your mind rove over the parts that you *are* sure of, because that's human nature, but the real progress is made when you allow yourself to feel the other bits, the bits you know aren't yet right.

If it takes three months for you to develop a plan, then good. I'd guess that three months would be a pretty typical development time for a first novel by a capable writer. If it takes longer, don't worry about it. If it takes you very much less than that, you are either unusually gifted, unusually lucky, or you're about to make a mess of things. Those three months don't have to be empty of any activity other than tinkering with your plan. On the contrary; the more you can read around your subject, the better. If I were setting out to write about John and Elly, I'd be reading a whole heap of things. Material on Chinese Medicine, history, and food. Books on and by Chinese-Americans. I'd want to find out about Oklahoma policemen. I'd want to learn about immigration issues. If possible, I'd go to Manhattan in winter. If not (and in any case), I'd try to read a big heap of winter-in-Manhattan lit. I might watch some movies too, but those would be more for fun than anything else. You're a writer, so it's words that you're searching for. Films may guide you to some of those words, but they're a clumsy guide most of the time.

Need More?

At Jericho Writers, we've developed a whole set of tools to help people write better and solve problems faster. In many cases, those things are worksheets – stuff you fill in as you go. If you'd like those tools (and they do help), then you're welcome to come and get them. They're free. Simply go here and help yourself:

jerichowriters.com/how-to-write-a-novel-free-resources

I'm dropping a mention of this in now, because we have an '**Idea Generator**' that helps you turn existing passions and knowledge into the basis for a commercially successful story. If you are unsure of your existing ideas, or you just want to come up with new ones, this tool will unquestionably work for you. It has *always* delivered for me. Oh yes, and the Generator comes in two different flavours. One for adult fiction, one for children's and young adult fiction. Both tools are available from the same link … and even though you think they can't possibly work, they really, actually and truly-ruly do.

Chapter Summary

- When planning, make notes on all fronts simultaneously.
- Any plan should have headings for 'story', 'character' and 'settings'. If you want to add some further headings, then do.
- Set down what you know – or think you know.
- Allow ideas to come to you as you proceed, try them out, and see how they impact other elements of your draft plan.
- Be ready to revise anything at all. Nothing should be set in stone. You're looking for a feeling of '*Yes!* That feels right'.
- Stay aware of gaps and inadequacies. Don't be afraid of them. Those are the gardens where your creativity will bloom.
- Take your time.
- Read voraciously anything that bears on your future book.
- Different writers work differently. It's OK if the working habits you evolve run differently from the approach taken in this chapter.

What is Your Plot?

As you get further into the development process, your notes will get fuller. The bits you know will start to expand and seem more solid. The uncertainties will slowly retreat, becoming more matters of detail and finesse. If your notes fill five or ten pages, you are probably finding a reasonable balance between planning things properly and not getting bogged down in detail. There's no template, though. No checklist that has to be completed before you can proceed. As long as you work in the way that is right for you – and don't kid yourself that you're further ahead than you truly are – you're doing fine.

In particular, the real test isn't the weight of your notes; it's how well you understand the crucial structural elements of your story. We'll talk in much greater depth about plot and character in future chapters, but for now let's focus on what it would be reasonable to know about your book at this early stage.

Knowing your plot

You don't need to know much about plot mechanics. In our story above, Elly needs to have seen some distinguishing feature of the car that knocked her down, in order that she can pursue it. But what that feature is and how she goes about the pursuit are issues for another day. If you happen to have answers to those questions, it's probably simpler to set them out in your notes so that they don't go on nagging at you. But if you don't have the answers, leave it. That's a worry you can come to when you reach the relevant chapter of your book. For now, it doesn't matter. Subplots are, likewise, largely irrelevant – as are timings, chapter-by-chapter schemes, and anything else along those lines.

Indeed, only one thing really matters at this stage, and that's *shape*. The shape of our Elly & John book started out very simply: *girl meets boy, falls in love, encounters problem, overcomes problem, lives happily ever after.* There was a big uncertainty about what that problem was going to be, but the sister facing a threat of deportation took us a long way towards a solution. The whole point about focusing on the *shape* of a story is to get to something tremendously simple. The plot of *Pride and Prejudice* has the following shape:

> Elizabeth Bennet wants to meet Mr Right. She meets Darcy and Wickham. She thinks Wickham is wonderful and hates Darcy. She destroys her relationship with Darcy. Then she discovers that Wickham is awful and Darcy is wonderful. Everything looks ruined. Except it isn't, and they live happily ever after.

That's fewer than fifty words, and some of those words could have been dispensed with.

You should aim to summarise your own novel in the same way, and in as few words. Because this is a tough exercise – much harder than it sounds – it's worth recognising some of the commonest mistakes.

- You are not writing a blurb for the back of your book. You're not *pitching* the novel. A good plot summary should reveal everything important about the plot in as few words as possible. That's not a treatment likely to make any book sound good, so don't worry if your plot summary sounds horribly bare. Bare is good. Bare is the point.

- By the same token, you do not need to explain anything about time, place, or character. If you look back at my brutally short summary of *Pride and Prejudice*, you'll notice that the book being described could equally well be set in Regency England or Flash Gordon's Mars. When it comes to a plot summary, that's how it should be. Focus on structure. Everything else is a distraction.

- Don't concentrate on the front end. That summary of *Pride and Prejudice* is equally weighted across the entire book. If you find yourself writing fifty or a hundred words explaining your book's set-up and then trail off with 'And then the adventure really begins ...', you don't yet know the shape of your plot. You shouldn't start writing in earnest until you do.

Why does shape matter so much? It matters because it is the structure that holds your book together. It's the foundation and the roof joists, it's the line of curving steel that holds everything else together. And, to switch metaphor, it provides you with a compass that points true north, even in the polar cold. If you know the structure of your novel before you start writing it, then although you *will* go wrong as you write, you can never go *far* wrong. If the chapter you're writing serves to nudge your plot forward by another few inches, it's doing roughly the right thing. If the chapter doesn't move that plot forward, it's pointless and needs to be deleted. You'll only be able to make those structural calls with confidence if you have a decent set of blueprints in your hand to start with.

Keeping it tight

As you shape your plot, bear in mind that *tight* is almost always better than *loose*.

Take, for example, the Elly & John tale we've been playing with. We chose a romantic problem in which Elly's actions (seeking the car that knocked her down) are threatening harm to her beloved's sister. Before we came up with that problem, the two protagonists were bound only by mutual attraction. Now they're bound together by:

- *Elly's secondary motivation* (finding the hit-and-run driver). Although she may be unaware of it, she now has two connections to John, not just the one.

- *John's anxiety about Elly's detective work.* That anxiety may push him away from Elly, but it's still a line that connects the two of them. And to mix 'push' forces with 'pull' forces is essential for any romance.

- *The fact that John's immediate family is now linked to the romance.* Suppose the person threatened with deportation was a work colleague of John's, nothing more. John would still have feelings about the looming deportation, but they'd be much weaker, too pallid to sustain an interesting romance plot.

Indeed, one of the continuing problems we have with our planned Elly & John story is that it hasn't yet achieved the right level of density. If the story is to be a romance, it can only have two real protagonists. Yet on the current plan, the person facing by far the biggest personal issue is John's sister. In a way, her story is the most interesting of the three, yet at the same time paying any attention to it will dissolve the energy in the romance. That's why the second version of the planned story contained a note that read: 'At the moment, John is risking nothing except his sister's safety. But maybe John has committed a felony by protecting her? If his immigration status were less than ironclad, then maybe the romance threatens him directly?'.

The more broadly you spread your energy, the more diffuse it becomes and the harder it is to sustain the reader's interest. Keeping a rich array of connections between your protagonists is helpful. So, very often, is keeping things within a family, because familial connections are the strongest ones of all. (Which is why, by the way, so much powerful literature makes use of them. When Darth Vader says, 'Luke, I am your father,' we know that what he says matters intensely. 'Luke, I used to work with your dad way back when, but we kinda lost touch' would not have done the trick.)

Plotting mystery novels

If you're writing a mystery novel – either a whodunit, or any other novel that relies in some way on uncovering a mystery buried in the past – then some of the foregoing comments may seem interesting and important, but also hard to use. The notion of chiselling away at your ideas in order to locate the shape of your novel seems like a very worthwhile challenge … but what *is* the shape of a detective novel? Isn't it always simply this?:

> A crime is committed. The detective follows the clues. Then he/she unmasks the villain.

That's it.

Indeed, one of the striking things about detective stories, the most classic of all mystery forms, is the way you get entire series founded on the same detective investigating largely similar cases and in a largely similar way. To be sure, with any long contemporary series, there'll be a soap-opera quality to them as well. In one book the detective gets married. In the next he has a child. In the next he has an affair. In the next he gets divorced, and so on. Yet these long-running storylines are an overlay over each novel's basic structure, which is indeed 'Crime – Clues – Conviction'.

In constructing a strong mystery, therefore, you need to approach things a little differently, and that means working backwards. Determine the crime. Determine what seems to have been going on (the story that most of the police will believe). Determine what has *really* been going (the story that your detective will uncover). If you want, you can start to piece together some of the clues that will take your detective towards a solution, but that may be more than you want to do at this stage. The *structure* of a mystery novel isn't the clues; it's what *seems* to have happened, what *really* happened, and whatever other things intersected, disturbed or complicated the thing that really happened. That's your structure – and these days, you can't allow yourself to pick anything too simple, because mystery writers have become so darn sophisticated in creating complexity.

Remember too that although crime fiction is the pre-eminent form of the mystery novel, mysteries can come in every possible package. Many ghost stories are, at their heart, mysteries. So is any story in which the protagonist comes to learn (or reveal) something highly significant about their past. So too are such masterpieces as *An Artist of the Floating World* and *Never Let Me Go*, a couple of books by Kazuo Ishiguro. The first of those two books, indeed, barely has a plot (it's a purer mystery novel, in that sense, than most contemporary crime thrillers). It hooks the reader via a series of revelations which gradually lead to a total inversion of our view of the protagonist. The human revealed by the end of the book is shockingly different from the picture we had when we started out. If you're writing a non-detective mystery novel, you would do well to study Ishiguro's technique.

Last, a book doesn't have to be either a mystery or not-a-mystery. On the contrary, many successful books are both. These are issues that we'll come back to in much more detail later on, but for now, take note. If your book deals with mystery in any form, you need to understand a little of its structure, as well as the structure of your more regular-looking plot.

Plotting your non-fiction

Narrative non-fiction needs to obey all the same rules as fiction. Perhaps it sounds forced to speak of 'plotting' your non-fiction, but that is effectively what you need to do, nevertheless.

In particular, you must not for one moment think that all you need to do is relate the events as they happened. That's not a structure, it's a splurge. Take, for example, the smash-hit *Eat, Pray, Love*, Elizabeth Gilbert's mix of travel, spirituality and true-life romance. Obviously enough, no bookstore sets aside shelving for 'Travel, Spirit & Romance True Stories'. Taken purely as a marketing concept, the book must have looked like a terrible idea. Except that Gilbert used the facts to tell a *story*. Her story was a personal one – about divorce, recovery, finding and receiving true love – and it was compellingly, wonderfully told. It was Gilbert's wonderfully deft combination of humour and emotional honesty which drew readers into her book; but it was her story that kept them there. (It was also, by the way, intricately structured and carefully controlled: an excellent example of memoir as craft.)

If your book doesn't obviously involve a story (such as travel, memoir, biography or historical narrative, for example), it most likely involves an *argument*. Malcolm Gladwell's bestselling book *The Tipping Point* didn't tell a story, but it led readers through a structured argument: what a 'tipping point' was, why they matter, what gives rise to them, and so on. In such instances, the argument plays the part of story: the rigorous structural element that holds everything else together. One of the commonest problems with new writers embarking on such work is that they like to fool themselves into thinking that if a reader is going to be interested in their views on (for example) how 'social epidemics' work, they're going to be interested in their views on everything else as well. So instead of a book that takes a clean line through some interesting material, they end up with an overstuffed ragbag of thoughts, observations, anecdotes and jokes. And a reader is not interested in your thoughts; they are interested in a topic. If you lose focus on that topic, you have lost your reader along with any chance of selling your manuscript.

Having said all this, it's probably also worth admitting that non-fiction is generally more loosely structured than a novel. If a chapter doesn't directly forward a story or argument, it may nevertheless be worth preserving. If the story lurks in the background, rather than grabbing the reader by the throat, that too may be OK. But don't use these comments as permission to neglect your story altogether. Elizabeth Gilbert and Malcolm Gladwell are both excellent writers of non-fiction. Their prose style, their ability to tell a joke (in Gilbert's case) or an anecdote (in Gladwell's) place them in the top bracket of popular non-fiction authors writing today. But if either of those writers had neglected structure, their books would barely have made a mark. If in doubt, do more structuring rather than less. You may have

Gilbert's wit, Gladwell's astuteness, and Bill Bryson's warmth, but I wouldn't count on it. A strong structure is any non-fiction author's best friend.

Chapter Summary

- Work to achieve a good understanding of the *shape* of your plot.
- You should be able to summarise your entire book (not just the set-up) in three or four dozen words.
- A plot summary doesn't need to say much about character or anything at all about setting. You're looking for *structure*.
- Work to achieve a kind of concentration in your plot. If your protagonists are strongly connected (even by forces that push apart as well as ones that pull together), that's a good thing. Loose connections between your protagonists may indicate a weak plot.
- Mystery novels (not just detective novels) have their own form of plotting.
- Narrative non-fiction needs a structure or an argument to hold it together.

WHO ARE YOUR CHARACTERS?

If you have ever read a book on writing screenplays, you'll have noticed a huge emphasis on story. Indeed, the most famous such book, by Robert McKee, is called simply that: *Story*. These textbooks often have a somewhat mechanical approach to storytelling, but at least you can feel the rigour that drives the machine.

On the other hand, with few exceptions, those books have almost nothing interesting to say about the development of character. It's as though their authors believe that they can concoct character simply by hurling together a few basic ingredients:

> **Dale**, 24, good-looking business school grad, has a gambling problem, still in love with high school sweetheart, superficially in control, easily panicked.

> **Yolande**, 42, Rwandan, entered the US illegally, restaurant waitress, studying human rights law, feisty.

These summaries aren't characterisations; they're more like those e-fit pictures issued by the police. Swift, purposeful summaries with everything individual left far behind. The essence of a person is nowhere to be seen.

That needn't bother a screenwriter too much. They've got dialogue to play with. The story arc will call for decisions to be made and character to be revealed. Most of all, though, screenwriters have at their disposal the ultimate special effect: a human actor. Give some dull lines to a Daniel Craig or a Jennifer Lawrence, and those lines will still vibrate with life. We novelists are not so lucky and, as we'll explore further in later chapters, the techniques that bring our characters to life have everything to do with the patient accumulation of detail. Character in the novel emerges the way snow settles: incrementally. Individual snow-flakes are neither here nor there. Taken together, they shape a landscape.

Finding the essence

We're not at the landscape-building stage, however. We're still at the planning stage, which presents us with a dilemma. We can't plan effectively without knowing our major characters; yet we can't know our characters properly until we start to write. Those bald e-fit type characterisations are not the way forward. Or rather, you may well start out with characters not all that different from Dale and Yolande, but before your plan progresses far you need to leave those crude models a long way behind.

The trick, as so often in writing, lies in knowledge. The more you know about your characters, the more they will start to live. You need to know all the big things, of course. To return to the Elly & John story, we might want to ask about Elly:

- *Age, gender, nationality, occupation, social group.* The basic data.

- *Family, partner, close friends, workmates.* Who's who in Elly's world? Who's important, who's not? What are her key relationships like? Are they close, fiery, formal, intimate, destructive, phoney, or what? And what is it that drives these relationships? When Elly comes to cherish John, why did her heart settle on him, not on anyone else? What was the essence of that attraction? And how often does she ring her mother? Does she watch ball games with her father? Why did she move away from her home town?

- *Desires, motives and fears.* What drives her? What terrifies her? What will make her happy? What does she believe will make her happy? Is she decisive in going after what she wants? Or indecisive? Impetuous or calculated?

- *Looks.* What does she look like? Is she tall or short? Attractive or unattractive? What's her dress sense like? Is she self-conscious about the way she looks, or quite the opposite? What would she look like to a stranger when she's sitting alone in a bar? What does she look like to her lover, as she's lying next to him in bed?

- *Attitudes.* What are her attitudes? What are her politics? Is she optimistic? Is she resourceful? Is she a risk-taker? Does she prefer men to be serious and disciplined, or does she love a party-animal? Is she ambitious? Does she believe in hard work and graft, or appearances and winging it?

- *Backstory.* What do we need to know about her past? Was she busted cheating in an exam? Did a schoolfriend of hers commit suicide? Has she had major love affairs we need to know about?

- *Reputation and stereotypes.* How people respond to a character depends in part on their prior assumptions. So, does Elly bring any stereotypes into the room with her? Does she look like a dumb blonde? Or like a tough policeman's daughter? Does she have any kind of reputation that people might be aware of? Is that reputation deserved or not?

- *Habits.* Is she tidy? Is she proud of her apartment? Does she go to the gym? Does she read Flaubert?

These, though, are fairly basic questions. You need to ask them all right, but you need to ask the quirky little ones too:

- Does she floss her teeth?
- What embarrassing thing happened to her in Mexico?
- How does she fidget?
- What odd little mannerism of speech is she teased about?
- Was she ever afraid of public speaking?
- What are her hands like?

- Has she ever fallen off a horse?
- Is she good at mathematics?
- Who was her childhood heroine?
- Can she play the guitar?
- Has she ever had a truly terrible haircut?
- What was her first encounter with snow?

And so on.

Different writers have different ways of tackling this kind of exercise. I know one author who writes down a list of at least a hundred questions about her major characters, then answers them. The questions you ask need to relate to the character and the book. There's no point asking about memorable railway journeys if the book is set in the later Roman Empire. Be sure, as well, to write the questions down before you start to supply any answers, otherwise you'll be seduced into framing only those questions to which you already know the answer.

It's also essential to make sure that you ask yourself a really long list of questions, because the whole point is to push your imagination to stretching point and beyond. You need to find the odd little facts (a horse-riding accident; a failed perm; a six-year-old girl with frozen fingers and a sense of wonder) that help an individual life start shivering into view. If you just fire the same battery of twenty questions at your characters (Hair colour? Eye colour? Age?) you'll never move far beyond the lifeless e-fit summaries with which we began this chapter.

Developing that list of questions is quite arduous, so I've prepared a starting set that you can just take and adapt to your own purposes. You can download it via the link below. I'm sure you'll get something from it.

Get Your Ultimate Character Builder Here

jerichowriters.com/how-to-write-a-novel-free-resources

If this particular route into character knowledge doesn't appeal for some reason, that's OK too. What matters isn't whether you complete a specific exercise, but whether you end up with wonderful characters. And alternative routes into that character knowledge are legion. Some writers write practice scenes or short stories as a way of warming up their characters, a kind of practice game before the big match. Others may just start to build them up from notes, much as we started doing with the Elly & John story in the chapter titled 'Planning'. It doesn't matter much how you choose to do it. All that matters is that you don't start writing your book until your characters are limbered up and ready for action – and that means *knowing* them, intimately and in detail.

How to know when you've done enough

In the case of plotting, there's a fairly clear stopping point, a moment where you know you're ready to proceed. Once you have the basic shape of your plot mapped out, you have your road map. If you want still more detail, then by all means go and find it, but you've got the essentials already. When it comes to characterisation, there's no such obvious stopping point. You could write fifty pages of notes or write almost nothing. How do you know when you've done enough?

In the end, you will have to judge this for yourself. I find that there comes a point where I know a character so well that I know I can answer – or instantly improvise, which is the same thing – any question you care to ask me about him or her. I used to say that you need to know your main characters as well as your best friend, except that you need to know them much better than that. After all, there's an awful lot you may not know about your best friend: what they dream of at night, how they first encountered snow, that embarrassing incident in Mexico, and all the rest of it. So forget the best friend. What you are after is *fluency*. You need to know your characters so well that you can talk about them with the same confidence that you have when you talk about yourself. Once you have that ease, that confidence, your character is warmed up, and it's time to get them out onto the pitch.

There's another way to know as well. Mostly, I find that characters of mine have a touchstone; some central image that is the key to much else about them. That touchstone is something you get to intuitively, not intellectually. You will reach it slowly, not fast. Quite often you only get there properly once you're a good way into your novel. What's more, the touchstone that makes sense to you might make no sense at all to a reader.

One of the protagonists in my novel *The Lieutenant's Lover* was a man called Misha. For me, there were two keys to his character: that he was an engineer and that he had long, pianist's fingers. Those things would strike anyone else as a nonsense. Who *cares* what his damn fingers were like? But your touchstone isn't there for anyone else. It's for you. For me, the fact that Misha was an engineer gave him a kind of practical capacity, a pleasure in doing; it gave him technical ingenuity and optimism. Those things were balanced by something inward and sensitive. Something capable of producing beauty and feeling injury. Pretty much everything in Misha's character related back – for me – to those things. You don't need to tell your reader what your touchstone is. You're obviously not going to conceal the fact that your character is an engineer, but you don't have to announce it with any kind of fanfare. That touchstone is for you and you only. If you work a different way, that's probably fine. If not, then lucky you.

Edge

It's not enough to create an authentic character. You also need to create an interesting one. That's a large enough subject that we won't go into it here, but you would be well-advised to spend time reading the relevant chapters later in the book before you advance too far. The chapter 'Finding Edge' will be particularly important to you.

Main characters, minor characters

Any character at the centre of your novel needs you to know them very well indeed. If you're writing a love story, you need to know the two partners. If you're writing about three sons, you need to know all of them. If yours is a single-person viewpoint book, you're lucky. You need to know just one person in infinite depth.

As characters decline in importance, the amount you need to know about them falls rapidly away. I spend a lot of time on my protagonist(s) but have never put together more than half a page of notes on any character even one step removed from the centre. If that half page strikes you as a little undercooked – well, it may well be. I don't much like taking notes, so I tend to get by with the least I can get away with. If you find it helpful to put together two or three pages on your subsidiary characters, you should do just that. If you find yourself putting together ten pages, however, I'd raise an eyebrow. There's a difference between planning and procrastination, and ten pages on a secondary character is more likely the latter.

With characters who aren't even secondary – a work colleague who'll appear for a chapter or two, an old boyfriend who pops up awkwardly towards the end of the book – I personally ignore them completely. Almost certainly, you'll find that you get more life, more *apposite* life, into those characters by going with the flow as you start to write the chapter in question.

Characters in non-fiction

Finally, a word of caution to the non-fictioneers. It's so easy to think that you don't need to attend to characterisation because you yourself are the protagonist; that you don't need to think about how other characters will appear because you will be writing about them from a position of knowledge and authority.

Yet that's not quite true. For one thing, your reader doesn't know you, and never will. All they encounter is the character who arises from the page. It's that character that you're seeking to create. It's that character we're in search of. For another thing, non-fiction is not truth. It's a selective, edited, *shaped* version of the truth. Take, for example, the classic travel stories of Eric Newby. In his *A Short Walk in the Hindu Kush*, he presents himself as a hapless buffoon blundering around in the wastes of Afghanistan. Yet he was nothing of the sort. During the Second World War, he served with the British Special Forces, won a medal for gallantry, was captured, escaped and was captured again. He was a bestselling author, edited the travel section of a national newspaper, and spent his life travelling extensively, often in its remotest places. Eric Newby the human being was as far from being a buffoon as a man can get. Eric Newby the *character* was a different matter altogether. That's not giving you license to lie, of course, but it does give you license to edit. And if the truth gets stretched at times – well, heck, everyone's better for a good stretch.

So, for non-fiction too, you need to plan out your characters – the ones who'll come to life in the pages of your manuscript, not the one you see in your mirror – with as much care as any novelist. The techniques described above may feel jarringly contrived in this context, in which case you should adapt them as seems fit. Just don't con yourself into believing that the whole issue is of no relevance to you. It is, it is.

Chapter Summary

- 'E-fit' style character summaries are useless to a novelist, except at the very earliest stages of planning.
- The key to strong characters is knowledge.
- You need to know all the big facts, of course, but you should make sure you learn lots of quirky little ones too. Those details lend life and individuality.
- You are aiming to achieve fluency in your knowledge of a character. You may find you arrive at some touchstone-like central image as well.
- Focus hard on your protagonists. Lesser characters don't matter nearly as much.
- Non-fiction needs characterisation too. That characterisation can't conflict with the core facts of your narrative, but that doesn't mean it needs to be coolly accurate either.

WHAT IS YOUR STAGE AND
WHERE IS YOUR CAMERA?

Plot and character are the pair of dancers who will create your book, but you can't altogether neglect the stage or the camera.

Finding your stage

Plot and characters emerge from a place and time. You simply couldn't set *Romeo and Juliet* in twenty-first-century London, for example. You couldn't set *Moby Dick* on a contemporary Japanese whaling ship. What's more, the setting you choose will almost certainly reverberate with your characters and plot in a way that enriches both. We noticed that reverberation starting to happen, when we picked *A Winter's Tale* as the theme of our Elly & John story. The notion of a romance set around a single New York winter led us to the idea of a winter of freedom in China and opened up a huge extra dimension of interest to explore with the two protagonists.

For these reasons, it's vital to spend time building up your own understanding of setting, at the same time as you're working with plot and character. The process needs to be iterative, and what you do under any one heading needs to influence what feels right elsewhere too.

Once you've found a way you like working when it comes to characterisation, you'll probably want to use something like the same technique to work on settings. You may not want to ask yourself a hundred questions about your setting ('So, Manhattan, have you ever fallen off a horse? And just what *were* you up to in Mexico?'), but you still need to tease out the elements of place that are likely to hide from view. Thus, for example, everyone knows that Manhattan is cold in winter, that the shops are twinkly, that skaters skate, that coffee is hot, and so on. But the same things are true of almost any city in a northern landscape. We need to know Elly's Manhattan, and John's Manhattan, and the city they jointly share. Does Elly have a thing about the icy Hudson? Does John go jogging round the reservoir in Central Park? Where do they meet when they eat sandwiches together? Do they get them at a deli, and if so, what else does the deli sell? Who runs it? Who frequents it? What do those people sound like, dress like? What do they complain about, comment on? You need to drive at the specific, the individual, the concrete, the detailed. Naturally, you want to build something that feels like a *cohesive* picture of your setting, but the cohesion will emerge from an accumulation of details, and many of those details will be quirky, or unexpected, and won't emerge in any obvious way from some twinkly, snowy, Hollywood version of the city.

What's more – and this is to repeat the lecture given to non-fictioneers at the end of the previous chapter – you need to give attention to your setting, no matter how well you know it. Perhaps you live in the same place as you intend to set your book. (Many first writers do, myself included.) Or perhaps you've seen a hundred movies of the place concerned. These things can help tremendously, but they're still not the same as seeing a place *in words*. You need to make the transition from an actual city (or village, or whatever) to the one that is going to appear in your book. Even if you don't twist the truth at all – and you're welcome to do so, if it suits your purposes – you still need to select the truths and observations that are right for your pages. A sprightly shopping-centred comedy will pick one set of details. A dark psychological thriller might pick quite another. Yet they could easily be set in the exact same spot. So, make notes on *your* setting, your version of the place in question. Let the setting emerge, just as your characters have already done.

Sci-fi and fantasy

If you are writing science fiction or fantasy, your setting will certainly be *a* major character in your work and may even be *the* major character. Anyone who's read China Miéville's *The City & the City* will remember its setting infinitely longer than they recall its somewhat ordinary central character. The America of Neil Gaiman's *American Gods* is utterly central to the whole reading experience. Ditto the Mars of Andy Weir's *The Martian*. And so on. Unsurprisingly, therefore, you need to develop the structure and atmosphere of your chosen world with especial care before you start writing. Three things in particular need some thought.

First, you need to determine the rules of your world. What kind of magic or technologies are possible? Who can deploy them and what are their limitations? If you don't set these rules carefully to begin with, you've potentially given yourself an authorial Get Out of Jail Free card whenever a situation looks perilous for your protagonist. Readers will detect that cheat, and any denouement you do achieve as a result will seem contrived and unsatisfying. So, figure out the rules beforehand and never stray from them. That doesn't mean that you need to reveal them upfront in three long chapters of exposition for the reader. On the contrary, you may well develop some mystery by withholding key elements of your constructed world until fairly late in the book. If you want to make use of that mystery, you need to hold on to your secrets.

Secondly, your rules need to cohere, to make sense. I recently dealt with a first novel by a capable writer who wanted to explore literary themes in a speculative universe. She set her novel in the late twenty-first century. She had spaceships and space stations. And unicorns. The unicorns made no sense. The writer herself felt that since she was writing speculatively, it didn't really matter what she chose to throw in. To a reader, however, the fact that the rules of this world seemed utterly arbitrary rendered the whole literary enterprise incredible. Indeed, something like the same problem occurred throughout the novel. The people in the book all had names like Zil, Tantor and Deelam. That was as much true of any elderly, English-speaking characters as it was of anyone else. But elderly English-speakers of the late twenty-first century are the children being born today. Children with names like Tom, Olivia and Alex. For sure, it's a stupid, picky, and unromantic point that I'm making, but my pickiness nevertheless reveals something true and important about this particular author's characterisation of her world: she hadn't thought it through, she hadn't cared enough. She was being lazy.

Third, there needs to be a reverberation between the story you are telling, the world you are creating and the characters who fill it. To take an example, Lois McMaster Bujold wrote a fantasy novel, *The Curse of Chalion*, about a world where the religion centres not on a Holy Trinity, but a Holy Quintet. Her world has a God the Father, God the Mother, God the Son, God the Daughter and (brilliantly) God the Bastard. This is a thrilling concept with which to launch a novel, but it would risk seeming entirely pointless if the book's narrative didn't tangle with the intricacies of this religion. The narrative has to explore the questions raised by the world you have created. You have to use your characters like elementary particles to bombard your world, testing out its paradoxes and limits.

Andy Weir's *The Martian* is a beautiful example of all of this. The story is set in 2035 and Weir (a computer scientist who is the son of an electrical engineer and a particle physicist) set out to research and build his world with as much precision as possible. The ruthlessly thought-through logic of his world made his character's struggles utterly plausible, utterly realistic. The world built the character, who built the book, which became a movie-adapted bestseller.

Positioning the camera

As you start to plan your novel, you'll also need to consider where to position your camera. Should you write in the first person or the third? Multiple viewpoints, or just the one? Will you write in the present tense or the past?

These questions are intricate enough that I'm going to defer them for later chapters. You, of course, cannot defer them. You can't sensibly start writing your book until you know what you're doing on these scores. For most writers, the answer will be obvious. In my first novel, for example, I knew I was writing about three brothers, with occasional chapters related from the viewpoint of the sister, who played a somewhat secondary role in the story. So I wrote in the third person ('he said ...', 'he saw ...', 'he felt ...'). I used multiple viewpoints, one for each protagonist. I chose to write in the past tense, because it felt more natural and more flexible. I didn't give much thought to what I was doing; I just did it and it worked out fine.

If you have a set of answers that seem obvious and natural, they're very likely the right ones. Perhaps, before you start writing, you'll want to check over the chapters that deal with these issues, but if you have a firm idea of how to proceed, you're probably in good shape already. Excessive analysis may well end up clouding a picture which was clearer when it was left simple.

If, on the other hand, you're not sure about these things, then you *must* read the relevant chapters later in the book – they're in Part Four, 'Placing the Camera' – before you move any further forward. If you make a mess of these issues, not only will your manuscript be a mess, but it'll be a mess that can only be put right with a tremendous amount of work. Few mistakes are as pernicious.

Chapter Summary

- Settings needs characterisation too.
- If you know your book's settings very well already, you still need to start harvesting the kinds of detail that will work for your book. You need to get from practical familiarity to a writerly familiarity.
- Sci-fi and fantasy writers need to take particular care with settings. Those settings need to engage with plot and character. The rules must be determined consistently in advance.
- If you know what you are doing in terms of viewpoint, then fine. If you're not certain, then make absolutely sure you read the relevant section of this book before starting your novel. You risk disaster if you don't.

WHO ARE YOU?

We've dealt with plot, and we've considered character and setting and camera angle, so we're almost ready to venture forth into the writing itself. Just one thing remains, and that is to consider who *you* are.

A particularly bloody killing

Writers are different. Some write in a state of personal struggle, others in a kind of euphoric bliss. Some write with their kids clattering in the next room, others in an ear-plugged, darkened silence. Some write in the early mornings. Others, at home after work. Still others – the obsessives – do it all the time, whenever they can squeeze a moment. I knew one young writer who was getting married and wanted to take his laptop on honeymoon with him. An older and wiser author advised him that to write on the honeymoon would be to write off the honeymoon, and the laptop stayed at home.

Some writers are notebook carriers, Dictaphone wielders, Post-it Note users. Others walk around without so much as a pen in their pocket and have never even had the thought that pasting colour-coded cards round their study walls might be a wonderful way to plot out a novel. Still others – the sort who have already built a spreadsheet, organised in four ways by chapter, character, plot point and emotional tone – are working out how to download a suitable mindmap app to their smartphone.

Some novelists are fast and furious when it comes to the first draft. I know one author who profoundly dislikes the act of getting that first draft down onto the computer. He works fast, disliking every sentence that comes from his fingers. In between writing, he paces round and round his (smallish) room, so much so that his study carpet has a rectangular groove in it where his pacing has worn it. Only once he reaches those final words, THE END, does he relax. It's not that he stops working; it's just that, for him, the fun bit can start: the editing, the questioning, the reshaping, the pruning. That editing process takes several times the length of time that the initial writing process did.

I know another writer who edits as she goes. She may go over a chapter some forty or fifty times before proceeding to the next. Her 'first draft' novel is more like a fortieth draft. There may still be some further editing to be done before the manuscript goes off to a publisher, but most of the necessary work has already been done.

Some authors write longhand to start with, then transfer everything to a computer for the editing process. Others (nearly all) write on computer from the beginning. I don't know any serious author who doesn't use a computer at all. (And the sensible ones save their manuscript in a single computer file. Some newer writers keep all their chapters in different files, which makes editing the book and skimming through to review structural issues almost impossible. Any computer, unless it's actually steam-powered, will easily handle manuscripts of 200,000 words and more. And do remember to back things up – the easiest way is to make sure that everything you write is auto-backed up into cloud storage somewhere. If you don't know what that means or how to accomplish that happy goal, ask someone who does.)

Some writers like their work. They're generous to it, forgiving, warm and respectful. Others live in a kind of horror at a malformed sentence. Booker-Prize-winning author John Banville has commented about his (deeply impressive) collection of published novels: 'I hate them all ... I loathe them. They're all a standing embarrassment'. His wife once described him during the act of writing as being like 'a murderer who's just come back from a particularly bloody killing'. Still other writers are bipolar. They love their work when they're writing it, then turn savagely critical as they're editing it. Plenty of authors (including, for a long time, myself) can't bear to re-read their printed work, because the impulse to start re-editing it becomes unbearable.

Some writers are word count fanatics. They set themselves a daily target and stop once they've reached it. Antony Trollope used to start work at 5.30 am and write for three hours with his watch in front of him. He aimed to produce 250 words in each quarter of an hour. If he finished a novel before 8.30, he took a fresh sheet and started a new one.

Still other writers have on occasion worked at a rate that would make Trollope seem idle. Robert Louis Stevenson's stepson recalls the creation of *Strange Case of Dr Jekyll and Mr Hyde* thus: 'I remember the first reading as if it were yesterday. Louis came downstairs in a fever; read nearly half the book aloud; and then, while we were still gasping, he was away again, and busy writing. I doubt if the first draft took so long as three days'. Libbie Hawker's bestselling *Take Off Your Pants!* is a book that encourages seat-of-the-pants plotters to get organised. She writes her own 90,000-word novels in three weeks and promises to show how you can do the same.

Some writers are so miserly with their output that they only ever produce one book. Harper Lee is one such writer – though since her *To Kill a Mockingbird* has sold thirty million copies and been translated into forty languages, it would have been a little hard to improve on. Aged eighty, she refused a speaking engagement, saying, 'Well, it's better to be silent than to be a fool'. Barbara Cartland, on the other hand, rejected the alternative of silence, writing over 700 books in the course of her career. (And, OK: there's also *Go Set a Watchman*. But that was just an early draft of *Mockingbird*, and wasn't much good, so I'm not going to count it.)

Back in the good old days, writers liked a tipple. F. Scott Fitzgerald was a drunk. So were Raymond Chandler and James Joyce. So were Tennessee Williams, Dylan Thomas, Dorothy Parker, William Faulkner, Charles Bukowski and Ernest Hemingway. You could add Jack Kerouac, Hunter S. Thompson, and Evelyn Waugh to the list, except that they liked drugs as well as the booze. The poet Allen Ginsberg campaigned against tobacco with the slogan 'No don't smoke the official Dope, Smoke Dope Dope'. (Despite the perky catchiness of the phrase, no government agency chose to adopt it.) Thomas De Quincey blew his brain with laudanum (a mixture of opium and alcohol), then wrote a book about it. Aldous Huxley blew his mind with peyote, mescaline and LSD, then wrote a book telling us to do the same. In 1997, the British novelist, Will Self, snorted heroin on the Prime Ministerial jet and was subsequently fired by the newspaper he'd been working for at the time.

These days, writers are less red-blooded than they were. For most of us, substance abuse is likely to consist of nothing worse than over-indulgence in peppermint tea and home-made fudge. Our rehab programmes of choice are long country walks or popping out to the gym. Confirming the trend, a Scottish psychiatrist, Dr Iain Smith, has argued that stimulants only create an illusion of creativity. 'Artists and writers often portray it as being the case that alcohol and drugs help their creativity,' he said, 'but the evidence suggests that the opposite is the case.' Even with highly alcoholic writers, Smith reports they mostly produced their greatest work when sober.

The only rules

There is no single working method that suits all writers. Indeed, there is no single working method that reliably works for any one writer. I, at any rate, jiggle my method around according to my taste and fancy of the moment.

You need to do the same. If you like to write fast and furious, please do so. If you like to move slowly, then do that. If mornings work for you, write in the mornings. If last thing at night is your thing, write then. And try different things. You're unlikely to find your most comfortable working method at the first attempt, so try out a few different ways. Try to evolve a rhythm that works for you. As you seek to evolve that rhythm, do bear in mind that you-the-writer is quite likely to resemble you-the-human-being.

So, if you are messily disorganised in everyday life, it is not highly probable that you are going to start filing index cards, updating spreadsheets and maintaining a system of colour-coded Post-it Notes on your study walls. Go with the person you are, not the one you think you ought to be.

That aside, I think there are only two rules that apply to pretty much every serious writer. First of all, you are only a writer if you *write*. Keeping a notebook is not writing. Admiring autumn leaves and raindrops on cobwebs is not writing. Joining online writing communities is not writing. Reading this book is not writing. Those things may all be valuable supplements to the main activity, but you only qualify as a writer when you start writing a book and each week, pretty much, that book gets longer.

Secondly, no serious writer is idle about editing. It doesn't matter whether you like to produce a first draft in a rush and edit at leisure, or whether you prefer to edit and re-edit as you go. But perfectionism matters. A willingness to radically re-appraise your work is essential. If, on review, you find that one character (and a large chunk of the book) needs to vanish, you need to do the evil deed – and do it again, and again, until the book is right.

Don't give up the day job

These may be the only two rules that matter, but I'd also advise a little prudence. Even for most published writers, writing is not a profession that pays much, or pays reliably. If you're not yet published, you face a cliff-face of uncertainty which you have to scale before you even reach the hostile plateau where pro authors must scratch out their living. So, pay attention to the day job. Give it as much care and dedication as you would do if you had never in your life dreamed about being the first person to go on Oprah, win a Pulitzer and accept a Nobel Prize all on the same day.

The same thing goes for your relationships. You *will* be un-faithful to your partner; you have to be. Your book will demand a certain kind of creative energy from you, and you will give it. But your loved ones are more important than your book. It's fine if you reduce their rations for a season or two, but you cannot withdraw your attention and commitment indefinitely.

And third, enjoy it! There's a thread among writers talking online and amongst themselves in writing groups which speaks of writing as something arduous but necessary, like shovelling snow or clearing gutters. I've never understood this. If you don't *enjoy* your writing, why the heck are you doing it? The chances of success are hideously small (though they'll be larger if you read this book, and larger still if you make use of it). The rewards of success are often puny, and authorial careers are down there with First World War pursuit pilot in terms of longevity and dependability.

In any case, writing *is* fun, so if you're not enjoying it, you're doing something wrong. Lighten up. Notice the pleasures as they come. When things feel like a slog – and they will – remember the times that have felt different. Find pleasure in your daily achievements. And if, over time, you notice that writing makes you feel worse, not better, stop doing it. Give it up. Play golf, knit a sweater, take a holiday, buy a dog. There's no honour in doing something hard and disagreeable that no one in the world needs you to do.

And dogs are lovely.

Chapter Summary

- You need to feel out the working method that suits you.
- But your working method *must* include actually writing, and it *must* accommodate serious editing and re-editing of your work.
- Have fun. If you aren't having fun, get a dog.

Some Common Mistakes

At the start of this section on planning, I said truthfully – if scarily – that many books are ruined before they're started. If you've made good use of this opening section, your chances of going badly wrong will be vastly reduced. When you set out on your adventure, dog sled harnessed, runners greased, and pemmican packed, you may even be heading within a degree or two of true north, skimming over the snow, full of a justified confidence that you'll wind up within an honourable distance of your target, and every chance of making it there in the end.

Going for it

Nevertheless, and in the interests of taking every precaution, you may just wish to check that you haven't committed any of the following common errors.

- *Writing a literary novel that isn't literary*. If you want to write a literary novel – the sort of thing that might win a Pulitzer or a Booker; the sort of thing talked about on culture shows and discussed in book groups – then make sure it's *literary*. A theme alone doesn't make a thing literary. If you are writing a novel about the way our society neglects our old folk, you have an important topic to write about. You and I can both agree that these things matter. But if your prose style is nothing more than competent, if your characters are efficient but nothing more, you have not written a literary novel and it will not sell. What you have is a heap of paper.

- *Writing a thriller that doesn't thrill.* Equally, if you are writing a thriller, then make sure it thrills. That's not code for 'entertains somewhat'. At Jericho Writers, we often receive 'thrillers' that are nicely mannered, where fights don't hurt anyone too much, where the cops are always decent and the villain is always going to get their comeuppance. When we tell their authors that they have written a manuscript that falls way short of commercial acceptability, we're told, 'Oh yes, but I hate all that violent stuff.' Fine, then write a different sort of book. A thriller *must* thrill. The standard of writing in this area – particularly in the US – is exceptionally high and you cannot fall short of it. A non-thrilling thriller is a contradiction in terms and it cannot sell.

- *Writing experimental, post-modern literary fiction.* Experiment, by all means. Then write a book that might actually sell. Experimentalism as a literary fashion is dead.

- *Rewriting classics. The Lord of the Rings* has already been written. It's been quite a success, apparently.

- *Turning your favourite computer game into a novel.* A computer game is not a novel and doesn't want to be one. And vice versa.

- *Writing the kind of book you loved as a child or young adult.* This is a common problem with writers of children's fiction that come to the game relatively late in life. But it's also a problem for anyone whose reading habits are still stuck in the past. And again, my editorial colleagues at Jericho Writers still receive a trickle of those slightly toe-curling novels about formidable duchesses, blustering majors, randy vicars and dithering postmistresses. Maybe once there was a market for such things, but there isn't any more (thank goodness). You must write for the market as it is today. If you don't like it, feel free to write for yourself and for your friends. Just give up any thought of commercial publication.

- *Writing a 'small book'.* Often new writers tell us that they realise their book isn't going to be hugely commercial, but they'd be perfectly happy to see their book published in a small way. That shows a delightful modesty – and a total lack of realism about the economics of publishing. A micro-publisher with any ambitions of launching a novel will still need to budget $25,000 or more to get it off the ground, and that's excluding any advance to you. Given that launching debut fiction is a desperately uncertain business, no sane publisher will commit that kind of money to any project unless they think it can sell in reasonable volumes. It's not the extent of your modesty which will determine a publisher's objectives, it's whether or not they stand to make money.

- *Thinking that self-publishing releases you from market pressure.* It doesn't. It just shifts the pressure from the agent/publisher to the reader. There are seven or eight million e-books on the Amazon store. That number is growing all the time. The majority of those books have each sold either zero copies or a single-digit number of copies. You'll only really start to make money when you have several titles in the top 20 to 30,000. Self-publishing doesn't release you from commercial pressure. It brings that pressure up close and personal. (Which is good, by the way. We're here to please readers. If we're not doing that, we're not doing our job.)

- *Forgetting that a book needs to be marketed.* A commissioning editor at any large publishing house will receive dozens of manuscripts, all perfectly competent, all sent in by capable literary agents, every month. If she's to acquire your book, that editor will need to champion it to others in the firm. She needs to build support across the departments: in editorial, in sales, in marketing. That's a tough job, and you need to do all you can to help her. No sales director is going to go all gooey inside because you've got a lovely prose style. Salespeople and marketers require angles. They require a USP (Unique Selling Point). Same thing for indie publishers. Yes, you can write your own book description, but Amazon browsers are brutal. If you can't successfully pitch your book in a hundred words or so, you'll never sell it at all. That USP matters. Don't build a book without it.

- *Misjudging the hook.* Writers who remember that their book needs a selling point often misjudge what a selling point might consist of. If your book is about a trip to Europe that went disastrously wrong, don't kid yourself that your market is 'all people who have ever been to Europe'. If you're not sure what a hook might be, go back to the chapter titled 'What Is Your Market?'. You need to read a lot of current, debut fiction in your genre and get a feel for what kind of books are selling. See what those authors are doing to get published. Then do the same – only make it new and different and a pace or two ahead of the pack.

- *Writing as therapy.* Writing *is* therapy if you are doing it for yourself and for your own healing. It's a terrific thing to do and the benefits have been clinically proven. But clinical proof has nothing to do with the ways of publishers. Publishers (and self-publishers) need work they can sell. That means you can't think about your work as therapy; you have to think about it as a product. If you don't want to do that, then don't. Writing is worthwhile, whether or not you ever choose to seek publication.

- *Writing to please your creative writing teacher.* If you've studied creative writing to any advanced level, then you'll have worked through a whole host of exercises about writing with your senses, using memory, individuating dialogue, and much else. You'll be a better writer as a result. But creative writing teachers have a natural tendency to encourage *creativity* rather than *marketability*. If creative writing teachers were in the market for manuscripts, you should bust a gut to please them – but they're not. Publishers are. Readers are. If you have to please creative writing tutors or the market at large, I suggest you please the one holding the cheque book.

- *Writing boring non-fiction.* There are lots of important and interesting subjects in the world, and perhaps you know a lot about one of them. Perhaps you even have some academic qualifications in the field. If so, you need to choose. You can write a worthy and important book for an academic press, which will quite likely price it at some crazily high price, and the book will never be widely read or sold. Or you can write an entertaining one for a trade publisher, and see your book priced to sell and actively marketed. Both options have their merits, but you can't expect to write a boring book and sell it to a trade publisher. They won't buy it.

- *Holding something back for the trilogy.* Your trilogy will sell if your first book blows people's minds. If your first book is lacking in any way at all, there'll never be a third book, or a second, or a first. So give that first book all you've got.

There are, on the whole, two threads running through these comments. The first is that *if you want to write for publication, you must write for the market.* That should be so obvious as not to need saying, but there's a persistent belief that somehow the literary world hovers above the world of sordid commerce. It doesn't. It's like investment banking, only without the money.

The second thread is that if you are to write for the market, *you have to go for it.* You have to make your thriller thrill. Your chick lit has to be funny and engaging; your weepie has to draw tears; your literary novel has to dazzle. When top agents are taking one in every 2,000 manuscripts to come their way, second best isn't even close to good enough. You have to excel, and you won't achieve that unless you go for it with everything you've got.

A word about words

On a slightly different score, writers sometimes go wrong by misjudging the length their book should be. The only decisive way to know how long *your* book should be is to go to a bookshop, find some comparable works and estimate their word counts. But for a quick guide, then the following rules apply to most authors most of the time.

- A typical **adult novel** is somewhere between 75 and 120,000 words in length. If you are writing something with an epic feel, you may certainly go longer still. My first novel was sold to publishers at 190,000 words and was still over 180,000 when it went to print. At Jericho Writers, we once helped an author cut her manuscript from 500,000 words to 220,000, then helped her secure an agent. The book was a fraction under 200,000 words when it was published (and promptly became a bestseller). For normal fiction, however, these very large word counts are rare exceptions. The further you creep above 120,000 words, the more carefully you need to scrutinise your text for excess verbiage. In most cases, there'll be a lot. At the other end of the scale, it's rare to see a commercial novel sell if it's much less than 75,000 words. A literary novel may well be as little as 50 or 60,000, but the shorter your book gets, the better it needs to be. For very short fiction, it's helpful if you have already won a major literary prize or two.

- If you are a **self-publisher**, and especially if you are writing series fiction with a view to earning a living from it, you will need to write a lot of books. The result is that a lot of self-published books are somewhat shorter than their trad-published cousins. Not *much* shorter, of course – you still need to please your audience – but the lower edge of self-published commercial fiction perhaps stands at 60,000 words or so, rather than 75,000.

- If you are writing **children's fiction**, you need to judge your book as carefully as you can against similar books written for a similar age group. Buy some comparable books. Count the words on an average page, then multiply up to get a total word count. You need to write material that falls in the same sort of range, or you will disqualify yourself from the market. Oh, and don't use the huge later books of J. K. Rowling to justify some gigantic word count. Once you're a global bestseller, you can do what you like. Until then, you play by the rules.

- If you are writing **fantasy fiction**, very long word counts are quite common. Even here, however, you need to ask yourself if you really need that 200,001st word. I bet you don't.

- If you are writing **travel** or **memoir** or **inspirational true-life story**, the standard word count would be somewhere in the 70 to 100,000-word range. If your manuscript falls far outside that range, you need to question whether you are correctly understanding the market for such work.

- For other narrative non-fiction – **history or biography**, for example – word counts can vary a fair bit according to topic. Anything much less than 75,000 words is a short book, but books as short as 50,000 words will be published if they're good enough and on a strongly marketable topic. Equally, very long books – 200,000 words or more – can sometimes be published if the topic is outstanding and you are superbly qualified to write it. But take care with any unusual word count. Don't rely on instinct. Go to a bookshop and check.

- Finally, and although it falls rather outside the scope of this book, **novelty** books can of course be very short indeed. So can some **motivational** or 'how to' texts. If in doubt, go to a shop.

- **Self-publishing** allows a much greater range of pricing and length. (Yet another great thing about it.) But you still have to deliver value. So, if you want to sell a 25,000-word novella, you certainly can. But if you price that bad boy at $6.99, you should expect terrible reader reviews, because you're not delivering the value that people expect. So check the market and price accordingly.

Mush, mush

If you've planned your novel properly, you've taken care to write for the market, and you're really going to go for it, you're all set to leave Base Camp. Pull on your balaclava and hitch up those huskies. It's time to write the first word.

Chapter Summary

- Check that you're not about to fall into any of the common traps.
- Familiarise yourself with the approximate lengths of books in your market.
- Then start mushing.

Part Two
Prose Style

When you open a novel – and I mean of course the real thing – you enter into a state of intimacy with its writer. You hear a voice or, more significantly, an individual tone under the words. This tone you, the reader, will identify not so much by a name, the name of the author, as by a distinct and unique human quality. It seems to issue from the bosom, from a place beneath the breastbone. It is more musical than verbal, and it is the characteristic signature of a person, of a soul. Such a writer has power over distraction and fragmentation, and out of distressing unrest, even from the edge of chaos, he can bring unity and carry us into a state of intransitive attention. People hunger for this.

– Saul Bellow

When a man's thoughts are clear, the properest words will generally offer themselves first, and his own judgment will direct him in what order to place them so as they may be best understood.

– Jonathan Swift

I got a sense of the power of restraint from Hemingway, which is the smallest way to put it, because I got much more than that from him. I learned the power of simple language in English. He showed what a powerful instrument English is if you keep the language simple, if you don't use too many Latinate words. And from Faulkner I learned the exact opposite, that excess can be thrilling, that, 'Don't hold yourself in. Don't rein yourself in. Go all the way. Go over the top. Overdo it.' And between the two, it's almost as if you've now been given your parameters. This is the best of one extreme and this is the best of another. And somewhere between the two you may be able to find your style in time to come.

– Norman Mailer

CLARITY

New writers often complain that agents don't read the work that comes their way. This is half right, but it's not the full picture.

Because agents deal with such a huge volume of submissions, they have to develop a system that quickly filters the no-hopers from the maybe-possibles. And, while most of the things that matter about books take time to reveal themselves, there are two obvious exceptions:

- *The quality of the concept.* If a book is clearly unmarketable – a thriller that's way too short, a literary novel that's ludicrously experimental, or whatever else – an agent can confidently reject it, perhaps from the covering letter alone.

- *The quality of prose.* You want to write a book. Books are made up of sentences. If your sentences are bad, your book will be bad, so it will be rejected. A skilled professional reader can make a fair estimate of your prose quality in half a minute, and often less. Those judgements are almost always correct. And, as ever, the same basic strictures apply to self-publishing too. It's true that readers are often less snobbish than agents, but prose still needs to be *effective*. It needs to convey the story. Bad prose will kill your book, no matter what your mode of publication.

We've dealt enough with the first of these two issues. This section of the book will deal intensively with the second. If you want to write a literary novel, your prose must be wonderful. If you want to write a commercial one, it must be competent. Both things are hard to achieve, and you must not fail to achieve them. There are still, however, far too many writers who somehow think that their work exists in some realm beyond that of words and sentences, that some genius quality of plot or concept will carry them over any number of speed bumps in the language itself. It won't. Not only will those speed bumps fatally disable the book, the genius of your concept won't even emerge from the stumbling execution. Prose style matters vastly, and the lesson begins here.

Beautiful clarity

The first task of language is communication, and communication needs clarity. That sounds like the simplest of all possible tasks – after all, you presumably manage to navigate your ordinary life without sowing confusion and doubt among those you talk to – but the printed page is less forgiving. Your only engagement with your reader is via words. You've got no gesture, no tone, no opportunity to interject or correct. Consequently, a simple-looking task is in practice quite complicated, and a significant proportion of new manuscripts are studded with numerous problems of comprehension. These problems may individually be minor, but cumulatively they are lethal.

Take the following snippet:

Men grappled at the night sky and the secrets that it begrudged to them.

This is a terrible sentence. We can just about make out what it means – but only just. Men *can't* grapple at the night sky: it's too far away, and in any case, it's made out of thin air and the interstellar void. There's nothing you can grapple *with*. There's a clue later in the sentence, however, in the word 'secrets'. Presumably, men are grappling with the *mysteries* of the night sky ... though they might do better to start by tackling the mystery of the second half of the sentence. If you begrudge something, you withhold it, you don't begrudge anything *to* someone. Perhaps the author means 'bequeath' – only that makes no sense of the first bit of the sentence. Probably, then, the author means this:

Men grappled with the mysteries of the night sky, but the sky begrudged its secrets.

Or if you prefer, then this:

Men grappled with the mysteries of the night sky, but the sky was grudging and gave them little.

Or this:

Men grappled with the mysteries of the night sky, but the sky was cruel and withheld its secrets.

I hope you can see that the second two formulations of the sentence are better than the first. All three versions are readily comprehensible, because we've connected the word 'grapple' with something that can (metaphorically) be grappled with, and because we've ditched the baffling phrase 'begrudged to' and replaced it with something that makes good clear sense.

The reason why the second and third versions work better is that the first sentence lacks a precise sense of closure. The sentence's opening creates a question: 'Golly, gosh, I wonder whether those men are going to figure out the mysteries of the night sky?' In the first version of the sentence, you don't quite achieve that closure. You can begrudge something, but hand it over nevertheless. So as things stand, there's a tiny doubt about the correct answer. The second and third formulations eliminate that doubt. They give a precise answer to the question that was raised – a few secrets in one case, none at all in the other.

Now you, of course, would never write such a hideous sentence as that first example. You're much better than that. But you might possibly write something like this:

Sergei hoisted the heavy chest up onto the deck of the twin-engined yacht and shut its heavy brass lock.

Do you know what that sentence means? You do, of course. It's obvious. At the same time, however, if you watch your feelings as you read the sentence, you'll encounter not one problem but two. (And a third, which we'll get to in a bit.)

First of all, that word 'lock' is wrong. You can't *shut* a lock. You can *lock* it, or you can *close, shut* or *fasten* a clasp. I imagine that the author is intending us to imagine a clasp. Because you are a sophisticated communicator, you probably made a little mental adjustment to the author's statement and would (if you'd had more text in front of you) have been ready to read further. But the damage has already been done. That mental adjustment required a moment's effort on your part. Your forward momentum was imperceptibly slowed. If, as you read further, you had encountered a number of similar problems – perhaps as many as a dozen on every page – then the act of reading would quickly seem like a strain, not a pleasure. If you had just downloaded a $0.99 e-book, you'd quit reading and turn to something else. If you were an agent, you'd stop reading and reject the book. Either way, that author's career is over before it's started.

The second problem with the sentence is grammatical. The word 'its' theoretically points back to the most recent noun, and the nouns 'deck' and 'yacht' are therefore jostling for attention more aggressively than the word 'chest', which is the correct option. Again, it's not hard for us to make the necessary mental adjustment, but we don't want to have to do any work at all. We're reading for fun, not exercise.

Restructuring the sentence is perfectly simple. For example:

Sergei hoisted the chest up onto the deck and locked it.

The little ripple of uncertainty that bedevilled the first version of that sentence is gone. The new one has nothing extraordinary to recommend it – it's not a thing of beauty – but it does its job, cleanly and simply, then gets out of the way. It's perfectly decent writing. (If you're worried by that grammatical problem – does the word 'it' refer to 'deck' or to 'chest'? – then relax. By eliminating one of the intervening nouns, 'yacht', and simplifying the entire sentence, we've effectively solved the problem. The first sentence sounded awkward. The refurbished model sounds just fine. That's all that matters.)

What matters here is attitude; your attitude as a writer. Almost certainly, as you read the paragraphs above, a little part of you was saying something like, 'Jiminy Cricket, aren't you making a meal of this? It's only a *word*'. And that part of your brain needs to die, I'm sorry to say. A word is never *only* a word. It's your means of communication.

The single largest part of developing your skill with words has to do with precision. Precision matters more than almost anything. And for your language to be precise, you have to become pedantic. You have to worry about whether you *lock* clasps or *fasten* them. You have to worry whether you begrudge things or begrudge them *to* someone. You have to worry about whether you can *grapple* with the sky, and whether the meaning of *its* could be confusing, given the context. It's only by attending to the details that you can ever hope to create a big picture that moves and compels the reader. A writer needs to be obsessed by words, just as an artist needs to be obsessed by paint.

Pedantry is your friend. Embrace it.

A task for every sentence

We've concentrated so far on word choice. The poor sentences above failed because their writers made wrong or lazy choices when it came to selecting the right word. But that's not the only way to baffle a reader:

> *The door was painted apple green, but it must once have been painted blue, because you could see the blue flecks showing through, not that I was noticing such things that time my father collapsed through it, blood spurting from a bullet wound over his stomach.*

There's no problem with word choice there, no problem with grammar, but it's still a ridiculous sentence, because its focus shifts so abruptly and so without logic. What's worse, the second part of the sentence rubbishes the information given in the first ('not that I was noticing such things ...'). If the narrator dismisses the door like this, doesn't the reader have a right to feel miffed for having had her time wasted?

The sentence above is comically bad, but muddled focus can create confusion in more subtle ways. Take our friend Sergei again:

> Sergei hoisted the heavy chest up onto the deck of the twin-engined yacht and shut its heavy brass lock.

In addition to the problems we came across earlier, there's an additional one. What is the focus of this sentence? What is it trying to communicate? Is it trying to describe a chest? Describe a ship? Describe a lock? Or report an action? It's doing everything at once, which means the reader isn't entirely sure which way to look or what point to take away. And we could just have said this:

> Sergei hoisted the chest up onto the deck and locked it. The yacht was twin-engined and fast.

We've ditched any description of the chest's lock – because it doesn't seem important – and separated out the action being reported from the description of where we are. A sentence that previously felt clunky and confusing now feels clean, simple and easy to understand. Where the first version felt sluggish, the second one feels swift. Our reader is on the move and keen to keep reading. The trick here is to make sure that every sentence has a task and that it does its task without confusion before giving way logically to the next. That sounds easy – and it is – but your book will contain some 5 to 10,000 sentences, and you can only allow yourself the merest handful of errors.

When you switch from reading bad sentences to something that's well-written, the relief washes over you. For example:

A thin blond man sat in the hard chair in Poitras's office. He wore brown slacks and brand-new tan Bally loafers with little tassels and a brown coarse-knit jacket with patches on the elbows. He had a dark beige shirt and a yellow tie with little white camels. Silk. He glowed the way skinny guys glow when they get up early and play three sets at the club. I made him for Stanford Law. Poitras dropped into his chair behind his desk and said, 'This is O'Bannon.' When Poitras looked at O'Bannon, his flat face hardened and his eyes ticked. (From *The Monkey's Raincoat*, by Robert Crais.)

Do you feel the perfect clarity of this writing? That's got a lot to do with the way each sentence has its own job to do. The first sentence introduces the key element of this little scene: there is a man sitting in Poitras's office. The next two sentences describe his clothing in some detail. The next one ('Silk.') completes the description, with a hint of disapproval. And so on. Each sentence is given its job; it does its job; then it ends. The result is that the reader always knows exactly the point that Crais is making, and the forward flow of the narrative is uninterrupted.

It's also important to understand that making your writing clear does *not* mean that it has to be unsophisticated. Crais writes thrillers – very good ones – and his writing has the brevity and snappiness of that genre. But his writing is always sophisticated. That final phrase 'his eyes ticked' is a wonderful metaphor that turns Poitras's eyes into ticking clocks, or possibly even into bombs. It drops a tiny seed of danger into a paragraph that has mostly been about a stranger's clothes. Or take the sentence, 'He glowed the way skinny guys glow when they get up early and play three sets at the club'. On the surface, the narrator is simply communicating something about O'Bannon's glow and its probable cause. Except that a couple of well-aimed jabs (the comment about skinny guys, the addition of 'at the club' at the end of the sentence) communicate something else entirely: namely, that the narrator reckons he could kick O'Bannon's ass.

Your writing can be clear, but also sophisticated. Each sentence can be clear, but it can be clear at two levels, not just the one.

Confusion bad, mystery good

'Clean and simple' is a good motto to have when writing, but that doesn't mean you can't throw in more exotic ingredients from time to time. It only means that you need to take care. Here's how *not* to do it.

> *It was luxurious to be there then, reclining at the poolside in those Tuscan hills, swatting irritably at the mosquitos.*
>
> *Edgar was a soft, furious man. He'd arrived late, because of some problem to do with the line, and was profuse with his gifts and his apologies.*

These snippets read quite gracefully, except that it's hard for the reader to make sense of the juxtaposition of 'luxurious' and 'irritably' in the first example, and 'furious' and 'profuse ... apologies' in the second. We could just eliminate the mosquitos from the first example and the word 'furious' in the second, but that would be to remove their most interesting elements. Instead, we just need to make sure that, having disconcerted the reader by introducing something unexpected, we help them out:

> *It was luxurious to be there then, reclining at the poolside in those Tuscan hills, sipping our proseccos and swatting amiably at the mosquitos, which we were too idle to hunt with any vigour.*
>
> *Edgar was a soft, furious man. He'd arrived late, because of some problem to do with the line, and was profuse with his gifts and his apologies. But always too profuse, too apologetic, as though a summer thunderstorm lurked ready to burst just beyond the apology's horizon.*

In the first example, we've kept the mosquitos, but have woven them into a fabric of contented laziness. In the second example, we've started to knit together the 'furious' and the 'apologies', with an explanation of how Edgar manages to combine the two.

This quality of sewing together unexpected elements, and doing so while retaining the reader's absolute confidence, is often a mark of genuinely excellent writing. These beautiful opening lines, for example:

> *I'm Homer, the blind brother. I didn't lose my sight all at once, it was like the movies, a slow fade-out. When I was told what was happening, I was interested to measure it, I was in my late teens then, keen on everything.* (The opening sentences of *Homer & Langley*, E. L. Doctorow.)

How well this works! And how simple it is! Anyone reading this book is, in principle, capable of writing those sentences. Doctorow (a literary author) isn't flaunting some amazing vocabulary, concocting some extraordinarily complex grammar, or deploying some abstruse but wonderful piece of imagery. He's just doing the simple things, really well – and a critical part of what he's doing is creating strong sensations in the reader and handling them appropriately.

Thus, Doctorow knows that we'll be captivated by the word 'blind', in the first sentence, so he gives us the further information we want: not 'all at once … [but] a slow fade-out'. This in turn provokes the question, 'What is it like to go blind?' So Doctorow tells us – but tells us something utterly unexpected. Instead of mentioning some huge sense of loss, the narrator says, 'I was interested to measure it, I was in my late teens then, keen on everything'. That's the last thing we were expecting to hear, but we don't feel *confused* (a problematic feeling) we feel *intrigued* and *mystified* (a wholly excellent one). We're just forty-four words into Doctorow's novel and he has us in his power. If an agent were to read those opening lines, he'd be excited already.

If I'm a casually browsing reader, I've already hit the 'Buy' button.

Chapter Summary

- Prose style matters intensely. Probably over 50% of manuscripts rejected by agents will be rejected because their writers haven't taken enough care with their writing style.

- The single most important virtue in any piece of writing is clarity – making your meaning clear.

- Make sure that you use precisely the right word for the job. Be relentlessly pedantic when you come to interrogate your own work. That pedantry is really no more than a quest for accuracy.

- Give each sentence one job to do. Don't overload a sentence with a whole set of different focuses. It won't work.

- By all means, create surprise and mystery in your writing – but take care to distinguish between mystery (which is excellent) and confusion (which is destructive).

- Remember to look after your reader. If you generate a question in a reader ('Gosh! What must it be like to go blind?'), then either answer it, or make it clear that you are intending to leave the issue mysterious for the moment.

ECONOMY

Brevity is the soul of wit. – **William Shakespeare**

Clarity may well be the first virtue of professional and effective writing, but if so, then economy is surely the second.

Should you require proof, look back at that opening sentence. It's terrible. I could have said:

> *If clarity is the first virtue of effective writing, economy is the second.*

The first sentence is twenty-one words long, the second one thirteen. That's a difference of eight words.

If you think it's petty to care about eight words, you haven't yet understood the degree of pedantry you need to cultivate as a writer. The longer sentence is over 50% longer than the shorter one, and it says the same thing. If you carry that same sloppy attitude into a manuscript that ought to be 100,000 words long, you'll have a manuscript of 150,000 words, of which fully a third are not required. Such a huge, purposeless cargo will sink the vessel.

A cautionary tale

One of the most remarkable publishing stories of recent years revolves around an under-edited manuscript. A fifty-year-old Swedish journalist had written three novels, initially for fun and only later with the thought of publication. He delivered them to his Swedish publisher, then died of a heart attack. The novels were accepted for publication in Sweden, but when it came to selling the international rights, Anglo-Saxon publishers were largely unmoved. The books were terrific, but vastly too long. Each manuscript really needed to be at least 30,000 words shorter, and the author was no longer around to make the necessary edits. All the major British houses rejected the manuscript. So did the Americans. The story was simply too baggy. Wonderful, but overweight.

In the end, a tiny British publisher acquired world English rights: that is, the right to publish an English translation of the book, anywhere in the world. Then, in a stroke of publishing genius, they changed the title of the first book to *The Girl with the Dragon Tattoo*, put a fantastic cover on it, and marketed their hearts out. The campaign worked. The book, as we now know, became a huge international success. The author, Stieg Larsson, became a bestseller almost on a par with J. K. Rowling, Dan Brown and Stephenie Meyer. Once that success was already starting to be visible, but only then, were the North American rights snapped up by Knopf, a part of Random House, which went on to profit handsomely from their bet.

There are two morals you could draw from this story. The first (hopelessly wrong) one is that economy doesn't matter, since you can succeed without it. The second (infinitely more accurate) one is that one of the best crime novels of recent years – an excellent heroine, a strong hero, a classic mystery puzzle, loads of atmosphere, a splash of conspiracy, and some fine set-pieces – almost failed because its author hadn't pruned it properly. A less excellent book would never have been published at all. Even as it was, the book required dazzlingly committed and imaginative marketing to avoid vanishing from sight altogether.

So economy matters. It matters vastly.

Word by word

Pruning your manuscript is one of the simplest exercises there is. You simply have to do it with sufficient rigour. That means analysing every sentence you write to make sure it is as lean as it should be. It means turning these monsters:

> *The snows came early that year, lying cold and white across the landscape.*
>
> *Rufus was the sort of dog that absolutely anyone could – and probably would – fall in love with.*
>
> *The station waiting room was twenty foot long by about half that amount wide, but on this occasion it was completely empty, except for a single red butterfly struggling feebly in the corner of the window.*

Into these beauties:

> *The snows came early that year.*
>
> *Rufus was a dog to fall in love with.*
>
> *The waiting room was empty, but for a red butterfly struggling in the window.*

I hope it's obvious why the second set of sentences is better. Snow is always cold and white, and it's got nowhere to lie but landscapes. The long straggle of words in the middle of the Rufus sentence adds nothing. In the case of the third sentence, readers don't give a damn about the size of the waiting room (unless it's about to play a critical part in what follows), so don't tell them about it. I also, however, hope it's obvious that the sentences have got clearer, as well as shorter. The essential meaning of each one has become more distinct, because it's not being smothered by a quilt of unnecessary verbiage.

The first draft of your manuscript will almost certainly contain monstrosities like those above. That's fine. That's what first drafts are for: they give writers something to tinker with. The only way to hone your draft is to get into the habit of scrutinising every word and every phrase in every sentence, and not just once but repeatedly. If that seems like a lot of work – well, it is. Welcome to the world of writing. There are no shortcuts, no spellcheck to help you. You simply need to go through your manuscript and delete everything that needs deleting. Because you won't catch everything the first time, you need to do it multiple times. That's just the way it is.

Nor is it just a question of hitting the 'delete' key a lot. You also need to tweak. In the waiting room sentence, I changed the initial *'except* for a single red butterfly ...' to a *'but* for a single ...', because I thought the rhythm worked better that way. The more you delete, the more you need to rewrite.

Sentence by sentence and paragraph by paragraph

You need to scrutinise your work at the level of words and phrases, but you also need to work at the level of sentences and paragraphs, scenes and chapters. Nothing comes with diplomatic immunity. Nothing is beyond review.

This means that you need, mentally, to operate at a variety of levels. At our annual Festival of Writing, I've occasionally asked students to condense the following paragraph:

> *Lucinda Roberts left the room ahead of her people who were still packing away their presentation papers and ring binders. She pushed the bell for the elevator, then entered when its doors swished open. She pressed the button for the ground floor and allowed herself a few moments of satisfied inspection in the full-length mirror at the back of the lift. She was still a slim size eight, and she knew that beneath her sleek silk shirt, her body was flat and gymtoned. She wondered about her lightweight cashmere navy suit, though. She'd bought the expensively pur-chased item year before last, and it was probably time to discard it from her wardrobe now with the changing fashions. At the bottom of its descent, the elevator came to a standstill and the doors opened up again. She stepped out.*

A good student might produce something like this:

> *Lucinda Roberts left the room and rode the elevator to the ground floor, allowing herself a moment of satisfied inspection in the mirror on the way down. She was still slim, her stomach flat. Her cashmere suit looked good but would soon need to be replaced. As the elevator came to a halt, she got out.*

That's taken a 138-word paragraph and turned it into one of just fifty-six words – a huge improvement.

But not huge enough. The truth is that the entire paragraph is tedious and needs to be deleted. The snippet does, admittedly, tell us something about Roberts's vain self-absorption, but the author will have other opportunities to convey this information when it becomes relevant. I'd suggest replacing the whole thing by the single word, 'Afterwards, ...'

If you only focus on words and phrases, then you're likely to miss sentences, paragraphs and even whole chapters that fail to contribute, so you have to make sure that you read with a narrow and wide focus at the same time. If you can't do that, then you'll need to separate out the tasks. Re-read one time, looking for sentences and paragraphs that can go. Re-read another time looking for surplus words and phrases.

In *On Writing*, Stephen King suggests that he removes about 10% of the manuscript when it comes to editing it. (The rule he adopted at a teacher's advice is: 'second draft = first draft – 10%'.) I think that's probably typical of an experienced professional author, especially one, like him, with a background in journalism, but it's not a reliable guide to how much you need to cut your manuscript. You need to make yours perfect, with not a word too many. That's the only guide you need. You may find yourself cutting 20% or 30% or even 50%, in which case, good for you. (You may also need to work some material back in, of course, as you work to deepen characterisation, or atmosphere, or whatever else may have been lacking in that opening draft, so you might cut 30%, add back 20%, and find that the novel is only 10% shorter. That's fine too.)

And one last example to rub it in. I remember reading a client's manuscript that was great, but just too long. It was over 130,000 words and it didn't have more than 90,000 words of story. I kept telling the writer to remove text without actually eliminating content. (So instead of four sentences describing a Moroccan *souk*, for example, she could have used just one – and that sentence could combine the very best ingredients of all four.) The writer concerned kept not understanding what I was after, and the wordcount ticked down, but by minimal amounts – 2,000 words here, 3,000 there.

At last, though, and one hefty re-edit later, the message hit home. The book slimmed down to a sprightly 90,000 words – and the author won a great book deal with a terrific Big Five publisher. Job done.

Long sentences

Do note that being economical with words is not the same as being against long sentences on principle. Here's a whopper from John Updike, one of his generation's most admired prose stylists:

> *All around them, up Eighth Avenue to Broadway, the great city crawls with people, some smartly dressed, many of them shabby, a few beautiful but most not, all reduced by the towering structures around them to the size of insects, but scuttling, hurrying, intent in the milky morning sun upon some plan or scheme or hope they are hugging to themselves, their reason for living another day, each one of them impaled live upon the pin of consciousness, fixed upon self-advancement and self-preservation.*

John Updike, *Terrorist*.

That's eighty-three words, and not one of them surplus. Although you could argue for deleting certain parts (why is it necessary to say 'up Eighth Avenue to Broadway'? do we really need all three parts of 'plan or scheme or hope'?), the truth is that the sentence swarms just like the city it is describing. The addition of 'Eighth Avenue to Broadway' gives a sense of location that the phrase 'great city' on its own can't supply. The multiple parallel descriptors ('scuttling, hurrying, intent') and nouns ('plan or scheme or hope') allow those little insect-like humans to teem with individual purpose and life. The whole point is the multiplication.

Not all of us will write like Updike, but any of us is allowed a long sentence if and when there's a call for it. Indeed, varying your sentence rhythms is a good way to keep your prose musical and interesting. The test is never *length*, but *purpose*. If a word (or phrase or sentence) has a purpose, then keep it. If not, delete it.

Double adjectives

When it comes to self-checking your work, there are a few bad habits to watch out for. One of the commonest of these is the double (or treble) adjective:

> *The thick dark wool of his sleeve caught on the sharp upright spike of the green-painted iron railing.*
>
> *A blanket of thick black cloud …*
>
> *The wet, grey, sodden embers …*

It's quite easy to write like this as you're compiling your first draft. Words are free and have a habit of sneaking in. That's fine, let them settle where they want. Then destroy them:

> *His sleeve caught on the railing.*
>
> *A blanket of cloud …*
>
> *The sodden embers …*

As these examples demonstrate, adjectives often seem to contribute, but don't. In the first example, none of the adjectives were worth having. In the second, the nouns 'blanket' and 'cloud' tell you everything you need to know, so again the adjectives can be discarded. In the last case, you do need one adjective, 'sodden', as it tells you something that you're not expecting, but if embers are sodden then of course they're wet, and of course they're grey.

Even where two adjectives do add information that isn't implied elsewhere, they can often fight against each other and bleed energy from the image:

A bleak stone farmhouse ...

A yawning, beardless sentry ...

In both these cases, it feels as though the writer is uncertain about what he wants to communicate. Does he want to stress the farmhouse's bleakness or its solidity? The sentry's tiredness, or his youthfulness? A more decisive writer might have achieved more with less:

A bleak farmhouse ...

Or: *A stone farmhouse ...*

A yawning sentry ...

Or: *A beardless sentry ...*

Decide what you want to say, and say it. If you seek to hedge your bets, you may end up losing them.

Emotional economy

Another tremendously common problem centres on trust: your willingness to trust your words to carry weight. Again, an example is the best way to illustrate the point:

> *Racked in agony, the prisoner's sobs and screams echoed the violence of his torment through the gloomy walls of the dungeons that had borne savage witness to such an eternity of suffering.*

This is such a horrible sentence, it's beyond improvement and needs to be deleted. Just count how many extreme words are choking it: *racked, agony, sobs, screams, violence, torment, gloomy, dungeons, savage, suffering.* Those words include some of the most extreme words in the English language and yet they're bunched up here like grapes on a vine, with the result that not one of them is having its due effect. You need to trust your character, trust your story and trust your words:

> *The prisoner shifted on his pallet. The dark weal on his leg was starting to stink, but seemed to be healing. In the yard below the window, he could hear ostlers or grooms moving food of some kind for the animals. He couldn't tell what animals or what food, because the neck chain that anchored him didn't let him stand up enough to see out.*

Whereas the first snippet repelled the reader with its density of dark language, the second one uses a softly-softly approach to draw the reader in. We start to connect with the prisoner and the place. The first book will be rejected instantly. The second one is still afloat.

Writing like a writer

Not all writers write like writers. Plenty of people write like this:

> *It's the type of location frequented by harassed-looking mums with kids in tow, rather than city high-flyers in suits, well that's apart from us. It's early autumn, quite sunny really, but not very warm, actually by my definition I would say cold. But even if it was another ten or fifteen degrees below, we would still be drinking outside on the freezing metal benches under a space-heater that doesn't create much heat, in our designer sunglasses to prevent squinting (actually, mine aren't designer at all, though I say they are – they're a thirty-quid temporary measure until I can find the time to get some decent replacements. I lost the last pair on holiday) all because Little Lu and Gemma smoke.*

At Jericho Writers, we do (sadly) see manuscripts like this from time to time, and I hope it doesn't need me to tell you that they stand no chance at all. If I were an agent, I'd have rejected this book before I hit the first full stop. The writing is so desperately lazy. Instead of that hideous second sentence, the author could have said, 'It's early autumn, sunny but cold'. But the entire paragraph needs radical pruning. There's nothing wrong with talking this way – none of us are poets when we talk – but writing this way is a crime. And one you, I'm sure, are not going to commit.

Chapter Summary

- Be relentless in your quest to eliminate wasted words. If you use thirteen words to say something that could be said in ten, then your finished manuscript could easily end up being 30,000 words too long.
- You need to scrutinise your work for needless words and phrases ...
- ... and for needless sentences and paragraphs.
- Remember to tweak your writing at the same time as you are deleting surplus.
- Double adjectives should generally be avoided.
- The same goes for an overload of emotionally intense language.
- As for writing the same way as you talk – never!

CLICHÉS: A FIELD GUIDE

All writers know they need to avoid clichés, but the task is much harder than it sounds. After all, think of what writing a novel consists of. You have to drag the entire thing from your imagination: characters, events, dialogue, places, smells, everything. And all this needs to feel fresh. A reader will quickly detect anything recycled. Or rather: anything recycled quickly feels generic, and novels work only when they seem specific, alive and individual. A lack of freshness is the kiss of death.

The same goes for narrative non-fiction. Although your manuscript is based on fact, you still have to find a way to dream those facts into words. Let's say that you are writing a book about naval warfare. You still need to imagine your way into the Battle of Midway or onto Nelson's quarterdeck at Trafalgar. That exercise is as much imaginative as it would be for any novelist, and a fresh approach is equally essential. (And at least a novelist is aware they have to use their imagination. Writers of non-fiction often forget they have to do the same.)

Unfortunately, however, writers are human. Imagination is *hard*. Almost always, the first idea to spring to mind will have its roots in something you've read or watched or come across before. You won't be aware of those roots. You aren't thinking, 'Hey, I could nick that cool bit from *Sex and the City*'. You'll be thinking, 'I know, I could make my character a sassy New Yorker, really into fashion, a journalist perhaps …' The cliché doesn't *feel* different from any other idea. They arrive in your head the ways anything else does. Yet unless you are scrupulous about finding and eliminating clichés, your manuscript will soon be overgrown with them.

The classic cliché

The classic cliché is easy to recognise:

> *She was grasping at straws.*
>
> *Her boyfriend, though, was like a wet blanket.*
>
> *They tasted the agony of defeat.*

Any phrase that comes pre-packed is a cliché, and any writing that has too many clichés will feel dead. Fixing the issue is simple. One option is to create your own images:

> *She was becoming desperate, a drowning woman in search of a lifebelt.*
>
> *Her boyfriend sat in the corner, inert as an empty beer crate.*
>
> *They were defeated and knew it, and the knowledge was a killing one.*

But you don't have to. Creating your own imagery may call more attention to the sentence than makes sense. In which case, just say what you mean:

> *Tiny facts now filled her with unreasonable hope.*
>
> *Her boyfriend, though, was both shy and awkward. Party spirit died in his presence.*
>
> *They felt shattered by defeat, shattered and hopeless.*

In most cases, you'll find the strongest solution is also the simplest. I quite like the 'inert as an empty beer crate' image above, but on the whole the third trio of sentences is better than the second. They are both better than the first.

The disguised cliché

Most clichés are not as obvious as the ones above, however. They generally prefer to enter your manuscript wearing some kind of disguise, however modest:

Her eyes were blue pools that he could swim in forever.

He was about six foot, strong-jawed and craggily handsome.

There aren't any pre-packaged phrases here, not like 'grasping at straws' or 'tasted the agony of defeat', anyway. All the same, the language is dead, because the imagination behind it was too lazy to forage for anything new.

If you want to stick with these rather time-worn types (the woman with the entrancing eyes, the craggily handsome man, etc), then at least freshen them up a bit:

Her eyes were pale blue. Paler than cornflowers, paler than her faded linen shirt, paler than the airmail letter she held questioningly towards him.

He looked like his Jeep. Tough, durable, even handsome in a shallow sort of way.

I'm not sure either of those sentences is going to win a prize any time soon, but at least they take something old and put a skim of something new on it. They're better than the clichés.

The situational cliché

Clichés don't only lurk in single phrases or sentences. It can lurk in the situations you set up:

A log fire was beginning to roar away. Joan was in the kitchen making brownies and listening to something classical on the radio. John eased his slippers off and pulled his armchair closer to the hearth, taking care not to disturb the spaniel, who was snoring contentedly before it. Was it too early for whisky, he wondered, already knowing the conclusion he was likely to reach.

The actual writing in this snippet is OK – and yet I hope you *felt* its inadequacy. This is a tediously perfect scene, is it not? The roaring fire, the snoring dog, the home baking, the marital peace, the promise of whisky. No doubt most of us would feel content in such a setting, but it feels unspecific and bland – as though the writer has borrowed some off-the-shelf version of contentment and dropped it straight into the manuscript without alteration.

Because the problem here isn't the language, you can't simply rewrite a few phrases and hope that the problem goes away. On the contrary, you have to reimagine the scene for yourself. You have to send the pre-pack version of contentment back to the warehouse and ask yourself how your characters arrange their own version of bliss. Perhaps they bake together. Perhaps they bicker amiably as they do the dishes. Perhaps they pull all the cushions off the chairs and make a huge pillowy pile in front of the fire, so that John and Joan and the spaniel can all nest together. You need to be true to your characters of course, but truth to your characters almost always means a more interesting – and persuasive – version of things than anything smacking of last season's TV ad.

The character cliché

Since we're creating a small menagerie of clichés, we can't avoid mentioning the character cliché – one of the commonest issues in first-time novels. Let's say for example, you have a young Irishwoman in your novel. A romantic heroine, no less. Excellent! So why not give her red hair, a passionate tongue and an impulsive nature? That idea could really go somewhere.

Or your protagonist is a cop? In which case, have you thought of making him a hard-drinking maverick? One who probably doesn't play by the rules. And he could be divorced, that might work. Perhaps some case from the past still haunts him.

Or you're writing a non-fiction memoir about your time in France. You need to depict the builder you've been working with on your house. So why not bring out his comic, rustic side? How about a few bucolic scenes at the grape harvest? Why not show how he can be difficult much of the time, but nevertheless has something important to teach you about the good life?

These crimes are easy to mock – and easier to commit. Remember: cliché has a habit of creeping in whenever you're not on guard against it, and sometimes even then.

Good writing will certainly help minimise the damage:

Sinead O'Riordan flushed with anger, as she impulsively leaned forwards and …

Sinead brushed a stray lock of coppery hair from her cheek. 'I'm damned if I'll …'

'Excuse me?' said Sinead. Her voice was almost inaudible. In the absence of sound, Bridget found a host of other details intruding on her attention. The enamel jug's chipped top. The pale gleam from the potato peelings. The distant rushing sound made by the wind playing in the flue. 'Excuse me?' …

The first two snippets here read like genre romance of the worst sort. The third – well, heck, this last version of Sinead is still a passionate and impulsive Irishwoman, but at least she's not all coppery hair and angry flushes. The third Sinead we can believe in, at least to an extent.

Better still, though, you should mix things up. If you have an impulsive Irishwoman, then make her dark-haired, give her bouts of self-doubt, or make her anxious about her friends' approval. If you have a maverick cop, then why not make him contentedly unmarried? Or have him married to a defence lawyer? Or make him teetotal? If you have a rustic Frenchman, try to find those aspects that individuate *your* comic Frenchman from everybody else's.

It's certainly true that genres – notably romances and cop stories – have rules which writers pretty much have to obey. You can't have an ugly romantic heroine whom nobody much likes or a weedy cop who plays everything by the book. Even so, you need to feel out the limits of your genre and live at those limits. The inner core is long dead, long gone.

Plot cliché

Finally, in our menagerie, you can have plot clichés as well. In fantasy manuscripts, it might be that a kingdom can only be saved if some artefact is retrieved. In detective stories, it might be a plot involving a serial killer who disposes of his victims in a succession of weirdly coded ways. In thrillers, it's a bomb that needs to be defused in thirty minutes, or else …

Very often authors get infected by movies rather than other books. This is a worse infection to suffer from, because movie plots are designed to work as movies. Since a two-hour feature film is much more compact than a 100,000-word book, its plot is simpler too, more like a novella than a full-length novel. Furthermore, Hollywood designs its plots to deliver a given quotient of car chases, explosions and special effects. Novels work differently. They work through *interiority* – getting into the minds of others – and tracing the thoughts and emotions of those other minds as events unfold. If your manuscript attempts to end like a movie – a few big explosions, followed by a face-to-face encounter with some adversary on the top of a tall building – it risks failing as a novel.

And having said all this, of course, there's a fine line between cliché and simply following the requirements of the genre. There's no certain way to know the difference, other than by reading widely and reading intelligently. The industry professionals – the agents and editors – that you will one day have to convince to take a risk on you will be deeply versed in whichever genre you are writing in, and you cannot afford to let these hyper-critical readers catch you out.

The cliché cure

There are a few different strategies for dealing with clichés, but they end up falling into one of three broad groups: avoid, subvert, and go large.

The 'avoid' strategy is simple. Just as you're about to write about your passionate, flame-haired Irishwoman, you change course at the last moment. You tone down her hair colour. Your tone down her passionate temper. You create a character with more light and shade on the page. This strategy is never the wrong one.

Option two is simply to subvert. So, let's say you're all set up for a marriage proposal in a beautiful rose garden ... but then you realise, that's all just too expected, too familiar. Instead, therefore, you set your rose garden by the side of a busy city street and the words of your proposal have to be shouted over the roar of traffic. Or the roses presented by your romantic hero are full of thorns (a strategy I once used myself – in fiction, that is). Or a sudden downpour sends your happy couple running and laughing and drenched to a local coffee shop. Or whatever. You can borrow some of the beauty of the expected location, but mark it with your own unique twist.

And option three? The hell with it! You take the cliché and give it some juice. So, let's say your thriller ends with a midnight shootout at some docks. And OK. Why not? That kind of setting has become so common for good reason. Thrillers need shootouts. Drugs need to cross borders. Docks are a logical place to unload drugs. So: shootouts at docks – that makes a kind of sense.

But don't let your midnight shootout seem like everyone else's. The easiest way to achieve individuality and conviction is to create your own setting, your own characters. So, if your docks feel intensely real, your shootout no longer feels like just another thriller cliché. And if the characters inhabiting your shootout talk and behave like your characters and not just some stock characters from an old Nicolas Cage or (worse!) an old Vin Diesel movie, then readers will be intensely present in your creation. They won't be able to half-look away, confident that they've seen this scene before. We'll talk much more about that process of intensity in prose and character creation, but take note. It's just about the most powerful tool you have as a writer – and you can deploy it everywhere.

Chapter Summary

- Your first idea is likely to be a bad one; it'll almost always smack of cliché.

- The worst clichés (eg: 'like a wet blanket') are easy to spot and easy to avoid.

- More often, clichés are disguised. The phrase itself may not be hackneyed, but the imagination feels stale.

- Clichés can also be situational (the spaniel snoring by the fire) or character-based (the passionate, flame-haired heroine).

- Plot cliché (the deserted warehouse scene; the coded serial-killings) are also common.

- Your three cliché elimination strategies are: Avoid, Subvert and Go Large. They're all good 'uns.

PRECISION

So far, we've reviewed prose style under the headings of clarity, economy and the avoidance of cliché. If you focus meticulously on these things, you will unquestionably improve your writing style. It can't help but improve. As you were reading, however, you may have noticed another theme stirring under the surface – a theme that will emerge again and again as we proceed.

That theme is *precision*; the art of saying precisely what you mean. And because what you mean is often vague until you set it down in words, precision is also the art of *seeing* precisely. Seeing character, seeing scene, seeing emotional tone. Look back at some of the sentences we have corrected in previous chapters:

1A) *Sergei hoisted the heavy chest up onto the deck of the twin-engined yacht and shut its heavy brass lock.*

1B) *Sergei hoisted the chest up onto deck and locked it. The yacht was twin-engined and fast.*

2A) *Her eyes were blue pools that he could swim in forever.*

2B) *Her eyes were pale blue. Paler than cornflowers, paler than her faded linen shirt, paler than the airmail letter she held questioningly towards him.*

3A) *Rufus was the sort of dog that absolutely anyone could – and probably would – fall in love with.*

3B) *Rufus was a dog to fall in love with.*

4A) *She was grasping at straws.*

4B) *Tiny facts now filled her with unreasonable hope.*

In each case, you'll see that one of the essential things we've achieved is an increase in precision. The second sentence in each pair locks onto the thing that the writer is seeking to communicate and communicates it precisely. There's no excess verbiage, no hoary old clichés, no muddled structures or word choices. Such precision is always a virtue. It's a virtue in genre fiction, where it permits the story to move fast and cleanly. It's a virtue in literary fiction, where it allows a writer to communicate subtle things with exactness.

Understanding your own image

The previous chapters have therefore already covered most of what this chapter would otherwise be about: the art of *writing* precisely. But underlying the art of writing is the art of *seeing*. As you develop as a writer, you'll find that the writing comes ever more easily. The bit that remains hard is seeing your world accurately enough to report it.

Sometimes, the problem is that you have an image in mind but haven't yet pinned it down with enough exactitude:

Just like a cloud passing across the face of the sun, thrusting its shadow-image on the ground below, the actors in the soap opera vanished behind my aunt's amply padded posterior.

As readers, we more or less know what the writer is getting at here. The aunt's bottom moves in front of the TV set, like a cloud passing in front of the sun. That may not be a brilliant image, as it happens (clouds and suns? doesn't that feel a bit stale?), but the worse problem is that the writer hasn't sorted out all the elements of what she's trying to say. There are two main issues. The first is that phrase 'thrusting its shadow-image on the ground'. Of course clouds cast shadows, and of course those shadows fall on the ground. But the connection in the writer's head is: 'cloud/sun' equates to 'aunt's bottom/TV set'. The cloud's shadow on the ground has nothing to do with this equation – it distracts from it, indeed – so it should be discarded:

Like a cloud passing across the face of the sun, the actors in the soap opera vanished behind my aunt's amply padded posterior.

This sentence is already better, but its new brevity makes the second problem more visible. The aunt's bottom is meant to be playing the role of the cloud, but it's the soap actors who are 'like a cloud' in this sentence. The author, in other words, has confused herself and got the image back to front. It should read like this:

Like the sun disappearing behind cloud, the actors in the soap opera vanished behind my aunt's amply padded posterior.

I still don't like this sentence. It feels dull: a forced joke, not a light one. But at least it accurately communicates what the author was intending. This third version of the sentence is much the best of the three, and its core virtue is greater precision.

Seeing the specific

At other times, the problem is a different one. It's not that the writer has failed to grasp their own image, but that they haven't yet seen their own scene clearly enough:

1) *All that day, the neighbours came round and wept on his shoulder.*

2) *The family was in good spirits that day, laughing and joking and cavorting around.*

These sentences may strike you as perfectly all right. 'Wept on his shoulder' is something of a cliché, but there are plenty worse. The writing is economical. It's clear. What's not to like?

The trouble is that in both cases, the writer has jumped in with a lazy *and probably false* generality. Suppose that first sentence, about the neighbours, was part of a tale about small-town Montana. Obviously some tragedy has happened and people are coming round to express their grief. But people vary. Some cry, perhaps even literally on someone's shoulder. Others are tight-lipped and angry. Others are simply blank with denial and shock. Others come round, and fuss, and cook pot-roasts and enjoy the hubbub. And so on. The generality kills the town, because it tries to cast the entire population in an identical mould.

The second sentence suffers from the same issue. I can believe that any family has days when everyone is in good spirits, but there's an absence of distinction in this phraseology which blurs everyone together. Characterisation suffers. The scene feels generic, not distinct.

The obvious solution to these problems is to start unpicking the generality into its component parts:

> *All that day, neighbours came round. All expressed regrets, some formally, in dark suits and sober ties. Others came just as they were when the news found them, with red eyes and only a blink or two away from tears. Mrs Chatterton — inevitably — was there almost instantly, equipped with pot-roast and moralising advice …*

But perhaps you don't want to spend time at this point in your narrative bestowing this level of detail on how the neighbours reacted. In which case, say what you mean but say it *with accuracy*:

> *The townsfolk expressed their grief too, each in their own way, some formally and without sincerity, but mostly with emotion evident in their faces. He felt their grief, and shared it, and the sharing was helpful.*

Avoiding hesitation

Still other times, imprecision arrives because the author herself is in two minds about what she wants to say.

> *The faint din of morning traffic rose like mist from the streets.*

I dreamed that I was walking across the frozen lake, which was starting to melt so that the rock-hard ice was now as fragile as a thin film of muslin.

These sentences are both muddled, because the author hasn't yet settled what she wishes to communicate. Is the traffic noise *loud* or *quiet*? At the moment – a 'faint din' – it's trying to be both. And is it *lying* on the streets ('like mist') or is it *rising* from them? At the moment, the author is trying to have it both ways.

The second sentence is worse, because it's clunkily construct-ed as well as being muddled in intention. We understand that the lake's ice is melting and fragile, but the sentence seems to be pointing in all directions at once, both 'rock-hard' and 'fragile'. What's more, that phrase 'a thin film of muslin' isn't helping at all. Muslin doesn't come in films, it comes in sheets. And it doesn't come thin or thick, it just comes like muslin, which *is* thin, but which is also soft and pliable (unlike ice) and which is actually quite strong given its bulk, and therefore not a good way to convey fragility.

In both cases, the writer needs to choose what she wants to say and then say it. Here are two versions of the first sentence, depending on whether you want to go noisy or quiet:

The din of morning traffic was already clamouring from the street below.

Or: *The murmur of traffic started to fill the streets like an early morning mist.*

For a beautiful version of the second sentence, try this:

I dreamed that I was walking across the ice on the lake, which was breaking up as it does in spring, softening and shifting and pulling itself apart.

Marilynne Robinson, *Housekeeping.*

It's worth noting, incidentally, that being *precise* is not the same as being *simple*. Marilynne Robinson is wanting to convey a fairly complex image here. She wants to create a dream picture in which the ice is simultaneously strong enough to walk on and utterly perilous. She's found a way to combine these ideas in a way that is precise and clear. The clarity comes partly from her writing, but most of all from her *seeing*. She has seen this image clearly, and that enables her to report it perfectly.

Did I happen to mention pedantry?

One of the services we sometimes carry out at Jericho Writers is intensive feedback on a client's prose. The way it works is this. A client sends in one fairly short chapter, and we rip it to pieces. Sentence by sentence. Word by word if necessary. Our points are often cruelly petty, cruelly pedantic. If a writer uses the phrase 'faint din', we'll pick them up on it. If they say that the townsfolk 'cried on his shoulder', we'll ask them if that's truly what they meant. If they compare ice to muslin, we'll point out that muslin, unlike ice, is flexible and is strong despite its thinness. We try, in short, to behave like the pickiest, most pedantic English teacher anyone has ever had, sentence after sentence after sentence. The client then corrects their work and sends it back to us – the selfsame chapter – and we do the same thing all over again. Sentence after sentence after sentence.

Writers react in two different ways to this exercise. Some (much the smaller group, fortunately) feel mad at us because we keep not looking at the bigger picture. 'But are my characters OK? Does my plot work?' they want to ask. These writers are unlikely ever to succeed. Character and plot emerge from accurate seeing and accurate reporting of what is seen. You can't have good characters if a writer reports their thoughts and actions in a blurry, muddled way. You will only ever have blurry, muddled characters. There is no more to these people's existence than your words on a page.

Other writers, the large majority, get it. They understand why we're being so picky. They see their chapter coming into focus, as if a camera lens had had the wrong focal depth and is now finding the correct one. The result of that tighter focus is better characters, more decisive plot manoeuvres, more precise emotional definition. The writer comes to understand what is needed, and rewrites not just that single chapter but the entire manuscript. Every single aspect of the book improves as a result. And it happens because of pickiness. Pedantry. An annoying attentiveness to an everlasting sequence of minor details.

You need to cultivate those attitudes in yourself. Not necessarily in your first draft. You may be one of those writers who likes to whack your first draft down to get it over with. But thereafter, the slapdash builder has to give way to the picky interior designer. You can't overlook a niggle because it's minor. Of course it's minor! It may only be one word among 100,000. But if it's the wrong word, it's the wrong word – and you need to fix it.

Yes, you can

If that seems like a frightening thought, then here's a reassuring one on which to end the chapter. You *can* write precisely. Look back at Marilynne Robinson's beautiful ice sentence. It's so simple. It starts off in the plainest way imaginable: '*I dreamed that I was walking across the ice on the lake*'. Nothing fancy about that. Anyone could come up with that. Then, she tells us about the state of the ice: '*which was breaking up as it does in spring*'. Again, how easy is that? How easy and how clear. Then admittedly you get to a little poetry – '*softening and shifting and pulling itself apart*' – but these are simple words that any of us has in our vocabulary. Robinson is one of the most admired writers of the modern age, but her craft has an awful lot to do with exactitude. Doing the simple things well, and never allowing a blurry, clumsy or muddled phrase to slip onto the finished page. If you're equally picky with your own work, your writing style will certainly be strong enough for publication. It may even, like Robinson's, achieve excellence. And it begins with precision.

Chapter Summary

- One of the greatest virtues in writing is precision.
- To achieve precision, you need a precise imagination. You need to *see* clearly.
- That means being specific in your choice of phrasing ...
- ... and avoiding muddle or hesitation.
- Pedantry is your friend. A relentless attention to detail will work wonders for your prose.

Some Technicalities

We've dealt with most of the major issues involved in writing clean, readable, professional prose. A few technicalities remain. A quick gallop through them, and you'll be fit to write like a bestselling author.

Nouns and adjectives

Every now and then, a writer is aware their prose lacks a bit of sparkle. For example:

> First version: *The room contained a table and a couple of chairs that stood beneath the window. The table held a pen and paper; nothing else.*

Those writers then try to compensate by working their adjectives as hard as they can:

> Second version: *The gracious room contained a scarred, pine wooden table and a couple of stiff-backed, rush-bottomed chairs that stood beneath a classic Victorian-paned window. The pine table held a black pen and creamy white paper; nothing else.*

The first version here is indeed dull, but at least it's clean and clear. The second version, far from being improved, is both dull and overwritten. It's become worse, not better.

The solution is simple. The first little snippet is boring in large part because its nouns are boring. Just look at them: *room, table, chairs, window, table, pen, paper*. These are very common words. They're also generic ones, broad and non-specific in feel. You can't solve the problem by trying to hide those words in a cloud of adjectives. You'll solve it by changing the nouns, by avoiding the obvious, and by picking up on some detail that gives individuality.

> Third version: *The study was furnished with a small writing bureau and a couple of rush-bottomed chairs, fraying from age or use. Pen and paper lay ready, creamy and inviting in the empty light.*

This version is the clear winner. It wins out for three reasons. The first is that our selection of nouns has improved. The boring word *room* has changed to the more specific *study*. *Table* has given way to the more specific *bureau*. Secondly, we've avoided some statements of the obvious. We haven't mentioned that the room has a window, since nearly all rooms do. Instead, we've drawn attention to the quality of light. Equally, we haven't bothered to mention that the pens and paper were lying on the bureau – where else would they be? – we've mentioned the feeling that those things generated. Finally, we've picked out a detail which intrigues the reader. In the final version, the rush-bottomed chairs are 'fraying from age or use'. That comment creates a little ripple of intrigue. Who has been using the chairs? And for how long? And why? The third version does, as it happens, make good use of adjectives, but no longer are the adjectives being asked to supply the interest single-handed.

If you look back at the first version of this snippet, then at the third version, you can see how huge the difference is – and how simple the changes are. The first version is unpublishably dull. The second is worse. The third has a reader turning the page with interest.

There is, though, a fourth alternative, namely this:

> Fourth version: *The room contained a couple of chairs, and a table with pen and paper. Nothing else.*

That's as dull as the first version, but it's short. It's conveying information swiftly and clearly, then standing back so the narration can get on to more interesting things. There's no easy way to judge when you need to go for the more ornate version of things and when to go for the cleanest and simplest. You need to judge for yourself – or rather, let your story guide you. The story never lies.

Verbs and adverbs

In the same way, you should usually let verbs do most of the work.

She said excitedly/She exclaimed ...

He called loudly/He shouted ...

She jumped high for joy/She leapt for joy ...

He ran quickly/He sprinted ...

Most of the time, you'll find that the simpler construction – the second one in each pair above – works better. The word *shout* means to *call loudly*, so why not use it? We have a word in English that means *jump high*, so why not *leap* at the chance to use it? The resulting prose is simpler, less cluttered, more exact.

There is, however, another alternative that will often be better still. What about:

She said ...

He called ...

She jumped for joy ...

He ran ...

In the first two cases, it's highly likely that the dialogue itself will indicate whether the first speaker was excited, or the second one was raising his voice, in which case the reader won't thank you for rubbing it in. In the last two cases, the extra emphasis of *jumped high* or *ran quickly* may be unnecessary. What matters is that the first person was jumping aloft in delight and the second person was bothering to run. It quite likely doesn't matter the distance cleared by the first person, or just how fast the second person was travelling. If in doubt, cut the adverbs. Your prose will improve.

Adjectives and adverbs

Adverbs don't only modify verbs (as in she 'ran quickly'); they can also modify adjectives:

A very exciting adventure

An absolutely incredible surprise

A truly exotic feast

It won't surprise you to learn that those adverbs – *very, absolutely* and *truly* – can all happily be deleted. They add nothing. Destroy them.

The senses

Hold your hand out in front of you, palm towards your face. Now bring your hand steadily towards you, until it is arrested, about an inch or so in front of your eyes, by a prominent fleshy obstruction. That thing in the middle of your face is your nose. You use it to smell with.

Likewise, if you grope around on the side of your head, you will find a couple more fleshy protuberances. These are your ears, and you hear with them. Further investigation will reveal that you are in possession of tools which allow you to sense texture, temperature, and taste. Many of your readers possess similar equipment.

So, use these things. Don't write descriptions which rely only on the visual. Use all your senses to create atmosphere. A really good exercise is to review a couple of descriptive passages that you've written and see if you've offered any information beyond the visual. If you haven't, you might want to make a habit of recording the smells, tastes and sounds of a particular scene. Often, you may find that the material you've added seems a little forced or contrived, in which case, by all means delete it. But you need to get into the habit of thinking in every sense. Only then will you find the best way to conjure atmosphere in any situation.

Punctuation

This book is not a book about punctuation. I mean, how boring would that be!? Dullsville, Arizona! And, to think some people actually like that kind of stuff ...!!

If you want a book on punctuation, then you can find any number of them on Amazon; take your pick. But I will say that you should almost never use exclamation marks (except in dialogue, and not often even then). You should never, ever use double or treble exclamation marks. Nor should you use exclamation mark / question mark combos ('?!' or '!?'). And if you find yourself using a lot of ellipses ('...'), then cut down. You'll get by fine without 'em.

(Incidentally, I realise that some readers will cry foul, because they've noticed I use quite a lot of exclamation marks in this book, so let me introduce one further rule: once you've published a dozen books or more, you can do whatever the heck you like.)

Repetition

It's easy for writers to get into a habit where – through habit more than anything – they find themselves repeating the same word in a paragraph or on a page. The habit is destructive, because the reader's attention swerves towards the constant, habitual repetition, and so stops noticing the sense of what's being said.

Where these repetitions are unintended, you need to rewrite the relevant chunk to avoid them. The word 'habit' in the paragraph above was needless and obtrusive, for example. But don't be too mechanical about these things. T.S. Eliot wrote: 'Time present and time past/Are both perhaps present in time future,/And time future contained in time past'. Here, the repetitions are deliberate and purposeful. The passage would not be improved by some contrived attempt to run through the thesaurus, looking for synonyms for 'time', 'present', 'future' and 'past'. So be alert to those repetitions, but don't be afraid of them. If it sounds right, it is right.

The abstract and the concrete

One of my editorial colleagues, a prize-winning author of some distinction, begins each of his editorial reports with a quotation from Strunk and White's *Elements of Style*: 'Prefer the specific to the general, the definite to the vague, the concrete to the abstract'. It's excellent advice. We've already discussed how specific words ('study') are usually better than their more general cousins ('room'). The chapter titled 'Precision' spent a lot of time preferring the definite to the vague.

It only remains then to point out that abstract sentences can be terrible:

> *He felt himself embraced by an intimacy that boasted a fine degree of tact, yet at the same time provided a resistance, forceful in its quiet power, to any negative assumptions that he might have generated given the disturbances of his own past delinquencies.*

What the heck does this mean? It's as though the writer has an idea that long words and abstractions make for good writing. And they don't. In this case, they make for a car crash. Here's what we could have said:

> *He felt loved. She was intimate and tactful, but he never mistook that tact for weakness. Once, preparing dinner one evening, work-ing beside her at the zinc worktop, he made some disparaging comment about his past misdemeanours. Half-joking, half-not. The easy thing would have been to let it go. Every woman he'd been with before would have let it go, or at most sighed or tutted at him. And she did neither …*

You can't escape from abstractions entirely, and you shouldn't want to. This snippet uses several: *tact, weakness, past, misdemean-*

our. But those abstractions are firmly rooted in the specific. The passage says, in entirely general and abstract terms, 'he never mistook that tact for weakness', then plunges straight into an example of what precisely that phrase means. The example is given a time ('one evening') and place ('the zinc worktop'), so that any whiff of the general is exterminated as the example unfolds.

It's obvious, I trust, that the second passage is much better than the first, and that it's better because it's less abstract, less general – but it's also worth noticing that the first passage does terribly little to characterise the man's lover; indeed, she isn't even mentioned. The torrent of abstraction has become so removed from the here-and-now that the woman herself has disappeared. The second passage doesn't merely rescue her – she makes an appearance as early as the fourth word – it starts to give her personality and individuality. We don't yet know how she corrected him – did she take his hands and stare into his eyes? did she tap him on the shoulder with her wooden spoon? did she interrupt and make a joke? – but we're all ready to find out how one specific woman responded to one specific man on one specific occasion. That's how novels work. That's how you need to work too.

Rhythms

All writing has a rhythm. The strongest determinant of that rhythm is simply sentence length. Short sentences sound simple, snappy, fast. Longer sentences feel more thoughtful, give more room for introspection.

There's no one 'right' rhythm; you simply need to find the one that works best for your book. On the other hand:

- Short sentences are fine. In moderation. If they're always short, they get dull. Like this. Not just dull. Irritating. Maybe worse. They drive you nuts. Crazy, even.
- Equally, long sentences generally benefit from alterations in rhythm. In the chapter titled 'Economy', we looked at

an eighty-three word sentence from John Updike, who is more than able to produce a few whoppers in the course of a book. But he's also happy to mix things up. The sentence which followed that eighty-three-worder was four words – and just fifteen letters – long: '*That, and only that*'. The very short sentence acted like a second full stop to the long one. It underlined its predecessor. It gave it room to breathe, to unfold its meaning. A book made up only of longer sentences is unlikely to be a good one.

Although full stops are the strongest determinants of rhythm, they're not the only ones. Consider, for example, these two sentences:

If you use a lot of parentheses (brackets – and dashes like these – are the main types of parenthesis), you will slow your narrative, perhaps fatally.

If you use a lot of parentheses, you will slow your narrative, perhaps fatally.

That's not to say you should never use brackets and dashes – you certainly should; they can be helpful little beasts – but keep an eye on yourself to make sure you're not overusing them.

There's one last rhythm issue worth watching out for:

A) *I am standing by the window. I am not certain whether the pills have started working already. I feel a fluttering in my heart but I cannot tell whether that's the pills already. I decide it will not hurt to take another, so I do. I continue to stand at the window. I gaze out, feeling my heart.*

B) *The knife flew through the air and struck the wood above the door. The wood didn't hold the blade and the knife fell to the floor. The stone floor made a ringing noise, then the room fell silent.*

This first passage is jarring because every sentence starts the same way: 'I am ...', 'I am not ...', 'I feel ...'. Even where a sentence comes in two halves, the second half of the sentence has the same type of opening ('… but I cannot tell …', '…, so I do.') The second passage does the same thing, only this time it's a succession of *The – noun – verb* openings ('The knife flew …', 'The wood didn't …') which grow repetitive.

In both cases, the writer just needs to mix things up. If you start a couple of sentences one way, then open the next one differently. Like most things in this book, that's not an absolute rule, of course. There'll be times you deliberately want to generate some repetition, but not many and never unintentionally.

Emphasis

Consider these sentences:

A) *She could see the clutter of the courtyard down below and, beyond it, a sea of apricot blossom, white and perfect in the sunlight.*

B) *She could see a sea of apricot blossom, white and perfect in the sunlight, and immediately below her, the clutter of the courtyard.*

I hope it's obvious that the first sentence is better, even though it says the same thing, and in the same words, as the second. The difference is emphasis. The visually arresting bit of the sentence is the bit about the apricot blossom. If you place that image at the end, it'll feel stronger because it's not immediately swallowed up by something else. The final full stop is telling the reader to pause a moment, to take in what he's just read. If you bury the key element of a sentence in the middle, you risk losing the effect altogether. (The start of a sentence also lends emphasis, but perhaps a little less than the end.)

By the same token, the start and end of paragraphs are stronger places than middles. If there's something big you want to say, then you probably want to say it first thing, or last thing, not leave it squidged unhappily into the middle.

Naturally, you can't apply these thoughts too mechanically. You can't simply go through your writing, altering any sentence or paragraph that has its most interesting bit in the middle. But if you read a passage and it's not feeling right, then it may be worth thinking about whether you're placing your emphasis in the right place. If not, it's an easy thing to fix. So fix it.

The schoolmarm is out

Plenty of new writers feel themselves paralysed by a handful of rules half-remembered from the old days. The good news is that most of those rules can be dispensed with.

- It's fine to abbreviate; you don't need to write phrases out in full ('it is' or 'do not', for example). Go with whatever feels right, given the tone of your work and the rhythm of your sentence.
- It's fine to use brand names: Hoover, Jell-O, Pernod.
- It's fine to use real places, if you wish. Fine to make places up, if you prefer. Or fine to make places up within real ones – a handful of fictional streets in an otherwise real London, for example. One good technique is to stay with real places when they're large (Manhattan, Washington), to use real places when they're famous (the Empire State Building, the White House), and to dissolve into the fictional when you get local or character-centred (for example, where a character lives or works).
- It's fine to name real people, real newspapers, real books.
- It's fine to swear, cuss, blaspheme, and generally use the kind of language that your grandmother would hate. Be careful, though. Swearwords look stronger on the page than they do when spoken, so you probably want to be sparing in their use. That's true even when you're writing about people (soldiers in wartime, for example) who are likely to swear about as often as they draw breath. Use swearwords, by all means, but don't go crazy. For what it's

worth, my crime writing, which is reasonably gritty, uses the word 'fuck' in some form about eight times in every 10,000 words. If you are way over that level, you might want to think again. If you are writing cosy crime, however, or sweet romance, then using that word even once is probably once too often.

- It's OK to use the word OK. You can also use words like 'thing' or 'stuff' and anything else that your schoolmarm told you not to use.

- Sentence fragments – that is, sentences without a main verb – are just fine too. No issue there.

Funny foreigners are out

Once upon a time, it was common enough for authors to transcribe regional dialects, or foreign accents, in a way which made the speakers seem like something from a freak show. Here, for example, is how Emily Brontë delivers the speech of Joseph, a rough Yorkshireman, in *Wuthering Heights*:

> *T' maister nobbut just buried, and Sabbath not o'ered, und t' sound o' t' gospel still i' yer lugs, and ye darr be laiking! Shame on ye! sit ye down, ill childer! There's good books eneugh if ye'll read 'em: sit ye down, and think o' yer sowls!*

These days, of course, that kind of writing would be embarrassing. It's hard to read, for one thing, and looks – and is – horribly snobbish. At the same time, Joseph's dialect and vocabulary are clearly different from those of the more educated members of the household, and a novelist needs to get to grips with that difference.

The modern way is more subtle, more accurate – and harder to do. Here's an example: a conversation between a black kid and a Muslim one, both American. (I've eliminated most of the surrounding text, so we can read the conversation more clearly.)

> *Tylenol Jones comes up to Ahmad in the hall … 'Hey, Arab,'*
> *he says. 'Hear you been dissing Joryleen.'*
>
> *Ahmad tries to talk the other's language. 'No way, dissing.*
> *We talked a little. It was she come up to me.'*
>
> *… 'She say you disrespect her religion.' …*
>
> *'Her religion is the wrong one,' Ahmad informs Tylenol,*
> *'and anyway she said she had no use for it but to sing in that*
> *foolish choir.' …*
>
> *Tylenol's face darkens and comes closer with a jerk. 'Don't*
> *you talk to me of foolish – you so foolish nobody give you shit,*
> *Arab.'*

John Updike, *Terrorist*.

The first point to notice is how perfectly this captures the timbre of the speech in question. Updike is as accurate as Emily Brontë was, and is a lot easier to read into the bargain. At the same time, both passages make use of dialect words. Emily Brontë's Joseph uses regional vocabulary (like 'nobbut' or 'lugs'), and Updike's Tylenol uses the African-American word 'dissing'.

Equally, both writers make use of grammars that differ from the mainstream. So Joseph says 'ye darr be laiking' (for: 'you there are lurking'), instead of using the Standard British English word order 'you are lurking there'. Updike's Tylenol also uses a grammar that reflects his culture (the grammar is African-American Vernacular English, not Standard American English). Thus Tylenol says: 'hear you been dissing Joryleen', instead of: 'I hear you have been dissing Joryleen'. There's nothing patronising about using these alternative grammars. Quite the opposite. African-American English does have its own vernacular grammar and there's no reason to accord that grammar less respect than any other. So if Tylenol uses it, we should certainly let him do so.

The crucial difference between the two passages – the reason why the first is embarrassing and the second isn't – is that Brontë tries to capture the sound of Joseph's speech by writing it out phonetically. So instead of writing 'and the sound of the gospel still in your lugs', she has Joseph say, 'und t' sound o' t' gospel still i' yer lugs'. Updike doesn't do that. His Tylenol, for example, may well not pronounce the first 't' in 'Don'**t** you talk to me of foolish'. If it comes to that, he probably wouldn't take care to pronounce the 'f' in 'of' separately from the 'f' in 'foolish'. But Updike knows he doesn't need to register such things. If he gets the rhythms, grammar and vocabulary right, then we, the reader, will insert the sound ourselves.

And that's the way to do it. Feel free to use dialect words. Feel free to use dialect grammars. But stop there. Don't make Yorkshiremen say 't' sound o' t' gospel', and don't ask black Americans to sound like something from a 1930s minstrel show. Neither they – nor a publisher – are likely to thank you for it.

The lawyer is in

Finally, there are a small handful of rules which are live and well and living in a courtroom near you.

- If you defame (say something derogatory and not demonstrably true) about a real, live person, you risk a libel action.

- If you say something intrusive (no matter how true) about a real, live person, you risk an invasion of privacy lawsuit.

- If you quote from someone else's work without permission, you risk an action for infringement of copyright or plagiarism.

Most readers won't need to worry about these issues. Novelists mostly don't libel people, because they're inventing their characters from scratch. Non-fiction authors mostly don't libel people because they're not writing that kind of book.

If you are potentially writing the kind of book where these issues matter, I'd suggest that you steer a roughly sensible course around these things as you're writing, but otherwise forget them. If you worry overmuch about legal matters now, you'll find it almost impossible to string a sentence together. So be sensible, write your book, and worry about the legal detail thereafter. If you want to quote other writers in your book, then quote away and seek permission if and when you get your book deal. You don't need it any sooner.

If you're still worried, there's a much fuller guide to all three legal issues in an upcoming addition to the series, that will answer all your questions.

Ghosts of greatness

Thus far, I've spoken of prose style largely as an exercise in competence: communicating clearly, precisely, economically and with specificity. That probably sounded like an easy enough task when we started out. I expect it feels a tad less simple to achieve now. Which is good. You won't deal with the task at hand unless you have a true understanding of what's involved.

At the same time, the goal itself feels a little downbeat. A little patronising. In my defence, I offer three justifications. The first is that there are countless bestsellers written by people who are immaculately professional prose stylists, but who never (or almost never) attain anything poetic. Secondly, we're about to talk about the rest of it – the magic – in the chapter that follows. And third, an admission. If you follow perfectly the rules we've dealt with so far, you'll achieve something wonderful. Take the following chunk from *The Cut* by George Pelecanos. The hero, Spero Lucas, is being introduced a few pages into the first chapter:

> *Lucas sat still for a long minute, looking at nothing. He closed his note-book and got up out of his seat. He stood five-foot-eleven, went one-eighty-five, had a flat stomach and a good chest and shoulders. His hair was black and he wore it short. His eyes were green, flecked with gold, and frequently unreadable. He was twenty-nine years old.*
>
> *Petersen watched Lucas stretch. 'Sorry. That seat's unforgiving.'*
>
> *'It's these wood floors. The chair sits funny on 'em cause the planks are warped.'*
>
> *'This house goes back to the nineteenth century.'*

'Your point is what?'

'Ghosts of greatness walk these rooms. I start messing with the floors, I might make them angry.'

A young GW law student entered Petersen's office and dropped a large block of papers on his desk. She was dark-haired, fully curved, and effortlessly attractive. Tom Petersen's interns looked more or less like younger versions of his knockout wife.

'The Parker briefs,' said the woman, whose name was Constance Kelly.

This is writing of a kind that gets better the more of it you read. It's almost shockingly clean, shockingly precise. It has a clarity so absolute that the clarity itself feels like a little work of art. And at the same time, the prose creates a setting in which humans can be as complicatedly human as they wish to be. Pelecanos himself isn't going to get into long character dissections – you wouldn't read him if he did – so you, the reader, have to gather all you can from the clues he offers, especially in dialogue. We'll talk more about dialogue in a much later chapter, but for now, simply appreciate a master at work. Look at the authenticity of those speech rhythms, the unexpected direction taken by the conversation, the way character is revealed through words. Pelecanos has done nothing more or less than adhere to the guidelines we've considered so far, yet the result comes close to perfection. If I had to pick a Pelecanos novel or a Hemingway one to read on a plane journey, I'd pick the Pelecanos.

Chapter Summary

- Check your nouns. Usually, boring nouns make for boring prose. Working your adjectives hard won't compensate.
- Don't state the obvious. Look for the telling or inviting detail.
- Similarly, try not to rely on adverbs.
- You have five senses. Use them.
- Avoid exclamation marks almost completely. Use ellipses ('...') sparingly.
- Watch for unintended repetitions.
- Abstractions are OK in moderation, but your prose should always keep one foot in the tangible.
- Check your prose for tediously repetitive rhythms (too many short sentences; too many similar sentence structures).
- Sentence endings and beginnings give more emphasis to a word or phrase than sentence middles.
- Most old-fashioned prescriptions on writing can be ignored, but not all – check the list earlier in this chapter.
- Don't use phonetic speech to capture the accents of foreigners or people with regional accents.
- Watch out for libel, for breach of privacy and for copyright issues.

LITTLE FLASHES OF GENIUS

If your prose style has achieved everything we've spoken about so far – clarity, economy, precision and the avoidance of cliché – then you are a competent writer.

If that sounds like a rather underwhelming compliment, it shouldn't. Many bestselling writers have a prose style that is utterly professional, utterly competent, but no more. They get their huge sales and committed readerships from other aspects of their work: a rip-roaring plot, memorable characters, a stunning concept. For these writers, prose style is important as a means to an end. It's about the efficient communication of a wonderful story. They don't need more from their prose style than that; it's not where their magic lies.

What's more, *you are capable of achieving this level of professionalism*. Although many new writers are let down by their prose style, that's because, in most cases, they have never really focused on it. You're going to. If you focus on the lessons so far in this section, and take time to apply them – and perhaps, if you want, get professional feedback as well – there's no reason why you shouldn't write as cleanly and capably as, say, a John Grisham or a Nora Roberts. It's within your grasp.

But many writers will not want to stop at mere competence, and this chapter will look hard at the skills that will take your work to a new level altogether. In some cases, you have to get to that level. If you're writing literary fiction, it's not enough to put together sentences in a clean, efficient, competent way. You need to add a little sizzle, a little class. You need some strut in your writing, a 'look at me' quality which will satisfy an audience more demanding than that for genre fiction.

On the other hand, there'll be many writers of more commercially orientated fiction who aspire to something similar themselves, to write a storming story, stunningly told. To achieve the literary excellence of a le Carré or an Elmore Leonard. Or to achieve the sales success and book-group style admiration that greeted Audrey Niffenegger's *The Time Traveler's Wife*, or Alice Sebold's *The Lovely Bones*.

All such writers should read on. Those who are happy to be a John Grisham can, if they like, skip this chapter and move on to the next one. But I hope you stay, because, for the first time in this section, we take a look at magic.

Making your images precise

A lot of writers think that good writing is all about flashy images.

> *'Tis the East, and Juliet is the sun. Arise fair sun …*
>
> William Shakespeare, *Romeo and Juliet.*
>
> *When the evening is spread out against the sky like a patient etherised upon a table …*
>
> T. S. Eliot, *The Love Song of J. Alfred Prufrock.*
>
> *… he looked about as inconspicuous as a tarantula on a slice of angel-food.*
>
> Raymond Chandler, *Farewell My Lovely.*

These fragments *are* all examples of fine writing, but it would be a mistake to read too much into them. Two of the pieces above come from poetry, not prose, and the speakers are gawkily teenage in one case (Romeo) and awkwardly self-conscious in the other (Prufrock) – and both are drawn, therefore, to the occasional overcooked image.

Raymond Chandler's narrator, Philip Marlowe, is neither gawky nor awkward, and when he presents an over-the-top image, he does so knowingly. Indeed, the sentence which ends with the tarantula image begins like this: 'Even on Central

Avenue, not the quietest dressed street in the world ...'. That understated introduction – 'not the quietest dressed street in the world' – tips the reader off that what follows is going to be merrily overstated.

So, let's discard the idea that flashy imagery is the way to go. If flashiness is not the key to success, then what is? The answer surely lies in our old friend, *precision*. Take a look at the snippets below, all from writers who, at their best, are outstandingly good at what they do:

> *If we were outside – the* [tornado] *drills happened sometimes at recess, which felt like a great waste – a teacher would lead us to a dip in the grassy hill behind the elementary school, and we'd lie flat on our bellies and join hands, forming an irregular circle or a human flower, our bodies the petals pointing out. In high school, we joked about the absurdity:* That was supposed to save us? I *pictured a net of children blown aloft, straining to hold on to one another.*

Curtis Sittenfeld, *American Wife.*

> *For the first time, her love for Edward was associated with a definable physical sensation, as irrefutable as vertigo. Before, she had known only a comforting broth of warm emotions, a thick winter blanket of kindness and trust. That had always seemed enough, an achievement in itself.*

Ian McEwan, *On Chesil Beach.*

These examples reflect much more accurately the way imagery generally works in fiction. Curtis Sittenfeld uses two images. The first is this: 'an irregular circle or a human flower, our bodies the petals pointing out.' It's as though her first attempt to describe the configuration 'an irregular circle' doesn't quite capture it, so her narrator goes on to the more exotic idea of a 'human flower'. It's not the exoticism of that idea which appeals, however, but its accuracy. The 'petals pointing out' part illustrates how the children were lying, in a way that the earlier phrase, 'irregular circle', failed to capture. Indeed, if you or I or Sittenfeld's narrator were asked to brainstorm a way to describe more accurately how the children were lying, I think we'd fail to do it. Deftly, and without any hoo-hah, Sittenfeld has given us the picture and moved on.

Her second image does call for a little more attention: 'I pictured a net of children blown aloft'. A *net* of children? You know exactly what she means – but at the same time the image is ludicrous. It's the sort of thing you'd expect in a Roald Dahl fantasy, and nowhere else. But again: that's the point. Sittenfeld has already told us that she recognises the 'absurdity' of the idea, so to give a precise picture of the situation, the image must carry an absurd quality, as well as a visually accurate one. That tiny word, a 'net' of children, does both things perfectly.

Sittenfeld's images are trying to capture a physical situation. McEwan is using imagery to define an emotional one. First off, that phrase 'irrefutable as vertigo'. How well that works! Florence, the woman McEwan is writing about here, is feeling her first twinges of physical desire and is taken aback by them. Vertigo is simultaneously a strange feeling, literally a giddy one, and yet it's also irrefutably there. Perhaps no other feeling is as strange and as undeniable. It precisely recognises the oddness of Florence's new feelings.

Contrast that image with the two that follow: 'a comforting broth of warm emotions, a thick winter blanket of kindness and trust'. Unlike the vertigo image, these are comfortable, easy ideas to take in. A comforting broth, a winter blanket. These images are so comfortable; indeed, they lie only a step or two away from cliché ... which is the point. Cliché is *familiar*. It may not be daring, but it is cosy. The homely simplicity of these images deliberately contrasts with the earlier 'vertigo' one, and they work in large part through the contrast.

Imagery: the second dimension

If precision is the major goal of your imagery, then you also need to be alert to its flavour. We saw both Sittenfeld and McEwan use images that were precise in two dimensions. The first dimension had to do with physical or emotional accuracy. A 'human flower' gave precise expression to a particular shape. 'Irrefutable as vertigo' gave precise expression to a particular feeling. The second dimension has to do with accuracy as regards mood, context or character. A 'net of children' worked because the image was ludicrous, at a moment where a ludicrous image was called for. A 'comforting broth of warm emotions' worked because the image itself was a familiar one, at just the moment when familiarity mattered.

Pretty much all good images work well in both of these dimensions. Here are a couple more snippets to play with:

> *The wind strikes the trailer like a load of dirt coming off a dump truck, eases, dies, leaves a temporary silence.*

Annie Proulx, *Brokeback Mountain*.

> *Tennis courts said to be the oldest in the United States neighbour the cricket field, and the park itself is surrounded on all sides by Victorian houses with elaborately planted gardens. For as long as anyone can remember, the local residents have tolerated the occasional crash of a cricket ball, arriving like a giant meteoric cranberry, into their flowering shrubbery.*

Joseph O'Neill, *Netherland*.

Annie Proulx's image gives a precise auditory explanation of the sound of the wind, but it's flavoured by the character of the man listening to the wind: a rough-and-ready cowboy living in his trailer and making a living labouring on the land. He's familiar with dirt and dump trucks. He mightn't think about wind in metaphorical terms, but if he did, he'd probably be talking about dirt and dump trucks.

Something similar is true of Joseph O'Neill's 'giant meteoric cranberry'. That's an utterly outlandish image – echoes of Roald

Dahl, again – but that's the point. The image is precise along dimension one, physical accuracy. A cricket ball is indeed the same colour as a cranberry, it is much larger, and the shooting parabola of its descent shares something in common with a meteor. But dimension two – accuracy to context – is more important here. The cricket ball arrives like something from another world. Indeed, cricket – an English game being played in New York – *is* from another world, and the people playing it are almost all immigrants. Neither they, nor the game, nor the cricket ball truly belong in these orderly Victorian gardens. That's the point. That's the meteor.

Good writers do not necessarily need to make extensive use of imagery. A good writer may go for pages on end without deploying it. What matters isn't frequency of use, but excellence. And excellence is about precision.

Atmosphere

If your book contains exotic settings, so much the better. You have that much more scope to revel in the creation of atmosphere, a more enticing array of details from which to pick. Skilfully done, such things enrich a book no end. There are a number of ways to approach such things. One obvious way is to revel in the foreignness of the place. (Or of the moment, if you're writing historically; or of the planet, if you're writing speculatively.) Barbara Kingsolver's *The Lacuna*, a historical novel set in Mexico, opens like this:

> *In the beginning were the howlers. They always commenced their bellowing in the first hour of dawn, just as the hem of the sky began to whiten. It would start with just one: his forced rhythmic groaning, like a saw blade. That aroused others near him, nudging them to bawl along with his monstrous tune. Soon the maroon-throated howls would echo back from other trees, farther down the beach, until the whole jungle filled with roaring trees. As it was in the beginning, so it is every morning of the world.*

This isn't simply a passage that describes a place (Isla Pixol in Mexico) and a time (1929) that's alien to us, it's a passage that makes the most of its exoticism: the biblical opening and closing to the paragraph, the imagery ('like a saw blade'), the vague but frightened adjectives ('monstrous'). Even the word 'howlers', which stands at the centre of the paragraph, is weirdly undefined, though in a menacing sort of way. After all, what *is* a howler?

This kind of approach can pay rich dividends. We're plunged into the exotic in such a way as we *feel* the exotic in every line. That sense of the foreign lends a sense of excitement to the writing. It offers a rich palette of colour to the writer that cares to make use of it. Having said that, however, you can't allow that palette to dominate your characters. Kingsolver's passage deploys the exotic as vigorously as it does only in part because the place is (to most of us) an exotic one. The bigger reason it takes the approach it does is that the characters involved (an American mother and her young son) are strangers in this world. The howlers are, in fact, local monkeys and are completely harmless. The two outsiders don't know this, so their reactions to a perfectly ordinary dawn chorus are biblical, vague and frightened.

That's a good way to approach things, but not the only way. Here, for example, is a snippet from another historical novel set in a non-Western country – Chimamanda Ngozi Adichie's *Half of a Yellow Sun*, a novel which depicts the civil war which unfolded in 1960s Nigeria:

> *Master found a rain-holder on the wedding day. The elderly man arrived early and dug a shallow pit at the back of the house, made a bonfire in it, then sat in the thick of the bluish smoke, feeding dried leaves to the fire.*
>
> *'No rain will come. Nothing will happen until the wedding is over,' he said, when Ugwu took him a plate of rice and meat. Ugwu smelt the harsh gin on his breath. He turned and went back indoors so the smoke would not soak into his carefully ironed shirt.*

To most Western readers, the episode described in this passage is exotic. It describes something that we haven't witnessed and invokes a job function (that of rain-holder) we hadn't even imagined. But look how opposite is Adichie's technique to Kingsolver's. There's no biblical language here. No metaphor. No anxious imprecision in the adjectives. Instead, the prose is simple, clear, factual – and still exotic. The central character Ugwu, a domestic servant, notes with equal lack of comment the rain-holder's technique and the presence of gin on his breath. In the space where you might expect a comment, the narrator simply tells us that Ugwu went inside to avoid contaminating his cleanly ironed shirt. Here, the 'exoticism' arises precisely from Adichie's anti-exotic technique. She reports her scene precisely and without literary flourish, thereby allowing the scene itself to make its mark. Her point-of-view character here is an insider, not an outsider, so her technique fits the character, just as Kingsolver's did.

Either way, readers are greedy to be taken to unfamiliar places, unfamiliar times and (for fantasy and sci-fi readers) unfamiliar worlds. Bringing these unfamiliarities to life in a compelling way will lift and enrich your work. That doesn't mean to say you should alter your story to go chasing after the unknown. If you are writing a crime thriller set in an ordinary office, in an ordinary town, in the present time – well, then, you are. You need to bring your scenes alive with as much vividness as you can muster, but that sense of the unusual will need to come from other aspects of your story.

The shocking and the edgy

One possible way of getting that edge of the unusual into your work is through the central character. Nick Cave's *The Death of Bunny Munro* opens in an ordinary hotel room, in an ordinary town, and the protagonist has the unromantic occupation of travelling salesman. The book opens like this:

'I am damned,' thinks Bunny Munro in a sudden moment of awareness reserved for those who are about to die. He feels that somewhere down the line he has made a grave mistake, but this realisation passes in a dreadful heartbeat, and is gone – leaving him in a room at the Grenville Hotel, in his underwear, with nothing but himself and his appetites. He closes his eyes and pictures a random vagina, then sits on the edge of the hotel bed and, in slow motion, leans back against the quilted headboard. He clamps the mobile phone under his chin and with his teeth breaks the seal on a miniature bottle of brandy. He empties the bottle down his throat, lobs it across the room, then shudders and gags and says into the phone, 'Don't worry, love, everything's going to be all right'.

The paragraph sets the tone for the book it introduces. Where Kingsolver and Adichie took the reader to the edge of the unknown in geographical and historical terms, Cave does something similar here in terms of psychic geography – taking us out to the limits of the known and describing the view with candid accuracy.

Even here, though, it's worth noticing that Cave does more than this. Hunter S. Thompson, William S. Burroughs and Jack Kerouac all helped drag literature into the age of sex, drugs and rock 'n' roll. Simply planting your character in that milieu no longer does enough to create an edge of vitality. What gives this paragraph its shiver of excitement is the wonderful contrast between the opening line and the final one. That's a contrast which beckons us forward into the book. Why is this man damned? Why is he telling his wife not to worry? Cave gives us a character who lives on the distant fringes of our own, rather more domesticated, psychic geography, but he's also shrewd enough to create a story that leaps from that geography to pull us in.

Invention

One aspect of the writer's craft which writers themselves tend to put a lot of store by is invention. Not the large-scale inventions of plot and character, but the line-by-line ones, the ability to deliver little pleasurable surprises to the reader with every line.

Here, for example, is a snippet from Cormac McCarthy's *Blood Meridian*, an exercise in high style:

> *At fourteen he runs away. He will not see again the freezing kitchenhouse in the predawn dark. The firewood, the washpots. He wanders West as far as Memphis, a solitary migrant on that flat and pastoral landscape. Blacks in the fields, lank and stooped, their fingers spiderlike among the bolls of cotton. A shadowed agony in the garden. Against the sun's declining figures moving in the slower dusk across a paper skyline. A lone dark husbandman pursuing mule and harrow down the rain-blown bottomland toward night.*

I hope it's obvious that this is fine writing – but look past the fineness of it and observe its capacity to create surprise after surprise. You might come up with a slightly different list from me, but I'd suggest that this short passage offers the following mini-surprises:

- *At fourteen he runs away.* A plain, short, simple sentence, but one that's shocking in what it says and – in contrast to the more ornate language before and after it – in its very simplicity.
- *Freezing kitchenhouse.* A lovely stroke that, to call it the kitchen*house*, not simply the kitchen. That choice of word makes it wonderfully explicit how alien this landscape is. We all have kitchens; none of us have kitchenhouses.
- *The firewood, the washpots.* The first two sentences are surely preparing us for something with more motion in it – they're about running, about what *won't* be seen again. But here we have something with zero motion (not even

a main verb) and about the things that *are* being seen again (in the mind) right now. It's a static touch that comes just when you're expecting movement. A little jerk of delay, beautifully timed, that mirrors the wrench involved in departure.

- *He wanders West as far as Memphis, a solitary migrant on that flat and pastoral landscape.* The next sentence moves from the intense, static close-up of the previous one to the vastly wide-angle – an angle so vast that it appears to take in the West, Memphis, and all the surrounding landscape. The boy himself has almost been lost. We were prepared for movement, but the radical zooming out takes us, yet again, by surprise.

- *Blacks in the fields, lank and stooped, their fingers spiderlike among the bolls of cotton.* Gosh, another surprise. A contemporary reader is (fortunately) not used to hearing contemporary authors talk about toiling 'blacks' in this flat, apolitical way. That's the first shock of this sentence, but McCarthy follows up by calling their fingers 'spiderlike'. That's a view so dehumanising, it verges almost on the racist ... but at the same time hammers home how different is the mental world of this boy and the people he comes from. (The beautiful fragment which follows about the shadowed agony also makes it clear that McCarthy hasn't lost his marbles. *He's* not insensitive to the suffering and he doesn't expect us to be.)

And so on. McCarthy's prose delivers a succession of micro-shocks to the reader. It's not that any individual shock is all that great, it's that you can't take your eye off the writing for a moment, you can't afford to relax, because you have no idea where McCarthy is going next. And that's not because McCarthy is shooting off in a whole series of random directions. He isn't. That little sentence about the washpots and the firewood is a perfect way to suggest the mind of the runaway boy. The sentence is simultaneously surprising and inevitable: a perfect combination.

It would be easy to think you only get this level of surprise and delight in the most finely wrought literary fiction. But you'd be wrong. You get it in abundance in J. K. Rowling. Here, for example, is a bit from the opening to *Harry Potter and the Prisoner of Azkaban*:

> *It was nearly midnight, and he* [Harry] *was lying on his stomach in bed, the blankets drawn right over his head like a tent, a flash-light in one hand and a large leather-bound book (*A History of Magic *by Bathilda Bagshot) propped open against the pillow. Harry moved the tip of his eagle-feather quill down the page, frowning as he looked for something that would help him write his essay, 'Witch Burning in the Fourteenth Century Was Com-pletely Pointless – discuss'.*

If the Cormac McCarthy prose felt like a fine brandy – golden, old and complex – Rowling's prose is like the box of chocolates that you scoff in bed on a Sunday morning. The opening couple of lines in the paragraph sets the scene simply and clearly, then the joyful surprises just keep on coming. '*A History of Magic*': perfect! What else would a wizardly schoolkid have to read on his holidays? And the author's name: the toothsome, absurd, repeata-ble 'Bathilda Bagshot'. Lovely. And while the reader might have guessed that Harry Potter would be using a quill, Rowling jumps beyond that simple idea and offers us the idea of an eagle-feather quill. Finally, that essay title is a delight, simultaneously po-faced and joking. You can hardly read it without smiling.

Rowling is writing for an utterly different audience to McCarthy's, but her prose is equally watchable: you have to keep your eye on it, because you never know what's coming next and you don't want to miss a thing. (Her capacity for invention is half the reason for her success. The other half is her warmth of tone. Even when her books get dark, her warmth is never far away.

Rowling's inventiveness brings readers to her books; her kindness keeps them there.)

Things unsaid

Consider this little passage:

> *As soon as she heard the front door open, Eilis went downstairs. Rose, in the hall, was holding her pocket mirror in front of her face. She was studying herself closely as she applied lipstick and eye make-up before glancing at her overall appearance in the large hall mirror, settling her hair. Eilis looked on silently as her sister moistened her lips and then checked herself one more time in the pocket mirror before putting it away.*
>
> *Their mother came from the kitchen to the hall.*
>
> *'You look lovely, Rose,' she said. 'You'll be the belle of the golf club.'*
>
> *'I'm starving,' Rose said, 'but I've no time to eat'.*
>
> Colm Tóibín, *Brooklyn.*

It would be quite easy to read this passage as bland. Certainly, it's efficient enough (all those things about clarity, economy and precision are handled perfectly), but where's the excellence? Where are the little flashes of genius?

The curious answer, in this case, is that the genius lies in what is *not* on the page. At this point in the book, which is set in the Ireland of the 1950s, Eilis has no job, no boyfriend, and a very restricted life. Her sister is more glamorous, prettier, and has a little money. And none of this is spoken about. Not in this passage, nor anywhere else, except indirectly. The book is written from Eilis's point of view, yet it spends little time dissecting her emotional life. When we do get little flashes of interiority, they are often bland ('She knew nothing about types of watches but thought the prices were very low') or frustratingly short on detailed insight ('She drank a cup of tea with the others, holding the letters [from home] in her hand nervously, feeling her heart beating faster when she thought about them …').

Yet the book, a small masterpiece, is about these silences. It's a love story set in an age and culture where people did not have a language in which to discuss their feelings, or even understand their feelings. Tóibín uses this fact to play a double game. At one level, he is reporting Eilis's story as she would have understood it or thought of it. At another level, he knows damn well that any modern reader is going to be filling in the gaps, making the necessary deductions – and will be shocked at the way the story unfolds towards its unhappy (and moving) conclusion. Tóibín's story gains its power by its restraint; the things it hints at but doesn't say. It's a profound and wonderful technique – and one that would go hideously wrong in clumsier hands.

The sound of music

In an earlier chapter, we encountered this sentence from Marilynne Robinson's *Housekeeping*:

> *I dreamed that I was walking across the ice on the lake, which was breaking up as it does in spring, softening and shifting and pulling itself apart.*

We admired that sentence for its deftness in conveying a complex picture. But its virtues go beyond simply that. Marilynne Robinson could have said this, for example:

> *I dreamed that I was moving softly over the frozen lake, which was starting to melt as it does in spring, breaking up, cracking, yanking itself to bits.*

Those two sentences say almost exactly the same thing, but they feel quite different. Why?

If you haven't stopped to answer that question, then you might want to pause a moment or two before reading on. If you have duly pondered the matter, then with a little luck, you have the answer: the sentences feel different because the second sentence inverts the balance of sound at work in Robinson's version.

Robinson's sentence has all the hard-edged sounds ('walking', 'lake', 'breaking') in the first part, and then side-slips into a succession of wonderfully gentle sounds to finish with ('softening and shifting and pulling itself apart'). The transition from hard to soft is a kind of auditory melting. The sentence is melting, just the way the lake is. In the second sentence, I placed the soft sounds early on and packed the last clause with all those spiky 'k' sounds. The sentence now has the opposite effect. It's as though the sentence is, musically speaking, calling attention to the lovely softness of that frozen world, in contrast to the shards and spikes of ice created by its destruction. (Robinson's choice, needless to say, is the right one.)

If you fancy another little puzzle, then ask yourself why Robinson chose to write this:

… softening and shifting and pulling itself apart.

Instead of this:

… pulling itself apart and shifting and softening.

All those things are going on simultaneously, so it can't be that Robinson's verbs are somehow echoing the chronology of the break-up. As far as chronology goes, those verbs could be in any order at all.

Again, the clue is in the sound. The sentence starts with two compact descriptors of what's happening to the ice: 'softening' and 'shifting'. It then moves to a much less compact description: the three words 'pulling itself apart'. That movement from the compact to the less compact reflects what is happening to the ice. The sentence itself is breaking up, just the way the ice is.

I've called attention to these things because any genuinely poetic prose is about sounds as well as meanings. You have to get the meanings right, of course, but the sound should be a musical accompaniment, endorsing and filling out the sense. It's a tough brief to master, but if you get it right, your writing will be magical.

Don't panic

By this point, some readers will feel a little freaked out. The chapters that have gone before provided a good, workmanlike but *achievable* checklist for writing well. In this section – well, jeepers! All of a sudden, it seems that our images need to succeed in multidimensional space, we need to invent something amazing in every line, our sentences need to be musical as regards both sound and rhythm, and we need to attend carefully to everything that we're *not* saying, as well as everything that we *are*.

But don't panic. For one thing, the standard set in this chapter is very, very high. Ian McEwan and Curtis Sittenfeld are lavishly gifted. Annie Proulx is a hero of mine, Marilynne Robinson a genius, J. K. Rowling a gazillionaire. You can write worse than these folk and still be very good indeed. For another thing, you don't have to get from where you are now to where you need to be all in one hop. Writers often get better. Practice makes perfect. (Marilynne Robinson, damn her, is an exception: *Housekeeping* was her debut. But then you don't need to worry about her: she's a genius. It also took her almost quarter of a century to write her next novel.)

What's more, the thing that's scariest about reading about other people's genius is that you have to analyse it word by word, and even sometimes letter by letter. That process of analysis can lead you to the ridiculous idea that authors work the same way, that they sit sucking the ends of their pencils as they try to figure out whether it would be better to start this particular sentence with a hard sound or a soft one, and whether the image they're toying with works properly in multidimensional space. And of course it's not like that. Stuff comes to you. You write it down. You see whether it sounds good, whether it feels right. If it does, you're happy and slightly amazed by your own good fortune in having such good material just float into your head. If it doesn't, you scratch it out, tinker around, or get impatient and go outside for a walk, then come back in and tinker again. Sometimes you get it spot-on, and you're pleased you went to all the trouble. Other times, it never quite feels just so, but that doesn't matter too much, because other sentences can do the heavy lifting, and this bit can simply avoid doing anything unmannerly, like containing clichés or clogging things up with unnecessary verbiage. Even wonderful writers can write ordinary sentences. Ordinary sentences are OK too.

Yet having said all *that*, the analysis helps. The kind of thinking we've been doing in this chapter turns us into more conscious writers and (just as important) more conscious readers too. You'll learn more from the material you read and be quicker to spot the difference between good and bad in the things you write. As you develop these analytical skills, you'll find they percolate, mysteriously but inevitably, into your own work. One day you'll look back at something you've written and analyse it the way we've done in this chapter. You'll notice, all of a sudden, that what you've written is very, very good. You'll notice a musicality in the writing, a deftness in the imagery that you never thought to put there, but which is there nevertheless. Enjoy that moment when it comes. It's what writing's all about.

Chapter Summary

- Most writers can achieve competence, if they work at it. Some writers will wish to seek excellence.
- The best images tend to be precise rather than flashy.
- They will also work in two dimensions: physical accuracy and an accuracy of mood or flavour.
- Atmosphere can be created by using rich, strange language or bare, simple language. Either way, introducing the reader to exotic or unfamiliar scenes will keep them attentive.
- Edginess is also a good way to produce saleable fiction. But you can't *only* be edgy; you need to find a way to bring something distinctive to your mood.
- Invention is one of the aspects of prose style most cherished by serious writers. You'll find inventiveness and playfulness in both high art and popular writing.
- You can communicate plenty by leaving things unsaid.
- Train yourself to become alert to the music of your words.
- Don't panic: practice makes perfect.

TONE

Writing isn't about striving for a Pulitzer or a Booker Prize. It's about writing well for your audience – and finding a way of writing that works well for the story you're telling, and the people you're telling it about.

Tonal variety

Thrillers are often thought of as sounding all alike. Tough and clipped, the bastard children of Ernest Hemingway and Raymond Chandler. And that assumption is at least half a nonsense, as the following extracts reveal:

> 'What did you do?'
>
> 'We buried them in the well. Quickly, before the soldiers came back.'
>
> I studied the old woman. Her face was brown corduroy. Her hands were calloused, her long braids more gray than black. Fabric lay folded atop her head, bright reds, pinks, yellows, and blues, woven into patterns older than the mountains above us. One corner rose and fell with the wind.
>
> The woman did not smile. She did not frown. Her eyes met no one's to my relief. I knew if they lingered on mine even briefly, the transfer of pain would be brutal.
>
> Kathy Reichs, Grave Secrets.

> Annabel was remembering her law tutor at Tübingen, discoursing on the arts of cross examination. Never under-estimate a witness's silence, he liked to say. There are eloquent silences, and guilty silences, and silences of genuine bewilderment, and silences of

creativity. The trick is to know what kind of silence you are hearing from your own witness. But this silence was her own.

'Is this part of your coordination, Herr Dinkelmann?' she asked playfully, while desperately collecting her thoughts.

The clown's smile again, the perfect curve. 'Don't flirt with me, Frau Richter.'

John le Carré, *A Most Wanted Man.*

I am sorry, as well, to present such a sketchy and disappointing exegesis of what is in fact the central part of my story. I have noticed that even the most garrulous and shameless of murderers are shy about recounting their crimes. A few months ago, in an airport bookstore, I picked up the autobiography of a notorious thrill killer and was disheartened to find it entirely bereft of lurid detail. At the points of greatest suspense (rainy night; deserted street; fingers closing around the lovely neck of Victim Number Four) it would suddenly, and not without some coyness, switch to some entirely unrelated matter. (Was the reader aware that an IQ test had been given him in prison? That his score had been gauged as being close to that of Jonas Salk?) By far the major portion of the book was devoted to spinsterish discourses on prison life – bad food, hijinks in the exercise yard, tedious little jailbird hobbies. It was a waste of five dollars.

Donna Tartt, *The Secret History.*

Even if you don't know these authors, you should be able to feel what kind of novel each snippet comes from. The first, by Kathy Reichs, is mass-market crime fiction. That doesn't mean the writing is inept. On the contrary, you'll notice (I hope) that Reichs takes some care to give us a visual impression of the woman being spoken to. The sentence, 'her face was brown corduroy', offers a simple but imaginatively precise image. It's good writing. At the same time, it feels as a crime novel should feel. The sentences are mostly short and always efficient. There's nothing much to slow the reader down. And sandwiching that short paragraph of description are elements ('We buried them in the well' and 'the transfer of pain would be brutal') which give the snippet a sense of toughness. As readers, we know that we're in a tough place where wrong decisions are liable to have bad consequences. The passage, short as it is, feels 'crimey'. The tone is spot-on.

John le Carré feels different. He too writes thrillers, but he's known for the intelligence and poise of his writing. Both things emerge clearly here. Because the book is a thriller, you feel a continual toughness of tone ('Never under-estimate a witness's silence'; 'There are eloquent silences, and guilty silences'; '"Don't flirt with me, Frau Richter."'). The sense of unrelenting hardness – in the world and those who inhabit it – is a core quality of a good thriller, and it's fully on display here. At the same time, le Carré is perfectly happy to demand literary sophistication from his reader. The phrase, 'The clown's smile again, the perfect curve' is the clearest example, but it's present throughout the passage. It's there in the fencing between the two speakers. It's there in the whole question of whose the silence is, and what kind. Kathy Reichs would be disappointing her audience if she wrote like that. Le Carré would be disappointing his if he didn't.

The third snippet is different again. Donna Tartt's book is a psychological thriller or, if you prefer, a murder mystery. The thread of murder and self-destruction isn't always as clear as it is in the passage above, but you always feel close to the edge of darkness. At the same time, the tone is entirely unlike anything you'd expect to find in a conventional thriller. Donna Tartt's narrator is snobby, intelligent, disdainful, and preppy. (Just listen to him sniping at those 'spinsterish discourses on ... tedious little jailbird hobbies'). There are no short sentences here, no attention-seeking attempt at toughness. Tartt has, in fact, adopted a tone that is entirely at odds with her genre and the genius of her book lies in that disparity. The book combines the narrative force and darkness of a thriller with the elegance and intelligence of a literary novel. It's a wonderful book.

You can take any literary genre you like and find similar variations of tone. Women's fiction can range from soap-bubble light chick lit through to serious and affecting literary novels. In non-fiction, you'll find a range of tone from colloquial to highbrow, from brisk to discursive. In short, it's not the genre which sets the tone of your book, but you. The choice is crucial.

How to choose your tone?

Many new writers – perhaps especially those starting out in genre fiction – don't give much thought to these issues. Thriller writers just decide to write the way they assume all thrillers are written. Authors of chick lit set out with a tone of bright, gossipy cheerfulness, on the assumption that all such fiction has to be written that way.

The truth, however, is that you need to be as careful in thinking about tone as you do when thinking about character or plot. And you can do anything you like, so long as your tone is:

- Right for your market,
- Right for your story,
- Right for your characters, and
- Right for you.

We'll take those bullet points in turn. First of all, 'right for your market'. Most writers will, most of the time, play the game the way Kathy Reichs and John le Carré have done: namely, adopting a style which clearly reflects their chosen market niche – mainstream crime thriller in Reichs's case, upmarket spy-thriller in le Carré's. That doesn't mean that you need to sacrifice all individuality of style – far from it – but it does mean that you will *generally* want to write a thriller in one kind of way (taut, snappy, hard), commercial women's fiction in another (confiding, warm, intimate), and so on. If, like Tartt, you choose to write in one genre (psychological thriller) while using the tone from another (literary novel), then you've got to be good enough to pull in readers from both genres and keep them hooked. Needless to say, that's a hard trick to pull off, but impressive if you can do it.

Second, 'right for your story'. What kind of tone suits your story? The le Carré novel quoted above plays out a drama of trust, betrayal and political ruthlessness. The book can be read as an attack on the moral compromises involved in George W. Bush's war on terror; both the plot-line and its political implications call for intelligent participation by the reader. Le Carré needed to find a tone that could handle all the aspects of his novel: thrillerish darkness and pace; psychological incisiveness; moral disgust and political insight. The elegant, edgy, intelligent prose blends these things almost perfectly. If he'd sought to handle the same story while writing like Kathy Reichs, he'd have lost entire dimensions of his story. It wouldn't have worked.

Third, 'right for your characters'. When it comes to character-isation, it's fairly obvious that if you are writing in the first person (as Reichs and Tartt do in the examples quoted), your writing style has to feel plausibly like the character who's meant to be speaking. So Reichs's narrator – forensic anthropologist, Tempe Brennan – needs to be reflected in the way she speaks. Tough, but perceptive. Emotionally aware, but not too introspective. Tartt's narrator also talks exactly the way he is: that's how we were able to start describing him accurately from one short extract. So, with first-person narration, the rule is fairly simple: *choices you make about your main character will also be choices about the way you write*. The one thing defines the other.

Something similar is also true when it comes to third-person narration, however. Take the le Carré story again. In theory, you might think the narrator could be one sort of person and the principal characters could be entirely different. But could they? Just imagine trying to rewrite the passage in teen chick-lit style. ('Annabel was remembering her law tutor at Tübingen, droning on and on about cross examination. Never under-estimate a witness's silence, he liked to say. But omigod, his clothes! Old jeans cut just tight enough to emphasise his fat thighs. And his hair …') That kind of writing would kill the book immediately. So while, as a third-person narrator, you *can* write in a tone that's different from your characters' own voices, you nevertheless need to find a tone that harmonises with them, which adds to the story instead of undermining it.

Finally, the last bullet point: 'right for you'. In the end, none of us pick out a writing style the way we choose a pair of socks. Although the emotional range of your book will vary from page to page and chapter to chapter, its tone – your style of writing – will remain largely consistent. You need to find a style that you're happy with, a style that you'll be happy to spend months with as you write your first draft, then a whole lot more months with as you edit it. That means that the style you write in needs to express something true of yourself. Not the whole truth by any means – Donna Tartt probably isn't a murderous, narcissistic snob, for example – but *a* truth.

Finding the right accommodation between who you are and what your book is can take time and be hard to achieve. We once had an editorial client who had come up with a wonderful plot for a thriller and had a strong lead character into the bargain. But the thriller needed an edge of darkness throughout, and my client's natural tendency as a writer was towards a kind of jovial, up-beat cynicism. Those two things were utterly at odds. The joviality was killing the thriller. It took a long time to achieve, but we had to work to develop a style of writing that felt true to my client but which was also appropriate for the story. Once we had done that, the thriller leapt to life and we found an agent for it without difficulty.

Many writers won't have a problem with the issues discussed in this chapter. For them, finding the right tone for their work will seem easy and natural; something they barely need to think about. Others, though, may find these issues the very knottiest ones they face.

Either way, it's OK. If you think there's a natural fit between your writing style, your story and your characters, you're probably right. Just make sure that you're not inadvertently copying some other author or (even worse) some generic idea of what your kind of book should sound like.

If you think you haven't yet groped your way to that natural fit, that's fine too. Simply being aware of the issue will help vastly. Get as specific as you can when you analyse your own work. When you take a random paragraph of your work and look at it in isolation, what messages is it sending? About the book and about the characters? Can you find other books in your particular segment of the market which send similar messages about themselves? If there is a discrepancy, then where exactly is it coming from? You don't need to find answers to these questions speedily, you just need to find them accurately. A solution *will* come. You may just need to give it time to emerge.

Tone in non-fiction

Before we leave this topic, it's worth re-emphasising that *all* writing needs to find a tone that works. That message is especially important for non-fiction authors, many of whom seem to believe that the intrinsic interest or importance of their subject matter mean they don't need to think about tone at all.

Not so! Remember, if you are writing non-fiction for a trade publisher – that is, a mainstream one, not a business or academic one – then your readers will be reading *for pleasure*. They may well have a strong interest in the topic you are writing about, but they'll only stick with it if you make the experience enjoyable and rewarding. That means you need to approach your craft with a novelist's sensitivity for story, pace – and tone. Take the two snippets below. They're both about social epidemics in relation to crime.

A) *Crime data provides persuasive additional evidence of a correlation between serious crime (homicide, rape, and other serious offences against the person) and a law enforcement policy that mandates broad tolerance of low-level social misdemeanours (such as graffiti, for example, or public intoxication).*

B) *On December 22, 1984, the Saturday before Christmas, Bern-hard Goetz left his apartment in Manhattan's Greenwich Village and walked to the IRT subway station at Fourteenth Street and Seventh Avenue. He was a slender man in his late thirties, with sandy-coloured hair and glasses, dressed that day in jeans and a windbreaker. At the station, he boarded the number two downtown express train and sat down next to four young black men. There were about twenty people in the car, but most sat at the other end, avoiding the four teenagers, because they were, as eyewitnesses would say later, 'horsing around' and 'acting rowdy.' Goetz seemed oblivious.*

The first snippet is an invention of mine. It's unreadably boring. No matter how interesting my subject might be, no one would read that kind of stuff for fun. And since such a book will have no readers, it'll have no publisher either. The second snippet is from Malcolm Gladwell's internationally bestselling *The Tipping Point* – and is written almost like a thriller. The tone is factual, direct, and clear, and the passage has an obvious forward momentum. This reads like a chunk from some type of crime novel – a police procedural, most likely – and you just know that something nasty is about to happen. (Which it duly does.)

Gladwell doesn't write like this all the time. He dips in and out of storytelling mode according to where he in his argument. But he is never that far away from a good story, because he knows that story is one of the strongest ways to grip his readers – and to give the more abstract points he's making sense and force. What's more, when he does tell a story, he *tells* it. He's not embarrassed to deploy the tools of a novelist, because he knows those tools have been shaped for powerful storytelling.

That's not the only way to write non-fiction, of course. Bill Bryson adopts a tone of humorous, avuncular relish in the facts he's conveying. Amanda Foreman's *Georgiana* found a wonderful intimacy with its central character, in part by making excellent use of letters and other original source materials. The huge political books of recent years – *Fire and Fury; Fear;* all the rest – varied hugely in tone, from journalistic, to gossipy, to almost academically precise, but all found different ways successfully to enter their subject matter. The key to finding the tone appropriate for you and your project involves the same bullet points as we examined above. It's a question of finding a tone that's right for your market, right for your story, right for the characters you're writing about, and right for you.

Chapter Summary

- All good writing has a tone, and every genre contains a multiplicity of alternative tones.
- You need to choose an approach which is right for your market, your story, your characters, and you.
- Give yourself time to find the right voice.
- Remember that non-fiction needs a tone too. Whether you sell your non-fiction or not will have at least as much to do with the approachability of your writing as with the subject you are discussing. You need to pay attention to both.

Part Three

Character

Before I write down one word, I have to have the character in my mind through and through. I must penetrate into the last wrinkle of his soul.

– Henrik Ibsen

It begins with a character, usually, and once he stands up on his feet and begins to move, all I can do is trot along behind him with a paper and pencil trying to keep up long enough to put down what he says and does.

– William Faulkner

Begin with an individual, and before you know it you have created a type; begin with a type, and you find you have created – nothing.

– F. Scott Fitzgerald

Showing, Telling, and the Riddle of Character

Characterisation is usually taught in logical order:

1. Choose a starting point: an unmarried climatologist, why not?

2. Start to accrete data about that person. So, she's a woman. Thirty-eight. Retrained after a short career as kindergarten teacher, because she was worried about the planet. One serious romance, which failed following her boyfriend's infidelity. Yadda, yadda, yadda.

3. Once we've got our character alive and kicking, then run a battery of checks to ensure that she'll be fit for purpose. Will the reader have empathy for her? Is her motivation going to be strong enough? Will the obstacles be formidable enough? What kind of emotional shift will she experience through the book? Blah, blah, blah.

4. Finally, run through the basic options regarding viewpoint. First person, third person, omniscient vs limited, and so on. Dull but important.

And that's it. Job done. According to the logic, that is all a writer needs to know about character.

Not seriously overweight

The logic is compelling enough in its way, except that the most important thing has been left clean out. Take a look at these notes on character:

BJ is a late-twenties woman. Mildly but not seriously overweight. Social drinker, but sometimes very social. Ditto, when it comes to smoking. Uncertain self-esteem. Longs to be loved. No steady partner. Occasionally decisive, more often not. Sometimes awkward when in company, especially so with men.

DC is a mid- or late-thirties man. A business type. Charming, but deceitful and untrustworthy. There to bed women, not commit to them. Witty, however, and with some money and power.

That seems good enough as far as it goes. Naturally there are more details to be added. We'll want to know about friends and family and backstory and all those other good things, but we've got time enough for that. DC perhaps seems a little underwhelming so far, so we'll make a mental note to give him an interesting backstory, and maybe some other twist: a limp, a fear of poultry, a sister in a wheelchair – we'll think of something. On the whole, we seem to be making steady progress.

Now look at this:

Huh. Had dream date at an intime *little Genoan restaurant near Daniel's flat.*

'Um … right. I'll get a taxi,' I blurted awkwardly as we stood in the street afterwards. Then he lightly brushed a hair from my forehead, took my cheek in his hand and kissed me, urgently, desperately. After a while, he held me hard against him and whispered throatily, 'I don't think you'll be needing that taxi, Jones.'

The second we were inside his flat we fell upon each other like beasts: shoes, jackets, strewn in a trail across the room.

'I don't think this skirt's looking well at all,' he murmured. 'I think it should lie down on the floor.' As he started to undo the zip he whispered, 'This is just a bit of fun, OK? I don't think we should start getting involved.' Then, caveat in place, he carried on with the zip. Had it not been for Sharon and the fuckwittage and the fact I'd just drunk the best part of a bottle of

wine, I think I would have sunk powerless into his arms. As it was, I leapt to my feet, pulling up my skirt.

'That is just such crap,' I slurred. 'How dare you be so fraudulently flirtatious, cowardly and dysfunctional. I am not interested in emotional fuckwittage. Goodbye.'

It was great. You should have seen his face. But now I am home I am sunk into gloom. I may have been right, but my reward, I know, will be to end up all alone, half-eaten by an Alsatian.

This – of course – is a chunk taken from Helen Fielding's marvellous *Bridget Jones's Diary*. It vibrates with life. Bridget's character sings off the page. Daniel Cleaver (the Hugh Grant character, if you've only seen the film) is deliciously awful, but in a more-ish way. This is a book that you want to go on and on reading, and which promises delight on every page.

When you compare the character notes we started with and this chunk from an actual book, you'll notice that the notes are perfectly accurate, yet at the same time seem to have left out everything important. So, yes, like countless women, Bridget Jones is a tad overweight, a tad insecure, a tad boozy, and so on. Those things were accurately summarised in the notes. But those notes haven't yet found their way to an *individual*. There are umpteen thousands of women who tick those boxes.

On the other hand, how many women in the world would, when they notice they're being exploited, stand up and say, 'That is just such crap. How dare you be so fraudulently flirtatious, cowardly and dysfunctional. I am not interested in emotional fuckwittage. Goodbye.' How many women, on getting home, would have the weirdly surreal thought that, 'my reward, I know, will be to end up all alone, half-eaten by an Alsatian.'

The same goes for Daniel Cleaver. The notes we wrote for him were perfectly accurate and, in a way, there's never much more to his character than those notes convey. No limp. No fear of poultry. No disabled sister. No big twist that Helen Fielding is holding in reserve. As far as the character notes are concerned, what we have in Daniel Cleaver is a walking, talking cliché. Except he isn't. He says things like, 'I don't think you'll be needing that taxi, Jones,' and – oh joy! – things like, 'I don't think this skirt's looking well at all. I think it should lie down on the floor.'

The wonderful things about these bits of characterisation is that they're hard to categorise in any way at all. What kind of a woman says, 'I am not interested in emotional fuckwittage'? And what exactly does it say about someone that they have a fear of being half-eaten by an Alsatian? And, come to that, why *half*-eaten? Why only *half*?

If all you do is pursue the logical path to characterisation – the one we set out at the start of this chapter, and one which will be visible throughout much of the rest of this section – your characterisation will certainly be competent and functional. It may also be dull and lifeless. You'll only get to vibrant life if you manage to leap beyond the theory to the kinds of details that seem both *surprising* and *inevitable*. When Bridget storms out of Daniel Cleaver's flat with her slogan about emotional fuckwittage, the reader is simultaneously startled by her turn of phrase and accepting of it. 'Yep, that's Bridget, all right.' The same again when it comes to the Alsatian. The same again when Daniel Cleaver wants to get her skirt to lie down on the floor. It's always surprising, but always precisely accurate.

Tequila gimlets and porcini bruschetta

Part of the reason why Helen Fielding's work so sizzles with life is that it's written in the first person. Every word, every turn of phrase, hints at character. When Bridget Jones talks about an '*intime* little Genoan restaurant', we know how to read that word '*intime*'. Our Bridget – the one who downs cheap white wine with her girlfriends and whose only reliable mathematical gifts are those that come from counting calories – isn't *au fait* with *la langue francaise*. She's not that posh, that stuck-up, or that cultured. So her use of the word '*intime*' is a pose. It's a word purloined from the kind of aspirational lifestyle magazines that she reads compulsively and which in their turn use the word as a pose. It's a shared pretence at a different sort of life. All that, from one delightfully chosen word.

Authors who write in the third person gain some advantages from their choice, but they lose some intimacy with character. A good third-person novelist can reveal character slowly, in layers, with subtlety and surprise, but it's rare that the page vibrates as it does when you have a character like Bridget Jones speaking direct. Nevertheless, the principles of good characterisation are the same. Here's a chunk from Lauren Weisberger's *Last Night at Chateau Marmont*:

> *A waiter arrived at the table and Leo ordered for the group without consulting anyone. Brooke normally hated it when people did that, but even she couldn't argue with his choices: another bottle of champagne, a round of tequila gimlets, and a bunch of snack plates, everything from truffled porcini bruschetta to mozzarella and arugula. By the time the first dish of crab cakes in an avocado puree arrived, Brooke had happily rediscovered her earlier buzz and was feeling almost euphoric from the excitement. Julian – her Julian, the same one who slept in socks every night had just performed on* The Tonight Show. *They were staying in a gorgeous suite at the infamous Chateau Marmont, eating and drinking like rock royalty. One of the most famous musicians of the twentieth century had announced he loved her hair. Of course her wedding was the best day of her life (weren't you required to say that no matter what?), but this was quickly clocking in as a very close second.*
>
> *Her cell phone screeched from her bag on the ground, a shrill fire-alarm-like ring she'd chosen post-nap to ensure she didn't oversleep again.*
>
> *'Why don't you get it?' Julian asked through a full mouth as Brooke stared at her phone. She didn't want to answer it, but she was worried something was wrong; it was already after midnight back at home.*

'Hey Mom,' she said as quietly as she could. *'We're all in the middle of dinner right now. Is everything OK?'*

This doesn't have the thrilling quality of *Bridget Jones's Diary* (and we'll come back to that issue in a subsequent chapter), but Brooke is already more alive than any set of character notes would convey. She's human enough – flawed enough – to choose a naff ringtone. She's girlish enough, innocent enough, to feel starstruck. (A rock star liked her hair! They're in the Chateau Marmont! They've got champagne and gimlets and porcini bruschetta!) She's anxious about her mother, but also seeking to quieten her down, to signal that now is not a good time.

Julian too, though barely mentioned, has already flickered into individual life. He sleeps in his socks. So what? What does that say about someone, precisely? And yet, it says *something*. The fact gives us a knowledge which may be hard to articulate but is nevertheless real. And when Brooke's phone rings, he asks 'Why don't you get it?', with his mouth full. He's unmoved enough by his surroundings that he simply doesn't get why his wife might be unsure of whether to answer her phone. Nor does he think much about how he comes across. Brooke may be in raptures because someone famous likes her hair. Julian, on the other hand, talks with his mouth full, because he doesn't really give a damn, no matter where he is.

Showing and telling in fiction

The reason why these passages are so alive is that they're shown, not told. The reader is *told* nothing about Bridget Jones's character, nothing about Brooke's. There's no sentence anywhere which says, 'Bridget Jones is prone to erratic behaviour when it comes to men, particularly when she's drunk'. There's no sentence which says, 'Brooke is overawed by her surroundings'. Either of those sentences would have killed the respective passages.

In any case, they'd be redundant. The reader already knows these things, because the author is *showing* them unfold, and the reader isn't so dumb that she hasn't cottoned on. A movie doesn't say in voiceover, 'Now this is a dangerous bit, where Brie Larson has to leap onto a moving vehicle while being shot at. She's nervous, but determined'. We don't need that. We just watch her jump.

It's the same with novels. *Showing* vibrates with energy. That's where drama happens. That's where characters come alive. That's where choices matter, where consequences seem at their biggest. That's not to say that telling is redundant. It isn't. All books will have both. 'It was ten years later, and Beth was a mother of three now, two boys just starting school, and a little girl on the verge of her first birthday.' That's a straightforward way of *telling* the reader something which could easily take fifty pages to *show*. (There'll be more about showing and telling in a later chapter, so don't worry if you still have questions. It's a good sign if you do.)

The big point, though, the one to come away with from this chapter, is this: the essential heart of characterisation – and, darn it, of all good fiction – is showing a scene unfold, moment by moment, picking up on the telling detail, recounting actions, thoughts, feelings, dialogue, choices, sensations and memories just as they come to the character in question. That's showing. That's characterisation. That's what we're aiming at.

Showing and telling in non-fiction

In non-fiction, the balance between facts and drama is a little different than it is in fiction, but the principles of characterisation are much the same.

If you are writing a travel book, let's say, with yourself as protagonist, you will need to tell and show, both in good measure. Since this chapter has a girly theme, let's consider the girliest travel book in the world ever, Elizabeth Gilbert's *Eat, Pray, Love*. I've condensed the text a little to make it manageable, but here's how it starts:

> *I wish Giovanni would kiss me.* [This is showing. You know it's showing because Gilbert is clearly referring to a specific

place at a specific time. It's not a general statement about her and Giovanni. It's her having the hots for him right now this minute.]

Oh, but there are so many reasons why this would be a terrible idea. To begin with Giovanni is ten years younger than I am, and – like most Italian guys in their twenties – he still lives with his mother. These facts alone make him an unlikely romantic partner for me, given that I am a professional American woman in my mid-thirties, who has just come through a failed marriage and a devastating, interminable divorce, followed immediately by a passionate love affair that ended in sickening heartbreak ... This is why I have been alone for many months now. This is why, in fact, I have decided to spend this entire year in celibacy. [This is telling, of the plainest, most direct sort. Gilbert doesn't mess around, she hits you with the facts that you need to know to get yourself orientated. There are other ways you could open a book, but this one works for me. Do notice, however, how dull this paragraph would be, if we hadn't opened with that first sentence about wanting to be kissed. Those opening six words created an instant ripple of suspense – will he kiss her? how will she react if he doesn't? – so that we absorb the subsequent block of information with relish, because we're greedy to see how this bears on the whole Giovanni-kissing situation. And then you get to the final sentence, which sets up the entire book as neatly as some high-concept Hollywood movie: gee, what's going to happen to an attractive woman abroad when she tries to live up to *that* resolution? Two paragraphs in, and most readers will already be hooked.]

Giovanni is my Tandem Exchange Partner. That sounds like an innuendo, but unfortunately it's not. All it really means is that we meet a few evenings a week here in Rome to practice each other's languages. We speak first in Italian, and he is patient with me; then we speak in English, and I am patient with him ... [More telling, but notice that we're already threading back to the Giovanni-kissing issue. Gilbert knows that she can't stay long away from that moment, because it's where the tension resides. There's *always* more tension in the shown drama than the reported one, always more drama to be found in the present moment than in the same moment reported after the fact.]

We have been eating and talking for many pleasant weeks now, sharing pizzas and grammatical corrections, and tonight has been no exception. A lovely evening of new idioms and fresh mozzarella.

Now it is midnight and foggy and Giovanni is walking me home ... Now we are at my door. We face each other. He gives me a warm hug ... [Bingo! We're back again to the shown, not the told. Again: we know we're being shown something, not told it, because we're back to one specific moment in one specific place. The scene-setting intro is over, and we're back to the drama of the present. We're back to the situation that gave us the first sentence of the book. Giovanni, by the way, does not kiss her and she's OK with that. She even says a prayer about it. Three, to be precise. It's that kind of book.]

Gilbert's book is an excellent book for any wannabe travel writer to read and learn from, but there's a broader point here. The way Gilbert moves fluently from showing to telling and back again is a model for all such movement in non-fiction.

There will nearly always be more telling in non-fiction than in fiction. That's fine. People come to non-fiction because they want facts, they want to learn things, they want to be told stuff. But if your book is true narrative non-fiction, it'll probably need to switch seamlessly from telling to showing and back again. The showing gives life and vivacity and authenticity. The telling delivers fact and thought and intelligent reflection.

Different types of non-fiction will strike the balance differently. If the book is about you – if it's travel or memoir – I'd expect the book to have a lot of showing. Less than an average novel, maybe, but still a lot. If you're writing historical biography, on the other hand, you'll be more limited in what you can show. You won't often be able to trace the intimate flow of thoughts, sensations, memories and all the rest, because you simply won't have sources that permit that kind of reconstruction. Even so, your sources will allow you to illustrate the points you're making. Thus you might say, 'Napoleon was famously impetuous in command. For example, there was a time when ...' The opening phrase delivers general information – it's a form of telling. The closing phrase makes ready to get specific about time and place, introducing an anecdote that illustrates (shows) the general point. If you're writing for a broad audience, then you'll always want to come back to the specific – particular events happening at a particular time and place.

Chapter Summary

- It is important to know your character, to gather data about them, to know their backstory and so on.

- But character springs to life in *showing*, not telling. The showing is everything.

- The heart of characterisation is showing a scene unfold, moment by moment, picking up on the telling detail, recounting actions, thoughts, feelings, dialogue, choices, sensations and memories just as they come to the character in question.

- Characterisation in non-fiction works much the same way, except there is probably a little more scope for *telling* the reader things.

FINDING EDGE

As we've already discussed in 'Who Are Your Characters?', the first step in creating strong characters is *knowing* them. You need to know your lead players intimately. Better than you know your best friend. Better than you know your wife or husband. You need to know their dreams and fears, their memories and thoughts, the itch between their toes and the longings in their hearts. Exactly what you need to know will vary from project to project and character to character, but the checklist we gave in that chapter is a good place to start:

- *Age, gender, nationality, occupation, social group.*
- *Family, partner, close friends, workmates.*
- *Desires, motives and fears.*
- *Looks.*
- *Attitudes.*
- *Backstory.*
- *Reputation and stereotypes.*
- *Habits.*
- *The quirky little details – the embarrassing incident in Mexico, falling off a horse, and all the rest of it.*

You probably want to go back to that chapter to refresh your memory of the list in full. (And if you haven't downloaded our Ultimate Character Builder, then you can do so here):

jerichowriters.com/how-to-write-a-novel-free-resources

Edge

Although knowledge is the most important part of characterisation, it's not the only one. After all, you could create a character that you know intimately – and who is as dull as ditchwater on the page. In the last chapter, we looked closely at two characters, Lauren Weisberger's Brooke and Helen Fielding's Bridget Jones. Both characters were well-handled from a technical point of view, properly individuated, with plenty of telling little details. But one character – Bridget Jones – soared off the page, while the other one didn't; she merely occupied it. True, *Bridget Jones's Diary* was told in the first person, which helped. It's also true that it was a comedy, and therefore had more opportunities to behave outrageously. Nevertheless, the question arises, how do you get a character to dominate the page? How do you get her to infect a reader's mind, so that they go on thinking about her, long after they've laid the book aside?

The answer has to do with finding edge. You need to find a character that creates some sense of danger, or tension, or shock, or alarm, or jeopardy in the reader. Take Bridget Jones, for example. The genius of her characterisation is simply this. The reader *empathises* with her, yet is constantly *alarmed* by her. We want her to be romantically happy, but then we see her acting in ways that promise (and generally deliver) chaos. We want her to avoid excruciating embarrassment, but – dear old Bridget! – we can rely on her to turn up at a party in a bunny costume when no one else is in fancy dress. The constant interplay of empathy and alarm is what gives rise to the vibrancy of her character.

With Brooke, the same interplay wasn't there. Yes, we wanted her to be happy and achieve her aims, but her situation didn't create much sense of danger. If you're not familiar with the book, Brooke's dramatic predicament is this. She works hard to support her musician husband. He then becomes a huge rock star. Their lives change. Brooke struggles with the frantic schedules and the media pressure and all the rest of it. Then her husband is found drunk in bed with a woman – with whom he has not had sex – and feels terrible about it. Brooke has to decide what to do.

Now, that won't strike many readers as a desperately edgy situation. Gee, your husband becomes famous and you're on the path to enormous wealth. That's tough. Your hubby commits one misdemeanour – for which he apologises profusely and sincerely, which happened under pressure, and which did not in fact involve sex – and you have to decide what to do. Too bad. Admittedly, no one's likely to enjoy their partner nearly cheating on them, no matter what the circumstances, but the situation still doesn't register high on the emotional Richter scale. Even if we have empathy with Brooke, her situation doesn't generate enough alarm for us to be properly concerned. The edge is missing.

Creating edge

There are broadly two options for making sure that edge is present.

The first is the obvious one. You create a character who brings turbulence through the door with them. So, for example:

- Bridget Jones creates turbulence by aspiring to more than her socially blundering character ever seems likely to deliver. In her wake: bottles of wine, cigarette ends and the occasional set of bunny ears.

- Patrick Bateman – the psychopathic and probably delusional investment banker star of *American Psycho* – creates another sort of turbulence, the sort that leaves behind a lot of mutilated bodies and a whiff of very expensive aftershave.

- Becky Bloomwood, star of the *Shopaholic* series, is also compulsive, but leaves nothing worse than a heap of credit card invoices and a mountain of adorable shoes.

- Jack Aubrey, the swaggering sea captain hero of Patrick O'Brian's series of naval adventures, has the kind of job and lives in the kind of age when adventure is always going to come a-knocking, yet the character himself has a swagger, an appetite for risk, which creates an excitement all of its own.

- Lisbeth Salander (Stieg Larsson's *The Girl with the Dragon Tattoo*) is an orphaned bisexual computer hacker with Asperger Syndrome and a capacity for violence. She could make stuff happen in an empty room.

- Alexander Perchov is the Ukrainian 'translator' from Jonathan Safran Foer's *Everything is Illuminated*, and you just know that he's going to cause mayhem as soon as you encounter his version of English. (His opening sentences run thus: 'My legal name is Alexander Perchov. But all of my many friends dub me Alex, because that is a more flaccid-to-utter version of my legal name. My mother dubs me Alexi-stop-spleening-me!, because I am always spleening her.')

Perhaps curiously, most novelists don't take this option. A much more common route is to insert a fairly ordinary central character in a situation that puts extreme pressure on that person. For example:

- Clare, in Audrey Niffenegger's *The Time Traveler's Wife*, is an ordinary person who happens to love a man prone to inadvertent time travel.

- Henry, in the same book, is also an ordinary person. Yes, it so happens that he's a (reluctant) time traveller, but his feelings about that condition are not so different from what yours or mine might be, if we found ourselves in the same situation.

- Bella Swan (the star of Stephenie Meyer's hugely bestselling *Twilight* series) is an ordinary teenage American girl. Who loves a vampire.

- Mary Boleyn is Philippa Gregory's *The Other Boleyn Girl*. She'd have an ordinary enough life, except that she has a love affair with Henry VIII, and her sister (and love-rival) becomes queen.

- Susie Salmon is the narrator of Alice Sebold's *The Lovely Bones*. Susie is as normal as you can get. Except she's dead.

- Eilis Lacey, the heroine of Colm Tóibín's *Brooklyn*, is an ordinary Irishwoman who is compelled to emigrate and who comes to be caught in a significant emotional dilemma as a result.

- Richard Mayhew is the protagonist of Neil Gaiman's *Neverwhere*. He's an ordinary businessman who just happens to tumble out of his regular life and into an underworld.

- Another Mayhew – Edward, in Ian McEwan's *On Chesil Beach* – is a man entirely typical of his era. A wedding night mishap sparks a conflict with his new wife, with disastrous consequences.

- Jack (the five-year-old narrator of Emma Donoghue's *Room*) is a completely normal little boy. It's just that he has spent his entire life, with his mother, imprisoned in a room that measures 11 square feet and that has a single skylight out onto the world beyond.

The world's bestselling novel may well be Tolkien's *The Lord of the Rings*, which features a very ordinary hobbit in a very unordinary situation. The world's bestselling series of novels is J. K. Rowling's *Harry Potter* books, and although Harry Potter may look un-ordinary – he's a wizard, for heaven's sake! – he lives in a world where there are plenty of wizards. In actual fact, when it comes to his personality, J. K. Rowling takes good care to make him very ordinary. His emotions and aptitudes seem very much as our own might be in similar circumstances. He's dazzled by Hogwarts, outclassed by Hermione, keen on sport, ignorant of much in the magical world, and so on. His ordinariness is crucial to his success.

A *pas de deux*

Characters of the first sort, the ones that bring their own turbulence, essentially supply their own plot. Becky Bloomwood, the *Shopaholic*, needs nothing at all to create mayhem except the opportunity to spend money. The only way Bloomwood would be a normal character would be to put her in a very unusual situation – let's say, a tribal village somewhere in the Amazon jungle that has no shop, no money, no internet connection, no credit cards.

Mostly though, character and plot dance a *pas de deux*, where each needs the other to succeed. And although it's true to say that the characters on the second list are normal, they're seldom *only* normal. Harry Potter finds an extraordinary capacity for courage and resourcefulness. That capacity is latent, rather than dominant. He's not a Jack Aubrey type, capable of starting a brouhaha pretty much anywhere. Nevertheless, put him under enough pressure and he'll rise to the challenge.

Bella Swan, too, would be a normal girl, leading a normal life, but for her dalliance with a vampire. But where most girls would think twice about romancing a partner who would love to drink her blood, Bella *likes* that about him. She likes the darkness, likes the risk, likes the presence of the dark side.

To create edge, therefore, you don't necessarily need to create an extreme character (a Bridget Jones, a Patrick Bateman, or whoever). But if you plump for an ordinary one, then:

- That person needs to be placed in a situation which puts them under extreme pressure.

- That person needs to find some latent characteristic which comes to the fore. That characteristic may be heroic (as with Harry Potter) or neutral (as with Bella Swan) or calamitous (as with Ian McEwan's Edward Mayhew).

- That latent characteristic *in combination with* the circumstances of the story needs to set the character off on a path that feels anything but ordinary.

Lauren Weisberger's *Last Night at Chateau Marmont,* in my view, didn't quite pull this trick off. Brooke was never sufficiently tested. As a result, she was never driven to find truly unexpected inner qualities or resources. The book felt competent, but never vibrant.

The same could not have been said of Weisberger's earlier work, and the one that made her name, *The Devil Wears Prada.* There a character, not dissimilar to Brooke, finds herself working for the fashion editor from hell (Meryl Streep, if you've seen the film). The heroine – Andrea – tries hard to accommodate her boss's unreasonable and bullying demands. She also tries to fit in with the norms of her fashion magazine, losing weight, wearing only designer clothes, promoting an unhealthy degree of self-loathing in the magazine's teenaged readers. This is pressure we *do* understand, and when Andrea finally finds the resources to tell her boss to fuck off, we cheer her on.

And that's the equation at its most successful. An ordinary person. An un-ordinary situation. Unexpected inner resources. Result: a book that pitched its tent on *The New York Times* bestseller list and stayed there for six months.

Ramping it up

If you think that your character and story haven't yet achieved the required energy, you need to ramp things up. Some classic options are:

- *Adding story pressure.* Let's say your novel is about corporate bullying. Your character is experiencing mean comments at the coffee machine and people sometimes nick her stationery. Such a story is too low-energy to survive. So add to it. The bullying now starts getting a physical or sexual edge to it. Or the protagonist's family becomes involved. Or one of the bullies is a family member. Or all of these things. You need to make sure you stay convincing and serious, but the situation must feel dangerous or it won't hold anyone's attention.

- *Complicating the story.* Alternatively, you can take the existing story and add a different dimension. Perhaps the person being bullied has a teenage daughter, on the brink of a serious eating disorder. When the mother is bullied, perhaps her emotions spill out at home, with life-threatening consequences for the daughter. That new dimension alters the story, of course. It's no good you simply going through the motions. The new dimension you've added has to occupy you heart and soul, just as the original one did. What's more, there needs to be some interesting mesh between the new story element and the old one. One plus one needs to equal three.

- *Genre-bending.* This is a version of the previous option, and an exciting one. The idea is that you take one genre (in this case a realistic tale of corporate bullying) and ram into it with another – let's say a ghost story. So maybe our victim is forced to work long hours in the office … and starts to hear strange noises and witness inexplicable events. All of a sudden, the possibilities of this tale seem larger and more unpredictable than they had done before. Again, you do need to make sure you write the new hybrid with conviction. You need to make your concoction convincing, evenly handled, and you need to find some interesting reverberation between the two parts. Done well, however, and you may have something unique and compelling.

- *Finding a twist.* You take a predictable response and invert it. The predictable response is that our victim *feels* victimised and acts out a victim-ish role. But what if she doesn't? What if she chooses to get even with the bullies? Or starts bullying someone else? Or takes firearms lessons and starts to get carried away? Any non-standard response adds immediate interest.

There's good news here too. If you write well, with conviction and accuracy, the reverberations between your new story element and the bones of the old one will start to happen of their own accord. The bullying story and (for example) the ghost story will cross-fertilise each other in rich and unexpected ways. That doesn't mean you can altogether forget about how to join them, but it does mean you'll get more than you bargained for. Watching that happen is one of the great pleasures and surprises of writing.

Ramping it up in non-fiction

All these comments are as true of non-fiction as they are of fiction. The only difference is that you can't simply choose to alter facts to improve your story. But you can:

- *Exaggerate.* Not too much – you can't alter or invent major facts – but a little hyperbole can become part of your style.
- *Delete.* If parts of your story are dull, drop them. If you spent five months getting to know Taliban warriors in Afghanistan, and two months kicking around a luxury hotel in Kabul waiting for a visa, your book should be almost entirely about the adventurous five months, with only enough about the tedious two months to make the narrative hold together. Your *life* needs to be lived minute by minute. A book can skip anything it doesn't fancy.
- *Weave.* If, as you were travelling in Afghanistan, your mother was very sick, in and out of hospital, and you were in touch with her as often as possible, then perhaps those stories can usefully collide. You might be able to find themes of life and death, comparisons of and attitudes to health care, and so on. You need to handle these things with care – after all, there is a clear market for adventurous travel books, and you stray beyond it at your peril – but you may well have a more interesting book at the end of it.
- *Enrich.* Finally, of course, if your book is a memoir of some sort, it should not only be a memoir. If you are writing about your travels in Afghanistan, then you'll want to

enrich it with facts about history, geography, the people, the politics, and so on. You still need to place your experience at the centre of things, but you can be liberal in bringing in other topics as they become relevant.

Chapter Summary

- Go back to the chapter 'Who Are Your Characters?' to refresh your memory of how to know your character in the right level of detail.
- Good characters need edge. Some characters bring turbulence with them (Bridget Jones, Patrick Bateman, Lisbeth Salander).
- Other characters get their edge by being ordinary people in desperate situations (Mary Boleyn, Bella Swan, Richard Mayhew).
- If your story lacks edge, then add to it. Think about adding story pressure, complicating things, genre-bending, or inverting the predicted response.
- The same thoughts apply to non-fiction too. If you have to apply a little (modest) pressure to the facts, then feel free.

The World of Interiors

People have feelings, thoughts, memories, and sensations. These things are in constant flux, sometimes overpowering, sometimes only just on the verge of consciousness. The novel is the only art form which deals head-on with this inner activity. It's what novels were invented to do.

That will sound achingly obvious to most, yet a surprising number of first novels seem to be populated by robots. If you worry that you might have a robot for a main character, there's a simple way to check. Take a two- or three-page chunk (which may include some dialogue, but shouldn't be all dialogue) and make a note of any fragments which reveal inner life. For example, from a randomly chosen couple of pages in Philippa Gregory's *The Other Boleyn Girl*, I came up with this list:

The last thing I wanted was for him to leave behind his curls and his baby plumpness, the last thing I wanted was to see any change in the way he held out his arms to be picked up, the steady rushing of his fat little legs.

... while I wanted to hold him in my arms, my baby forever.

... our favourite place, on the stone bench facing towards the moat ...

I wondered how much Stafford knew of our marriage.

That was about as honest and tactful as I could manage, ...

... showing me that he was cleverer than I had allowed.

I was reluctant to discuss my future ...

It was such a bleak and accurate summary of my life that I rather choked at the vista he opened up for me.

... stung into honesty ...

And also these:

... there were tears in my eyes.
That made me chuckle.
I hesitated.

The first set of examples all reveal information that only the narrator, Mary Boleyn, could know. Other people might guess (for example) that she was reluctant to discuss her future from the way she hesitated or from the tone of her voice, but they would be guessing. Only Boleyn herself could know for sure. The second set of examples show Boleyn observing herself as others might observe her too: visible tears, an audible chuckle, a stutter of hesitation. The two groups aren't completely distinct – is 'stung into honesty' an internal or an external observation, for example? – but it doesn't matter how precisely one draws the line. What does matter is that a good novelist typically dips in and out of a character's mind, often multiple times on the course of a single page.

What's more, nothing is off limits. We know about Boleyn's love for her child, her favourite seat, her view of her life, her thoughts and musings, her instant responses and her deeper ones. We see tears, laughter and hesitations all mingled on the page. As it happens, nothing in this section talks about physical sensations – 'I was always hungry', 'my knees were sore' – but it could very well have done. Any aspect of a person's mental life is potentially matter for a novelist's pen.

Creating inner life

Creating inner life is remarkably easy. There are no special techniques, no special skills required. All that matters is that you remember to do it. Three kinds of omission are common.

• *Forgetting to include any inner life at all.* Many writers come to the novel under the influence of film or TV drama. They *see* their book as a film, their characters as actors. That approach has its strengths – it often, for example, delivers a strong and energetic storyline – but it has one enormous weakness. Films are about exteriority. We watch the actor's face for clues about inner feeling. We gauge character from dialogue and action. Novels have this exterior element too, but they mustn't stop there. Although there are some literary and thriller-ish exceptions to the rule, in general you can't write a successful novel without talking about the world of the interior. So do it. Just make sure that your protagonist has feelings, thoughts, memories and sensations. If you're unsure whether you are pitching things about right, then compare a few pages of your novel with a published book in a similar market niche. Don't get too mechanical about this, however. There's no golden formula that you have to target. Some chapters will be more interior than others. The truth is, if you're alert to the importance of the issue, you're unlikely to make a mess of it.

• *Locating inner life only through the external.* In the list of examples from Philippa Gregory's novel, some of Boleyn's inner life was depicted externally: 'there were tears in my eyes', for example, rather than 'I felt tearful'. There's nothing wrong with that at all. On the contrary, Gregory's use of the external felt natural and appropriate in context. But some writers may find that they tend towards using the external almost to the exclusion of anything else. It's as though they know they're meant to be saying something about the character's inner life, but haven't found the language with which to say it.

This is a problem I've come across even with intelligent and capable writers who are writing in the first person. Again, once you notice the problem exists, it's easy to fix it. You just make sure that you make reasonably frequent mention of your character's thoughts and feelings, and you do so in the ordinary language of your novel. If you look back at the snippets from Gregory's work, you'll see how simple it can be: 'I wondered how much Stafford knew of our marriage'. If you want to get more involved and complex than that, then do, but even simple is better than nothing at all.

- *Locating inner life only through the bland.* Perhaps the commonest mistake is to give your character an inner life, but only of the blandest, least interesting sort: 'I was hungry', 'I worried about the possible consequences', 'I remembered my mother's welcoming arms and loving smile', 'I felt sad'. Naturally, there'll be plenty of places where you want to note a feeling briefly, without much dissection or analysis. That's fine, but it's fine because it gives you the opportunity, at other points in your text, to take some fragment of your character's inner world and explore it properly.

  So use that opportunity. Taken on its own, that sentence about the mother's welcoming arms is a thoroughly tedious one. We'd probably have to condemn it on the grounds of cliché – unless it acts as an introduction to a fuller exploration of *this* person and *their* experience of mothering: '... her loving, but always hesitant, smile. I never understood that hesitation, as a child. I didn't understand it now ...'. Those explorations open up a character, which in turn opens up a story. It's what good writers do.

A better sort of gravel

Some writers veer away from doing this because they have the idea that they're writing an action-adventure novel, not some tediously introspective arty novel. They have the idea that any introspection will slow their novel down, to the point of killing any suspense. This idea is so entirely untrue that one can only assume those who hold it haven't read very much action-adventure fiction. Here, for example, is a snippet from *Casino Royale*, Ian Fleming's first James Bond adventure:

> *He explored his present physical sensations. He felt the dry,*
> *uncomfortable gravel under his evening shoes, the bad, harsh taste*
> *in his mouth, and the slight sweat under his arms. He could feel*
> *his eyes filling their sockets. The front of his face, his nose and*
> *antrum, were congested ...*

I don't, as it happens, like Ian Fleming as a writer, but his books are both wildly successful and chock-full of introspection. And just look how minute that introspection can be. 'He could feel his eyes filling their sockets', for heaven's sake! Or: 'He felt the dry, uncomfortable gravel under his evening shoes'. This is a man who can't just discern the granularity of the surface beneath his shoes, he can tell whether it's wet or dry. He probably knows which quarry it's from.

The point isn't that introspection is tedious; the issue is *who* is introspecting about *what*. If the person whose brain we're looking into is James Bond, and the question he's rotating in his mind is how to rob the Casino Royale, there's nothing tedious about it. How could there be? Hollywood can deliver bigger, better, shinier explosions than the pages of a book, but it can't tell you what it is like to *be* James Bond, or Jason Bourne, or Alex Cross. Writers can. That's why thriller-readers read Fleming and Ludlum and Patterson. There are exceptions to every rule, of course, and Elmore Leonard, for example, makes remarkably little use of interiority. But he *is* an exception and he *is* Elmore Leonard, which you quite likely are not. So if in doubt, tell us what your character is feeling. Your reader wants to know.

Whose interior?

The last question that worries some writers is *whose* inner worlds they are meant to be depicting. Ian Fleming tells us in great detail about James Bond's interior life, but that's where he stops. In the opening chapter of *Casino Royale*, all we know of Le Chiffre's interior life is that he has a 'curious, impressive profile'. That, and that his poker chips are untidily arranged and numerous. All we know of the person who runs the *caisse* is that they are 'generally nothing more than a minor bank clerk'. All we know about the doorman is that he is 'bored'.

That's not because Fleming writes in the first person – he doesn't – but because he keeps the spotlight of interiority firmly fixed on his main character. If you have several protagonists, you may find yourself peering into a number of different heads, but you should never do so promiscuously. The camera is a flirt; she can step out with whoever she likes. The writer isn't like that. You need to pick your targets of interest and cling to them tenaciously. There's more to be said here, and we'll say it in due course, but for now the simple rule is the one to follow. Stick with Boleyn, ignore Stafford. Stick with Bond, ignore the clerk.

Non-fiction

Novelists have it easy: they can just make stuff up. Philippa Gregory doesn't really know what Mary Boleyn was thinking; she invented it. If you were a historian writing a narrative history of the same episode, you can't allow yourself the same licence.

Nevertheless, anyone writing narrative history, or any other kind of narrative non-fiction, has to create as much interiority as the facts permit. Typically, the choices are:

- *Your book is about yourself.* If you're writing a memoir of some sort, you will write about yourself very much as a novelist would. Thoughts, sensations, memories, feelings. If you don't *precisely* remember what you were feeling at the *precise* moment you are talking about, don't worry about it, just make something up. That something needs to be broadly correct, but that's all. For the rest of it, your only obligation is to call the moment to life, just as a novelist would.

(Oh, and just because you're writing about yourself, don't think that you couldn't possibly fall into one or all of the traps outlined above. Strangely enough, there are a fair few memoir writers who come across as robots. I suspect that because the individual concerned knows darn well what they were thinking/feeling/experiencing, they forget the need to inform the reader. You can't allow yourself that forgetfulness. We want to know about your inner world, which means you have to tell us.)

- *Your book is about people you've interviewed.* In such magnificently well-researched books as Bryan Burrough and John Helyar's *Barbarians at the Gate*, or Bob Woodward's *Fear*, his brilliant account of Donald Trump's White House, there are frequent references to what some third party is thinking, feeling or remembering. You may even find people's recollections of particular physical sensations during particularly fraught or important moments in the story. Because these books have been massively researched, and because the relevant interviews and sources are documented exhaustively in the end-notes, a reader simply stops asking where the writer gets his information from. We trust that the information is solidly based on interviews (or letters or whatever) and that the writer is diligent and honest enough to advise us where there is room for doubt. There's no question that books such as these read better for their multiple interior perspectives, but if you're planning to take that route then make sure you've got a sturdy voice recorder. It's going to take some punishment.

- *Your book is about people you haven't interviewed.* If your book is not, for example, Bob Woodward's *Bush at War* but more like, say, Robert O'Connell's *Revolutionary: George Washington at War*, you're going to need more than a sturdy voice recorder to collect any contemporary interviews. All the same, readers will be as greedy as possible for any fragments of interiority you can supply. If your book is only about grand strategy and lines of battle, it will most likely be an unengaging read. Amanda Foreman's *Georgiana* is a lovely example of how *personal* a work of history can be. *Team of Rivals*, Doris Kearns Goodwin's book about Lincoln, is also a fine example of bringing the dead to sparkling life.

Chapter Summary

- Characters need inner worlds. That means thoughts, memories, feelings and sensations. These things should be present on most pages of most books.
- The commonest problems with inner worlds are (i) forgetting to include any internal language at all, (ii) dealing with feelings etc only through external observations, and (iii) dealing with them only in bland and unmemorable ways.
- Adventure stories need inner worlds too.
- Protagonists need inner worlds; lesser characters don't.
- In non-fiction, your access to inner worlds may be more limited, but even so you should seek to create personal engagement with your characters by finding as much interiority as you can.

Faces, Bodies, Mirrors

The previous chapter covered the interior, but exteriors can be difficult too.

A straw-haired man of thirty

In the good old days, things were simple. If you wanted to describe someone you just went ahead and did so, almost feature by feature. Here's F. Scott Fitzgerald's narrator describing someone in *The Great Gatsby*:

> *Now he* [Tom Buchanan] *was a sturdy straw-haired man of thirty with a rather hard mouth and a supercilious manner. Two shining arrogant eyes had established dominance over his face and gave him the appearance of always leaning aggressively forward. Not even the effeminate swank of his riding clothes could hide the enormous power of that body—he seemed to fill those glistening boots until he strained the top lacing, and you could see a great pack of muscle shifting when his shoulder moved under his thin coat. It was a body capable of enormous leverage—a cruel body.*
>
> *His speaking voice, a gruff husky tenor, added to the impression of fractiousness he conveyed.*

In this passage, Fitzgerald's narrator thinks it necessary to tell us about Tom Buchanan's build (sturdy), hair (straw-coloured), mouth (hard), manner (supercilious), eyes (arrogant, shining), attitude (leaning aggressively forward), clothes (effeminate, swanky), boots (glistening), body (enormously powerful, great pack of muscle, enormous leverage, cruel). By this point, we need a new paragraph to prepare us for the further information about his voice (gruff, husky, tenor) and the impression conveyed (fractious). Phew! Time for a tea break.

Fitzgerald's list will leave most readers reeling. Or, more accurately, few readers will even attempt to absorb or digest the mass of information they've been given. We'll simply condense this whole chunk for filing, remembering something like, 'Tom Buchanan is a strong, swanky son-of-a-bitch'. Indeed, if you start to tease apart Fitzgerald's description, puzzles quickly loom into view. *Supercilious* implies a kind of cool haughtiness. *Fractious* implies something petulant. *Arrogant, aggressive* and *cruel* together imply nothing short of outright brutishness. It's not at all clear to me how those descriptors are meant to fit together. I think they don't. It's not only the reader who's overwhelmed by the mass of information; Fitzgerald is too.

The modern way is altogether lighter in touch. To stick with New York for the moment, here is Joseph O'Neill's narrator in *Netherland* describing the residents of his Manhattan hotel:

> *There was also an old and very sick black gentleman (now dead), apparently a legendary maker of prints and lithographs. There was a family with three young boys who ran wild in the hallways with tricycles and balls and trains. There was an unexplained Finn. There was a pit bull that never went out without a panting, menacing furniture dealer in tow.*

That's little more than half the length of Fitzgerald's description, yet it finds space to describe a lithographer, a family of five, a Finn, a furniture dealer and a dog. Each of the descriptions is about as long as our capacity to remember them – and as a result, a huge amount of potential information has been left out. We don't know whether the furniture dealer's mouth is hard, aggressive, supercilious, fractious, arrogant, cruel or anything else. We know nothing about his nose or hair colour. We would be unable to describe this character to the police. And yet he's alive. More alive than Fitzgerald's Buchanan, because the overload of description in that first passage ended up killing it. O'Neill's throwaway line about the 'unexplained Finn' is almost a joke about our capacity for remembering things: 'I, the narrator, can't keep track of all these people, and I know you can't either, so let's just call him unexplained and leave it at that. Frankly, neither of us care enough to keep tabs on every last Finn'.

O'Neill's technique is, give or take, the right one to employ in your own writing. He's a literary sort (with some fancy admirers: Barack Obama is a fan) and you can feel the literary knowingness in the snippet above. But more commercial writers approach the challenge in a broadly similar way:

> *Dr. Peter Saul looked very much like his dead brother Montague, slender and cerebral in owlish glasses, brown hair thinning towards inevitable baldness.*

This sentence – from Tess Gerritsen's *The Mephisto Club* – makes the necessary introduction, but swiftly, economically. We're essentially being given a stereotype: 'the guy is brainy but weedy, so let's give him specs and thinning hair, the reader will get the picture'.

This isn't *good* writing, but it *is* efficient writing, and thrillers will do fine if a rip-roaring plot is delivered fast and efficiently. What's more, Gerritsen is too adept to be happy with the more clichéd end of cliché. 'Slender and cerebral' is not a bad phrase. 'Owlish' may not be an original term, but we know what she means, and the adjective is more interesting than many. A clumsier writer might have said the same thing in a worse way:

> *Dr. Peter Saul looked just like his dead brother Montague, a thin man, looking brainy with little round glasses perched on the top of his bald head.*

I hope you don't need me to tell you that that is a pretty horrible sentence. Good writing matters here, just as much as anywhere else.

The reflections of this section suggest that there's a fairly simply recipe for writing good, swift, and memorable character
descriptions. As a rough summary:

- Keep your descriptions short (as a general rule, anyway).
- Home in on one or two features of interest; it's fine to
  ignore all the rest.
- Pay attention to your prose style. It matters here as much
  as anywhere else.

If you stick carefully to those rules, you'll be doing fine.

Owlish and cerebral

If you want to go beyond these basics, however, another trick is
worth noticing. The best descriptions often hover in the no-
man's-land between the physical and the personal.

Take Gerritsen's word 'owlish', for example. Owls have large
round eyes, so 'owlish glasses' says something about the size and
shape of the lenses. On the other hand, owls are also supposedly
wise. So although you could have a complete dunce in owlish
glasses, you would never say so. The word works because it says
something physical and something about a personality at one and
the same time.

O'Neill's description of his furniture dealer as being 'panting,
menacing' occupies a similar space, half-physical, half-not. Indeed,
even Fitzgerald is trying to play a similar game: the 'effeminate
swank' of those riding clothes is notionally saying something
concrete about the clothes themselves, but is also talking about the
dangerously mixed personality of their owner.

In positioning your description appropriately, it helps to remember that your description may well be completely useless as a
way of picking people out of an identity parade. As it happens,
Gerrtisen's description of Dr Saul would be moderately helpful at
an identity parade, but you wouldn't get far with O'Neill's 'family
with three young boys who ran wild in the hallways'. You
wouldn't get far with his Finn, either. Sometimes, of course, it

matters what a person looks like. Other times, it really doesn't. A reader needs some way to label the person in question, but the label – 'unexplained' – can be almost meaningless and still work fine.

A deer grazing in snow

A further trick emerges from this one. When you're picking the characteristic you want to call attention to – that thing hovering between the physical and the personal – you're also providing your reader with a key to that particular character, a mnemonic almost, a quick way to remember the essence of the character in question. That essence can be fairly obvious – Fitzgerald's description of Buchanan's brutishness, for example – but it doesn't have to be. You can, in fact, hint at some of the deepest themes in your book while seeming to do no more than describe a person.

In an earlier chapter, I spoke about a character of mine, an engineer with long pianist's fingers. Here's the moment (from *The Lieutenant's Lover*) where that character (Misha) meets his future beloved (Tonya):

> *Misha was about to bend down to check the stove, when he realised that the door out onto the corridor wasn't closed and the space outside wasn't empty. He straightened. There was a girl there, dark-haired and serious. There was something very still in her manner, and something remarkable in her stillness. She was still in the way that a white owl is, or a deer grazing in snow. But there was also something watchful about her, untrusting. She didn't come or go. She didn't speak. She didn't even look away when she saw Misha looking at her.*
>
> *'Zdrasvoutye,' he said. 'Good day.'*
> *'Good day.'*
> *She didn't move.*

This is, as it happens, another 'description' which would be pretty much useless at an identity parade. You'd know to look for a dark-haired girl, and that's all. She could be tall, short, fat, thin, blue-eyed, brown-eyed, pretty, ugly – anything at all. Some of those details are filled in later, but not many. I doubt if any reader either noticed those omissions or cared. They'd have created a picture in their mind's eye, and I was happy enough to let them get on with it.

So much for what I didn't say, but look now at what I did. 'She was still in the way that a white owl is, or a deer grazing in snow. But there was also something watchful about her, untrusting'. One of the themes of the book is the contest between Misha's trustfulness and Tonya's grittily realistic untrust. I didn't want to be too crude in the way I approached that contest, but nor did I want it to be buried. So I dropped it in there, right at the moment of meeting. Because the facts alone might not have been memorable enough ('there was also something watchful about her, untrusting' – accurate, but dull), the passage needed some image to anchor it. The key sentence seems to be groping for the right image, just as Misha himself must have been groping for it. A white owl? Sort of, but not quite. Ah, I know, a deer grazing in snow. Yes! Like that, she was like that.

Since neither I nor most of my readers live close to the Arctic Circle, the image is odd enough to be memorable. Where I come from, deer don't graze in snow, they graze in well-tended Oxfordshire parklands. So the image is odd, but (I hope) also apposite. In Russia, where this scene is set, deer *do* graze in snow, they *are* watchful, they *are* untrusting, they *do* have a kind of beauty which goes beyond mere physical appearance, which relates simply to their deer-ish-ness, if that makes any sense. If my description worked for you, then you had a fact to carry away with you (Tonya doesn't trust), and an image (the deer in snow) to help anchor that fact. In a couple of lines, I attempted to give the reader the essence not merely of Tonya, but of the book itself.

You may not want to go as far as that. Perhaps the themes of your book will emerge at another point altogether – and it's absolutely fine if they do. But if you want to add freight to your descriptions, go right ahead. Pinpoint something crucial about a character. Nail a theme. Hint at a weakness. Raise a question. Foreshadow an ending.

Don't hammer away at these things. Don't be too crude or too loud or too direct. Just drop a silver penny into the reader's mind and let her subconscious do the rest.

The mirror in chapter 1

To revert to rather plainer fare, you wouldn't believe how many new writers who, writing in the first person, are seized by anxiety about three pages into their novel. 'My readers don't know what the protagonist looks like! And I, the novelist, can't tell them, because I'm writing in that person's voice. Crisis! Ah, I know what. I'll have my character encounter a mirror. What a wonderfully brilliant and original solution, even if I do say so myself.' That sort of thinking usually produces writing like this:

> *I stop in front of the hall mirror. I see a thirty-something woman, a bit plump maybe, but not too bad for her age. Blonde hair in a feathery bob. Good cheek-bones, and a lovely new tan suit from Karen Millen, but a frazzled look in her eyes ...*

Oh dear. There's a lot wrong with this snippet, but the wrongness starts with the anxiety, the feeling that you have to establish everything key about your character early, and her looks most of all. But you don't have to. It's not a race. You've got a whole book ahead of you, so take your time.

The thing that's worst about that anxiety is that it ends up pulling you away from your character. Let's say your protagonist is rushing to pick up her child from school and knows that she's left it a few minutes late. That accounts for the frazzled look, but she's *being* frazzled, not thinking about looking frazzled. Your character isn't going to pause to identify her hairstyle, to appraise the cut of her suit, or to consider whether her weight is acceptable. Listing these things is pulling you away from the being frazzled, which is what this passage should be about.

Relax. Stay with your character and with the experience of being that character. At some point there'll be a moment where looks matter, in which case say whatever matters at that point and, until then, leave it. If you find that you've left something major out for a very long time – well, that's fine too. I am currently about halfway through writing the seventh book in my Fiona Griffiths series: that's about 750,000 words, and change. I didn't reveal my character's hair colour ('dark') until about the 100,000-word mark. I have still said almost nothing tangible about her face. I still haven't mentioned her eye colour and maybe never will. (Truth is, I haven't yet decided, probably because I don't care much either way.)

That's not because I've got some weird tell-the-reader-nothing game going on. I haven't mentioned her eye colour because no story incident has yet called upon Fiona to reflect on the colour of her eyes. On the other hand, I do mention – with reasonable frequency – that she is short and slight. Those facts are relevant to the story and so they're something that she thinks about. Since her other physical attributes are mostly irrelevant, she doesn't especially talk about them. Many new writers are uncomfortable about silences of this sort, but you shouldn't be. If you withhold some major pieces of information about your character (and do so while writing well and telling a strong story), your reader has only two ways to respond:

- *Eagerness to find out the relevant info* – which is good, because it means you've created a little mystery and a reason to read on.
- *Imaginative filling out of the character* – which is also good, because the reader needs to engage imaginatively with your character anyway, so giving them some space to play in can't be bad.

It's win-win.

Being him, feeling her

Finally, there's another reason why that stopping-in-front-of-the-hallway-mirror description didn't work so well, and that was the *stopping*. The story simply braked to a halt while the description did its stuff, and then (let's hope) got going again afterwards.

And descriptions don't have to be like that. There's no reason why a description shouldn't be charged with energy. Compare that hallway description with the Misha-Tonya one. The latter description was motionless, in the sense that no one was moving around, saying or doing very much – but it was energised, because the atmosphere was full of charge. There's something strange about a woman who doesn't alter her gaze when someone looks directly at her for the first time. Something strange about a woman who echoes that person's '*zdrasvoutye*', but without giving any indication of why she's there or what she's doing. She was there on Misha's doorstep, a mystery.

Put another way, the description of Tonya was part of the story. The story didn't stop unfolding so as to allow space for a nice description. Rather, the story unfolded *through* the description. The sentences about Tonya's appearance were integral to the suspense. They, more than anything else, were creating the suspense.

You should aim to do likewise. You'll generally find it easier to bring the descriptions into the story if you offer them up at the moment when characters interact. If the two characters are significant rather than bit-part players, so much the better. If the moment of meeting has real plot significance, that's better still. What's more, you'll find that these techniques help keep you close to character, rather than pushing you away from it (as in the hallway mirror scene). With that Misha-Tonya scene, we weren't just looking at Tonya, we were being Misha looking at Tonya and experiencing whatever Misha himself was experiencing. We *were* him and we *felt* her. If you write a description that is an essential part of your story, and which brings you closer to your character or characters, you've done well. You've done all you need to do.

Chapter Summary

- Avoid the list!
- Lightness of touch works better. Home in on one or two specific features or aspects.
- Good descriptions often hover between the physical and the personal.
- The characteristic you choose to highlight often hints at some essential quality to the underlying person.
- Avoid mirrors, especially in the first chapter. It's OK to leave things hanging.
- Try to insert character descriptions when they're called for, when the story demands them.

MEETINGS

So far in this section, we've figured out that characters are best portrayed through showing, rather than telling. We're reminded ourselves to check that we know enough about our characters before we start writing them. We've ensured our characters have edge, that they have fully furnished inner worlds, that they have faces and bodies and (as far as possible) avoid the mirror in the hallway. So we're pretty close to done, right?

Not quite. Characters in novels only exist vibrantly in relation to story and in relation to other people. Story is the most obvious of these two relationships. We're not really interested in Bella Swan, the star of Stephenie Meyer's *Twilight*, in the round. We don't care about her political views, her skills at mathematics, her interactions with most of her classmates, or an awful lot else. We care about her in relation to her developing romance and otherwise almost not at all.

Meyer knows this perfectly well. One day, she has Bella doing nothing much, beyond preparing some homework on Macbeth. She relates the experience thus: '*And so the day was quiet, productive – I finished my paper before eight.*' No inner life. No physical descriptions. No memories. No physical sensations. Just a few words pushing us through time to the next moment of drama. Bella – the true Bella – emerges through those dramatic moments. Her decisions will shape the drama and the drama will shape her. Watching those things happen is why we read fiction. If you allow your story to go static, your character will go flat. They only live through each other.

Suddenly rigid

We'll deal with those issues more fully when we consider plot, but characters are also crucially defined by their relationship to other people.

It's a cliché of Hollywood screenwriting that lead characters need best friends. If you watch a standard rom-com, for example, then both the guy and the girl will have best friends. Maybe one each. Maybe a little group of two or three. Those friends will typically be same-sex, but you'll also get such radical innovations as gay best friends, goofy best friends, ethnically diverse best friends, embarrassing best friends, or whatever else. Now admittedly, those Hollywood friends solve a technical problem that screenwriters have and novelists don't: they do away with the need for stilted interior monologues. The guy or the girl can complain or sigh or yearn or laugh in company. But it goes beyond that. I said that a static story will kill your character – and it will – but the same is true if you allow your character to drift away from important human relationships.

Often, that means your protagonist will be sharing page space with their significant other. Here for example is Bella Swan's first proper 'meeting' with Edward Cullen, a vampire. (I've compressed the passage in the interests of brevity.)

> *In fact all the tables were filled but one. Next to the center aisle, I recognized Edward Cullen by his unusual hair, sitting down next to that single open seat.*
>
> *As I walked down the aisle to introduce myself to the teacher and get my slip signed, I was watching him surreptitiously. Just as I passed, he suddenly went rigid in his seat. He stared at me again, meeting my eyes with the strangest expression on his face – it was hostile, furious. I looked away quickly, shocked, going red again ...*
>
> *I kept my eyes down as I went to sit by him, bewildered by the antagonistic stare he'd given me ...*
>
> [During class] *I couldn't stop myself from peeking occasionally through the screen of my hair at the strange boy next to me.*

During the whole class, he never relaxed his stiff position on the edge of his chair, sitting as far from me as possible. I could see his hand on his left leg was clenched into a fist, tendons standing out under his pale skin. This, too, he never relaxed.

No words are exchanged at any point, but the passage is nevertheless crammed with the relationship between Bella and the mysterious Edward.

The same is equally true when Edward is nowhere to be seen. The scene above is taken from the first chapter of *Twilight*. Here are some bits from the start of chapter 2:

The next day was better … and worse.

It was better because it wasn't raining yet […]

It was worse because I was tired […] And it was worse because Edward Cullen wasn't in school at all.

All morning I was dreading lunch, fearing his bizarre glares. Part of me wanted to confront him and demand to know what his problem was […]

But when I walked into the cafeteria with Jessica … I saw that his four siblings of sorts were sitting together at the same table, and he was not with them.

[…]

He didn't come, and as time passed I grew more and more tense.

[…] I held my breath at the door, but Edward Cullen wasn't there either.

Present or absent, the chapter is full of Edward Cullen and Bella's thoughts and feelings about him. Indeed, if you had to single out the thing that best accounts for Stephenie Meyer's success, you'd have to say it was this: her ability to create a relationship that dominates the page, whose overwhelming importance fills the book even when one of the two main characters is not even present.

Problematic, unstable and turbulent

Your book may not be a romance – still less a romance for teenagers – so you don't necessarily have to approach these things with Meyer's (erm) full-blooded intensity. But you do need to keep your characters in constant relationship. Those relationships need to be dynamic and changeable, not static and repetitive. You need dialogue, because speech is where our interactions are most alive, most fully located in the present moment. You will also, almost always, want to make sure that your protagonist is richly endowed with human relationships, because an impoverished set of relationships will make it much harder for you to keep your character alive and engaging.

None of this should be taken to mean that those relationships need to be happy, successful, stable or loving. On the contrary: they will typically be problematic, unstable and turbulent. Even the 'easy' relationships are likely to have their ups and downs, their difficulties and challenges. And, naturally, the relationships in question include the nasty ones: Sherlock Holmes and Moriaty, James Bond and Blofeld, Harry Potter and Voldemort.

In some cases, the critical relationships are institutional as much as human. Robert Langdon, the hero of the Dan Brown's *The Da Vinci Code,* has a relationship with the Parisian police, though the person of Bezu Fache. He has a relationship with Opus Dei via a series of chase sequences involving Silas, an albino killer. In a sense, Langton's critical relationships are with the institutions, not the individuals. If Fache weren't trying to arrest him, someone else would be. If Silas weren't trying to kill him, someone else would have a go. But that logic extends only so far. Drama requires a human face. If *The Da Vinci Code* had involved a whole sequence of different policemen and killers, with no single character in the frame for more than a chapter or two at a time, it would have lost a crippling amount of dramatic energy. That energy is only retained because the key institutional relationships are carried forward by the same human characters.

A snakeskin skirt and a mini tank top

Most writers will have no difficulty with these issues. Your emerging novel is, quite likely, fine as you've planned it. But these things are easy to test. Check that you have a decent amount of dialogue in your book. (Genre fiction typically has more than literary fiction, so make sure you compare like with like.) Check that there is a good degree of intensity in your character's core relationships, that those relationships dominate the book, that you skip rapidly over segments of time when little is happening, and so forth. If you find passages that are necessary in terms of story, but which are lacking in terms of important human relationships, then find a way to get those relationships in there. Remember, you can do that whether or not the relevant counterpart is on the page or not.

You can do it, as Stephenie Meyer did it, by making the page echo with an absence. Or you can do it by trickery of another sort. In Lauren Weisberger's *The Devil Wears Prada*, for example, there's an opening chapter – a prologue, in effect – which shows Andrea Sachs being bullied by her fashion magazine boss, Miranda Priestly. Chapter 2 then leaps back in time to the moment when Andrea first got the job. The Andrea-Miranda relationship clearly forms the heart of the book, yet you'd think it would be hard to say much about it until the two characters have met. Not so. Riding the elevator up to her interview, Andrea hears one snakeskin-skirted employee saying to another, 'She. Is. Such. A. Bitch! I *cannot* deal with her anymore.' The person being spoken about is not, as it happens, Miranda Priestly – except that it is! By the magic of association, we intimate (correctly) that this office is a bitch's paradise and that the Queen Bitch is Miranda Priestly. As the story heads moves towards the moment when Andrea first encounters her, there's a rising chorus of people talking about her, like worshippers of some occult deity. It's twenty pages into the book before Miranda first makes her appearance, but she's been the dominant presence throughout, nevertheless.

Most writers won't have a problem with these issues – building convincing human relationships often comes as one of the most natural and least worried-about aspects of writing – but it's worth checking your work nevertheless. If you can find a way to squeeze more human interaction, more relationship intensity into your pages, it's highly likely that your book will be better as a result.

Keeping it tight

If you put a certain volume of gas into a given space, it'll bounce around, happily gassy, doing whatever gas does. If you then constrict the space – same amount of gas, but just less space to bounce around in – the gas will start jiggling harder and faster. In more technical terms: the pressure increases.

That is, obviously, a delightful piece of knowledge in its own right, but it gets better: the same thing is true of stories. If you compress the number of characters with whom your character is in relationships, you will increase the associated story pressure too. So, for example, let's say your detective character (like mine) is a maverick who gets into constant trouble with his or her bosses. If there are three or four such incidents over the course of your book and she interacts with a different senior officer on each occasion, the whole thing feels repetitive and slightly pointless. If you keep the interaction with the same officer, there's a whole unfolding relationship drama overlaid on the naughty-cop-in-trouble one.

Likewise, if your character has to take evidence from four different and unrelated individuals in the course of a book, that just feels like beads on a string. Thing, then thing, then thing, then thing. If you can contrive things so that the individuals are (for example) members of the same family, then again you have a drama that adds to the mere evidence-taking process you started with. Family relationships are in general the most urgent ones you can play with, but any deep, long relationship will suffice.

You can't be stupid about applying these observations, of course. You can't sacrifice the plausibility of your story just to engineer some closer relationships. But if you think the story can take it, deep relationships between relatively few characters will tend to drive a more forceful story than looser relationships between a relatively large number.

Chapter Summary

- Characters emerge fully only through interaction with others.
- You can fill a page with a relationship, even in scenes where both characters are not present.
- Even human–institutional relationships (eg: Robert Langdon/ the French police) need to be personalised.
- You can also use metaphor and association to create the echo of key relationships.
- Keep it tight. Deep relationships between relatively few characters are likely to deliver greater intensity than weaker relationships between rather more characters.

EMPATHY

Most of the time, when agents reject a manuscript, they do so without any explanation. A standard form letter or email is typical. That's not rudeness; it's efficiency. It isn't their job to do more. Sometimes, though, an agent will ask for a full manuscript, read it, vacillate, and end up rejecting it with a formula that says, in effect, 'we just didn't feel enough empathy for your main character'.

Now I personally dislike this formula, because it has so much potential to mislead. So, let's be clear: *main characters do not need to be nice.* Lisbeth Salander in *The Girl with the Dragon Tattoo* is not likeable. Gatsby in *The Great Gatsby* was criminal. Captain Ahab, of *Moby Dick* fame, was a vengeful obsessive. Sherlock Holmes was an arrogant, misogynistic drug addict. John Updike's *Rabbit* series of novels stars a wife-beating adulterer who consorts with prostitutes. If an agent tells you that your main character is not empathetic, you will achieve nothing by making your protagonist volunteer at his local church or making her keen on home baking and flowered pinafores.

An alternative to home baking

Let's start by looking at one of literature's all-time nasty protagonists: Patrick Bateman, the psychopathic (and – worse – the investment banking) star of Bret Easton Ellis's *American Psycho*. Here's a typical bit of Bateman-speak, slightly compressed to keep the example compact:

> *Jean, my secretary who is in love with me, walks into my office without buzzing, announcing that I have a very important com-*

pany meeting to attend at eleven ... Jean is wearing a red stretch-silk jacket, a crocheted rayon-ribbon skirt, red suede pumps with satin bows by Susan Bennis Warren Edwards and gold-plated earrings by Robert Lee Morris. She stands there, in front of me, oblivious to my pain [a cocaine hangover]*, a file in her hand.*

After pretending to ignore her for close to a minute, I finally lower my sunglasses and clear my throat. 'Yes? Something else? Jean?'

'Mr Grouchy today.' She smiles, placing the file timidly on my desk, and stands there expecting me to ... what, amuse her with vignettes from last night?

'Yes, you simpleton. I am Mr Grouchy today,' I hiss, grabbing her file and shoving it into the top desk drawer.

She stares at me, uncomprehending, then, actually looking crestfallen, says, 'Ted Madison called and so did James Baker. They want to meet you at Fluties at six.'

I sigh, glaring at her. 'Well, what should you do?'

She laughs nervously, standing there, her eyes wide. 'I'm not sure.'

'Jean.' I stand up to lead her out of the office. 'What ... do ... you ... say?'

It takes her a little while but finally, frightened, she guesses, 'Just ... say ... no?'

'Just ... say ... no.' I nod, pushing her out and slamming the door.

Before leaving my office for the meeting I take two Valium, wash them down with a Perrier and then use a scuffing cleanser on my face with premoistened cotton balls, afterwards applying a moisturizer.

I hope two things are clear from this. First, Bateman does not volunteer at his local church. Second, Easton Ellis is a very, very good writer.

The description of Jean is wonderful. Nothing about what she looks like, only what clothes and what brand names she is wearing. At the end of that description, Bateman adds that she is 'oblivious to my pain' – though he himself is oblivious to everything that is human about her. He then bullies her, pointlessly, noticing only the little details of her suffering. That noticing may or may not have a sexual edge to it. It's hard to say for sure, but the possibility is unsettling. Having then pushed her out and slammed the door, he moisturises calmly, without a second's reflection on what has just happened.

As readers, we take all this in from two standpoints. The first is Bateman's own. Easton Ellis takes us directly inside Bateman's head. It's a weird place to be. We don't *like* what we find, but there's a thrill attached to being there nevertheless. It's like being left alone in someone else's house, free to snoop. We may not like their décor – all black silk wallpaper and giant mirrors – but we have a freedom of movement that can't help but excite us.

The second standpoint is our own. Bateman's perspective has a hypnotic attraction to it, but that doesn't mean we completely lose our critical faculties. So just as part of us is sitting in Bateman's head as he bullies Jean, another part of us is with Jean being bullied. That conflict creates a tension, but an exciting one. The passage feels vibrant with life, despite the emotional deadness of its narrator.

Now, pretty clearly, if 'empathy with the narrator' is taken to mean something like 'I'd love to have him round to dinner; maybe he could read a story to the kids', no sane adult is going to feel empathy for Patrick Bateman. On the other hand, if the phrase means 'I'm fascinated by this repellent human being and find myself eager to read on', then *American Psycho* is a masterpiece of empathic communication. Your challenge is to match it.

Where things go wrong

Nearly always, if a reader fails to connect with your main character, it's because of a technical flaw in the writing: a problem that can be identified precisely and which can – in principle – be remedied. That's the good news. The bad news is that the problem could lie almost anywhere. If your writing isn't quite working somewhere along the line, it's rather like having a slow leak somewhere in your heating system. You're always going to struggle to maintain the pressure you need to keep the boiler firing. Having said that, a few problems are more common than others. They are:

- *Challenge.* You haven't given your main character a sufficiently challenging brief.

- *Interiority.* You haven't got inside your main character's head sufficiently.

- *Human relationships.* Your protagonist's key relationships are missing, dull, or otherwise low-energy.

- *Individuality.* Your character still feels a bit bland, a bit generic.

- *Motivation.* It's all very well to create a challenging situation, but your character needs to feel the challenge. If they aren't consumed with the importance of what faces them – or if they think, 'Oh well, if this doesn't come off the way I'm hoping, at least my fallback position isn't so bad' – your reader will lose interest too. That also means that your character needs to take *action* in order to avoid the bad outcome and achieve the good one. If he comes over as passive, he looks like he doesn't care, no matter how much he might protest otherwise.

- *Movement.* If the main character's essential position in relation to their goal doesn't change much from chapter to chapter, then you lose any sense of dynamism and the reader's interest quickly stalls.

- *Location.* Sometimes a writer will do a good job with their characters but forget to locate the story properly in a given time and place. Such stories can start to feel as if they're being acted out on a white stage under conditions of unvaried illumination. Unsurprisingly, it's hard to care for people under those circumstances.

Because everything in writing is connected to everything else, some of these issues leak out into other areas altogether. Some of these things we've already talked about. Others, we'll talk about elsewhere. And if you reckon your book already ticks these boxes, you're in good shape. Your characters are alive – and no agent will think to complain about empathy.

Chapter Summary

- You do not create empathy with your characters by ensuring that your characters are nice. They may well not be.
- You do create empathy with your characters by writing well.
- If you find that professional readers are not connecting sufficiently with your characters, the problem could lie in almost any aspect of your writing.
- Review the checklist in the last section of this chapter to locate some of the more common issues.

Part Four

Placing the Camera

Since each story presents its own technical problems, obviously one can't generalize about them on a two-times-two-equals-four basis. Finding the right form for your story is simply to realize the most natural way of telling the story. The test of whether or not a writer has defined the natural shape of his story is just this: After reading it, can you imagine it differently, or does it silence your imagination and seem to you absolute and final? As an orange is final. As an orange is something nature has made just right.

– Truman Capote

A novel must give a sense of permanence as well as a sense of life.

– E. M. Forster

FIRST PERSON, THIRD PERSON

So far, we've spoken of character while avoiding the whole question of viewpoint. Helen Fielding brought Bridget Jones to life in the first person, as an 'I'. Lauren Weisberger brought Brooke Alter to life in the third person, as a 'she'. On the other hand, both novelists concentrated relentlessly on their central character. Bridget Jones is never off the page, nor is Brooke.

And it doesn't have to be like that. Audrey Niffenegger's *The Time Traveler's Wife* is written in the first person, but there are two narrators: Henry (the time traveller) and Clare (the wife) take it in turns to narrate. They each say 'I' when they're speaking. Each section opens with a simple 'HENRY: ...' or 'CLARE: ...' to denote who's saying what.

Equally, you can have multiple third-person viewpoints. Richard Mayhew is the protagonist of Neil Gaiman's *Neverwhere*, but that doesn't mean that he's never off the page. On the contrary. There'll be some scenes (a majority) that follow Richard Mayhew intently, but plenty of scenes that follow other characters altogether. Many thrillers, for example, will cut from the hero, to the antagonist, to some side-kick helping the hero, back to the hero again, and so on. Thus in John Grisham's *The Firm*, the person who 'owns' most of the page space will be Mitch McDeere (the Tom Cruise character, if you've seen the film), but there'll be plenty of scenes occupied by secondary characters too: Bill DeVasher (a Mafia thug on McDeere's trail), Abby McDeere (Mitch's wife), Tammy Hemphill (a secretary who helps McDeere), and so on.

There are other options too – odd, but possible:

- **Second person singular ('you').** *If On A Winter's Night A Traveler*, a novel by an Italian literary author, Italo Calvino, makes the reader the protagonist of every odd-numbered chapter: 'You are doing this, you are about to read that'. Every even-numbered chapter is a chunk from the book that 'you' have chosen to read. Jay McInerney's *Bright Lights, Big City* does something similar: 'You are not the kind of guy who would be at a place like this at this time of the morning. But here you are'.

- **First person plural ('we').** *The Virgin Suicides* by Jeffrey Eugenides is a recent example of this rare form. ('That was in June, fish-fly season, when each year our town is covered by the flotsam of those ephemeral insects ... Mrs. Scheer, who lives down the street, told us she saw Cecilia the day before she attempted suicide.')

- **Purely interrogative.** A recent book by Padgett Powell, *The Interrogative Mood: A Novel?*, consists of a series of questions addressed to the reader.

Still other alternatives exist, though they're rarer than hen's teeth.

If you research these matters online, however, you'll notice that these issues are only the beginning. Is your narrator omniscient or limited? Subjective or objective? Reliable or unreliable? What's his or her (or its) position on stream of consciousness? And what use should you make of free indirect discourse? Should you write in the present or the past? And where do you stand on chronological linearity? You don't have to get far into these questions for your blood to start heating up. It's as though writing a book is akin to doing a PhD in nuclear physics, when all you wanted to do was to tell a story.

Worry not. In the end, these things come down to a handful of either/or choices, where the right answer is normally the most obvious one. We start with the most elementary choice of all. Do you write in the first person or the third? The other, more exotic, choices can be ignored. If you're not confident, you shouldn't go near them. If you are confident, you won't listen to me anyway.

Defining terms – first person

A first-person narrator writes as 'I'. Helen Fielding is the author of *Bridget Jones's Diary*, and for the purposes of the book she writes as though she were Bridget Jones. She writes, as we saw in an earlier chapter, like this:

> *Huh. Had dream date at an* intime *little Genoan restaurant near Daniel's flat.*
>
> *'Um … right. I'll get a taxi,' I blurted awkwardly as we stood in the street afterwards. Then he lightly brushed a hair from my forehead, took my cheek in his hand and kissed me, urgently, desperately. After a while, he held me hard against him and whispered throatily, 'I don't think you'll be needing that taxi, Jones.'*

On every single page of the book, it is Bridget speaking. She talks about things she saw, said, did, and heard. If Daniel Cleaver gets up to some mischief in a place where Bridget can't see it or hear it, then the author can't tell us about it – or at least, not until Bridget herself gets the news from some third party.

Just to be clear, though, using the first person does not mean that you need to use the word 'I' or the pronoun 'me' in every sentence – nothing of the sort is the case. It's perfectly fine to use sentences like, 'The room was large, echoing and empty.' All that matters is that when the protagonist refers to herself, she says, '*I* stepped forwards …', not '*She* stepped forwards …'.

Defining terms – third person

A third-person narrator, on the other hand, is like some invisible storyteller. That storyteller, most likely, isn't defined. The narrator is unlikely to be given a name or any other kind of identity. There's usually no reason given for why this invisible person suddenly starts blurting out a story. The relationship of the narrator to the reader is left completely unspecified. Even to talk about a 'narrator' is a little misleading. In effect, we're simply talking about a convention of storytelling, a shared assumption which allows us to write and read novels in the first place.

If that sounds mysterious or ethereal, it really shouldn't. On the page, it just feels normal: what you expect from a story. As Lauren Weisberger handled it in *Last Night at Chateau Marmont*, it looks like this:

> *A waiter arrived at the table and Leo ordered for the group without consulting anyone. Brooke normally hated it when people did that, but even she couldn't argue with his choices: another bottle of champagne, a round of tequila gimlets, and a bunch of snack plates, everything from truffled porcini bruschetta to mozzarella and arugula. By the time the first dish of crab cakes in an avocado puree arrived, Brooke had happily rediscovered her earlier buzz and was feeling almost euphoric from the excitement.*

It's as though Weisberger (or some alter ego of hers) were sitting at our side telling us a story about a woman called Brooke and her husband called Julian. We don't bother to ask how Weisberger could possibly know all these things (after all, we know she's just making it up), so we just let her get on with it. Our interest is in the story. We don't, to be brutally honest, give a damn about the person telling it.

Writing in the third person

Most novels are written in the third person – unsurprisingly; it's how most formal storytelling has always proceeded. The classic opening for a story is 'Once upon a time, there was …', not 'Once upon a time, *I* was …'.

Stories work this way for a reason. Third-person narration offers numerous advantages, including:

Flexibility of standpoint

A third-person narrator is a flexible narrator. Lauren Weisberger can tell us whatever she cares to. In the snippet above, she told us about how Brooke was feeling in the restaurant. She could, if she'd wanted, have followed that scene with one that showed Julian taking a solitary walk in the garden afterwards. Or she could have jumped away from the Brooke/Julian pair altogether and talked about Julian's publicist, or a rogue waiter ... or, if this were a different kind of book, a flight-lieutenant in bomber command, the leader of a zombie army, or anyone else at all. In short, she can talk about who she likes, when she likes.

This flexibility yields huge benefits when it comes to plotting. You can cut from your protagonist, to their enemy, back to the protagonist, over to the protagonist's spouse, and so on. Crucially, this enables you to create types of suspense that aren't available with first-person narrators. Alfred Hitchcock famously distinguished between surprise and suspense as follows:

We are now having a very innocent little chat. Let's suppose that there is a bomb underneath this table between us. Nothing happens, and then all of a sudden, 'Boom!' There is an explosion. The [film-going] public is surprised, but prior to this surprise, it has seen an absolutely ordinary scene, of no special consequence. Now, let us take a suspense situation. The bomb is underneath the table and the public knows it, probably because they have seen the anarchist place it there. The public is aware the bomb is going to explode at one o'clock and there is a clock in the decor. The public can see that it is a quarter to one. In these conditions, the same innocuous conversation becomes fascinating because the public is participating in the scene. The audience is longing to warn the characters on the screen: 'You shouldn't be talking about such trivial matters. There is a bomb beneath you and it is about to explode!'

In the first case we have given the public fifteen seconds of surprise at the moment of the explosion. In the second we have provided them with fifteen minutes of suspense. The conclusion is that whenever possible the public must be informed.

[Conversation between Truffaut and Hitchcock, reprinted in *Hitchcock,* by Truffaut].

In third-person narrations, it's easy to create suspense of the kind Hitchcock is talking about. You simply write one scene in which an anarchist plants a bomb. You then write another, in which you sit your main character down and serve him tea. Job done. A first-person narrative simply cannot achieve this kind of suspense. The audience knows what the character knows. If the character doesn't know that there's gelignite under his chair, then the reader doesn't either. You'll get the surprise, but not the suspense.

Flexibility of narrative voice

A first-person narrator always has to sound like themselves. Bridget Jones is allowed to write sentences like, 'I may have been right, but my reward, I know, will be to end up all alone, half-eaten by an Alsatian', because they sound like her. She isn't ever allowed to say things that don't sound like her. So she couldn't, for example, say anything like this: 'It was a sombre truth, yet one I now recognised as such. The sole reward for all my virtue would be simply this: a lonely life, a lonely death, unremembered and unlamented'. She can't say that, because she's not that sort of person. If she wrote one single sentence like that in the entire book, it would feel strained and out of place.

A third-person narrative has much more flexibility. Because the narrator isn't normally endowed with a distinct personality, their voice can exist independently of any of the characters in the novel. You could be a highly literary writer writing in beautiful language about people with only the most rudimentary education or verbal abilities. What's more your tone can vary according to the mood of the particular passage. You don't need to justify fluctuations in tone according to the emotional state of your characters. You can just do whatever seems right for that particular moment.

Flexibility of camera angle

With a first-person narrator, there's only ever one possible camera angle: the eyes and ears of the character himself.

Writing in the third person, you have more flexibility. You can narrate in intense close-up. Ian McEwan, ever gifted at the close-up, notes one such moment in *On Chesil Beach*:

> *He was gazing at his wife now, into her intricately flecked hazel eyes, into those pure whites touched by a bloom of the faintest milky blue.*

In that sentence, McEwan is carefully analysing one pair of eyes and a moment of scrutiny that may have lasted just a few seconds. If McEwan's pen were a camera, then it's positioned just inches from the face of the actress. Time itself seems to be running in super slo-mo.

A couple of pages further on, however, and the camera has been reset to extreme wide-angle:

> *In just a few years' time, that* [running down to the beach with a bottle of wine] *would be just the kind of thing quite ordinary people would do. But for now, the times held them.*

In this extract, McEwan's narrator happily starts talking about huge social changes that lie some years into the future. Clearly, neither of his two protagonists could have known what the future held, but nor would they have been in possession of that god-like vantage point. In this case, that god-like vantage point gave a view into the future, but it could equally well have looked on the hotel from above or viewed the entire bay in a single snapshot.

Writing in the first person

Writing in the first person sacrifices all this lovely flexibility and offers only two real advantages.

Individuality

Third-person narration offers certain sorts of flexibility in abundance, but it's limited in one crucial respect. A third-person narrator needs, mostly, to merge into the background. You don't want the force of the narration to distract from the story being told. Imagine, for example, how *Last Night at Chateau Marmont* would read if told in a voice as loudly distinctive as Bridget Jones's:

> *A waiter, the cutest guy, adorable brown curls and long soppy sideburns arrived at the table. Leo, Mr Big Shot, did his whole chest-beating thing and ordered for the entire group. Typical. He didn't even think of consulting Brooke or Julian who – duh! – were meant to be the stars, right? Still, Big Shot knew how to order and …*

That, pretty much, says the same thing as the passage I started to quote above – except it doesn't. Brooke herself feels like a shadow, driven aside by the force and personality of the narrative voice. For Brooke to be in command of her own story, the narrator has to step away from the spotlight.

Intimacy

The other great advantage of first-person narration is intimacy. If the great virtue of third-person narration is the flexibility of camera position and standpoint, the great virtue of first-person narration is that the camera never shifts. We are utterly intimate with Bridget Jones, because we never leave her for a second. We maintain our 'empathy' with Patrick Bateman, because we are constantly in his head.

That intimacy runs very deep. In an earlier chapter, we saw the way that Bridget Jones's use of the word *'intime'* about a restaurant told us volumes about her. (How she didn't really have the sophistication that the word implied; how she likes to play-act at being sophisticated nevertheless; how she probably gets the word from women's magazines which also have a phoney kind of relationship with that kind of sophistication.) Because every word in a first-person narrative is 'owned' by the narrator, the reader knows exactly how to read them. In a third-person narrative, the whole issue is a little more nuanced. As we'll see in a subsequent chapter, even in third-person narrations, the narrative voice tends to get coloured by closeness to the major characters. So sometimes a word 'belongs' to the character in question. Sometimes it 'belongs' more to the narrator. That gives you fluidity, but it detaches you, at least a bit, from the central characters.

Indeed, you could say that the whole first person/third person distinction comes down to one thing and one thing only. A third-person narration offers the writer a broader range, more flexible choices. A first-person narration sacrifices flexibility but offers intimacy instead.

Choosing between first and third person

On the whole, few writers will come to this chapter uncertain of whether they want to write in the first person or the third person. For the most part, it'll be obvious and, for the most part, the obvious choice will be the right one.

If you are in doubt, however, then the default setting for most writers, most of the time, will be third-person narration. It's like wearing a suit to an interview, or a little black dress to an evening event. It may not be daring, but you can't go wrong. Jonathan Frantzen, the acclaimed literary author, says simply, 'Write in third person unless a really distinctive first-person voice offers itself irresistibly'. That's not a bad rule to follow (though it isn't, as it happens, one he follows himself). There are exceptions, perhaps, but it's still much more true than not.

It may also be helpful to think about what kind of story you are telling.

- *Thrillers, and any book where the story motivation is primarily external.* In a Tom Clancy novel, the question driving the plot might be something like: 'Will the Red October submarine make it to port in America?'. The way that question is resolved will have emotional consequences for the story participants, but the question itself is an external one, answered by whether or not a big wet chunk of metal arrives safely in the United States. Such books almost always want a third-person narration. That allows you to create suspense, Hitchcock-style, with any number of bombs-under-tables. You don't have to get hung up on the intimacies of any one character's emotional state. You can tell the story with freedom, range and verve.

- *Romances, and any story where the motivation is primarily emotional.* In a romantic novel, the question driving the plot is likely to be some variant of: 'Does the girl get the guy?'. There may be an external tale here (one that will presumably end with wedding bells and a big white dress), but the main issue is an internal, emotional one: does Miss Unattached find Mr Right? Most romantic novels are still written in the third person, but the case for the first person is potentially stronger. You may not need the freedom to go placing your cameras round the world (*à la* Tom Clancy), and the benefit from a truly intimate relationship with the central character may well be worth any sacrifice involved.

- *Literary fiction.* Literary fiction demands a lot of your prose style. It doesn't necessarily have to be flowery – there are hundreds of other ways to write good prose – but you may not want to be constrained by creating the kind of protagonist who would write lovely English. If not, third-person narration probably beckons.

Combining first and third

There's one further wrinkle worth teasing out before we leave for other things. I've spoken so far as though use of the first person means that the narrator *is* the protagonist. That, nearly all the time, is accurate.

But not always. The Sherlock Holmes stories (by Arthur Conan Doyle) are narrated in the first person by Dr Watson. A typical extract runs: 'I had seen little of Holmes recently. My marriage had drifted us away from each other …'. In a sense, this is classic first-person narration. The voice, the tone, the camera position are all firmly locked onto the fictional Dr Watson. At the same time, though, it's not Watson who holds the reader's interest, but Sherlock Holmes. Even in this tiny extract, we can feel his pull. The reader is looking out through Watson's eyes all right, but we're only ever gazing at Holmes. We don't know much about Watson's marriage, because we don't care and he doesn't tell us. This is first-person narration as a sneaky back-door route to a third-person narrative. The Holmes/Watson stories are probably literature's most famous examples of this technique, but they're by no means alone. *The Great Gatsby*, which we quoted a few chapters back, is narrated in the first person by Nick Carraway, but it's Gatsby, of course, who holds the reader's eye.

This is a neat technique, but it needs to be used well. Both Gatsby and Holmes are mysterious and powerful characters. That mystique is a precious commodity, easily bruised by too much intimacy. The use of a subordinate character as the viewing lens creates the required distance, and it does so in a way that *adds to* the primary character's magnetic allure. The intimacy of the first-person voice means that the reader is there with Carraway as he orbits Gatsby, is present with Watson as he orbits Holmes. We're kept at arm's length and entranced, both at the same time.

Beware, beware that siren call

Now, as you know, I love literary agents with a passion. They are the mightiest, most beautiful, most wise and most perfect race ever to have walked upon God's green earth. But they can also be wrong. They can give terrible advice. They can be wildly reckless with other people's time, hopes and dreams.

Let me explain myself.

A number of our editorial clients at Jericho Writers have told me about an experience that follows roughly the following sequence. (A) A writer writes a novel. It's pretty good. (B) They get it out to literary agents. Two or more agents ask for the complete manuscript, always a pretty good sign that the writer is roughly in the right zone for success. (C) One agent seems to get quite excited by the story, but they hesitate. It's not quite there. Something's wrong. (D) The writer and agent get into a bit of dialogue. The agent says, 'You know what, I *do* like this, but I think it would work so much better in third person [if it's written in first], or first person [if it's written in third]'.

So (E) the writer goes away and reworks the whole damn novel. And switching from first to third or vice versa is not a purely grammatic change. It's vastly more extensive. It's one of the biggest rewrites you can undertake. Then – hooray – (F) the writer sends the manuscript back to the agent in a flurry of excitement, only to find (G) that the agent still doesn't like it. And, normally, because the agent is a bit embarrassed by the whole episode, they are rather curt and unhelpful in their communications.

Great.

The writer had one pretty decent manuscript. They now have another version of the same thing. And neither is acceptable.

I have several comments on this, only some of which don't involve swearing. But first, never take editorial advice from anyone unless it makes sense to you. The right reaction to a piece of editorial advice should (after a period of reflection, perhaps) be, '*Yes!* I knew something was wrong, but I couldn't put my finger on it. Now I know exactly what the issue is and I know precisely what to do'. If you are following a piece of advice just because it comes from an agent and not because it echoes deep inside you, you are probably on a fool's errand.

Second, you need to ask yourself whether an agent has skin in the game, or not. If you are a client – an actual, signed-up client – then that agent has skin in the game. If the agent has done a detailed, detailed read of your book and given you extensive advice on it, they have skin in the game. If they are rejecting your manuscript in that wistful, sorry-I-can't-say-yes kind of way, but toss out an editorial suggestion in two or three lines of a short and business-like email, then that agent has no skin in the game and their editorial suggestion shouldn't be given particular weight.

Yes, they're an agent, but they're not acting as your agent or your editor. They're acting like someone a bit embarrassed about saying no to something, but trying to soften the blow with something constructive. That is not, even remotely, the basis for wholly altering your novel.

Just read those agency comments. See if they chime with you. If they do, great. If you're not sure, then ignore them. Enlightenment does not lie that way.

(And if you do want professional editorial help, then agents aren't the solution anyway. They are there to sell manuscripts. That's their primary function. Yes, they do some final polishing before sale, but that's the very final stage of editorial work. If you're at an earlier stage of things and you want pro editorial advice, that's the kind of thing that Jericho Writers offers as its primary service. Other firms offer much the same thing, of course – we're very good at what we do, but we're hardly alone. We'll talk more about how all that works in a later chapter.)

Chapter Summary

- The art of placing the camera – first person/third person, limited/omniscient, etc – is a subject that seems fraught with technicalities.

- Many writers won't need to worry about those technicalities. The most natural-seeming choice is usually the right one.

- As a rough guide, writing in the third person gives you the most flexibility ...

- ... but writing in the first person gives you the best chance at intimacy.

- Some stories may pull the Holmes/Watson trick, where a first-person narrator tells a story which is about some third party, thereby delivering a kind of narrative hybrid.

- Beware, beware any casually tossed out advice from agents. If the advice doesn't echo deeply with you, ignore it.

ONE, FEW, OR MANY

The next question facing you as you position your cameras is how many people you intend to follow.

Defining terms

We'll run through the options in a moment, but first let's clarify some terms.

- The **protagonist** of a story is the hero, the central character, the person on whom the reader's attention is fixed.
- The **narrator** of the story is the person who tells it.
- The only **point-of-view character** is the person though whose eyes the story is seen. (This is often shortened to POV character. You can also talk about a viewpoint character.)

As we saw in the previous chapter, the protagonist and narrator don't have to be the same person. Third-person narrators stand outside the story and tell us about what's happening to the protagonist inside. Even first-person narrators (like Dr Watson) may not be the protagonist (Sherlock Holmes).

The POV character is a different thing again. John Grisham's blockbusting *The Firm* had Mitch McDeere as the protagonist, or hero. It had an invisible third-party narrator. But a fair few of its scenes unfolded through the eyes of subsidiary characters, Abby McDeere, Bill DeVasher, Tammy Hemphill and so on. Those scenes were ones in which Mitch himself was typically not even present. If a scene is told from Abby McDeere's point of view, the narrator is restricted to narrating things that Abby herself can see, can hear or knows about.

The Firm only has one protagonist – Mitch McDeere. In the end, he's the only one that the reader really cares about and attaches to. He dominates the action and the page space. But those other POV characters are like external cameras positioned to pick up flashes of action that matter very much indeed to the core story. They're supplementary, but an essential part of the narrative technique.

If this starts to seem complex, it really shouldn't. Most writers will get these things right by instinct. We'll begin at the beginning.

One

The simplest model of all is that your cameras follow just one person.

This will be the typical, but not compulsory, model if you are writing in the first person. Emma Donoghue's *Room*, for example, is told exclusively from the first-person viewpoint of Jack, a charming five-year-old boy. Jack is simultaneously:

- the protagonist
- the narrator, and
- the only POV character.

Plenty of other first-person narratives proceed in just the same way, from Raymond Chandler's Marlowe novels to Aravind Adiga's *The White Tiger*.

Something similar can also be achieved through third-person narration, except that of course the narrator is now some invisible party, standing somewhat outside the story. The narrator is one entity. The protagonist and POV character are one and the same. Thus, for example, Colm Tóibín's *Brooklyn* focuses exclusively on Eilis Lacey. There is not a page in which she doesn't feature. There is no information reported which Eilis is not herself aware of. There is no view described which Eilis could not see with her own eyes at the moment being described. For example:

> *Double doors opened into a bedroom, and, since one of the doors was open, Eilis could see that the bedroom was decorated in the same heavy, rich style. She looked at the old round dining table and supposed that that was where the game of poker was played on Sunday nights.*

Tóibín doesn't tell us more about the bedroom than Eilis can see. He doesn't tell us more about the poker game other than reporting Eilis's supposition about it. Just as Jack was, Eilis is both protagonist and the only POV character.

One and a bit

You can also have books which *almost* restrict themselves to a single point of view, but don't quite. In Robert Crais's *The Watchman*, Joe Pike is featured on nearly every page, but there are very occasional short chapters which feature only his partner in crime-fighting, Elvis Cole. It's not really a two-POV book; it's more like a one-and-a-bit-POV one.

The one-and-a-bit format works well for Crais, because Cole and Pike are series characters and most readers will have met Cole before. They understand that, in this particular book, he plays a subordinate role, but in the series as a whole, he's Pike's equal. If you are not writing a series of books (and are not a fine bestselling author midway through that series), then that technique is unlikely to work for you, simply because the subordinate character's chapters are likely to seem purposeless in comparison when set beside those belonging to the central character.

Two

You can also have two POV characters in a book.

Audrey Niffenegger's *The Time Traveler's Wife* is a good recent example of a book in which there are two first-person narrators.

Obviously, because both narrators refer to themselves as 'I', there is potential room for confusion. So Niffenegger keeps it simple. Henry and Clare (the two protagonist-narrators) have alternating sections in the book. A typical such section begins:

> HENRY: *I'm almost calm as I follow Clare down the stairs, through the dark cold hall and into the dining room.*

As it happens, this opening from Henry immediately uses the word 'I', but that's just coincidence. Niffenegger is (quite rightly) equally happy to open a section like this:

> CLARE: *Mama's room is white and bare.*

It doesn't matter that Clare doesn't immediately start using the word 'I'. All that matters is that we know Clare is standing in her mother's room, looking at how white and bare it is. And in a sentence or two, the description over, Clare starts telling us where she is and what she's doing. The word 'I' has reappeared. If ever the reader gets confused as to who is talking at a particular point, they just have to turn their eyes to the head of the relevant section, and they'll get the reminder they need in nicely printed capital letters. Ideally, Henry will sound like Henry and Clare will sound like Clare. You should be able to tell just from the feel of the prose who is talking at any given point.

A wonderful example of this technique, but with a twist, is Gillian Flynn's extraordinary *Gone Girl*. That, wonderfully written, book gave first-person narration to both Amy and Nick. The big twist, however, is that, in the first half of the book, Amy's voice is delivered in the first person but via a set of diary entries. In the second half, the diary falls away and we get Amy in full narrator mode ... and we discover that the diary itself is carefully faked – its apparently candid first-person narration is all a fraud designed to conceal the real Amy's evil manipulations. What's particularly sweet about this method is that Flynn uses the apparent candour of that first-person narration as a kind of authorial ju jitsu. The intimacy tricks us into believing, so the mid-book twist is all the more shocking as a result.

But the same basic double-handed technique works just as well in third-person narrations. For obvious reasons, any book that centres on a relationship is quite likely to have two points of view involved, and Ian McEwan's *On Chesil Beach* is an example of a two-hander written in the third person. There are sections that relate things from Edward's point of view. There are sections that relate things from Florence's point of view. There's no great mystery in how this works. When McEwan talks about Richard, he says something like this:

> *Rising from his plate, mingling with the sea breeze, was a clammy odour, like the breath of the family dog. Perhaps he was not as joyous as he kept telling himself he was.*

When McEwan talks about Florence, he says something like this:

> *She would have reached over her shoulder to help, but her arms were trapped, and besides, it did not seem right, showing him what to do.*

Easy.

From three to many

And so on. You can in principle have as many narrators as you want. Guy Gavriel Kay's excellent *The Lions of Al-Rassan* has three principal POV characters. He tells his story in the third person, as do most writers who use multiple viewpoints, but you can find examples of multiple first-person narratives. Excellent recent examples include Matthew Kneale's *English Passengers*, and the remarkable *Maynard and Jennica* by Rudolph Delson.

The trouble is that as you multiply viewpoints, you tend to weaken the bonds of empathy with any one character. When Colm Tóibín follows Eilis Lacey throughout every word and sentence of his book, the reader doesn't merely 'have empathy' with Eilis. We actually feel, as we read, that we *are* Eilis. What she sees, we see. What she hears, we hear. What she feels, we feel. The emotional power of the book lives entirely in the completeness of this identification.

But what if Tóibín were writing a book about an Eilis, a Fionnuala, a Gráinne, a Hetty, an Iona, a Joan, a Kerry, a Lily, a Máirie, and a Niamh? At some point, that power of empathetic absorption in a particular character and a particular tale is going to weaken. That absorption starts to erode the very moment you start adding POV characters to your tale. A well-written book can certainly handle two POV characters. It can probably handle three. At a pinch, it might handle three and a bit. Perhaps even four. But if you go past four POV characters, you've sacrificed something that you won't get back. You may, in the process, make some other gains which are worthwhile, but the flipside of breadth is dilution. Dilute too far, and you may not have a story at all.

The expansive narrative

We'll have a think in a moment about what it means to keep your narrative tightly focused on a group of two or three characters, but first it's worth thinking about the expansive narrative. A Tom Clancy novel typically has multiple viewpoints. It is also, typically, large in scope. The 2000 thriller *The Bear and the Dragon* revolves around a war between Russia and China. The United States becomes involved, with nuclear consequences. It is, in fact, the story of a third world war. The story unfolds through the eyes of Jack Ryan, Sergey Golovko (the chairman of the SVR), Major Bob Teeters of the NSA, Tom Barlow at the CIA, Dr Benjamin Godley (an intelligence officer), and so on, and on, and on. There's a vast cast of characters, many of whom appear only for the briefest of moments.

These things are related: the scale of the narrative and the multiplicity of narrators. Certainly, you can tell the story of one person's war by using that person's viewpoint, and no one else's.

But if you want to tell *the* story of the war, you have to jump around. A frigate commander here. A marine captain there. A defence analyst here. A diplomat there. And so on. The number of viewpoints inevitably means that we don't care about many of the people we're hearing about. We're not *meant* to care about them. Some of the characters aren't just disposable in principle; they're soon disposed of in practice – as the missile comes in, as the bullet strikes, as the artillery starts up.

Clancy's huge narratives work as well as they do because his attention is largely external. The questions raised by *The Bear and the Dragon* are along the lines of 'What will happen if China invades Russia?'. They're not 'How will Jack Ryan feel about things if China invades Russia?'. That's not to say the latter question is completely neglected. It isn't. Ryan is the hero of this particular story, so we're going to spend plenty of time in his head, thinking his thoughts and feeling his feelings. But the question of his feelings is, and should be, subsidiary. This book isn't an interior book about Ryan's emotional state. It's about a third world war, for Pete's sake. There's a time and place for complex, subtle emotional investigations, but *The Bear and the Dragon* is neither the time nor the place. At the action–adventure end of the market, stories do tend to be external rather than internal. They also tend to have a fair few points of view. (The same goes for much fantasy fiction.)

It's not only big-scale thrillers where a large number of POV characters make sense. Matthew Kneale's *English Passengers* was a much-praised literary novel, which also had an external focus: Tasmania's brutal colonial past. The various narratives had interest in themselves, but the reader's interest in any one of the narrators was inevitably curtailed by the fact that none of them dominated the page space. In less capable hands, the narrative would have been too dilute to have succeeded, but Kneale brought his strands together to build a picture of a time and a colonial process that left shockwaves in the reader. Had Kneale's external focus been something less impactful, the dilutive quality of his narrative approach would have killed his story.

Finally, although these broad, external narratives may proceed through multiple viewpoints, there is almost always a central character (or two) who acts as the fulcrum for everything else. So although *The Bear and the Dragon* is not about Jack Ryan's emotional life, it is nevertheless Ryan who holds everything together. (In narrative terms, I mean; he also saves the world). If that central figure weren't there, the novel would seem to lack a centre. It would be hard for the reader to engage. That's a strange fact, on the face of it: why should we need to feel connected to one individual, in order to care about the fate of the planet? But we don't need to solve those mysteries, we just need to acknowledge their reality. It doesn't matter how drivingly important your story is, it still needs a centre. Without that centre, all you've got is words on a page. You don't have a novel at all.

If you use multiple points of view and are uncertain as to whether you may have over-diluted your novel, it's simple enough to check. Find books in a comparable genre and check how they handle things. In any genre, there will be a variety of approaches, so you need to pick your comparable texts with care. John Grisham's *The Firm* is typical (of a thriller) in the way it strikes a balance between focusing on the protagonist and supporting the main story with other viewpoints. If you are writing a thriller and the balance between protagonist's viewpoint and other viewpoints is about the same as Grisham's, you're doing fine. Tom Clancy's narratives, on the other hand, stand at the extreme end of viewpoint-multiplication. In Clancy's most diffuse texts, Ryan is still central ... but not very. Clancy can get away with that, in part because of his track record, and in part because of the crashing geo-political significance of his stories, but you should be wary of following his model. It's not impossible to get away with it, but it *is* hard. Grisham will be a safer model for most.

The focused narrative

Most books, though, do not have an external focus. They deal with one, two or perhaps three protagonists. Those protagonists are closely followed through the course of the book. Typically:

- We see plenty of those characters' inner lives. They mind about their feelings, and the reader is expected to mind as well.

- The story *is* the story of those characters. The story may take place against some tumultuous background – a world war, an intergalactic revolt, a plague, a revolution – but the story remains personal, not political.

- Any character whose point of view occupies a significant proportion of the book (let's say a quarter or more) is a protagonist. As such, their story needs to be important. It needs to matter to the reader, which means it has to matter to the writer.

- Each such story needs to be properly formed. It needs a beginning, a middle and an end. It needs a question to be answered, a motive to be achieved, an obstacle to be overcome. Almost certainly, there will be some tussle between some inner challenge and external events. (We'll go into these things in more detail when we consider plot. For now, all that matters is that each protagonist needs their own proper story.)

These things are worth spelling out, because one mistake commonly made by new writers is to give loads of page space to minor characters, or to major characters who nevertheless do not have their own proper story. These problems can spell death to a novel and can only be remedied by ripping down two thirds of the novel and starting again. There are two common mistakes here, and they're both lethal.

Killer mistake #1: minor characters have loads of page space

Let's say you have just finished reading John Grisham's *The Firm*. A flash of genius inspires you with the following plot idea: a newly qualified doctor joins a medical firm ... which turns out to be run by the Mafia. A story so blindingly excellent simply has to be written, so you choose a character (Deere McMitch) and let rip. Deere has easily the most page space in the novel. Sections told from Deere's point of view amount to some 30% of the total word count. There are a load of minor characters (including Deere's wife, Gabby; a thug called DeBasher; and so on), but none of these accounts for more than 15% of the word count. You figure that you're rounding out Deere's story by seeing it from many different points of view. In effect, you've included Deere's wife, brother, sister, secretary, nurse, and so on in order to make Deere himself more real. That's your theory, anyway.

And it's wrong. The reader doesn't in the end care about anyone except Deere. When he's occupying the page, the reader is interested. When he isn't, she's not ... and Deere only dominates the page for a slender 30% of the book.

Now, it would have been fine to make relatively short jumps away from Deere, in order to watch events unfold that are of critical importance to Deere's happiness and safety. Grisham does just that in *The Firm*. In effect, though, these jumps away from Deere's *viewpoint* aren't jumps away from Deere's *story*. It's still him the reader cares about.

That logic, however, tells us that it is emphatically not OK to make lengthy sojourns away from Deere in order to watch Gabby bake bread and muse about how she met her husband ... or watch DeBasher being pointlessly mean to a kid in a shopping mall. The reader cares about your protagonist. The reader does not care about anyone else. If you start telling a scene from some third party's point of view, that scene has to have consequences that matter a lot to your protagonist. If you spend time away from your protagonist and force your reader to watch scenes that truly do not matter to the protagonist, you are not enriching your book. You are killing it.

Killer mistake #2: major characters have no story

The second lethal mistake is this. You, the writer, are mostly interested in Carmela, a reporter who stumbles into a murder-mystery plot. But Carmela has an on-off relationship with Bobby, and there are bits of the story that happen to Bobby, not to Carmela. So you give 50% of your page space to Carmela, 30% or 40% to Bobby, and the rest is divided up amongst some minor characters.

This approach could work, as long as you get the reader fully as engaged with Bobby as with Carmela. That means you, the writer, need to care the same amount. Bobby needs his own fully developed inner life, his own overwhelming motivations, his own obstacles and challenges, his own resolutions and disappointments. His story needs to be crafted with the same care and intensity that you've lavished on Carmela. If the simple fact is that Bobby only exists in the story as a useful narrative device and as a way to amplify various bits of Carmela's character, the reader will see through you. They'll throw the novel away, because you've spent too much time talking about a character who doesn't matter.

Mixing first and third

Finally, though it's not a common technique, you can mix first and third person. Herman Melville did that (albeit chaotically) in *Moby Dick*. A more recent, and more fluent, example is Alice Sebold's *The Lovely Bones*, where the narrator is dead and in heaven. When she's talking about her new life in heaven, her narrator sounds like any other first-person narrator: 'When I first entered heaven I thought everyone saw what I saw.' When she's looking down on earth and relating what's happening there, the narration becomes effectively third-person: 'While everyone else slept, Lindsey stood at the mirror in the bathroom, looking at herself'. It's true that first-person narration keeps popping up ('In the mirror she saw something different and so did I …'), but the narrator is so removed from the action that most of the book *feels* pretty third-person. Barbara Kingsolver's *The Poisonwood Bible* is another successful recent example of a writer who mixes first and third.

On the whole, though, this is an exotic technique, and if you need to read about how to use it, you're probably better off leaving it well alone.

Playing it safe

If all the foregoing seems too complex and more than a little scary, then let's keep it simple. Your options are:

Easy and safe

These are options which don't throw up any major technical challenges when it comes to handling points of view. Most writers will handle these techniques with ease. And 'easy' doesn't mean that you can't write a wonderful, complex and challenging book. It just means the complexities lie elsewhere.

- First-person narration
  One single viewpoint (eg: *Room*)

- Third-person narration
  Strictly one viewpoint only (eg: *Brooklyn*)
  One main POV + some minor ones (eg: *The Watchman*)
  Two main POVs + minor ones to taste (eg: *On Chesil Beach*)

Pretty easy and pretty safe

You're still on pretty safe ground with the options in this group, but the technical demands on your writing have grown a little. In first-person narration, you need to make sure each voice is distinct. (That is, each character has to sound like themself.) In both first- and third-person narration, you have to make sure that each major character has a fully defined and compelling story of their own. You can't have characters who are there only to support the others. With thrillers and comparable work, you have to make sure that your additional points of view are always driving the main narrative forwards.

- First-person narration

  Two alternating viewpoints (eg: *The Time Traveler's Wife*)

- Third-person narration

  Three POVs, more or less alternating (eg: *Lions of Al-Rassan*)

- Thriller (or other externally driven story)

  Multiple POVs, but strong, decisive centre (eg: *The Firm*)

Requires deft handling and technical confidence

As you multiply viewpoints, you greatly increase the risk of your manuscript dissolving into an uncentred mess. You'll avoid that outcome by having a high-impact story and excellent characters. If you're writing in the first person, you'll need a talent for ventriloquism. If you're writing in the third person, you'll need a story that demands a large cast list and supplies cast members who can be drawn swiftly, memorably – and then discarded. If you're doing anything more exotic than that, you'll need a bagful of talent to pull it off.

- First-person narration

  More than two alternating viewpoints (eg: *English Passengers, Maynard & Jennica*)

- Third-person narration

  Very large number of POVs (eg: *The Bear and the Dragon*)

- Mixed first- and third-person narration

  Different narratives modes in same book (eg: *The Lovely Bones, The Poisonwood Bible)*

- Second-person narration, 'you' (eg: *Bright Lights, Big City)*

- First-person-plural narration, 'we' (eg: *The Virgin Suicides)*

Chapter Summary

- Whether you are writing in first person or third, you can have one, two or many protagonists.

- The more you have, the more you risk losing focus. Two or three protagonists will be the upper limit for most novelists.

- Make sure you don't give minor characters too much page space or fail to give a story to your major characters.

- If in doubt, go for an easy/safe option. You don't win points for technical trickery. You do win points for writing a terrific story.

Up close, Far out, and the Myth of Omniscience

I had been a novelist for some time before I'd heard anyone talk to me about the omniscient narrator. I'd written five novels. I'd set up a thriving editorial company. I had my first non-fiction book chugging its way towards completion. And an editorial client asked me whether I thought limited third person or omniscient third person was the best away to go for their book. That question baffled me then and baffles me now. I hope that by the end of this chapter, it will baffle you too. But let's start by explaining terms. (Unless you are writing in the first person, that is. If you are, the themes of this chapter don't pertain to you. First-person narration is always narration from a personal, limited, human perspective. Other than under exceptional circumstances, it can't be otherwise. Everyone else, though, should read on.)

Chasing whales

In the good old days, when Melville was out chasing whales, Dickens was London's darling, and Tolstoy was trying to think of a catchy title for his book about Napoleon's invasion of Russia, narrators were omniscient. They knew everything. Dickens famously opened his *A Tale of Two Cities* with the lines, 'It was the best of times, it was the worst of times, it was the age of wisdom, it was the age of foolishness, it was the epoch of belief, it was the epoch of incredulity, it was the season of Light, it was the season of Darkness.' It's as though his narrator is hovering above London (or all of England?), seeing everything, judging every-thing, knowing everything.

Such grandeur has fallen out of fashion. The modern narrator tends to stick much closer to their protagonist. Khaled Hosseini's *A Thousand Splendid Suns* is an epic account of love and friendship in modern Afghanistan. In its way, its scope is every bit as grand as *A Tale of Two Cities*, yet its approach is intimate right from the very first sentence: 'Mariam was five years old the first time she heard the word *harami*. It happened on a Thursday'. It's as though Hosseini's narrator simply knows less than Dickens's, has fewer resources, sees less.

To put the same thing in cinematic terms, Dickens is like a director for some massive-budget Netflix epic. He opens his book with a wide-angle panning shot from a helicopter-mounted camera. If he wants to see into the bedrooms of chambermaids, the dressing rooms of dukes, or Her Majesty's royal parlour, he's got crews available to do just that. There's nothing he can't know or can't see. Hosseini's position seems to be the exact reverse. He's a micro-indie filmmaker, able to afford nothing more than a handheld camera. He has no lens to handle anything more distant than a medium range shot. More often than not, he's shooting his story in close-up. It's become conventional to say that where the Victorian narrator was omniscient, the modern narrator is limited. It's become conventional to say that limited narration works better for the modern novel. It sounds duller, but that's just that way it is.

Limited, schlimited

There are just two problems with the omniscient/limited way of looking at things. In the first place, it isn't true. In the second place, it doesn't help.

Let's start with the truth. A page or two on into *A Thousand Splendid Suns*, Hosseini says:

> *It was true. She didn't remember. And though she would live the first fifteen years of her life within walking distance of Herat, Mariam would never see this storied* [pistachio] *tree. She would*

never see the famous minarets up close, and she would never pick
fruit from Herat's orchards or stroll in its fields of wheat.

That's not as grand as Dickens, I grant you, but it's still omniscient. Hosseini's narrator can survey fifteen years at a glance, no
matter that ten of those years lie in the future. He knows about
the orchards and wheat fields of Herat, even though Mariam
herself is completely unaware of them. He knows about the
history of Herat's famous pistachio tree. He knows about the
town's minarets and their international reputation. He doesn't
make a big song and dance about knowing these things, but he's
not short of knowledge.

It's not just Hosseini's narrator who turns out to be a heck of a
lot more knowing than he first appears. A couple of chapters
back, we looked at this comment of Ian McEwan in *On Chesil
Beach*:

> *In just a few years' time, that* [running down to the beach
> with a bottle of wine] *would be just the kind of thing quite
> ordinary people would do. But for now, the times held them.*

McEwan's narrator is predicting the future – and predicting it not
simply for one girl, as Hosseini had done for Mariam, but
predicting it for the entire British people, perhaps even for the
whole of Western civilisation. Even Dickens didn't attempt that.

The touch of the intimate

So, let's forget the whole idea of omniscience. All third-person
narrators are as omniscient as they care to be. The only question is
why Dickens and his contemporaries often chose to go big and
why Hosseini and his contemporaries generally choose to go
small.

We've already hinted at the answer. In the last chapter, we
saw that as you multiply the number of viewpoints in a book, you
risk diluting the reader's identification with the main character (or
characters). What you gain in scale, you may lose in impact. And,

indeed, since novels only work by creating intense identification with the protagonist, your losses are potentially much greater than your gains.

Something similar is true when it comes to narration. The more intrusive your narrator, the more your character risks being thrust into the background. It can happen very quickly and very insidiously. Let's take another, rather longer, look at Hosseini's passage about the orchards of Herat. Including the bit before and the bit just after, that passage runs like this. (I'll come to the underlinings I've added in a moment.)

> *'There is a pistachio tree,' Jalil said one day, 'and beneath it, Mariam jo, is buried none other than the great poet Jami.' He leaned in and whispered. 'Jami lived over five hundred years ago. He did. I took you there once, to the tree. You were little. You wouldn't remember.'*
>
> *It was true. She didn't remember. <u>And though she would live the first fifteen years of her life within walking distance of Herat, Mariam would never see this storied tree. She would never see the famous minarets up close, and she would never pick fruit from Herat's orchards or stroll in its fields of wheat</u>. But whenever Jalil talked like this, Mariam would listen with enchantment. She would admire Jalil for his vast and worldly knowledge. She would quiver with pride to have a father who knew such things.*
>
> *'What rich lies!' Nana said after Jalil left. 'Rich men telling rich lies. He never took you to any tree.'*

An ordinary reader reading the novel will barely notice the interruption – yet what an interruption it is! Up until the underlined section, and then again immediately afterwards, we are completely absorbed into Mariam's experience. We share her fascination, her enchantment. We feel the brutality of her mother's correction. The underlined section rips us away from that closeness. We're no longer with Mariam – we couldn't be, because she doesn't know her future and she's never been to Herat. Instead of intimacy, we have something very far removed from it, far from character. In this case, it's as though Hosseini is giving us a snippet from some Afghan version of *Snow White* – a fairy story, not a novel.

Furthermore, it's not even clear why Hosseini thinks he needs to jump into the future like this. He's about to tell us about those fifteen years and he's about to give us a tour of Herat. There's no information which matters to Mariam which he can't tell us simply by staying close to her story and telling us whatever is important to her at any given moment. In due course, we'd have learned about all the things Mariam didn't do. In due course, we'd have learned all we needed to know about Herat.

It's the same with the McEwan. In the first half of his novella, McEwan repetitively tells the reader that the social world of his protagonists was a few years away from fundamental re-ordering. But why bother to tell us? Perhaps there are some readers unaware that the 1960s saw some rather important changes in society. If so, there are probably better places than *On Chesil Beach* to find out about them. For everyone else, it's the same deal as with Hosseini. McEwan's narrator intrudes on the story. He talks over his characters. Every time his narrator starts to tell us about how the 1960s were going to pan out, his characters shrink and fade until the narrator shuts up and allows them to get on with their story.

These examples might tend to suggest that omniscient narrators simply can't work today, even if they ever did. But that's not right. It's simply a question of understanding the trade-offs and understanding the techniques.

We'll start with the simplest model: intimacy, pure and simple.

The Baltimore Beltway

If you don't want an intrusive narrator, one option is simply to ditch the helicopter and the Steadicam, to ditch the boom mikes and the directional mikes, to ditch all the paraphernalia of omniscience. Colm Tóibín's *Brooklyn* is one novel where the camera never leaves its protagonist's face. Anne Tyler's Baltimore-set *Noah's Compass* is another one where you can read the entire book looking for a single sentence – a single phrase – which betrays the narrator's quiet supremacy. You won't find it. Although *Noah's Compass* is (beautifully) told in the third person, not a line of it has the narrator telling us anything that the protagonist, Liam Pennywell, can't see, know or feel himself. It reads like this:

> *His mattress was comfortably firm, and the top sheet was tucked in tightly on either side of him as he liked. His pillow had just enough bounce to it. The window, a couple of feet away, was cranked open to let the breeze blow in, and it offered a view of a pale night sky with a few stars visible behind the sparse black pine boughs – just a scattering of pinpricks. He was glad now that Damian had taken such trouble to situate the bed right.*
>
> *Most probably, he reflected, this would be the final dwelling place of his life.*

Writing like this is not remotely broad in scope. Quite the opposite. It's a perfectly painted miniature, utterly intimate with its single protagonist. The narrative viewpoint is restricted, not because Tyler's narrator has given up on omniscience, but because she has chosen to embrace intimacy. If Tyler's protagonist has some very boring thoughts ('his pillow had just enough bounce in it'), Tyler will simply stick up close as he has them. If Tyler's protagonist is incapable of poetic, lyrical expression, Tyler will eschew it too. Her aim is to stay anonymous, to avoid the limelight. If she ratcheted up her performance levels – if she invited you to notice that she was there at all – she'd have failed in what she set out to do.

And to be clear: these comments aren't intended as disparagement, but as praise. Tyler has the courage of her convictions and is prepared to accept the consequences. The result of her doggedness is a jewel of close observation and intimacy.

That's the first option.

Cricklewood Broadway

The second option is to welcome the ghost of Dickens. To embrace that rambunctious, noisy, splashy spirit, but to do so in a way that doesn't sacrifice intimacy *when needed*. Zadie Smith begins her smash-hit debut, *White Teeth*, with the account of an attempted suicide. Here is her opening paragraph:

> *Early in the morning, late in the century, Cricklewood Broadway. At 06.27 hours on 1 January 1975, Alfred Archibald Jones was dressed in corduroy and sat in a fume-filled Cavalier Musketeer Estate face down on the steering wheel, hoping the judgement would not be too heavy on him. He lay forward in a prostrate cross, jaw slack, arms splayed either side like some fallen angel; scrunched up in each fist he held his army service medals (left) and his marriage licence (right), for he had decided to take his mistakes with him. A little green light flashed in his eye, signalling a right turn he had resolved never to make. He was resigned to it. He was prepared for it. He had flipped a coin and stood staunchly by its conclusions. This was a decided-upon suicide. In fact it was a New Year's resolution.*

What a terrific opening that is! The very first sentence announces Smith's intention to make her narratorial presence felt. She's funny. She's mocking. She's disregarding her character – leaving him face down on the steering wheel, in fact – in order to highlight the various inadequacies of his situation. (His car is a bad one, his clothes are regrettable, and Cricklewood Broadway is as unlovable and embarrassing as its name somehow suggests.)

Smith's non-intimacy with character pervades everything in this paragraph. 'Early in the morning, late in the century' suggests a narrative standpoint at least as grand, high and remote as Dickens's 'best of times, worst of times'. Even when she comes to discuss the suicide itself, she stands *outside* the would-be victim, looking down at him from above. We don't, at this stage, have any interior insight into his thoughts, feelings or sensations. All we're being offered is the jauntily mocking viewpoint of a loftily distant narrator. We don't know what it's like to *be* Alfred Archibald Jones getting ready to die in his corduroy clothes, in his crappy car, in the wrong bit of London. We don't know because Smith hasn't deigned to tell us.

Had she maintained that opening tone for long – if she'd maintained it for two or three pages, even – it would have begun to grate. It would have felt as though she was grandstanding. Neglecting her characters in order to solicit our applause. But Smith is way too smart for that. If the first paragraph gives us the lofty view, the second one zooms in for an extreme close-up. Here (edited for length) is how Smith continues:

> But even as his breathing became spasmodic and his lights dimmed, Archie was aware that Cricklewood Broadway would seem a strange choice. [...] It was not a place a man came to die. It was a place a man came in order to go other places via the A41. But Archie Jones didn't want to die in some pleasant, distant woodland, or on a cliff edge fringed with delicate heather. The way Archie saw it, country people should die in the country and city people should die in the city. Only proper. In death as he was in life and all that. It made sense that Archibald should die on this nasty urban street where he had ended up, living alone at the age of forty-seven, in a one-bedroom flat above a deserted chip shop.

Already, in those closing lines, Smith has us as intimate with her Archie as Tyler had us with her Liam. They came by different routes, but the end-point was the same.

This is option two.

Changing focus

Now let's look a little more closely at how Zadie Smith does what she does. That second paragraph of hers moves through three layers of increasing intimacy:

243

- *'Even as his breathing became spasmodic'*. We're no longer hovering somewhere above Archie Jones, splayed out on his steering wheel; we're right by him, listening out for the changing rhythm of his breathing.

- *'Archie was aware that Cricklewood Broadway would seem a strange choice'*. We've now crossed a threshold, from being right next to Archie but outside him, to being right inside his head. We're aware of his thoughts and ruminations, right now, in the moment of his dying.

- *'Only proper. In death as he was in life and all that'*. You might think that if we're already right inside his head, there's no place more intimate to go. But there is. When Smith says 'Archie was aware that …', the structure of the sentence externalises Archie. It calls attention to the fact that there are two entities: Archie *being* aware and the narrator *telling* us about it. In this final step, Zadie Smith has killed that distinction altogether. Those thoughts – 'Only proper. In death as he was in life and all that' – belong to Archie. The narrator has stepped out of the equation altogether. We are getting unmediated access to Archie's dying thoughts. We are as intimate with Archie as it is possible to be. For fictional purposes, we have temporarily become Archie. (If you like to know the technical term for this type of writing, it's 'free indirect discourse'. But you don't need to know the term. All that matters is that you can feel when something works and when it doesn't.)

Two things are crucial to notice in all this. The first – the big thing, if you like – is that she does get intimate, and fast. One and a half paragraphs into her book, and we're hearing Archie's dying thoughts as our own. That's intimate.

The second is that there's a rhythm to these things. Zadie Smith moves from extreme distance to extreme close-up quickly, *but not jerkily*. She avoids jerks by doing it in stages. From 'late in the century' to 'face down on the steering wheel'. From the steering wheel to those spasmodic breaths. From breaths to an awareness. From an awareness to the living stuff of thought itself.

Just imagine how crunchingly awkward this would have sounded if Smith had tried to skip some of these intermediate gears. If we simply cut some intervening chunks, we could, for example, produce this:

> *Early in the morning, late in the century, Cricklewood Broadway. At 06.27 hours on 1 January 1975, Alfred Archibald Jones was dressed in corduroy and sat in a fume-filled Cavalier Musketeer Estate ready to die. It was only proper. In death as he was in life and all that. It made sense that Archibald should die on this nasty urban street where he had ended up, living alone at the age of forty-seven, in a one-bedroom flat above a deserted chip shop.*

I hope you can feel how grating this feels. (If it doesn't feel grating, it may be that the passage feels over-familiar to you by now. If so, mark this chunk and read it cold in a day or two.) It feels awkward, because Smith hasn't yet earned the right to quote Archie's inner thoughts. The first two sentences belong, very clearly, to the narrator, not to Archie. Inevitably, then, the reader will read the next sentence in the same voice. When we read 'It was only proper', we understand the narrator herself to be commenting on the action. Somewhere in the course of the next sentence or so, we'll probably figure out that the viewpoint has switched, but by this point, the damage has been done. We've been tripped up in the very first paragraph – and though an agent may stumble on for another page or two (that is one heck of an opening sentence, after all), her hand is already moving the manuscript towards the rejection pile.

If you want to know why Hosseini and McEwan stumbled in their attempts at omniscience, it's because they stumbled jerkily from intimacy to distance and back again. The reader was unprepared for the sudden shift and the shift, in any case, was too fleeting, too provisional to contribute much to the book. Smith handles her omniscience much better, because she moves smoothly through the gears and makes much more purposeful use of her narrator's power.

The entertainer

Three final thoughts to close the chapter.

First, there's not much point in making a big song and dance about your narrative voice, unless you've got a voice that sounds good when singing. Zadie Smith's *White Teeth* was a sensational debut largely because her narrative voice was funny, provocative, original and confident. Having claimed the stage, she then went on to own it. If you demand the stage, but your narrative voice has nothing much to recommend it, your audience will leave disappointed. (You can be quiet and classy too, of course; it's the classy part that matters.)

Secondly, although I've spoken as though there are only two options available to the writer, that's not true. There's a whole range of options, with Zadie Smith at one extreme and Anne Tyler at the other. Most contemporary authors nestle closer to Tyler than they do to Smith, but that's not to say that their end of the spectrum is better than the other. It's all a question of what your story is and how best to tell it. It's your call.

Third, this is a long chapter, but the essence of it is simple. If you're feeling slightly dazed at this point, read the summary. And if anyone asks you about the limited third person versus the omniscient third person, then express bafflement and confusion. You're a writer: of course you're omniscient.

Chapter Summary

- Contrary to what you may read elsewhere, the omniscient narrator is not dead – nor is omniscience a useful concept in thinking about your book.

- The issue isn't omniscience, but intimacy. Is your third-person narrator going to be very intimate with your main character (*à la* Anne Tyler)? Or is your narrator going to be capable of being very distant (*à la* Zadie Smith)?

- If you go for the first of those two options, you need to commit to it. That means you need to make the narrative voice unobtrusive, you need to stick like glue to your character's perspective, and you need to minimise any gap between how your character talks/thinks/perceives the world and how your narrator does. There doesn't have to be any gap at all.

- If you go for the second of those options, remember that intimacy with character *always* stands at the heart of a novel. If you have passages that are narrated at extreme distance from your characters, you have to compensate by getting up close and personal very soon afterwards. And you need to spend much more of your time being intimate than being distant. That's what novels are for.

- If you're going to go for it, then feel free to go for it. It's fine if your narratorial voice is loud, classy, and entertaining. Swagger is good.

- As you move from intimacy to distance, or vice versa, you need to do so smoothly. Zoom in smoothly, zoom out smoothly. If you try anything too abrupt, you'll trip your reader up. (A chapter break doesn't count though. That's like a stage-curtain going down. You can set up the stage any way you like when it rises again.)

- Tyler and Smith represent two ends of a spectrum. If you want to occupy the middle ground, you can.
- If you're hesitating about how to write your story, then remember: (A) If you don't have a strong narrative voice in mind, then there's not much point in seeking to promote it. (B) The Anne Tyler end of the spectrum poses fewer risks to the first-time writer.

PAST OR PRESENT?

From the complexities of narrative voice to the simplicities of tense.

The options

There are two ways you can write a book. In the present tense, like this:

> *Inside the changing room for female staff, I toss soiled scrubs into a biohazard hamper and strip of the rest of my clothes and medical clogs. I wonder if Col. Scarpetta stenciled in black on my locker will be removed the minute I return to New England in the morning. The thought hadn't entered my mind before now, and it bothers me.*

Patricia Cornwell, *Port Mortuary*, 2010

Or you can write it in the past tense. Like this:

> *The Monday I carried Ronnie Joe Waddell's meditation in my pocketbook, I never saw the sun. It was dark out when I drove to work that morning. It was dark again when I drove home. Small raindrops spun in my headlights, the night gloomy with fog and bitterly cold.*

Patricia Cornwell, *Cruel and Unusual*, 1993

As Patricia Cornwell's own transition suggests, the past tense used to be the standard tense of storytelling. Pretty much every writer adopted it as standard. Those who didn't were deliberately doing something showily different. And quite recently, perhaps just in the last decade, that's changed. It's changed in the books that line the bookshelves. It's changed in terms of the manuscripts that arrive on the desks of literary agents or editorial consultancies. I don't know why it's happened.

The unexpressive scream

And not everyone likes it. Philip Pullman, author of the bestselling *His Dark Materials* trilogy, has argued:

> *If every sound you emit is a scream, a scream has no expressive value. What I dislike about the present-tense narrative is its limited range of expressiveness. I feel claustrophobic, always pressed up against the immediate [...].*
>
> *I want* [storytellers] *to feel able to say what happened, what usually happened, what sometimes happened, what had happened before something else happened, what might happen later, what actually did happen later, and so on: to use the full range of English tenses [...]*
>
> *It's an abdication of narrative responsibility, in my view. The storyteller, in film or novel, should take charge of the story and not feel shifty about it. Put the camera in the place from which it can see the action most clearly. Make a decision about where that place is. Put it on something steady to stop that incessant jiggling about. Say what happened, and let the reader know when it happened and what caused it and what the consequences were, and tell me where the characters were and who else was present – and while you're at it, I'd like to know what they looked like and whether it was raining.*

[*The Guardian*, 14 September 2010]

Pullman clearly has a point. Your writing will not become vivid just by altering a tense. If it was bland in the past tense, it will be bland in the present tense. If it was compelling and immediate in the past tense, you won't burst through to some new ionosphere of excellence by shifting gear to the present. On the other hand, most of what Pullman is objecting to here is not present-tense writing, but *bad* present-tense writing. And it's easier to write badly in the present tense than in the past.

How to write badly

Back when we were thinking about prose style, we agreed to loathe the following snippet:

> *I am standing by the window. I am not certain whether the pills have started working already. I feel a fluttering in my heart but I cannot tell whether that's the pills already. I decide it will not hurt to take another, so I do. I continue to stand at the window. I gaze out, feeling my heart.*

We didn't like that, because of the rhythmical monotony. *I* this, *I* that, *I* the other. But it's not just the monotony of sound that makes this a terrible passage; it's the monotony of viewpoint. That sense which Pullman identifies as being always pressed up against the immediate. There are only a few dozen words in the text above, but it's already painful to read. A whole novel of it would be like being forced to eat a bowlful of brick dust.

When flipping from present to past, or vice versa, you can't just switch tenses on some kind of grammatical autopilot. You have to keep an ear out for what works and what doesn't. Here, for example, is a reasonably sympathetic rewriting of that passage, but switched back into the past:

> *I stood at the window, uncertain whether the pills had started working. My heart was fluttering, but it would have been any-way. I couldn't tell about the pills. I decided it wouldn't hurt to take another, so I did. And there I stayed: leaning up against the living room window, gazing out, feeling my heart.*

Compare the two passages. You should be able to see exactly why Pullman would prefer the second version to the first. The present-tense passage:

- Only ever has one grammatical subject ('I am standing …', 'I am not certain …', etc).

- Only ever has its camera trained on the immediate, the personal, the stream-of-consciousness thought/feeling/ sensation.

- Only ever has one unit of time: the moment-to-moment 'now'.

The past-tense passage, by contrast:

- Has a variety of grammatical subjects ('I stood', 'the pills had…', 'My heart was …', etc).

- Has a rather broader range of focus. Although this passage is clearly focused on a particular train of thoughts and feelings, that final sentence ('And there I stayed: leaning up against …') externalises things a bit. By presenting the same information in a more neutral, less subjective, and more external way, it removes some of the icky teenage-diary feeling of the first passage.

- Uses a variety of temporal periods. In the second passage, time is no longer a single dot of present-tense consciousness. It's become variable, elastic. It can shrink to a precise, fleeting moment: so, for example, the phrase 'so I did' refers to the tiny moment of time it takes to pop a pill. But time, in the past tense, can also easily expand. 'I stood at the window, uncertain whether the pills had started working.' Does that sentence refer to a minute or an hour? It could be either. If it was helpful to specify the exact period, then it would have been easy to do so, but the point is that the past tense releases time from the imprisoning present moment. If, for example, you say 'I *was* a good mother', you might equally well be referring to yesterday's beautifully arranged birthday party – or to thirty years of patient, thoughtful love. The past accommodates any unit of time with ease, without awkwardness.

How to write well

These sound like overwhelming arguments for the past tense. And, I'll admit, I'm somewhat old-fashioned in my sympathies and, despite the shifting fashions, I continue to feel that the past is and should be the default tense for any novel. Quite apart from anything else, that's how stories have always been told. In short, if you don't have a strong reason for working in the present tense, choosing the past can never be wrong.

But I'm not a zealot. We've just compared two passages and strongly preferred the variety and flexibility of the past-tense version. But the problem with the present-tense version is that it was written in such a way as to squeeze out every last drop of expressive flexibility. It wasn't the tense which did that; it was the lousy writing, as though the writer has been captured by the tense, not the other way around.

It doesn't have to be that way. It could be like this:

> *You can think what I tell you a confession, if you like, but one full of curiosities familiar only in dreams and during those moments when a dog's profile plays in the steam of a kettle. Or when a corn-husk doll sitting on a shelf is soon splaying in corner of a room and the wicked of how it got there is plain. Stranger things happen all the time everywhere. You know. I know you know. One question is who is responsible. Another is can you read* [the sign]*?*

This excerpt comes from Toni Morrison's *A Mercy*. And though Philip Pullman may have collected a Whitbread Prize and a Carnegie Medal for his writing, Toni Morrison has bagged a Pulitzer and a Nobel Prize for hers, which beats Pullman's haul and rather suggests that Pullman's comment about a 'limited range of expressiveness' has more to do with the writer than the tense.

To see how you can write fluidly in the present, take a close look at Morrison's prose. It's grammatically varied. There's no loss of rhythmical variety or texture. Quite the opposite: that phrase 'the wicked of how it got there' is both expressive and unexpected. The entire passage is every bit as varied and flavoursome as any well-written fiction, past or present.

Nor does the work lack focal variety. Although the passage is first-person present tense, the focus isn't always me-me-me. Indeed, the word 'I' is only twice mentioned, and both times in relation to someone else. That icky teenage self-absorption is nowhere to be seen.

Nor does the unit of time any longer feel like a single moving dot of consciousness. 'Stranger things happen all the time everywhere', her narrator says. Technically speaking, I suppose, that means now, this instant. Except it doesn't. That's not how we read it. The sentence reads like a universal statement, something true of all time, all places. The single moving dot of consciousness has expanded to fill all time, all space.

How to write like you

The moral of this chapter, I think, is simple. The present tense can be every bit as flexible and expressive as the past tense. It won't bring you any instant gain in immediacy, but nor will it bring any automatic losses either. It all depends on how you use it.

What's more, you have a *choice*. Writing in the present may be more fashionable than it used to be, but that doesn't mean you have to write that way to stay on trend. Harlan Coben writes in the past tense. So does Linwood Barclay. So does George Pelecanos. So does Michael Marshall Smith. So does R. J. Ellory. So does – but I don't need to continue. These writers are among the very best exponents of the contemporary thriller. If the present tense were truly necessary to create immediacy in our modern age, presumably these guys would be using it. And they're not. They write in the past tense. Patricia Cornwell may have made the change in her writing, but you're not her. You can do what you like.

Having said that, less capable writers are more likely to make a mess of the present tense than of the past. The narrow focus, the press of the immediate, the self-absorbed 'I' – all these things are more likely to be problematic when a writer is using the present tense. That's not my prejudices speaking, it's my experience of seeing countless first-time manuscripts cross my desk. Even quite good amateur writers seem to stumble with tense. I've seen writers convert a somewhat creaky present-tense manuscript into a past-tense one, and in the process find a fluency and inventiveness that had been absent before. For what it's worth, I'd say the past tense is still the safer option for beginners.

If you're still hesitating, experiment. If you've started writing in the past tense, take a random scene and rewrite it in the present tense, or vice versa. Play around. See what you like, see what works for you. It's certainly far better to spend a day or two conducting the experiment than to write an entire manuscript in a voice that doesn't work for you.

And you never know. You might just surprise yourself. For a long time, I was firmly in the Pullman camp. Present-tense writing set my teeth on edge. Like him, I'd tend to avoid novels that used it. And then – I wrote a novel in the present tense. Then I wrote five more. I'm currently writing another. I made the choice deliberately and with aforethought. (In my case, I was narrating from the viewpoint of someone with a scanty hold on her own past and future. I *wanted* the dot of consciousness effect. It was a core part of what makes my protagonist who she is.) And I liked the result. I've been converted from a past-tensophobe into a tense-agnostic. I like it better that way.

Chapter Summary

- Present-tense writing has become more common.
- Writing in the present tense is not some magical way to make your writing vivid or immediate.
- Good writing in the present tense will (i) have a variety of grammatical subjects, (ii) have a broad range of focus, and (iii) make use of a variety of temporal periods and ranges.
- If you're not sure which tense would work best for you, then try it both ways. Go with whichever style suits you better.
- And if you're still in doubt, stick with the past tense. It's generally safer.

The Time Traveller's Reader

If the eighteenth century created the novel, and the nineteenth century turned it into arguably humanity's most important art form – the only one capable of tackling every possible social, political, emotional and philosophical issue – it was left to the twentieth century to tackle the art form itself. Which of its features were essential? Which contingent? What would a novel look like if some of the standard tricks of the trade were abandoned or twisted out of shape?

In a surge of experiment, a large number of modernist works of fiction were written. Some great. Some unreadable. Some great *and* unreadable. Some modernist devices became standard fare for everyday novelists today; others have remained literary curiosities, museum pieces rather than living art. One of the great and lasting innovations, however, has been the introduction of non-linear narrative.

In a standard, linear narrative, things are simple. The story starts from the beginning and runs through to the end, relating everything important that happened en route, in chronological order. Obviously enough, that's how we experience time. Obviously enough, that's the natural way to tell a story. But not the only way. In Joseph Conrad's path-breaking *Lord Jim*, for example, the story is told by one character (Marlow) about a second one (Jim). Marlow is talking to a group of listeners, and those listeners interject with their own stories about Jim. Not only are these secondary stories nested within the overall Marlow story, but they are not arranged chronologically. One speaker might jump back in time, another jump forward. The effect is as of a collage slowly taking shape – a patchwork of different bits of evidence, which don't necessarily all point to the same set of conclusions. *Lord Jim* is a terrific novel, of course. Not merely a masterpiece in artistic terms, but a galloping good read too. Fiction at its very best.

Nor is non-linear storytelling any longer a province of high art. It's become a perfectly common part of storytelling on film: *Pulp Fiction* is one well-known example. Others include *Annie Hall*, almost anything by Robert Altman, *Memento*, *Inception*, and plenty of others besides. Like all literary techniques, however, non-linearity has its place. A novel isn't better for being non-linear. It's better for being better. A non-chronological narrative might be essential part of why a novel works, or it could well be an irritating distraction. The question for the novelist is knowing when to fool around with time and when to leave it well alone.

Flashforwards

Donna Tartt's splendid *The Secret History* tells the story of six classics students at an upmarket college in New England. It's a murder story, but one with a twist. The victim ('Bunny' Corcoran) doesn't die until midway through the book, yet Tartt's opening sentences tell us:

> *The snow in the mountains was melting and Bunny had been dead for several weeks before we came to understand the gravity of our situation. He'd been dead for ten days before they found him, you know. It was one of the biggest manhunts in Vermont history — state troopers, the FBI, even an army helicopter; the college closed, the dye factory in Hampden shut down, people coming from New Hampshire, upstate New York, as far away as Boston.*
>
> *It is difficult to believe that Henry's modest plan could have worked so well despite these unforeseen events. We hadn't intended to hide the body where it couldn't be found. In fact, we hadn't hidden it at all but had simply left it where it fell in hopes that some luckless passer-by would stumble over it before anyone even noticed he was missing.*

This is only a snippet of non-linearity. The rest of the book starts at the beginning and runs through to the end. All the same, it's a bold and crucial gamble, because – duh! – this is a murder mystery. Why give away the mystery on line one, page one? Isn't that the opposite of what these books are meant to do?

But look carefully at what Tartt has done. She's transformed the nature of the question the reader will be asking themselves about the unfolding narrative. Without this opening, the reader would have been asking themselves a question like, 'What is this group of introverted and over-intense college students going to get up to next?' With this opening, however, the question becomes, 'Why do these students murder Bunny?'. It's pretty obvious that the second of these questions is stronger, darker and more compelling. The book relies on it. (Or rather: the first half of the book. After the killing, the question becomes 'Will these students get away with it?' The book isn't a whodunit; it's a whydunit, then a whathappenstothosewhodunit?)

Tartt's book is a particularly good example of how a flashforward (however brief and however partial in the extent of the information revealed) can transform the essence of a book, but flashforwards of this kind are relatively common. Aravind Adiga in *The White Tiger* does exactly the same as Tartt: his narrator tells the reader that he is a wanted criminal. The question is no longer, 'What is going to happen?', but 'How did this man come to commit a serious crime?' Non-chronological moves of this sort add an entire layer of interest to a novel, and can work wonders for it. Donna Tartt's book would have been a vastly weaker book had it not been for that question-shifting prologue.

In *The Devil Wears Prada*, Weisberger's narrator does something that looks similar, but isn't. In her prologue, the narrator (Andrea Sachs) describes just how awful it is to work for her boss (Miranda Priestly). The prologue is fun, but it's not at all clear it alters the book's fundamental question. If the prologue is meant to raise the question, 'How does nice girl Andrea Sachs end up working for this dragon?' – well, that's answered by the first chapter. If the point is to indicate that this woman, Miranda

Priestly, is terrible – well, that's amply indicated by the first chapter as well. The flashforward does almost nothing to shift the way that the reader absorbs the story that follows. Indeed, all Weisberger's prologue really does is make a slightly desperate promise to the reader: 'If this book starts slowly, please don't worry, because there's some juicy stuff to come.' Needless to say, if that's the issue, you need to fix the slow start. Adding a prologue in simply delays things further. (I should confess that I'm guilty of exactly this sin myself. My oil-industry novel, *The Sons of Adam*, throws in a flashforward for no reason other than to put some action early in the book. I didn't like it at the time and don't like it now.)

In short, as a rough rule of thumb, flashforwards early in a book work if they transform the reader's interpretation of what follows. If they don't, they're probably redundant.

Flashbacks

Flashbacks have less potential than flashforwards to confuse the reader, because we all have the capacity to time travel backwards through memory. So if you're talking about your protagonist, Jane Doe, and you want to include a scene or two from her student days, the shock to the reader is not so acute as it would be if you included a flashforward to something in her future.

All the same, every departure from chronology interrupts the forward flow of your story. Most of the time, your reader will be reading about Jane Doe and wanting to know what happens to her next. Every time you jump back into the past, you are refusing to answer that question. The temptation for the reader will always be to skip some pages to get back to the story itself. Naturally, a shorter flashback will be less intrusive than a longer one. Less frequent flashbacks will be less intrusive than numerous ones.

Because non-linear narrations have become so commonplace in storytelling these days, these rules aren't always followed. There are plenty of thrillers, particularly, which will tell a regular action-adventure story (Ed McToughguy on the trail of Sean O'Nasty, let's say) but interweave a whole series of short, italicised snippets about Ed McToughguy's past. (He saw service in the Middle East. He saw things no one should have seen. He dealt with loss and trauma. He's got a sensitive heart, bless him, for all his collection of Glock semi-automatics.) This type of structure is now common enough that I can't pretend it will debar you from publication. But do you really need it? Does it add to the book? Are there not less intrusive ways of bringing McToughguy's past into the narrative?

The best answers may be the simplest ones. Instead of having a two-page italicised flashback, you could incorporate some of the more telling information in one or two paragraph chunks in the ordinary flow of the narrative. The reader will absorb those paragraphs not as formal flashbacks, but as information that fills out the character on the page *now*. The story isn't interrupted. The information is greedily absorbed. I'd say that for every five books I've read that include a large number of flashbacks, maybe only one of the five truly justifies the author's interference with chronology. Remember: readers want to know what happens *next*. Flashbacks give them the exact opposite. They're nice for authors, but seldom right for the reader. And the reader always, always has to be the boss.

Dual narratives

Another common example of non-chronological storytelling is where two non-synchronous narratives are spliced together. Recent(ish) examples include A. S. Byatt's *Possession: A Romance* and Jonathan Safran Foer's *Everything is Illuminated*.

In the latter book, the basic story is of a character (named Jonathan Safran Foer) who goes to the Ukraine to look for the woman who saved his grandfather's life. The narrative is split into two principal parts. One chunk is narrated by Foer's bizarre, but wonderful, Ukrainian translator. Another chunk is fragments from Foer's own historical novel, which relates the history of his family's community in the Ukraine from the 1790s onwards. (A third and smallest strand involves letters sent by the translator to Foer, once the latter has returned to America.) Each strand is told chronologically, but the switching around between the two means that the reader is constantly having to jump in time.

The book twists around and towards its own heart of darkness: the Nazi liquidation of Trachimbrod, Foer's family's shtetl. Each of the strands is both drawn irresistibly to that centre – by straightforward chronological progression in the case of the novel strand, and through a journey of discovery into the past in the case of the translator strand. Yet it's also as though each of the two strands seeks to resist that movement. Foer's historical 'novel' is magical-realist. It seeks to avoid the ugly but simple reality of what we know is coming. The translator strand is so bizarrely voiced and so full of outrageous comedy that it too is almost seeking to turn its face from the truth. When that truth finally is faced, it seems more powerful than ever, because these long acts of resistance have finally been overcome.

For me, Foer's novel is only partly successful. The comedy of the Ukrainian translator is handled with wonderful vigour and inventiveness, but the historical novel felt derivative and under-whelming. Nevertheless, from a structural point of view, it certainly works. There are two strands winding remorselessly towards the same terrible event, one winding back from the future, the other forwards from the past. The sense of avoidance and inevitability is beautifully done. If you were asked to find any simpler narrative structure to produce the same effect, I think you'd fail.

The dual-narrative plot of *Possession* is likewise a complex one. One narrative is connected with a doomed but passionate romance between two Victorian poets. The second narrative has to do with an investigation of that romance by two contemporary scholars. Inevitably, the two narratives end up reverberating together: the past illuminated by present-day researches, the present altered by the process of discovery.

In addition to straightforward chronological narration in each of the two strands, Byatt adds in a collage of diaries, letters and poetry which work (like the sub-narratives in Conrad's *Lord Jim*) rather like submissions of evidence in a court of law. These fragments of evidence stand outside ordinary chronology. The order in which they appear has to do more with the slow revelation of clues in relation to an unfolding mystery.

It's no coincidence that both books have a mystery at their heart (the fate of the shtetl on the one hand; a Victorian romance on the other) and that both books drive at that mystery in two ways: forwards from the past and backwards from the present. That dual approach to a mystery is probably the single greatest justification for these two-time-strand novels. If your story has a mystery that you want to approach both forwards and backwards, this double-stranded approach may well be right for you.

But note what Foer and Byatt do *not* do. They don't monkey around within each strand. So their books are essentially chronological; it's just that there are two chronologies to play with. If Byatt had started to drop lots of flashbacks and flashforwards into her text as well, the whole book would have become a confusing mess. The key to handling chronological complexity well is to do it simply and clearly. The reader needs to be presented early on with the way the novel works and then you need to stick to the bargain you've made. No further wrinkles or complexities of chronology. (The plot, of course, can get as complex as you like.) That way the reader can buy into the basic deal – 'Ah, I see! There's a Victorian strand and a modern-day one. Yes, I get it.' – then read on confident that no further tricks are about to be pulled. Complexity, more than anything, needs to be kept simple.

The collage

And that's a warning that needs to echo a little as we review the last – and most complex – non-chronological narrative technique of the chapter. It's the collage effect, as used by Conrad in *Lord Jim* and as used by Matthew Kneale in *English Passengers*.

Kneale's book is about the impact of English colonial rule in Tasmania. The Tasman aboriginal viewpoint is voiced by Peevay, whose story opens in 1824. The book's opening chapters are arranged as follows. Each chapter or section is narrated in the first person by one of around twenty different narrators, and the dates of each narration are given in brackets. Just to add a little complexity, some of the 'narrations' take the form of letters or other documents.

Chapter 1
- Captain Illiam Kewley (1857)
- Rev Wilson Geoffrey (1857)
- Kewley (1857)
- Wilson (1857)

Chapter 2
- Jack Harp (1820)
- Peevay (1824–8)
- George Baines (1828)
- Peevay (1828)

Chapter 3
- Kewley (1857)

Chapter 4
- Harp (1821–4)
- Peevay (1828)
- Sir Charles Moray (1828)
- George Alder (1828)
- Peevay (1829)

This is already enough of the structure to reveal Kneale's plan. The main element of the structure is the dual narrative. As we saw with the previous examples, the end-point is, as it has to be, a collision of sorts between the two narratives. In this case, the collision is a meeting. The earlier (1820s, 1830s) strand of the narrative gallops forward in time to meet up with the slower (1857) narrative. In the final chapter, the voices are located in 1858 and thereafter.

But whereas the classic, 'simple' dual-narrative structure requires that everything within each strand is strictly chronological, Kneale allows himself to jump around within each strand. Thus, although Peevay's voice closes chapter 2 in 1828, when we return to this strand in chapter 4, we've leapt back again to 1821. This departure from strict sequence is made easier by the multiplicity of narrators, which forces readers to piece together the story for themselves from the rich assortment of fragments in front of them.

Kneale's technique works brilliantly, but it is hard to pull off. It requires a powerful central story and a strong and empathetic central character (Peevay, in this instance). Done well, and you have a book that can win the most prestigious literary prizes around (the Whitbread, in Kneale's case). Done badly – or done anything less than well, in fact – and you have a mess. The risks are multiple:

- A dual narrative can be harder for a reader to 'get into' than a single one.

- Any departure from chronological ordering risks creating confusion, and thereby an obstacle to the reader's desire to read on.

- Using multiple narrators risks meaning that the reader has no one in particular to empathise with, so he ends up empathising with no one.

- Using multiple narrators also requires that the author be a fine ventriloquist, able to adopt a whole series of convincing but distinct voices within the confines of a single book.

Even in the most capable of hands, the demands on the reader are such that you can't build a thrusting, jet-fuelled commercial narrative in this way. This technique, in other words, is something that literary novelists may want to fool around with;

everyone else should stay well clear. And don't be tempted to use the technique just for the sake of it, a kind of literary showing off. You don't win points for using fancy techniques. You win points for writing wonderful books. Pick the right technique for the right book. If you happen to plump for the simplest possible technique (one narrator, one story, strict faithfulness to chronology, and so on), that's fine. Just be sure to write a wonderful book.

How to lose the reader before you've even started

The commonest problem with non-chronological narratives is a simple one. The writer simply forgets the need to start their story. So, for example, we at Jericho Writers quite often receive stories that proceed roughly like this:

1. *Prologue.* Flashforward. Corinne is tied to a chair in a cellar. She's seeking to free herself from the ropes that bind her.

2. *Chapter 1.* The present. Corinne goes to her ordinary job as (let's say) a dental hygienist. Her boss tells her that they're closing the office at 4.00 pm that day for a special client.

3. *Chapter 2.* The present. This is a dual-protagonist story. Corinne is the lead, but her significant other is Dwayne, a talented dancer. This chapter introduces Dwayne via a scene of him rehearsing for a big opening at the end of the week.

4. *Chapter 3.* Flashback. It's important for the reader to understand that today's calm, sensible, ordinary Corinne had a wilder past, so this is a flashback to that past – a student time of sex, drugs and rock 'n' roll.

5. *Chapter 4.* The present. Important to get the narrative moving again, so we now pick up the story of Corinne in her surgery at 4.00 pm when the special client – a local crime boss – arrives to have his teeth whitened.

You only have to present the story like this to see its weaknesses. You can see the logic that the writer used at every step. (That prologue: well, my story starts slowly, so I'd better get an action scene in early. That chapter 2: well, Dwayne is going to be important, so we'd better introduce him too. Chapter 3: well, we need to establish who Corinne is as early as possible.) All the same, the result is a disaster, a pudding, a mess that no reader will want to wade through.

The actual start of the novel, the place where a story discernibly kicks in is chapter 4 which, because of that prologue, is effectively chapter 5. Even then, no reader is going to feel settled – 'Ah, *now* the story starts!' – because there's been so much bumping around that the reader will be bracing themselves for yet more. And the writer could simply have done it like this:

1. *Chapter 1.* Corinne goes to her office and has to whiten the teeth of a local crime boss.
2. *Chapter 2.* Dwayne is threatened on the street by a thug who seems to have links to the same crime boss.

Just two chapters in, and already the story is more advanced than it was. No need for a prologue, because you have the promise of action from the opening chapter. No need for a flashback, because you're going to slip the necessary information in as and when it's most appropriate. No confusion in the introduction of Dwayne, because the structure is now so clean and simple that readers will instantly grasp how you're planning to proceed. I've illustrated these issues in relation to a fairly conventional story, but I'd say that the problem arises most frequently in fantasy-type material. Because writers of such work often have dual narratives (this world and some other world), plus fragments of poetry/myth/prophecy from the other world that they want to include, the openings of such novels are often a hodge-podge of material that arrests and confuses the forward progress of the underlying story.

When we put points like this to our editorial clients, the most typical reaction is twofold. The first part of that is a gloomy recognition that we're right, that a given opening structure is just too convoluted. The second part, often, is a resistance: 'Yes, but I need to do that because …' The thing that makes up the 'because' may make good sense or none at all, but it's characteristic that the sentence starts '*I* need' rather than 'the reader needs'. And what *you* need doesn't matter. The reader doesn't care. The reader is like an imperious diner at an upmarket hotel. She wants what she wants. That may be simple to produce or it may be hard, but the reader doesn't care either way. Your role is that of chef and waiter rolled into one. You simply need to give your reader what she wants and be damned to anything that you might need or want along the way. You're not the boss. The reader is.

Time travel – the basics

The central message of this chapter is a simple one. If in doubt, straightforward chronological narrative is the best way to go. It's what readers expect. It's how stories have always been told. Give or take the odd flashback (and perhaps an annoying flashforward in a prologue), the vast majority of commercial novels stick to ordinary timekeeping. So do the vast majority of literary novels.

If your story demands you do something a bit different, make sure your story truly does require it. You need to be led to the right technique by your story. Don't think of a glitzy technique and then try to squash your story in to fit.

Finally, be honest with yourself. Does your story jump around more than it should? The simplest way to check this is to do as we did for the Corinne/Dwayne story above. Simply write down in a sentence or two what happens in each of your opening chapters and note down when the action is happening. (You may want to do this with your entire manuscript, in fact, but it's opening chapters where these problems are most prevalent.) If you have an easy forward flow, you're in good shape. If not, you need to doubt yourself. Is your structure arising from your needs or from the reader's? Especially where openings are very cluttered, and perhaps especially in dual world fantasy manuscripts, it's a fair bet that the reader's needs are being neglected. You can't let that happen. If you neglect the reader, agents will neglect you.

Chapter Summary

- Storytelling no longer has to be chronologically linear.

- Prologues often involve flashforwards. The best of use of such prologues is to alter the nature of the questions that drive the story.

- Flashbacks are also common – including in plenty of published work. Often, however, such flashbacks intrude on a story's forward flow, and it may be better to use short snippets (a paragraph or two) of flashback, rather than whole pages.

- Narratives with dual time strands often converge on the same event, one working forwards from the past, the other working backwards from the future.

- The collage effect is technically challenging but can work well in the right hands. You'd be well-advised to have a strong central story, however, to keep the narrative on track.

- Make especially sure that the opening chapters of your story don't jump around too much. Every jump involves a loss of story momentum, and readers may not have the patience to wait while you sort yourself out.

MADMEN, LIARS, AND ROGUES

From the complexities of non-chronological narrative structure to the simple delights of madmen and liars.

In the good old-fashioned Victorian novel, the narrator told you what was happening and you trusted him or her to tell the truth. Even in credulity-stretching first-person narratives (*Gulliver's Travels*, for example), you trusted the narrator not to be making things up. If he said something astonishing happened, then – blow me down – happen it did.

In the twentieth century, and particularly in the second half of the century, that assumption was picked apart. In Knut Hamsun's *Hunger*, the narrator is a would-be writer who lives in acute poverty because of his failure to find secure employment. Hunger makes him increasingly delirious and at one point he thinks of eating his own finger.

Or does he? He's delirious. Perhaps he does indeed bite down on his own finger with a genuine thought of eating it, or perhaps that whole episode is just a neurotic fantasy. We don't know. There's no reliable narrator standing outside the story to tell us.

This margarine really does taste better

If Hamsun was one of the first writers to feed us a story via an unreliable narrator, he's by no means been the last. Bret Easton Ellis's *American Psycho* would have been a very good book if its narrator had been entirely dependable. As it was, his narrator, the loathsome Patrick Bateman, is anything but. Much of the book is given over to scenes of murder, torture, rape, cannibalism and necrophilia. (And no: it's not a book to give your grandma.) When he's done with a victim, he generally stashes the corpse in an upmarket Manhattan apartment. Late on in the book, he goes back to the apartment, which looks a little different. There's a new doorman in the lobby. The locks have changed. A bright real estate broker is in the apartment offering it for sale. There's a smell of roses, not corpses. Bateman is confused.

> *On the TV, in a commercial, a man holds up a piece of toast and tells his wife, 'Hey, you're right ... this margarine really does taste better than shit.' The wife smiles.*
>
> *'You saw the ad in the* Times?' *she* [the real estate broker] *asks.*
>
> *'No ... I mean yes. Yes, I did. In the* Times,' *I falter, gathering a pocket of strength, the smell from the roses thick, masking something revolting. 'But ... doesn't Paul Owen* [Bateman's alter ego] *... still own this?' I ask, as forcibly as possible.*
>
> *There's a long pause before she admits, 'There was no ad in* The Times.'

It's a brilliant bit of writing. Clearly, there is not an ad on the TV in which a man compares some margarine to shit, so Bateman is delusional, at least to some extent. But how far? Bateman can't tell us (because he's inside the delusion) and Ellis won't. He could have contrived an ending in which Bateman is bustled off to a psychiatric hospital and told that it's all been in his imagination. Or he could have given us an ending in which Bateman is arrested on numerous counts of murder and rape (thereby proving that it wasn't all in his imagination). He does nothing so crude. He leaves no easy way out for the reader – and tells them as much: the last words in the book are, 'THIS IS NOT AN EXIT'.

Some ambiguous endings are merely annoying; they feel like an authorial cop-out. As it is, turning Bateman into the least reliable of narrators lifts Ellis's work to the level of masterpiece. Bateman lives in the obnoxious world of the New York yuppie. Does that world simply not see Bateman's actions as crimes? Is his madness so widely shared that it's no longer seen as madness? Are others acting in the same way themselves? Is Bateman's own collapse a purely personal reaction to a world that has lost all sense of value? Is Bateman's madness the only sane act available to him? Did Bateman perhaps act out some of his crimes and not others? The genius of Ellis's ending is that you could answer 'yes' to any of these questions and the book makes sense of your answer ... except that no answer is quite complete. The book evades solution. This is not an exit.

My own current crime series features a first-person narrator who's a lot less repulsive than Bateman, but almost as unreliable. Especially in the first book of the series, my narrator, Fiona Griffiths, is quite content to conceal extremely important facts from the reader and, though she seldom lies outright, she's also happy to present some episodes in a deliberately misleading way – sufficiently misleading that the reader ends up with a wholly unrealistic picture of what actually happened. My story is a detective story, with a conventional whodunit at its core. But as you read further into that first story and start to notice that its narrator can't be relied upon, a second mystery opens up: the mystery of who Fiona Griffiths really is, and what is and isn't true about her. It's a delightfully simple way to introduce a second major plot-engine into a mystery story and, given that such stories are all about the detection of truth and falsehood, it's also a lovely way to put those themes right at the heart of things.

'Unreliable narrators' arise only in first-person narrations. (Or at least I'm darned if I can think of a counter-example.) Again, it's not a technique to use for the sake of it. It's a technique to use if your particular story and your particular narrator calls for it. Indeed, it's not quite a *technique* in the way that, say, a dual-stranded narrative is a technique. It's more that if you follow the logic of your narrator's personality through to its conclusion, you may end up with the narrator telling the reader things that may or may not be true.

And if you have such a narrator, then a couple of tips. First, take it slow. Don't reveal your hand too early. You have the entire book in which to reveal your character's duplicities, and the longer those duplicities take to reveal themselves, the more time you have to tease and tantalise the reader. So by all means, start dropping clues or hints or disconcerting inconsistencies in the first third of your book, but you may well want to wait until the final chapters to reveal the largest parts of your deception. In essence, you are using the first chunk of your book to hint at a mystery, the middle chunk to build it up, the final part to reveal as much or as little of it as you fancy. You can throw the big stuff in early, of course, but you will quite likely be sacrificing some narrative tension if you do.

Secondly, you can afford to be subtle. Readers are highly alert to the clues you drop, so you don't need to thump home evidence of inconsistency. Just place your markers, build them slowly, let the reader's own intelligence do the rest.

One of the sweetest things about this technique, from the author's point of view, is how little you need to do. You place your markers – then do nothing. The less you reveal, the more you delay things, the more tantalising is the mystery. Because authors are all lovely truth-telling people by instinct, this deception can be hard to do. There's almost an instinct to rush out your secret before it's had time to stew. So take your time. The best stews cook slow.

Chapter Summary

- Some first-person narrators may not tell the truth. They may lie, or they may be delusional.
- If you have such a narrator, then give yourself plenty of time in revealing the extent of your character's unreliability. There's no need to rush these things.
- Let your character determine whether your narrator will be reliable or not. Most narrators are reasonably reliable.

IRONY

'Irony' is one of the most complex and shaded terms in literary criticism. It's a term that has bred a whole race of sub-terms: verbal irony, dramatic irony, situational irony, tragic irony, post-modern irony – pretty much any sort of irony you care to think of.

The heart of the concept, however, is simple enough. It has two aspects:

- The words on the page permit two levels of interpretation: a surface meaning and an underlying meaning, which is sharply at odds with the other.
- The character is oblivious to at least one of those levels, so that, in effect, the author and the reader are exchanging knowing glances behind the character's back.

If that sounds complex, it shouldn't. When Shakespeare's Othello praises his evil snake of a buddy as 'Honest Iago', we in the audience know damn well that Iago is a loathsome reptile. Othello's words say one thing. Reality says something else. The irony lies in the shiver created by that discordance.

In a way, though, quoting Shakespeare is liable to mislead you, by suggesting that irony belongs only to the realm of high art. It doesn't. Any storyteller can make use of irony. In James Cameron's *Titanic*, Cal Hockley (the bad guy) swaggers on board the doomed vessel saying, 'It is unsinkable. God himself could not sink this ship.' Ha! He *thinks* it's unsinkable. We *know* it's not. His words say one thing, we know something different. That's irony right there at the heart of one of the world's biggest blockbuster movies.

Irony in the novel

In almost every book of quality, there'll be a frisson of irony somewhere along the way. That's clearest, perhaps, and easiest to introduce when you have a strongly voiced third-party narrator, such as Zadie Smith's narrator in *White Teeth*. Consider again that bit about Archie's would-be suicide. Here, I've added some of the text I missed out earlier:

> [...] *Cricklewood Broadway would seem a strange choice.* [...] *Squeezed behind an almighty concrete cinema complex at one end and a giant intersection at the other, Cricklewood was no kind of place. It was not a place a man came to die. It was a place a man came in order to go other places via the A41.*

This paragraph is mostly one in which the narrator gets ever closer to Archie's dying thoughts. In a sentence or two, those thoughts are voiced direct as though the narrator had temporarily merged with Archie. But look at that sentence, 'It was a place a man came in order to go other places via the A41'. That surely feels like Zadie Smith's voice intruding again. A narratorial smirk at Cricklewood's awfulness. It's not that Archie isn't thinking about Cricklewood's unloveliness – he *is*. But is he making a joke about the A41? I doubt it. The passage is pulled in two directions at once. There's Smith's jaunty viewpoint and Archie's more pathetic one. The tension between both points of view co-existing at the same moment and in the same paragraph is a large part of what makes the passage so delightful. Had the passage been *only* owned by Archie, it might have been tear-jerking. Had it been *only* owned by Smith, it might have been funny. As it is, it's both things at once – and, better yet, since those things are opposites, the passage has a life, an unsettledness, a shimmer of movement that makes it feel alive. Those things make us greedy to read on.

Quiet irony

It's easy to hear the irony at play in *White Teeth*, because you've got a narrator keen to get noticed, but irony of the quiet sort is just as common. Here's a snippet from Annie Proulx's *Brokeback Mountain*:

> *Ennis, high-arched nose and narrow face, was scruffy and a little cave-chested, balanced a small torso on long, caliper legs, possessed a muscular and supple body made for the horse and for fighting. His reflexes were uncommonly quick and he was farsighted enough to dislike reading anything except Hamley's saddle catalogue.*

That last sentence contains a little jab of irony. Ennis has just been described as 'muscular', 'supple', and 'uncommonly quick'. So any reader encountering the adjective 'farsighted' naturally assumes that Proulx is continuing to describe him in flattering terms. 'Farsighted enough to put a little money by for old age', perhaps, or 'farsighted enough to own a clean trucking licence'. But no: not only is Proulx switching back to a description of his physical failings, she's using it to pick up on his acute educational limitations too. Or is she? Maybe she's suggesting that true wisdom lies in ignoring all books except those connected with riding equipment.

You can interpret the word how you like – or better still, you can interpret it in every possible direction and relish the alternative meanings it throws off. The point is that the word 'farsighted' jolts you into reading the sentence in at least two different ways, and irony lies in the ambiguity. It takes a plain (though beautifully written) paragraph and introduces the shimmer of movement that irony always supplies.

Silent irony

Proulx's irony is quiet, but at least it's audible – she gives you a word to nudge you. Sometimes, though, irony is no noisier than a pair of raised eyebrows in a library ... yet you can hear it even in a shootout. In the opening chapter of Robert Crais's *The Watchman*, Joe Pike is acting as bodyguard to a rich, spoiled girl. They enter a safe-house, but no sooner have they settled in than they're under attack. Pike kills three men and fires at a fourth before getting himself and the girl out of the house and into their Jeep. In the process, he loses one of his two guns, but the pair make a safe getaway:

> *They had been at the house in Eagle Rock for twenty-eight minutes. He had killed three more men, and now they were running. Again.*
> *He was sorry he lost the Colt. It was a good gun.*

There's no word or phrase here that suddenly blurs into ambiguity. The writing is as un-ambiguous as you could possibly ask. Yet that second paragraph is ironic nevertheless, because the simple narration is so at odds with our own reactions. If you or I had just shot three people and only barely escaped from the house alive, we'd have some feelings about it. I don't know about you, but my heart rate might accelerate. My hands might be shaky. I might express relief. I might even let rip with a swearword or two. Because humans are humans are humans, that's what we readers are expecting from Pike. But not a bit of it. 'He was sorry he lost the Colt. It was a good gun.' Two sentences, twelve words, thirteen syllables. It's not just that Pike is unexcited, the language is too. Completely unruffled. Not a raised heartbeat to be seen.

So Crais – a very good novelist, albeit one whose techniques are less visible than some considered in this book – creates irony by doing nothing at all. He creates irony simply by not doing the predictable thing, so that one train of interpretation goes scooching off on the line we *expect* (raised heartbeat, cussing, shaky hands), and the other train of interpretation continues to roll forward on the line he lays down (pity about that Colt). Two viewpoints, one ironic passage, and that sense of life, of unsettledness that always marks fine writing.

First-person irony

Irony is always easier to create in third-person narration than first, simply because you have a voice separate from any of your characters. That allows you to swoop in on your characters when you want intimacy, but to zoom out again for an external perspective when you want more distance. Your swooping and zooming can happen in a highly visible way (*à la* Zadie Smith) or in a subtle, nudging, suggestive way (*à la* Annie Proulx). But either way, having the dual viewpoints of character and narrator gives you all the ironic machinery you need. It's easy enough to hold a conversation with the reader behind the character's back.

But what if you are writing in the first person? You can't ever, for a moment, leave the voice of your narrator, because that would be to destroy that narrator's credibility. So you, the *writer*, have no separate voice with which to make your presence felt. Creating irony sounds like an impossible brief, no?

Except it's not. Crais created irony by doing nothing, and any first-person narrator can create irony in exactly the same way. It's a kind of authorial ju jitsu: using the expected motion of the reader's reaction and using that motion to tip her off-balance. Here's Emma Donoghue's five-year-old narrator, Jack, in her bestselling *Room*:

> *I count one hundred cereal and waterfall the milk that's nearly the same white as the bowls, no splashing, we thank Baby Jesus.*

The reader is kept constantly off-balance in this sentence. Who *counts* cereal out? And who uses the word 'waterfall' for 'pour' (though we can also see what a good word 'waterfall' is)? And who has to make special note of the fact that they've poured milk out without splashing it? And that 'we thank Baby Jesus' is perfect: we first read that as Jack's way of expressing relief that he hasn't splashed the milk … except that we realise he doesn't punctuate his thoughts or his sentences the way we do, and in fact his mother is probably just saying grace with him the way they presumably always do. We're reading Jack's voice and his meanings in just the way he means them. But simultaneously we're listening to him with an adult ear and can share Emma Donoghue's laughter at some of Jack's turns of phrase. Donoghue doesn't once allow her voice to intrude on Jack's, yet she keeps that ripple of ironic duality vibrantly alive throughout.

Comic irony

Comedy and irony are intimately linked. I haven't particularly sought to hunt down examples of *comic* irony for this chapter, yet there's no coincidence that all the examples I've used so far have a comic edge to them. Zadie Smith's comedy is immediately visible. Proulx's is quiet, but 'farsighted enough to dislike reading anything except Hamley's saddle catalogue' is a joke nevertheless. Crais's ice-cool comment about the gun isn't laugh-out-loud funny, but there's surely a smile on his lips as he makes it. And there's certainly a smile on Emma Donoghue's face as she lets Jack count his cereal grains and waterfall his milk.

It's not hard to see the link between comedy and irony. Comedy is all about creating expectations and then thwarting them. It's all about dual expectations, dual interpretations. So, for example, my favourite joke of the moment goes like this. Q: You're American when you go into the bathroom. You're American when you come out of the bathroom. What are you when you're in the bathroom? A: European. (Say the last bit out loud if you don't get it straight away.) You wouldn't quite call this *ironic*. Irony generally implies something a little more subtle, a little less in-your-face than this, but you can see the family resemblances. That word 'European' could refer to nationality, or it could refer to what you're doing in the bathroom. The listener is expecting one kind of answer and receives another. Or rather: the listener *does* get the kind of answer they're expecting, but only makes sense of it by placing another interpretation on it. There's the little shock of seeing an ambiguity opening up underfoot. All that, comedy has in common with irony.

No wonder then, that for some authors comic irony shimmers brightly throughout their work. Here, for example, is an extract from Neil Gaiman's *Neverwhere*:

> *There are four simple ways for the observant to tell Mr Croup and Mr Vandemar apart: first, Mr Vandemar is two and a half heads taller than Mr Croup; second, Mr Croup has eyes of a faded, china blue, while Mr Vandemar's are brown; third, while Mr Vandemar fashioned the rings he wears on his right hand out of the skulls of four ravens, Mr Croup has no obvious jewellery; fourth, Mr Croup likes words, while Mr Vandemar is always hungry. Also, they look nothing at all alike.*

Everything about this paragraph is a delight. The tone of that opening clause is nicely formal. Croup and Vandemar are both referred to as 'Mr'. The phrase 'four simple ways for the observant' suggests a certain straight-faced quality in what is about to come. And what comes – though still on the face of it formal (those 'Mr's are never dropped) – is riotously untamed. 'First, Mr Vandemar is two and a half heads taller than Mr Croup'. Huh? Two and a half *heads* … that's two and a half feet, give or take. Why on earth do the 'observant' need a guide to distinguish two people, one of whom must be a giant, and one of whom must be very short indeed? But the passage runs on without a blip. 'Second, Mr Croup has eyes of a faded, china blue, while Mr Vandemar's are brown'. Here, Gaiman returns to the straight-faced; no trickery, no surprises. He's lulling us back into accepting the even formality of his tone. And then we get, 'third, while Mr Vandemar fashioned the rings he wears on his right hand out of the skulls of four ravens, Mr Croup has no obvious jewellery'. The last bit about Mr Croup's lack of *obvious* jewellery sticks with the formal tone, yet once again the reader is shrieking out a protest: Vandemar has rings made out of *what*? By the time we reach, 'fourth, Mr Croup likes words, while Mr Vandemar is always hungry', the game is up. Gaiman has been playing with us all along and we're not going to trust his neutral tone any longer … and he cheerfully admits as much right away: 'Also, they look nothing at all alike', thereby telling the reader that the whole paragraph has been a wild goose chase, dropped in for nothing but fun – and, of course, as a delightful way to give a vibrant (if elusive) visual characterisation of his two monstrous hitmen.

Gaiman's wonderfully inventive prose is full of such delights. He doesn't create punchlines quite as crashingly direct as 'European', but crashingly direct punchlines work well in bar-room anecdotes and work badly (or at least only temporarily) in fiction. Gaiman's playful tone – a tone that never quite acknowledges that a joke has even been made – can keep going through an entire book and still leave the reader wanting more. He's a master of the comic ironic tone.

How to insert irony in your novel

I've said, and I've meant, that there's pretty much no good book that isn't also an ironic one. In any good piece of writing, you'll find the shimmer of dual interpretation somewhere within it. So how do you insert irony in your work?

Answer: you don't. At least, I don't think you do. Perhaps it works differently for some authors, but for nearly everyone, I think, irony arises naturally from good writing. It's something that can certainly be cultured, invited, nourished and welcomed, but not really something that can be shoe-horned in by authorial diktat. If you get too direct about it, if your authorial nudges become too overt, you're likely to get something that smells too much of the bar-room: the man who sits too close to you and tells you beery anecdotes whose endings you've already guessed.

The purpose of this chapter is simply to call attention to the issue. To make you more conscious of it. To help you see the flicker of irony in every good book you read. If you have that consciousness, you'll find that irony creeps naturally into your work. It'll be something you discover in your writing after you've written it, not something you engineer into it from the start.

That's my theory anyway, so I thought I'd better test it by seeing whether my awareness of irony manifested itself in my work. Here's an extract from the first of my detective novels. Bear in mind that this is a first-person narration, so you won't find the very obvious ironic dualities that you find in Zadie Smith, for example. The narrator is a young detective, Fiona Griffiths.

> *I make the turn and, shades on against the sunlight, I speed up the drive in a stupid attempt to minimise my lateness. A last twist in the way catches me out and I emerge into the large grav-elled parking area in front of the house doing about thirty miles an hour, when under ten would have been more appropriate. I brake hard and go for a long curving slide on the gravel until my speed falls away. I only just manage to stop the engine stalling. A wide spray of ochre dust hangs in the air to mark the manoeu-vre. Silent applause. Fi Griffiths, rally driver.*
>
> *I give myself a few seconds to get my head together. Breath-ing in, breathing out, concentrating on each breath. My heart's going too fast, but at least I can feel it hammering away. Pulse rate falling off now. These things shouldn't worry me so much, but they do. There shouldn't be such a thing as poverty and starvation, but there is. I wait till I think it's OK, then give it another twenty seconds.*

The first example of irony comes at the end of the first para-graph. Griffiths drives too fast and stops in an uncontrolled and dangerous way. She's aware she hasn't covered herself in glory and says, 'Silent applause. Fi Griffiths, rally driver.' If we take the literal meaning of the words, she's congratulating herself – except that we know she isn't. She means the exact opposite of what she says. We saw her drive like an idiot and here she is acknowledg-ing the fact. This, technically, is an example of irony, but it's not one that we're going to count in this context. Fiona Griffiths is using irony in an ordinary human way. There's no gap between her and the reader, no separation between her viewpoint and ours.

Not so when it comes to the second paragraph. 'These things shouldn't worry me so much, but they do. There shouldn't be such a thing as poverty and starvation, but there is.' Normally when we speak about poverty and starvation, we do so with some empathy for the poor or the starving. Or perhaps, if we're in a hurry or have something else preoccupying us, we might not really feel any empathy, but we know that we at least have to pretend otherwise. We certainly can't just be flip about it. And here is Griffiths not being flip exactly, but being baldly uncaring. 'There shouldn't be such a thing as poverty and starvation, but there is.' She doesn't even go on to say, 'So there you go. What can you do about it?' – because she doesn't stop long enough to say anything at all. She just goes back to considering her breathing and her pulse rate. The poor and starving don't get a look in.

In this case, we do have that precious gap between character and reader. It's as though Fiona Griffiths is just talking away, being herself, but when she makes that remark about the poor and starving, the reader and the author are exchanging glances behind her back, saying to each other, 'Did she *really* say that?' (Of course, you'd get the reader and author muttering at each other behind the character's back if she had said something *directly* awful – 'I don't care about poor people', or something like that. But irony never exists at the level of the literal; only at the level where the literal and the implied part company. And Griffiths has, after all, merely stated a fact.)

Now I'm not suggesting that I write like Annie Proulx (I wish I did), but I *am* suggesting that the arrival of the ironic in that passage was completely unconscious. Not only did I not seek to engineer it in place, I didn't even notice it was there until I went looking for it. If you push too hard for the effect, you'll almost certainly overdo it. If you're aware of that lovely ironic shimmer in other people's work, then soon enough you'll find a shimmer in your own. What's more if you stick close to character (and if you've chosen a character interesting enough to have a little edge, the ability to be outrageous), the gaps between what you think and what your character thinks or says or does will arise of their own accord.

But enough of all this. Enough of irony. Enough of camera positioning, and character, and even prose style. It's time to explore the very heart of the novel. It's time to look at story.

Chapter Summary

- Irony (in the sense we are using it in this chapter) occurs when a gap arises between the character's interpretation of a situation and our own. Typically, it's a moment where the reader and author are exchanging glances behind the character's back.

- A strong narrative voice (such as Zadie Smith's in *White Teeth*) creates ample opportunity for irony.

- Even a quiet narrative voice (such as Annie Proulx's in *Brokeback Mountain*) creates opportunities for quiet irony.

- It's harder but possible to create that shimmer of unsettledness, a sense of duality even, in first-person work.

- Irony and comedy are intimately linked. If your work is ironic, it'll have a comic edge as well ... and not one likely to undermine your other story goals.

- Don't try to force irony into your writing. If you write well and pay attention to character, irony will make its presence felt.

Part Five
Story

It must be admitted that the art of story as I see it is a very difficult one. What its central difficulty is I have already hinted at when I complained that in The War of the Worlds *the idea that really matters becomes lost or blunted as the story gets underway. I must now add that there is a perpetual danger of this happening in all stories. To be stories at all they must be a series of events: but it must be understood that this series – the* plot, *as we call it – is only really a net whereby to catch something else.*

– C.S. Lewis

I guarantee you that no modern story scheme, even plotlessness, will give a reader genuine satisfaction, unless one of those old-fashioned plots is smuggled in somewhere. I don't praise plots as accurate representations of life, but as ways of keeping readers reading. [...] One of my students wrote a story about a nun who got a piece of dental floss stuck between her lower left molars, and who couldn't get it out all day long. I thought that was wonderful. The story dealt with issues a lot more important than dental floss, but what kept readers going was anxiety about when the dental floss would finally be removed. Nobody could read that story without fishing around in his mouth with a finger.

– Kurt Vonnegut, Jr.

I don't make plots in advance. I [...] try to throw people into a messy life and see how they'll sort it out while I'm writing. So the whole adventure is one I share with the reader.

– John le Carré

THE CLASSIC PLOT

Elsewhere in this book, it's been easy enough to look at examples. If we want to understand something about good prose, we need only look at a few sentences from a good writer. Good characterisation might need a few paragraphs to leap into life, but still reveals itself quickly. Plotting is different from that. The machinery of plot is so huge, so cumbrous, that it's hard for a 'how to' book to dissect it without melting into vagueness and generality. Nevertheless, we need to try.

In this chapter, we'll focus relentlessly on a single book: Jane Austen's *Pride and Prejudice*. Obviously enough, the novel is not a recent work by a contemporary author, and its selection is therefore at odds with my policy so far in this book. On the other hand, most people will either have read the book or seen a film or TV adaptation, and it's helpful to discuss a plot with which most people are broadly familiar. There is, additionally, another excellent reason for my choice: Austen's masterpiece is a near-perfect example of classic plot structure.

By 'classic', I don't mean either great or old. Classic, in this context, simply refers to the model to which most novels still aspire, the model still followed by the majority of stories, no matter if they're literary or commercial, for adults or children, for men or for women. It's also the model loosely followed by a tremendous amount of narrative non-fiction. (Life has an unfortunate habit of not always serving up stories in the classical format, but it's the writer's job to ensure that they are nevertheless presented as if they did.) In short, most books still follow the recipe that Jane Austen herself followed two hundred years ago, and understanding her recipe is a wonderful way to understand the art of plotting.

We start, simply enough, with beginnings.

Start early

Pride and Prejudice begins:

> *It is a truth universally acknowledged, that a single man in possession of a good fortune must be in want of a wife.*

You can't start any faster than that. On chapter 1, page 1, line 1, Jane Austen informs the reader just what the story is going to be about: a man getting married to a woman. To be sure, the sentence tends to suggest that a *man* lies at the heart of the story, but it becomes rapidly clear – within a page or two – that the story is likely to be told from the woman's perspective. We don't yet know much else. We're not certain who the protagonist is going to be (though Austen does drop a strong hint that we should keep our eye on Lizzy). Nor do we yet know who her romantic partner is going to be. But these things don't matter: they're reasons, if anything, to keep reading.

What does matter, crucially, is that Jane Austen promises us a story in the very first line of her book; she tells us what kind of story she is going to be telling; and everything that follows from here on will keep faith with these early promises.

It's also worth noting that Jane Austen relies, as any author can, on some intelligence in her readers. She doesn't actually say anywhere, 'Elizabeth Bennet really, really wants to get married; that's the thing that matters to her more than anything'. Indeed, she almost does the opposite. When Jane and Lizzy are discussing the ball in chapter 4, it's clear that Lizzy is a livelier, more independent, less homely girl than her sister. Naturally Lizzy does want to get married, but it's not at this stage an all-consuming matter for her. Jane Austen nevertheless lets the reader know what to expect, thanks to:

- Some well-placed nudges, including that opening sentence;

- The reader's knowledge of the conventions of the novel, which lead them to interpret those nudges in the appropriate way; and

- A shared knowledge about the world of the novel: a world in which anyone of Lizzy Bennet's age, sex and class would almost certainly be thinking hard about marriage.

You can do the same. You *do* need to establish your story early. You do *not* need to do that in an overly direct or ham-fisted way.

Identify your protagonist

It's common enough at the start of a book for an author to start with a wide focus, pulled back from the action, or to start with a secondary character who leads us to the main character. Thus the first page or two of a book may often be a misleading guide to where the main action is going to unfold. Nevertheless, contemporary fiction tends not to waste much time before focusing in on the main character. It's, in effect, part of that opening promise to the reader: *this* is what the story is going to be about, *this* is the person who's going to be our principal focus.

Jane Austen is fast and clear in identifying her protagonist. We already know that this is going to be a girl-meets-guy story, but we don't yet know which girl, or which guy. And then, 2,400 words into the book, we get this:

> *Elizabeth Bennet had been obliged, by the scarcity of gentlemen, to sit down for two dances; and during part of that time, Mr. Darcy had been standing near enough for her to hear a conversation between him and Mr. Bingley, who came from the dance for a few minutes, to press his friend to join it.*
>
> *'Come, Darcy,' said he, 'I must have you dance. I hate to see you standing about by yourself in this stupid manner. You had much better dance.'*

*'I certainly shall not. You know how I detest it, unless I am
particularly acquainted with my partner. At such an assembly as
this it would be insupportable. Your sisters are engaged, and there
is not another woman in the room whom it would not be a punishment to me to stand up with.'*

*'I would not be so fastidious as you are,' cried Mr. Bingley,
'for a kingdom! Upon my honour, I never met with so many
pleasant girls in my life as I have this evening; and there are
several of them you see uncommonly pretty.'*

*'You are dancing with the only handsome girl in the room,'
said Mr. Darcy, looking at the eldest Miss Bennet.*

*'Oh! She is the most beautiful creature I ever beheld! But
there is one of her sisters sitting down just behind you, who is
very pretty, and I dare say very agreeable. Do let me ask my
partner to introduce you.'*

*'Which do you mean?' and turning round he looked for a
moment at Elizabeth, till catching her eye, he withdrew his own
and coldly said: 'She is tolerable, but not handsome enough to
tempt me; I am in no humour at present to give consequence to
young ladies who are slighted by other men. You had better
return to your partner and enjoy her smiles, for you are wasting
your time with me.'*

*Mr. Bingley followed his advice. Mr. Darcy walked off; and
Elizabeth remained with no very cordial feelings toward him.*

This is the first time that one of the Bennet daughters has
been allocated any real page space, and it's the first time that
either Darcy or Bingley have been given real page space. What's
more, the first *significant* interchange of any sort is that between
Elizabeth Bennet and Darcy. You couldn't ask for a clearer
announcement of *who* the protagonist is going to be, nor of which
man is likely to entangle her emotions. (We can't, as it happens,
yet be certain that Darcy will end up being The One – there
might be any number of developments which could complicate
matters – but he is clearly going to be an important part of the
evolving romance.)

Fewer than 3,000 words into her book, and Jane Austen has announced the nature of her story, identified her protagonist, and set up the encounter which sets the whole story rolling. If I were being pedantic, I'd say that a modern editor would be likely to want to be in this position by the end of the first chapter; not (as in *Pride and Prejudice*) by the middle of the third chapter, although that *is* a rather pedantic complaint, since Austen's opening chapters are very short. In any case, the key point to notice is that very early into the book, we know the protagonist and her objective, and we have already witnessed the encounter which is to set this particular ball rolling.

Austen has even given us the first – and principal – obstacle in the way of the protagonist achieving her goal. She's met Mr Right: rich, handsome, and the talk of the ball. And then on her first meeting with him, she discovers that he's awful. He's stuck-up. He's rude. He doesn't like her, nor she him. Very early into the book, we have a protagonist, an objective and a problem. In other words, we have a story. The challenge now is to keep it developing.

Establishing the rules

The set-up phase also needs to introduce the issues which are going to become critical later. That feels obvious in the context of artificial or esoteric worlds – fantasy planets, sci-fi futures, twelfth century Bhutan, or whatever. So, if you're writing about a world in which certain magical things are possible, and if aspects of that magic will play a part in the final showdown, you need to have established your rules early on. If you only reveal them close to the moment of truth, they'll feel contrived and the ending will feel lame. That's true of magic. That's true of advanced technologies. It's true of whatever rituals, practices or beliefs will play a part in your ending.

The rule, however, is universal. It doesn't just apply to speculative or exotic settings. It applies to Jane Austen too. We are only 400 words into *Pride and Prejudice* before the author (via Lizzy's mother, Mrs Bennet) tells us one of the crucial facts of the whole set-up:

> *When a woman has five grown-up daughters, she ought to give over thinking of her own beauty.*

Little more than a page into the book, we learn that Mrs Bennet has five (*five!*) daughters to marry. That's one giant fact for the reader to absorb, but there's another one coming up. We're fewer than 8,000 words into the book when Austen tells us directly that:

> *Mr. Bennet's property consisted almost entirely in an estate of two thousand a year, which, unfortunately for his daughters, was entailed, in default of heirs male, on a distant relation; and their mother's fortune, though ample for her situation in life, could but ill supply the deficiency of his.*

In plain language, Mr Bennet's property would pass away to someone else (Mr Collins, from Planet Idiot) on his death. That would potentially leave one lady and five unmarried girls in dire financial straits. They wouldn't starve, but the girls would almost certainly be unmarriageable to any gentleman of quality. Jane Austen doesn't completely spell out these implications, but she doesn't have to: her readers would have understood them instantly. In short, and right at the start of the novel, Jane Austen has marked out the playing field on which her game is to be played.

What Jane Austen does, you should do too. If there are facts crucial to your premise, or elements of story-logic that become important later, you should reveal them early on. Not necessarily by the end of chapter 1 or even chapter 3 ... but still early enough that those facts feel part of the set-up, not an authorial Get Out of Jail Free card, played late.

Maintaining story movement

The key to maintaining movement is simple. A story is constantly triangulating between the same three landmarks: protagonist, objective, obstacles. You maintain movement and interest in your story if those interrelationships are constantly changing. If a chapter leaves those relationships constant, then it has not advanced the story and should probably be deleted. If a chapter alters those relationships, then it's probably advancing the story and should be retained.

There are, of course, a million ways to alter those relationships. An existing obstacle might get worse or it might disappear. A new obstacle might arise or a new ally might offer help. Information might arrive that seriously worsens an existing problem or utterly alters the conception of what the core objective is. The simplest way to understand these things is, as always, by example. Here's how Jane Austen does it. (Oh, and do note that although I've arranged the material below by chapter, the length of those chapters is not remotely uniform. The longer chapters have more meat than the shorter ones. In a modern novel, some of Austen's individual chapters would probably show up simply as sub-sections within a single, longer chapter.)

P&P, chapter 1 (850 words)

What happens? Bingley arrives at Netherfield. Mrs Bennet wants the newcomer to marry one of her daughters. Mr Bennet singles out Lizzy as being special.

Story development: The story – a girl-meets-guy romance – is established straight away. Lizzy Bennet is implicitly identified as our heroine.

P&P, chapter 2 (800 words)

What happens? Mr Bennet sets the social ball rolling with Bingley: thereby setting up the key encounter.

Story development: Lizzy Bennet is a step closer to meeting the intriguing newcomers. This is a chapter which might feel a little slow in a contemporary context – though it *is* short.

P&P, chapter 3 (1700 words)

What happens? Lizzy meets Darcy. He's horrible. They dislike each other. Additionally, Lizzy's sister, Jane, meets and gets on well with Bingley. A possible romance beckons.

Story development: The big meeting takes place. The girl has met the guy. The obstacle (the guy's pride and general obnoxiousness) is also established. The nascent Jane–Bingley relationship is also critical, as it forms an indirect relationship between Lizzy (Jane's sister) and Darcy (Bingley's best friend).

P&P, chapter 4 (1050 words)

What happens? It is established still further that Jane is serious about Bingley. We also learn that Darcy is an exceptional man – cleverer than Bingley, for example – but prideful.

Story development: The chapter takes the somewhat tentative Jane–Bingley relationship and makes it somewhat more emphatic. The stronger it becomes, the stronger the links between Lizzy and Darcy. Additionally, Darcy's virtues and his faults are painted in stronger colours. He's already by far the most interesting male presence in the book and will remain that way throughout.

P&P, chapter 5 (950 words)

What happens? We learn (via friends of the Bennets) that Bingley is very interested in Jane. Lizzy meanwhile declares that she has absolutely no interest in Darcy at all: her most emphatic statement so far.

Story development: The Jane–Bingley relationship grows once again: we now know that both partners are very interested in the other. At the same time, just as the force linking Lizzy and Darcy has become stronger than ever, we have her declaration that nothing would induce her to contemplate him as a partner.

P&P, chapter 6 (2350 words)

What happens? Lizzy worries that Jane isn't doing enough to hint to Bingley that she welcomes his advances. Meantime, Darcy starts to become interested in Lizzy and approaches her at a ball, seeking a dance. She refuses him.

Story development: The Jane-Bingley linkage is possibly weakening: at any rate, it seems more doubtful than it had done. Meanwhile, Darcy's position *vis-à-vis* Lizzy has altered. Her attitude to him certainly hasn't … but has her refusal possibly altered *his* outlook?

By the end of chapter 6, we're still only about 6% of the way into the book – 8,000 words out of a total 122,000. Yet just look how much movement has already taken place. Our Mr and Ms Right have met – disliked each other – shunned each other. Then Mr Right decides he might be wrong and makes an advance, which is rejected emphatically enough that his interest may well have been permanently spiked. And though the book isn't going to focus on the (rather bland) Jane-Bingley relationship, that liaison affects the degree to which Lizzy and Darcy are connected and it too has already sprung into existence, has seemed to be strengthened by avowals of interest on both sides, and has then been imperilled by Jane's excessively open and cheerful temperament.

The really striking thing in all this is how much *movement* takes place. Nothing stays static. Lizzy's relationship to her goal (of getting married) is in constant flux. Every chapter alters that relationship. The two longer chapters (3 and 6) alter that relationship in emphatic, decisive ways. It's a valuable lesson. Some would-be literary authors believe that their craft is too dignified, too important to chase after the trivialities of story. And that's nonsense. Jane Austen is one of literature's greatest novelists, and *Pride and Prejudice* is one of its greatest novels. Yet the book adheres as closely to the classic rules of plotting as any novel by Dan Brown or James Patterson.

At the same time, it's important to notice that what's happening is simply movement, a constant change in Lizzy's relationship to Darcy. There are no car chases here. No explosions. No shootings or kidnappings. The entire novel will go by without swearing, sex, or violence. That partly reflects the novel's period, of course, but it's important to understand that a story can be *simultaneously* quiet *and* plot-driven. What matters is less the loudness of the incidents you are describing, and much more the constancy of change. Naturally, if you're writing for the James Patterson end of the market, that change will need to be punctuated with plenty of explosions, car chases and the rest of it. If you're writing for the literary end of the market, the changes in question are likely to be subtle rather than crass. But the art of plotting is the same: figure out where your protagonist stands in relation to their core objective at the start of the chapter and make sure that they're in a different place at the end of it.

Checking your story

If you have any worries about the strength of story in your own novel – and you probably *should* have such worries, given how vital it is to get it right – you can do no better than to treat your story the way we've just treated Jane Austen's. Make a list of your chapters. Write down in one column what happens on the page. In the next column, write down what implications that has for your protagonist and his/her core objective. Then take a look at what you've got. What you *should* see is that the protagonist's relationship to his objective is constantly varying. That may be a big step forward (like Darcy asking Lizzy to dance) or a big step backwards (like when he insulted her earlier). Or it may be something else altogether (like the burgeoning Jane–Bingley relationship which creates a tie, like it or not, between the two principals). What you should *not* see is waffle or excuses:

- Chapter X introduces us to character A, who's going to be really important later.

- Chapter X fills in the protagonist's backstory, which helps fill out what kind of experiences made her the person she is.

- Chapter X delivers a lot of vital information about the political/social/educational/romantic/military background in Renaissance Venice/Revolutionary Boston/the Planet Zauron.

- Chapter X describes an amusing or dramatic incident that happens to character B who, although they're not the protagonist, are nevertheless very close to the protagonist and will play a part later in the book.

In all these cases, the solution is simple: eliminate the chapter. To be sure, you may need to filter some of the relevant information into the book elsewhere (though typically not at anything like the length you first imagined). Stories don't get better by having more in them. They get better by concentrating relentlessly on the matter in hand. Will Lizzy get Darcy? Will James Bond save the world? That's what the reader wants to know. That's what you've got to tell them.

Inner journeys

A lot of the theorising about story comes from the world of movies. That's partly because the sums of money involved in film are so large, studio execs feel the need for an analytical apparatus with which to determine whether a story works or not. In addition, screenplays *are* story in a way that just isn't true of the novel. As a result, many of the most influential works on story come from the world of film: Joseph Campbell's *The Hero with a Thousand Faces* and Robert McKee's *Story* being two notable examples.

These works can be helpful to prose writers, but novels are not films. Indeed, whether fictional or not, prose narrative possesses a dimension that films cannot have, namely the internal. Thoughts, feelings, memories, sensations, associations: these are all things that film can't deal with directly and that a novel or a non-fiction narrative has to address. That has a huge implication for the way that story is handled in prose. Although an *external* journey will be at the heart of most novels, it will nearly always be complemented by an *internal* one.

Pride and Prejudice illustrates the point perfectly. At one level, its story is one that unfolds in the external world. Darcy won't dance with Lizzy. Then he wants to. Then she refuses him. And so on and so on through the book, until finally he asks her to marry him and she says she will. All this is external: it can be filmed without any event being missed.

But there is also an inner journey, the one alluded to in the title, about Darcy overcoming his pride and Lizzy overcoming her prejudice. The snippet below (which I've lightly edited for length) is about 300 words long, or roughly one page of an average mass-market paperback book. It recounts a crucial moment in the story: Darcy's revelation of Wickham's wickedness. And it's jammed with language (highlighted in bold) which relates to emotions or thoughts.

*If Elizabeth, when Mr. Darcy gave her the letter, did not **expect** it to contain a renewal of his offers, she had formed no **expectation** at all of its contents. But such as they were, it may well be supposed how **eagerly** she went through them, and what **a contrariety of emotion** they excited. Her **feelings** as she read were **scarcely to be defined**. With **amazement** did she first **understand** that he **believed** any apology to be in his power; and **steadfastly was she persuaded**, that he could have no explanation to give, which a **just sense of shame** would not conceal. With a **strong prejudice** against everything he might say, she began his account of what had happened at Netherfield. She read with **an eagerness** which hardly left **her power of comprehension**, and from **impatience** of **knowing** what the next sentence might bring, was **incapable of attending to the sense** of the one*

*before her eyes. His **belief** of her sister's **insensibility** she instantly **resolved** to be false; and his account of the real, the worst
objections to the match, made her **too angry** to have **any wish** of
doing him justice. He expressed no **regret** for what he had done
which **satisfied** her; his style was not **penitent, but haughty**. It
was all pride and insolence.*

*But when this subject was succeeded by his account of Mr.
Wickham—when she read with somewhat **clearer attention** a
relation of events which, if true, must overthrow **every cherished
opinion** of his worth, and which bore so **alarming** an affinity to
his own history of himself—**her feelings were yet more acutely
painful and more difficult of definition. Astonishment,
apprehension, and even horror,** oppressed her [...]*

*In this **perturbed state of mind**, with **thoughts that could
rest on nothing**, she walked on.*

It's not that screenwriters can't tackle these moments. They
can and do. But a screenwriter needs to handle them from the
outside, via an actor's face in close-up, wracked by emotion. The
trouble is, of course, that the best actress in the world could
hardly express everything that's going on in the above passage.
Were she to attempt to do so, it would come across to the viewer
as fifteen seconds of outrageous hamming, emotion succeeding
emotion, thought succeeding thought, in relentless and ludicrous
sequence. Actors avoid such things by choosing to leave most of
the detail to the audience's imagination. The emotional drama is
implied, never stated.

(I have a telling example of this from my own experience.
One of my Fiona Griffiths novels was adapted for TV. I didn't
write the screenplay; someone else did. But no question, it was a
hard task. My novels are written first-person and they're very
interior. Fiona is discursive and eloquent about her own inner life.
And at one point, the screenwriter just froze. There was a stage
direction, given to the actor playing Fiona, saying, 'She remem-
bers the history of conflict with her father'. The actor laughed
about this with me. She was a talented and experienced actor.

That's why she'd got the part. But no human's face convey the simple information contained in that stage direction, let alone the vastly more complex and nuanced material in my book. Needless to say, the stage direction was changed.)

And to be clear, novelists have to get explicit about the inner. The drama of the external world will provoke a drama of the internal one ... and vice versa, as the protagonist's emotional position will determine her actions and her choices. The two stories will echo and reflect each other. They'll be in constant communication, often hard to tease apart. And the crucial element of that communication is usually this: the major external challenge which faces the protagonist is mirrored in some major internal challenge. To accomplish the one, she needs to accomplish the other and (usually) vice versa. So, for example, in *Pride and Prejudice*, we have the following structure:

Starting position

External: Penniless young woman is of marriageable age, at a time when good marriages really matter.

Internal: Happy, clever, and surrounded by loving relationships – but lacking a certain wisdom or maturity.

Challenge/motivation

External: Find Mr Right and marry him.

Internal: Become a whole human being. In particular, Lizzy needs to overcome her prejudice (or, in more exact terms, her self-regarding overconfidence in her judgements of people).

Obstacles

External: Darcy seems like a bad guy and Wickham seems like a good guy. Additionally, Lizzy's family is, for the most part, unhelpful to her cause. But all these things wouldn't have mattered, if Lizzy had been slower to judgement and wiser in the judgements she's made. In the end, her own inner imperfection is the only absolute impediment to getting what she wants most in life.

Internal: Her own immaturity and self-regard.

Resolution and denouement

External: She gets the guy! And note that this external denouement arrives late: 115,000 words into a 122,000-word novel. This is the point at which Darcy asks Lizzy to marry him for a second time, and on this occasion she says yes.

Internal: She grows up! The internal denouement arrives significantly earlier: 100,000 words into the novel. This is the point at which Lizzy gets the letter which proves that Darcy is a very good guy and therefore that she has been wrong about him all along.

There are a few things to notice about all this. First of all, there'll be plenty of novels – perhaps even most novels – where the internal challenge is, in effect, 'become a whole human being'. The exact path to wholeness will vary from character to character, but the basic journey is from incompleteness to wholeness.

In our own personal lives, we know things aren't quite so simple. Personal growth isn't a one-off thing. However passionate and important a romance may be, we know that the lessons learned along the way will only be one small part of that individual's lifetime journey. In novels, though, that tedious truth takes a backseat. Any reader who reads *Pride and Prejudice* will feel complete, will feel that Lizzy has completed the greatest act of personal growth that life will ever demand of her. Everything that follows will seem of secondary importance. She's had her 'hour upon the stage' and then, as far as the reader is concerned, she needs to be heard of no more. That's why – for novels that follow the classic pattern of storytelling described in this chapter – sequels are very rare, and generally unsuccessful when they do exist. Although modern hands *have* crafted a sequel to *Pride and Prejudice*, who the heck would want to read it? It's not just that those modern hands are unlikely to have Jane Austen's deftness. It's also that Lizzy and Darcy have completed their journeys. They're done. The modern sequel, *Pemberley*, is going to be about as interesting as *Sex and the City 2*, a tired rehash of a once-wonderful brand.

Secondly, one of the crucial obstacles to Lizzy's triumph – arguably *the* crucial obstacle – is Lizzy herself. She jumps too fast to a conclusion about Darcy, and that error of judgement bedevils her subsequent choices and seems to spell disaster for her. This too is typical of any classically plotted novel. In the ultimate analysis, the protagonist is their own worst enemy.

Thirdly, the table draws attention to another common feature of the internal and the external journey, namely that the *internal* one completes sooner. They sometimes complete at the same time, but – for reasons we're about to consider – I don't think I can recall any example in which the internal journey completes later than the external one. This is a point of enough importance that it requires its own section:

Jeopardy and the winter of hope

We like to think that our inner journeys affect our outer journeys ... but we know that other forces are also active and also potent. Perhaps our inner healing will bring about our desired outcome, or perhaps it won't. We may feel (*will* feel) that our inner healing deserves to be rewarded, but we know that life ain't fair and we may not get what we deserve.

These worries create the perfect opportunity for a novelist to create tension. Jane Austen gives us the new, mature, wise Lizzy on the stroke of 100,000 words. At this point, in effect, she has 'earned' Darcy. She's completed the act of personal change necessary to deserve him. She's felt regret and humility, the two qualities most lacking in her initial make-up. But will that be enough? For 15,000 words it looks as though the answer is no. Then – presto! – as if by magic but also with delicious inevitability, Darcy arrives and asks for Lizzy's hand in marriage. A happy ending is now in full flow.

The mechanics of this deserve close study, as they're typical of every well-crafted 'classic' novel.

- Lizzy grows up; she completes her act of personal change.
- She now cares more about Darcy than anything else on earth. Her life can never be complete without him. Whereas Lizzy began the book as wanting marriage in a rather general, unspecified, uncommitted way, she now wants marriage in a heart-and-soul way. It's become by far the biggest deal in her life. The 'jeopardy' (a term borrowed from screenwriting) has therefore increased. In the early chapters of the book, Lizzy didn't have much at stake. Now she has everything. The journey from there to here hasn't been one of smoothly rising jeopardy – the trajectory has been bumpier, more up and down than that – but the shift from 10% commitment to 100% commitment is nevertheless all but universal. (It's also true that the odds of success bump around as well. Sometimes the protagonist may look like they're on top; sometimes their prospects will look bleak. It's unusual for the odds to change in any smooth way through the course of a book.)
- Just when jeopardy reaches its maximum pitch, the odds of success reach their all-time low. In the case of *Pride and Prejudice*, Darcy's heroic act is that of rescuing Lizzy's airheaded sister, Lydia, from a disastrous elopement. In Regency England, Lydia's act would have disgraced Lizzy's family and thereby made Lizzy unmarriageable to any real gentleman – and most certainly any gentleman who happened to own half of Derbyshire. So in one stroke (i) Lizzy learns that Darcy is a true gentleman and a true hero, and (ii) knows that he can never be hers. Everything is at stake, but success seems hopeless.
- The 15,000-word gap between the inner denouement and the outer one now makes sense. This gap gives the novel-

ist her winter of hope. It's the long moment of awfulness, before …

- A happy ending! When the external resolution comes about, Lizzy is still in the position of thinking that nothing on earth matters more than getting hooked up with Darcy … yet in a wonderful (and fairly swift) reversal, her apparently hopeless position becomes one where Darcy asks her to marry him. Jeopardy is still on its maximum setting (that is: there's a lot at stake). What's changed is that the odds of success flip from close to zero to a glorious 100%.

The lessons for you are simple. Nearly always, you need to complete your protagonist's inner journey before their outer journey is complete. Nearly always, you need to make your protagonist long absolutely and completely for their main goal, before they have attained it. Nearly always, that goal should seem most distant at precisely the point when it is most desired. Then, most of the time, you'll sock it to the reader with a happy ending. Easy – and always delicious.

Unhappy endings

Unhappy endings are less common than happy ones in fiction, but they are perfectly acceptable within the boundaries of the classic structure. If, for example, Jane Austen had chosen to break the hearts of her readers, she might have proceeded like this:

- Lizzy grows up; she learns humility and abandons prejudice.
- At the same time, she thinks Darcy is lost.
- Then, by a miracle, it seems that she's wrong. Darcy isn't lost at all. She just has to (let's say) come and find him before he enters a formalised and loveless liaison with a woman he doesn't really love.

- She races to London, comes to his lodgings, finds him at home. She's ecstatic. She's not too late! ... but she has arrived only to find that the marriage has already taken place. Everything is lost.
- She goes away, her heart broken.

A structure such as this works perfectly, but do note the double twist. First, the odds of success collapse almost to zero, then they shoot up to 90% – success is imminent! – then everything collapses, and this time for ever. The standard happy ending involves one abrupt reversal in fortunes. The unhappy ending *must* involve two. The reader wants the novelist to toy with their emotions. Even if we were OK with the idea of an unhappy ending, we simply wouldn't accept one in which Lizzy got Darcy's letter, and thought 'Well, darn it, I was wrong about Darcy, my life is now shattered, but everything is now hopeless; I'd better retrain as a bitter old maid'. There's no climax to such an ending. Everything in the book up to this point would seem barren and pointless. We'd feel tricked.

And in any case, these matters probably don't concern you, because you are (I know) planning a novel with a happy ending. Whatever your artistic soul may prefer, publishers – and readers – prefer stories with happy endings. On more than one occasion, I've handed my publisher a novel with a sad or ambiguous ending. They've told me that they like the book, admire my storytelling ... and would I kindly now please grow up and deliver the happy ending that I know everybody wants. And I've always done as they've asked. The rule perhaps doesn't apply quite so forcefully with literary novels. And thrillers can certainly end on a note of darkness as well as triumph. For a broad but accurate rule of thumb, however, happy endings sell better than sad ones. They sell better at the tills. They are more desired by publishers. They are more likely to get picked up by agents. And if you're self-publishing, those happy-ending novels are more likely to get recommended by readers, more likely to kickstart interest in a series, more likely, in fact, to launch a credible career.

And for all the many successful counterexamples, where books with downbeat endings have done well, we know that readers and publishers and agents are broadly right. Had Jane Austen *not* brought Lizzy and Darcy together, her novel might still have been great, but it would not be the stuff of non-stop publishing success, it would not have provided endless material for Hollywood and TV – and it would not be the subject of this chapter.

Ending quickly

We saw earlier how rapidly Jane Austen began her story: the reader is plunged into the central drama of the story from the first line (implicitly), and directly within a couple of thousand words.

The same goes for the ending. *Pride and Prejudice* is 122,000 words long. By the time the climactic Lizzy–Darcy scene has finished, barely 5,000 words remain. Those final chapters make room for some tying-up of loose ends – and nothing else. No new incident happens. No new subject is started. Jane Austen is tidying the house before closing the shutters and bidding it farewell. And these days, in truth, to allow 5,000 words for such housekeeping would seem overlong. I think the average contemporary author would feel that anything more than 2 or 3,000 words would seem unnecessarily sluggish.

This shouldn't seem surprising. After all, once the Big Question is solved, the reader is done. Bond needs to kill Dr Evil, blow up the underwater lair, bed the girl – and that's it. We don't need to watch his debriefing with M. We don't need to watch his wounds heal. We don't need the 'It isn't you, it's me' conversation when he goes on to dump the girl. The questions that launched the story are answered, so the story is now done. Anything that happens from now on isn't *story*, it's just events. And you're telling a story.

Subplots

Authors like subplots. They give work a complexity, density and variety that you can't achieve from more linear plots. And yet the wicked little secret is that subplots don't really exist.

Pride and Prejudice illustrates both points. If we were to summarise the book's plot in its simplest possible form, it would look like this:

- *Motivation.* Lizzy Bennet wants to marry for love.
- *Structure.* She meets Darcy and Wickham. She dislikes Darcy and starts to fall for Wickham. Wickham turns out to be a bad guy; Darcy turns out to be a good guy. She now loves Darcy.
- *Outcome.* She marries Darcy.
- *Subplot 1.* Jane Bennet (Lizzy's nice sister) loves Bingley. Bingley vanishes. He reappears. They get hitched.
- *Subplot 2.* Lydia Bennet (Lizzy's idiot sister) elopes with Wickham. She's rescued.
- *Subplot 3.* An idiot, Mr Collins, proposes marriage to Lizzy. She says no. He subsequently proposes to her friend, Charlotte, who says yes.

The book's core structure is fabulously simple. Two men arrive in Lizzy's life. She picks the wrong one. When she discovers her mistake, all looks lost – but it isn't, and she gets her guy. If Jane Austen had left it there, the book would feel too scanty for a full-length novel. It simply wouldn't have the depth and complexity needed to build a story of the right weight and emotional substance.

Enter the subplots. With subplots added, the book now feels like a proper novel. Complex, but not bewildering. Rich, but not overloaded. Even now, *Pride and Prejudice* represents a pretty good benchmark for plot complexity. If your plot is much simpler than *P and P*, it may well be too simple. If it's much more complex, it's quite likely too complex. (Detective and espionage stories may be an exception here, but more of them in the next chapter). Overall, the lesson that beckons many an unwary author is that Subplots are Good, and they should be added freely.

Which is where the other part of the lesson arises: that subplots don't exist. They don't exist, because they only matter to the reader – only matter to the novel – insofar as they affect the core story. The reader does not care about Jane Bennet. Yes, she's a lovely, pretty, sweet-natured girl. And yes, her potential partner, Bingley, is a lovely, good-looking, sweet-natured guy (who also happens to have pots of cash). Yet we don't care about either of them. Or rather, to be precise, we only care about them insofar as they affect Lizzy, and we only really care about Lizzy in relation to the burning question: *will she find Mr Right?*

When Jane draws close to Bingley, it matters because it creates some kind of connection – like it or lump it – between Lizzy and Darcy. When Bingley disappears, the circumstances suggest strongly that Darcy is a rotter, a development which directly affects Lizzy's own fortunes. When Bingley returns to Jane, we're delighted, because this heals one of the wounds between Lizzy and Darcy (and lends further weight to the hypothesis that Darcy's own journey of inner redemption is largely complete). All this only matters because we care about the Lizzy-Darcy relationship to the exclusion of everything else.

The same goes for the other subplots. We don't give a damn about Lydia, who is a spectacularly silly girl and deserves everything she gets ... except that her disgrace is also Lizzy's disgrace, Wickham is exposed as the very worst sort of bounder, and the stage is set for Darcy to pull off a dashing rescue act. Nothing in the Lydia story matters, except as it relates to Lizzy and Darcy.

Like Lydia, Collins is also spectacularly idiotic – albeit from a very different part of Planet Idiot – and his unwanted proposal to Lizzy (and Charlotte's acceptance of his subsequent proposal to her) illustrate what you get if you choose to marry for sensible financial reasons without any love involved. But again: this third subplot bears directly on the main story. Collins is the obsequious protégé of Lady Catherine de Bourgh, who is Darcy's aunt, and all Lizzy's dealings with Collins echo back up the chain to the only place that truly matters.

Naturally, good writers don't create plot just for the sake of it. All the subplots in *Pride and Prejudice* illustrate something about love and marriage – the heart of the book's concerns – and contain moral and emotional lessons for the reader. They enrich the book thematically; they're not just adding structure for the sake of it.

But the lesson is clear. If you jam in subplots *only* for didactic purposes, you will instantly leach energy from your story. Stories start to die almost immediately if you remove their nourishment – the Big Question that launched them – and a single poorly designed subplot can kill a book. And this, in essence is the secret of the subplot: the only time a subplot works is when it isn't really a subplot at all. All twists and turns in the story need to bear directly on the main object of interest. They need to keep alive that sense of continual movement in the protagonist's fortunes. If they don't, they need to be eliminated. If they do, they are welcome to do so in any way they like and achieve whatever other subsidiary goals they can.

Consistency

The previous section focused on the essential unity of plot. This one offers a short homily on unity of purpose.

I've spoken so far about the Big Question on which the book depends (will Elizabeth Bennet find Mr Right?). I've sometimes spoken about Lizzy's core motivation (wanting to find Mr Right). Either way, I've implied that she has the same purpose all the way through, which is at best only half true.

Part of the untruth is that, early in the book, Lizzy's affections are not particularly engaged, and although, yes, she would like to marry and marry well, she is a well-rounded young woman with a perfectly ordinary range of interests and concerns. As things develop, it's true that her focus becomes increasingly consumed by matters of love, but it doesn't start out that way.

That's the first part of the untruth. The second is that, at a slightly less elevated level, Lizzy's motivations are shifting all the time. Roughly speaking, her evolution runs thus:

- 'I hate Darcy. I want nothing to do with him.'
- 'I'm interested in Mr Wickham.'
- 'Golly gosh, I'm *very* interested in Mr Wickham.'
- 'Oh no! Wickham is the worst of all bounders, and Darcy is the noblest of all heroes. I love Darcy after all – *he's* the guy I want.'

At this somewhat more practical level of motivation, Lizzy's motivations shift all the time. In an action story, transitions of this kind are common too. So, for example, James Bond might be sent off on a boring errand to track some missing money – then discover that a senior British diplomat has been killed – then uncover a plot to blow up the world. In the course of these transitions, Bond's motivations alter, just as Lizzy's did:

- 'What a boring assignment, but still, I'd better go and track down the missing cash.'
- 'Hey up. Old Sir Barnaby-Boring has been killed, I'm on the track of a killer now.'
- 'Aha! Not just a killer, but Dr Evil himself. High time I blew up an underwater lair, I reckon. And I wonder if I can find someone pretty to take to bed.'

There are three crucial points to notice about transitions of this sort. First, viewed at a certain higher level, the motivations never alter. Lizzy *is* always interested in love and marriage. Bond *is* always interested in saving the world.

Secondly, the protagonist's motivations *never* vary simply through vacillation or shifts of mood. They vary following the direct causal logic of the story itself. Thus, Bond only gets involved in Sir Barnaby-Boring when the logic of his investigation forces him there. Lizzy's affections only shift from Wickham to Darcy, when she uncovers information that force her to change her opinion. Either way, the changes that take place feel necessary, not whimsical.

Third, through all these changes, the reader never feels complete until the final chapter. Take that possible Bond story. Supposing that Bond was sent down to track down some money lost from a British consulate in St Lucia. He flies to St Lucia, tracks down the missing money, arrests the person responsible and is relaxing in a restaurant afterwards – let's say 20,000 words into the book – when he witnesses the drive-by shooting of Sir Barnaby-Boring, *in an incident totally unconnected with the previous material.* Pretty clearly, this is a plot that will never fly. The reader was prepared to engage with the money-plot only because they assumed it would lead somewhere more interesting than a relaxing dinner in a restaurant. If you betray that assumption, your reader will betray you by flinging your book across the room. (Or, if it's an e-reader, jabbing the off switch in a particularly forceful way.) Either way, the problem is that you've raised some story expectations, then completed them way before the end of the book. That must never happen, no matter what kind of story you're telling.

In short, no matter how the lower-level motivations may change, the big one never can. You need to initiate your Big Question early and answer it late. Along the way, you must never leave your reader with a sense of quiet satisfaction that the protagonist's job is done. It *can't* be done. You're in the middle of a story. Perhaps at times the protagonist *thinks* he's done, but the reader needs to know otherwise.

Quite likely, you've read this section with a sense of incredulity. Switching motivations and challenges halfway through the story? Surely that sounds like a terribly basic mistake, one that *you* couldn't possibly make. Well, maybe. But you have to remember that we at Jericho Writers see a lot of first-time manuscripts by first-time writers. And we do in fact come across a fair few stories that are either very episodic, with adventure after adventure following in no particular sequence, or that take the form of a chain of events in which the protagonist meets – and deals with – a series of linked challenges. Either way, your story won't work. Novels need structure. The episodic narrative worked fine for Miguel de Cervantes and *Don Quixote* (and indeed for most long-running TV dramas). It won't work for agents today. Similarly, the chain-of-events type narrative (for example, where a woman has cancer and deals successively with financial, creative, family and health concerns) also lacks a kind of structural integrity. It offers too many potential stopping points for the reader. It invites a reader to get halfway through the novel and think, 'Well, this woman has now solved her financial issues, and her creative ones. I daresay if new problems crop up, she'll deal with those too. I'll stop reading here.'

Your story must stay moving. To be static is to die.

A word about conflict

One of the slogans heard often in the movie business is that drama *is* conflict, a proposition which has inevitably influenced much of the writing about plotting in prose narrative.

And the slogan is true, up to a point. Take a simple situation – let's say, a couple washing up after having had friends round to dinner. There are three rough levels of interaction possible:

- *Harmonious.* The husband and wife discuss the evening. They find no serious points of disagreement and chat happily as they tidy up. Any such dialogue quickly risks feeling tedious.

- *Divergent.* The two discuss the evening, but the husband believes that Jemma, one of the guests, was inappropriately flirty and sexual as she got more drunk. The wife thinks Jemma behaved just fine. The couple are not in conflict exactly, but they do disagree. This conversation is instantly more interesting. A reader will be scanning this dialogue for clues, in order (i) to try and understand whether Jemma was or wasn't behaving inappropriately, (ii) to understand what the husband's position says about him, (iii) to understand what the wife's position says about her, and (iv) to see if the disagreement is going to lead anywhere in terms of what the couple *does*.

- *Conflictual.* The final level is where disagreement spills over into conflict. Normal social rules are breached. Perhaps the couple start yelling at each other. Perhaps crockery is broken. Perhaps – who knows – a marriage ends or violence is committed. Pretty clearly, dialogue of this sort is most likely to grab and hold the reader's interest.

On the whole, therefore, you should avoid too many harmonious scenes, have plenty of divergent ones (even if the divergences are small), and make full use of the occasional outright conflictual ones.

Having said all this, it's very easy to overdo things. Suppose you write a book about a couple who always argue. They argue about dinner parties. They argue about the gardening. They argue about their children. They argue about everything. Unless something happens to disrupt this status quo, you have a story that is full of *conflict*, but bereft of *change*. And it's change, not conflict, that lies at the heart of any drama.

What's more, focusing on conflict is likely to draw your attention to all the wrong things. Go back to the opening of *Pride and Prejudice*. It's absolutely true that, in the first couple of chapters, there is a low-level conflict of sorts between Mr Bennet (sensible, but distant) and Mrs Bennet (a nitwit). Yet that 'conflict' *isn't* the drama. It's background colour, which will go on, unchanged, through almost the entire course of the novel. Mr Bennet will go on being sensible but distant. His wife will go on being a queen of nitwits. Nothing much changes.

At the same time, the drama is obvious. Mr Bingley is coming to Netherfield! So is his super-rich friend Darcy! Five girls, two men: the race is on. The centre of the drama is blazingly obvious and has nothing whatsoever to do with conflict. Later on, of course, there will be moments in the text when the drama lies in direct, obvious conflict. When Darcy first proposes to Lizzy, she refuses him with asperity and the two go on to have a heated argument. But conflict is just one of the ways in which drama can manifest. The sole reliable universal of drama is change. Change in the protagonist's relationship to their goal. If you have that, you have a story.

The multi-protagonist story

Although Darcy is clearly a crucial character in *Pride and Prejudice*, he is not a protagonist. No scenes are related from his perspective. The book is Lizzy Bennet's book, and Darcy's importance arises only because he is (or becomes) so important to her. There are, however, plenty of books with multiple protagonists. *The Time Traveler's Wife* deals even-handedly between its two leads. *The Lions of Al-Rassan* deals even-handedly between its three.

The key rule in plotting such books is a simple one: each protagonist needs his or her own story, and each individual story must follow all the rules of the classic plot. So, if you have three protagonists, you will have three plots, each of which ticks the boxes enumerated in this chapter. Each character needs an inner and an outer journey. Each one will face mounting jeopardy and worsening odds. There will be the same basic pattern of challenge, adventure and resolution. By picking two or three protagonists, you are forcing yourself to write two or three books, not just the one.

What's more, those plots need to intersect and talk to each other. Typically, the actions of protagonist A will impact the story of protagonist B, and vice versa – but that doesn't need to be true in any very direct way. In A. S. Byatt's *Possession*, the characters who led one strand of the story lived and died in a completely different century to the protagonists in the other strand. Nevertheless, the stories spoke to each other. The discoveries of the researchers in the contemporary strand of the tale shed light on the romance depicted in the Victorian one. And the romance in that second strand is echoed and reflected in the deepening romance unfolding in the first. Such reverberations are quite enough to knit two stories into a single book.

These comments might sound rather scary. After all, writing a book seems a tough enough proposition without having to write two or three books simultaneously and to engineer things so that those different stories all intersect and complement each other. And perhaps it *is* a little scary. Certainly, the multi-protagonist story is more challenging from a technical point of view than the single-protagonist one. On the other hand, you have simplified your life in one respect. Because a two- or three-handed book needs two or three stories to sustain it, each of those individual stories will be fairly simple – probably too simple, in fact, to fuel an entire novel on their own.

I know this from experience. My first novel, *The Money Makers*, involved three protagonists. Each of the three had their own journey, their own jeopardy, their own climaxes and so on. The three stories ran in parallel and directly influenced each other. The book was a whopper – 180,000 words – so it had plenty of room to develop plenty of scale and complexity. Nevertheless, each individual story was a scant 60,000 words. There was no room for the treble subplots of *Pride and Prejudice*; no room for the twisting bluff and double-bluff of a modern espionage novel. Although readers certainly wouldn't have felt any lack of complexity (because, after all, those readers had to keep track of three parallel stories as they read), the fact is that each individual story was relatively simple: more novella-like than properly novel-like.

Non-fiction

Some writers of non-fiction may have felt a breath of impatience with this chapter or – worse still – started to skip bits. If you're among their number, you need to go back to the start and read every word. Non-fiction narratives must obey these rules too. Each one. Yes, of course, your story is *true*. So what? You still have to tell a story and the structures elucidated in this chapter *are* the structures of story, period.

Naturally, if you are writing memoir, there will be a host of life events – of huge drama and significance to you – which simply don't fit this relatively simple schema. Fine. So ditch them. You need to sift your life experience, find your story, and ignore the rest. (Perhaps you want to write those other parts down anyway. You and your family will and should treasure them. But they're not publishers. They're not ordinary readers from the wider public.) You may find this a shockingly brutal approach, but it's the only way to go, nevertheless. Jericho Writers has handled plenty of memoirs, of which several have gone on to become top-ten bestsellers. These memoirs were impeccably true. They also had impeccably novel-like structures. They had Big Questions, constant movement, inner and outer journeys – everything mentioned in this chapter, in fact. What's more, they were ruthlessly edited. The authors had had long, productive, busy lives. Yet each book revolved around a period of just two or three years. Those years were where the story lay. Everything else – well, it was just events. As ever, if you want to understand how your particular genre works, you need to get yourself down to a bookshop and buy a selection of books in a similar area. (If memoir is your thing, don't make the mistake of buying celebrity memoir. That's not the same genre. Every single little thing that Elizabeth Taylor did is of interest because she was Elizabeth Taylor. You're not.)

Having said all that, I will allow one small difference between narrative non-fiction and a novel, which is this: whereas the plotting of a novel needs to be tight, the structuring of a true-life story can be a little looser, a little more discursive. What would simply be slackness in the novelist reads like truthfulness in the memoir-writer. So yes, you can be a little more discursive. You can be a little less rigid in the application of the rules. But only a little. Story is story.

Want More Help?

Course you do. Plotting isn't just hard. It's also central to your success as a writer. So naturally we came up with a plotting worksheet, designed to keep your story on the straight and narrow. It's completely free, and you can get it right here:

jerichowriters.com/how-to-write-a-novel-free-resources

Chapter Summary

- The classic plot dominates storytelling. It's the single most widespread way of telling a story that exists.

- Make sure you get stuck in early: get the story rolling straight away, identify your protagonist, establish any important rules.

- Your story needs to move in every single chapter. If you allow the story to go static, it'll start to die. (You can check your story movement is sufficient by making sure that every chapter has a job to do.)

- Your external story (what happens in the world) needs to be complemented by an inner story (what happens in the protagonist's mind). Those two stories are intimately interconnected.

- As you move towards the climax of your book, the stakes (or jeopardy) need to increase. At the point of maximum jeopardy, the odds of success also need to seem abysmally low.

- You can end happily or sadly ... but happy endings tend to be more commercially successful.

- Once the Big Question that drives your story has been resolved, end it quickly.

- Subplots are essential (to give your novel the right degree of complexity) but they don't exist (because all subplots should serve to drive the development of your main story).

- Your protagonist needs to have essentially the same set of motivations throughout. The specific expression of those motivations may alter, but there will be a unity and consistency to them all the same.

- Conflict can be an important part of storytelling – but movement is a better concept to focus on.

- Finally, the multi-protagonist novel is also a multi-plot novel. Each of the rules in this summary need to apply to the stories relating to each of your protagonists. What's more, those stories need to interconnect. If that sounds tough, then remember each plot in a multi-protagonist tale can be simpler than it would need to be if it were a novel in its own right.

THE MYSTERY PLOT

The type of storytelling we looked at in the previous chapter undoubtedly represents the single most important model in world literature. Its themes and techniques are so universal that they transcend time, place and culture. If you go into a bookshop and pick novels at random off the shelves, the chances are that they will obey (or seek to obey) the rules we've just examined. And to read some accounts of plotting, you'd think these rules are universal. That they apply to *every* novel and *every* story.

And they don't. If you don't believe me, you can conduct the following simple experiment: go down to your local bookshop, wander into the crime section, put out your hand at random and pick two or three books off the shelf. It's almost certain that at least one of the books in your hand – and quite likely all three – will breach one of the key rules established above.

Sherlock Holmes and the mystery of the missing journey

On the whole, crime novels obey the rules given above. They get the story started straight away. They identify their protagonist and a goal (typically, a detective and a murder case to be solved). Any rules of their particular world are quickly established. Story movement is of the essence. And so on.

But the parallels don't go the whole way. There are at least two major differences between the 'classic' novel structure and the mystery novel structure. They are as follows …

Importance of motivation

Classic: To Lizzy Bennet, marrying Darcy became the be-all and end-all of her life. Nothing in the world was more important to her. Although it's not directly stated, you feel that the drama described in *Pride and Prejudice* will be *the* drama of Lizzy Bennet's life.

Mystery: To a detective protagonist – be it Sherlock Holmes, Philip Marlowe or Kay Scarpetta – the whodunit is just a murder investigation and investigation is what they do: their day job. They may or may not get emotionally involved in a case (Sherlock Holmes almost never did; modern detectives often do), but whether they do or not, they're never *that* involved. Another case will come along tomorrow.

Character change

Classic: To accomplish her goal, Lizzy had to change. She had to overcome her prejudice. She had to mature as a person. Again, and although it's not stated, most readers will feel as though that act of personal growth will be the defining act of Lizzy's adult life. By the end of the book, she is essentially complete as a human being. Though, presumably, her future life will throw plenty of challenges and problems her way, we feel that her great, lifetime act of personal completion is already behind her.

Mystery: To accomplish their goals, Messrs Holmes and Marlowe never change at all. They are essentially the same characters at the end of the series as they were at the start. They don't even have any visible change in their life circumstances (no partner, no change of address, no transformative family incident, etc). Kay Scarpetta does, as it happens, have an ordinary life story (romantic partners, job moves, etc), but it's an *ordinary* one: none of the high, intoxicating drama of Lizzy's journey in *Pride and Prejudice*.

Because the character change involved in *Pride and Prejudice* seems so huge, so life-defining, it follows that novels which follow the classic plot structure pretty much *can't* have sequels. If you've already plunged your protagonist into the defining drama of his or her life, then why would a reader want to spend any further time with that character? With the mystery novel, on the other hand, the logic runs exactly the other way. Sherlock Holmes and Philip Marlowe are terrific characters. Their business is the detection of crime; readers like reading about crime-detection; a series therefore beckons. That's why the great protagonists of classic fiction – Lizzy Bennet, David Copperfield, Huckleberry Finn, Captain Ahab – appear, for the most part, in one-off novels. It's why detectives – Sherlock Holmes, Hercule Poirot, Sam Spade, Philip Marlowe, Kay Scarpetta, Harry Bosch – appear in series, often very long-running series.

The mystery of the unwaxed moustache

There's a further set of differences between the classic novel and the mystery. In the classic novel, the Big Question looks forward into the future. *Will* Lizzy marry Darcy? *Will* Bond save the world? The issue is one of suspense, a question of what is going to unfold. In mystery novels, the Big Question typically has to do with the past. Who killed Sir Charles Baskerville? What happened to Little Velma? The issue is one of mystery, a question of understanding something that has already taken place.

Because of this difference in focus, the two different types of plot evolve in different ways. In the classic, suspense-driven, forward-looking plot structure, the story is driven by events. Bingley and Darcy come to Netherfield. They hold a ball. Darcy makes a cutting comment. At a subsequent ball he nevertheless invites Lizzy to dance. She refuses him. And so on. Naturally, there will be times when the revelation of information becomes absolutely central (eg: Darcy's revelation of Wickham's wicked-ness), but information isn't the centre of things. Events are.

Most contemporary mystery novels have plenty of incident, of course, but the critical plot evolution centres on the revelation of information – on clues, in fact. To acquire those clues, no doubt, the detective has to be active and inquisitive. There'll be times when the search for information means that the detective will be shot at, thumped, knocked out, blown up and so on. But those things are secondary. In an English crime story of the 'Golden Age', detectives moved through their investigation at an unhurried pace, waxing their moustaches as they elicited crucial details from housemaids and underbutlers. Information, not events, is the key.

The mysterious Mr Ono

Although the mystery story is most often associated with crime, pretty much any novel can have elements of mystery. Indeed, some novels may be pure mystery novels even though they don't involve themselves with crimes or detectives.

Any ghost story, for example, will certainly involve a large element of mystery. Those spooky goings-on up at old Miss Vanderhoek's mansion – are they because of a haunting, or is there a more human/rational explanation? Or think about Dan Brown's *The Da Vinci Code*. Robert Langdon is not a detective, and concealment of the Holy Grail is not a crime. There's certainly an action–adventure strand to Brown's novel, but the core of it is a classic mystery plot – just one that doesn't involve an ordinary crime or an ordinary detective. In the same way, the first two thirds of Stephenie Meyer's *Twilight* is at least as much of a mystery story as it is a classically structured one. For sure, there's a blossoming romance taking place, but whereas the classic romance (the Elizabeth Bennet/Darcy one, for example) involves a permanent shifting in the relationship between the two protagonists, in *Twilight* that relationship seems remarkably static. Bella fancies Edward. Edward fancies Bella (albeit in a slightly weird way). The novel overcomes this static quality because of the mystery which underpins it: just who is this mysterious, handsome, talented Edward Cullen? How come he can stop moving cars with his bare hands? And just why does he so assiduously avoid sunlight?

Mystery can dominate literary novels as well. As it happens, I'd regard Raymond Chandler as being one of the best American writers of the last century. His novels are crime-mystery stories, but they are also great and enduring works of art. You don't, however, have to share that opinion to agree that some obviously literary novels such as Kazuo Ishiguro's *An Artist of the Floating World* are essentially mystery stories. In Ishiguro's book, the narrator, Masuji Ono, is an elderly man, reflecting on his past. Ono has a high regard for himself and his achievements, but it becomes increasingly clear to the reader that he was, in fact, deeply implicated in the rise of Japanese fascism in the course of the 1930s. In essence, then, the novel is a mystery: what did Ono get up to before and during the war? There are a host of ancillary questions of course – is Ono a trustworthy narrator? how should we judge Ono's actions? – but the mystery is central.

And, of course, these things aren't all-or-nothing. Even if your novel is predominantly a classic novel in format, there's no reason why you shouldn't consider bringing hefty amounts of mystery-style plotting into your work. That means plotting which works via clues and investigation of the past, rather than events and the attempt to shape a future. Bringing both elements into your work will tend to add depth and interest. Naturally, you need to avoid clutter and confusion – which in turn means making sure that you take extra care with all the genuinely universal rules of plotting; that is, all those rules shared between the two different styles of novel. You also need to make sure that your novel has a proper centre. The hybrid nature of Meyer's *Twilight* works because the entire novel centres on the 'will they, won't they' question of the romance. The early mystery element, in which Cullen's vampire nature is gradually exposed, is as central a part of that question as the more event–driven developments later in the book.

The mysterious death of Miss Marple

The 'Golden Age' of crime fiction spanned the 1920s and 1930s. It was an international flowering, albeit one dominated by British authors. Famous names of the era include Margery Allingham, Dorothy L. Sayers, Freeman Wills Crofts, Georges Simenon, Ngaio Marsh, John Dickson Carr – and the queen of them all, Agatha Christie. Murders were typically upper-class affairs: baronets killed in the smoking rooms of their secluded country houses. Many of the novels were technical masterpieces. Authors would cause suspicion to fall on a succession of different characters, before revealing with a flourish that the actual murderer was the one person whom everybody least suspected.

The novel became simultaneously technically adept and excessively formalised, even lifeless. Indeed, a number of writers produced sets of rules which writers needed to follow, one of the best-known lists being the 'ten commandments' of British author Ronald Knox:

1. The criminal must be mentioned in the early part of the story, but must not be anyone whose thoughts the reader has been allowed to know.

2. All supernatural or preternatural agencies are ruled out as a matter of course.

3. Not more than one secret room or passage is allowable.

4. No hitherto undiscovered poisons may be used, nor any appliance which will need a long scientific explanation at the end.

5. No Chinaman must figure in the story.

6. No accident must ever help the detective, nor must he ever have an unaccountable intuition which proves to be right.

7. The detective himself must not commit the crime.

8. The detective is bound to declare any clues which he may discover.

9. The stupid friend of the detective, the Watson, must not conceal from the reader any thoughts which pass through his mind: his intelligence must be slightly, but very slightly, below that of the average reader.

10. Twin brothers, and doubles generally, must not appear unless we have been duly prepared for them.

These rules give you a sense of how contrived some of these 'golden' stories were. No *Chinamen*? No undiscovered poisons? Twin brothers and doubles allowed, but only if declared? Not more than one secret passage? It would be a strange story today that made use of any of these contrivances – except that today we might regard a Chinese character as being a person rather than a contrivance.

The Golden Age came to an end, murdered in broad daylight by Dashiell Hammett, Raymond Chandler, and other American authors who put murders back where they belonged – out onto the mean streets of whichever city the detective happened to patrol. The unreality of those interwar novels was part of the problem that brought about their demise, but they suffered from another ailment too, and one that was possibly more toxic in the long run. The *pure* mystery novel is a rather comfortable affair. The detective is not under threat. Other people may be, but readers care about protagonists far more than any other character, so those threats aren't all that material. The whole novel becomes an intellectual exercise, a kind of extended crossword puzzle. Although books like that still exist, they are generally categorised as 'cosy' crime and have a deliberately whimsical, playful tone – hence the number of such books that deal with cats or quilting or (very likely) both.

Mainstream crime has essentially abandoned this kind of writing. These days, crime novels are essentially crime thrillers; hybrid novels that combine the intellectual puzzles of a mystery with the suspense-driven drama of a classic novel. Needless to say, this change in market mood has brought about contrivances of its own. The classic novel, as we've seen, is largely a one-off affair. It doesn't lend itself to series characters and repetitive plots. If mystery stories want, nevertheless, to adopt some of their cousin's narrative structures, compromises are inevitable. Those compromises are well-known. The serial killer who starts to become obsessed with the detective. The final confrontation with the villain in a situation where the detective's life is suddenly in peril. The antagonistic relationship with the police chief, so that the detective's career seems in permanent jeopardy. Unstable personal relationships, which permit a host of 'will they, won't they' romantic questions to be raised.

In the end, dodges of this sort will only partially fool the reader. Although most romances do end happily, there is always the possibility that on this occasion Lizzy Bennet will not marry her Darcy. On the other hand, if you're reading the twentieth Kay Scarpetta novel, you've already been given quite a sizeable clue that any dangerous showdown with an armed killer in the deserted warehouse late at night is going to end happily for Ms Scarpetta. It's ended happily nineteen times before. Nevertheless, partial success is still success. And if you can make *your* deserted warehouse scene genuinely atmospheric and your villain genuinely menacing, the reader will give you the benefit of the doubt. In any case, if you choose to be purist about these things – if you're determined that your crime novel will be a true Golden Age gem, equipped with lustrous moustaches, hidden passages, Chinamen and all – you will be purist but unpublished. And if you choose to self-publish, you will be published but unread.

The market today demands jeopardy; mystery *and* suspense; Agatha Christie *and* Jane Austen.

Chapter Summary

- Mystery novels obey most of the rules of the 'classic' plot …
- … but there is often not the same sense of overwhelming motivation or inner character journeys.
- The mystery novel uses clues and information to drive back to some past event (the mystery), whereas the classic plot uses events and actions to drive forwards to some large unresolved question (the suspense).
- Essentially all crime novels have mysteries at their heart, but there are plenty of non-crime novels which are mysteries too.
- Equally, the modern crime novel is a crime thriller: powered both by mystery and suspense. If you are writing a crime novel, you must make sure that it is suspenseful as well as mysterious.

THE LITERARY PLOT

Suspense and mystery; future and past; events and information; challenges overcome and puzzles solved. You might think that between them, the two dominant novel forms cover pretty much everything that a novel *can* cover. And perhaps that's true. Or perhaps it isn't. I'm not sure.

From swerve of shore

There is, admittedly, one obvious type of novel that doesn't fit into either of these categories, namely the experimental. The modernist movement, which had its heyday in the interwar years, rejected conventional, nineteenth-century structures in every type of art form, including novels and poetry, but also in painting, sculpture, architecture, music, and so on. You can get a sense of the rule-breaking in question by reading Robert Musil's unfinished 1,700-page monster *The Man Without Qualities*. Or, if you don't have the stamina for that, you can dip into an equally famous novel, James Joyce's *Finnegans Wake*, which opens thus:

> *riverrun, past Eve and Adam's, from swerve of shore to bend of bay, brings us by a commodius vicus of recirculation back to Howth Castle and Environs.*
>
> *Sir Tristram, violer d'amores, fr'over the short sea, had passencore rearrived from North Armorica on this side the scraggy isthmus of Europe Minor to wielderfight his penisolate war: nor had topsawyer's rocks by the stream Oconee exaggerated themselse to Laurens County's gorgios while they went doublin their mumper all the time: nor avoice from afire bellowsed mishe mishe to tauftauf thuartpeatrick: not yet, though venissoon after, had a*

kidscad buttended a bland old isaac: not yet, though all's fair in vanessy, were sosie sesthers wroth with twone nathandjoe. Rot a peck of pa's malt had Jhem or Shen brewed by arclight and rory end to the regginbrow was to be seen ringsome on the aquaface.

Novels such as this today may be called several things: experimental, innovative, perhaps post-modern. But really the adjective which best describes the attitude of mainstream agents and publishers is *unpublishable*. The adjective which best describes the attitude of most readers is *unreadable*. That's not to say that there's anything wrong with fiction of this sort. Any lively art form needs to have radicals at its boundaries, exploring the limits of the possible. Twentieth-century literature would be vastly poorer had it not been for experiments like these. All the same, if you want to write fiction of this type, you are strongly advised to write shorter fiction and seek publication in experimental or online magazines. Mainstream agents and publishers will reject your work, because ordinary readers reject it too.

A book without plot

So, let's set such work aside and go back to the original question: whether there's a type of fiction that neither follows the model of the classic novel nor that of the mystery story. And perhaps there is, or perhaps there isn't.

Take, for example, the plot of Ian McEwan's short book *On Chesil Beach*. In its entirety, the plot is as follows:

On the night of their wedding, Edward Mayhew is about to have sex for the first time with his new wife, when he has a premature ejaculation. The couple argue and their marriage ends.

That's it. I haven't left out a single detail. It's not even a book *about* the argument and subsequent break-up. The ejaculation happens on page 100 of a 166-page book. There then follows a lengthy excursion back into the past. The couple's argument runs from pages 139 to 157. Their subsequent life stories are speedily summarised on the handful of pages that remain.

McEwan's novel is very short: a novella, in fact. Even so, the constant yo-yo motion of a true novel – the 'will they, won't they' type question – is notably absent. All that stuff about jeopardy and the winter of hope is essentially absent. The book just doesn't have enough plot movement to allow for it. With its frequent lengthy forays into the couple's pre-history, the novel doesn't feel like a sequence of dramatic events building to a climax. The feeling you have when you read it is more like that of a slow, inevitable zooming in, a single critical moment explored in ever more relentless close-up. And perhaps that's the secret. If the classic novel deals with the future, and the mystery novel with the past, then perhaps there's a third form altogether – the literary novel – whose progress is measured in terms of a slow intensification of focus, a steady increase in magnification or understanding.

The length of *On Chesil Beach*, however, makes it a doubtful foundation for any such theory. A better possibility is Joseph O'Neill's *Netherland*, a beautifully written book which was hugely admired by some of today's most influential critics. The book opens with two pieces of information which seem to promise a good old-fashioned yarn. First, we learn on page 4 that Chuck Ramkissoon, a friend of Hans, the narrator, has been found murdered. Secondly, we learn on page 22 that Rachel, Hans's wife, wants a trial separation and is intending to return to London from New York, taking their young son with her. A mysterious death and a marriage break-up: that seems like promising material for a story. Just the sort of Big Questions we need.

The trouble is, O'Neill sabotages both questions early on. The bit on page 22 about the trial separation is told in flashback and we know from page 3 of the book that the narrator is in fact contentedly married to Rachel. So the possible Big Question – will Hans succeed in getting back together with his wife? – has already been answered. Equally, even before we're told about Ramkissoon's death, Hans comments, 'I didn't wonder very often about what had become of a man named Chuck Ramkissoon, who'd been a friend during my final East Coast summer and had since, in the way of these things, become a transitory figure'. In other words, Hans is letting us know that he doesn't really regard the question of Ramkissoon's fate as being a Big Question at all; it's more of a minor footnote. (That also means that although Ramkissoon is the book's largest, most colourful presence, he's not one that we care about all that much – unlike Gatsby, his most obvious literary forebear. It's not what happens on the page that matters, or who fills the page – what matters is how those things impact the protagonist who is witnessing them.)

So what is the book about? What is its Big Question? The clue is present in the set-up and the conclusion. When Rachel says that she wants to separate, Hans tells us:

> There was another silence. I felt, above all, tired. Tiredness: if there was a constant symptom of the disease in our lives at this time, it was tiredness. At work we were unflagging; at home the smallest gesture of liveliness was beyond us. Mornings we woke into a malign weariness that seemed only to have refreshed itself overnight … Rachel was tired and I was tired. A banal state of affairs, yes – but our problems were banal, the stuff of women's magazines.

This is the problem at the heart of the book. It tells the story of a middle-aged, middle-class man's struggle to self-realise, to come properly into life, his own and his family's. The resolution is told in the final pages, on a family trip to the huge London Eye Ferris wheel:

> I notice, meanwhile, that Jake has started to race around and needs to be brought to order, and that Rachel is standing alone in a corner. I merely join my wife. I join her just as we reach the very top of our celestial circuit and for this reason I have no need to do anything more than put an arm round her shoulder.

The narrator then has a reminisce (one of many) about a child-hood incident in New York, where he was sightseeing with his mother. The book ends thus:

> *Which makes me remember my mother. I remember how I turned and caught her – how could I have forgotten this until now? – looking not at New York but at me, and smiling.*
>
> *Which is how I come to face my family with the same smile.*
>
> *'Look!' Jake is saying, pointing wildly. 'See, Daddy?'*
>
> *I see, I tell him, looking from him to Rachel and again to him. Then I turn to look for what it is we're supposed to be seeing.*

This clearly isn't the sort of Big Question which would keep a thriller pounding away. It's not even the sort of Big Question which would have satisfied Jane Austen or Charles Dickens or Herman Melville or any of the great pre-Modernist authors. But, if you care to see things this way, *Netherland*'s structure does, formally speaking, tick the boxes for the classic novel structure we looked at in the chapter on *Pride and Prejudice*. Faint ticks to be sure, but ticks nevertheless.

But perhaps that's not the only way to look at it. *Pride and Prejudice* has an urgent, obvious story. When you explore the movement in its plot – the way the story is advanced chapter by chapter; the way the subplots all pay homage to the novel's central question – the technical elements are clearly defined, unmissable. When you have a Big Question as evasive as Joseph O'Neill's, however, it's just not clear that the same analytical apparatus has much value. Whereas you can't possibly understand Jane Austen's plotting without thinking about classical plot structures, it's not clear that those structures lend any real insight into O'Neill's methods at all.

So perhaps it does make more sense to define that putative third type of plot: the intensifying, magnifying, type, one that revolves constantly round a central set of themes. If there is a central question here, it'll be one with answers that are vague rather than precise, ethereal rather than concrete. So where Jane Austen asks, *Will Elizabeth Bennet marry Darcy?*, O'Neill asks, *Will Hans overcome his tiredness, those 'banal' problems which are the 'stuff of women's magazines'?*

As soon as you accept that O'Neill may simply be plotting in a different tradition to the classic one, plenty about his approach makes sense. For example, both he and McEwan make extensive use of flashbacks and flashforwards. Such things threaten the purposeful forward drive of a classic plot. (*Pride and Prejudice* has no flashbacks and no flashforwards.) If, however, the purpose of a story is to drive deeper, if the storyteller doesn't much care about that purposeful forward movement in the first place, then you may as well use as many flashbacks and flashforwards as you choose.

Additionally, the notion of a different form of plotting makes sense of the way we talk about such books. According to *The New York Times*, *Netherland* is 'a resonant meditation on the American Dream'. The *USA Today* called it 'a meditation on despair, loss and exile'. And meditation, after all, is not the most dynamic thing you can do, as even the novel's fans agree. James Wood, for example, an admirer of the book, wrote in *The New Yorker* that, 'One suspects [Rachel's] absence from New York to be merely the necessary fictional trigger for Hans's hospitable sloth. But ... one can forgive a lot of stasis when the verbal rewards, page after page, are so very high'.

These thoughts then suggest we have three forms of plot: the classic plot, the mystery plot and the meditative plot. Authors can take their pick.

A word of advice

But before any would-be literary authors among my readers decide that the meditative plot sounds cool, a word of advice. First of all, if you don't have much of a story to speak of, the quality of your writing needs to be exceptionally high. Not just good-enough-to-carry-a-story strong, but good-enough-to-carry-a-novel-in-its-own-right strong. Very few writers achieve this standard. Indeed, for all the praise that *Netherland* received in some quarters, the view in others was that the book was simply too static – too dull – to be regarded as a success. Publishers, of course, are more interested in sales than in acclaim for its own sake, and O'Neill had real difficulty in finding a publisher for his book. He could write a nice sentence, but where was his story? Even fantastic prose may not be enough.

Indeed, if you want *my* conclusion to this trio of chapters on plotting, it's this: that the oldest methods are still the best. The modern crime novel uses plenty of mystery-style technique, but it is no longer a pure mystery novel. These days, even a crime novel needs the forward-looking, suspense-based drive of the classic novel to engage its readers. The same is true of the literary novel. If you write a book as static, as introspective, as O'Neill's *Netherland*, your writing needs to be very strong indeed; you need to be in the very top echelon of contemporary prose stylists to be accepted ... and even then, as O'Neill found, it may be tough. Personally, if I'd been a publisher, I wouldn't have bought his book. I thought it was boring. I'd rather eat a bowl of sawdust or glue grains of rice to a sheet of cardboard.

In short? Traditional plotting isn't a cop-out. It's the way we tell stories. It's Homer's way and Shakespeare's, Dickens's and Austen's, Hemingway's and Fitzgerald's. In the end, it's not the structure you use which will distinguish your stories. It's the way you tell 'em.

Chapter Summary

- The experimental novel is close to unsaleable these days.
- Some literary novels almost abandon classic novel structures, and instead focus with increasing intensity on a particular theme or emotional transition.
- Such novels are often non-chronological in structure. Their 'Big Questions' often seem ethereal or indistinct.
- They're also tough to sell. You'll only succeed if you are a very good prose writer ... and even then, you might do better to make greater use of classic plot structures.

Perspectives From Film

Although story is central to the novel, much of the recent theorising on plotting has come from the movie business. That's partly because films cost vastly more than books, so studio executives feel the need for an analytical apparatus which will allow them to identify successes and failures in advance. Additionally, though, films are much leaner than novels. Their stories are more compact. There's less room for subplot, less room for dialogue; they're more like perfectly crafted novellas than full novels. In consequence, story is even more central to film than it is to the novel. One famous screenwriter, William Goldman, coined the slogan 'screenplays *are* structure', something that no one could plausibly say about the novel.

On the other hand, although much of Hollywood's theorising is interesting and illuminating, it's also dangerous to import it too literally into your own novel or non-fiction narrative. Films are films, books are books, and the two things work differently.

Aristotle goes to Hollywood

More than twenty-three centuries ago, Aristotle's treatise on *Poetics* laid down the essential structure of dramatic storytelling. His thoughts have been disputed, refined and embellished, but studio executives in today's Hollywood still analyse story in a broadly Aristotelian way – Robert McKee, for example, the best-known theorist of story in the movie business, explicitly places himself within that tradition. And, according to the theory, story has three parts:

- *Set-up.* The first part introduces the characters, the location, and the situation.

- *Confrontation.* In the second part, the protagonist is faced with a challenge. It might be to save the world (if we're in a Bond movie) or to get the guy (if we're in a rom-com). But whatever the challenge, it's not a simple one. The middle act of a drama involves the protagonist battling against these obstacles.

- *Resolution.* The protagonist may succeed or may fail, but either way, there's a resolution. The world is or isn't saved. The girl does or doesn't get the guy.

So far, so simple. In the cinematic version of this tradition, the middle act is about twice the length of either of the others. So, in a two-hour, 120-page screenplay, you'd expect the transition from act 1 to act 2 to occur in around the 30th minute, the transition to act 3 to arrive in about the 90th.

The notion of the three-act structure may clarify things for certain prose writers, but it's essential not to take it too literally. A Hollywood rom-com may well have its two leads meet as late as the 20th minute of a 100-minute film. In prose terms, that could be 20,000 words into a 100,000-word novel. And that's far too late! Jane Austen, remember, set up her basic premise in the very first line of *Pride and Prejudice*, and she brought her two characters together 2,500 words into a 122,000-word manuscript. In effect, the 'set-up phase' of a novel doesn't really exist. A novel *starts with* instability. You see the world of the old status quo only as it is already disappearing. If, therefore, your novel begins with a long slow introduction to various characters, their interrelationships, their backstories and so on, you have doomed the book before it's begun. If you need to write those introductory chapters to get yourself into the flow, then by all means write away – just remember to delete them afterwards.

The hero's journey

There's a second issue with Aristotle's basic outline, which is that it offers very few tangible lessons to work with. It doesn't seem to offer much usable 'how to' style advice to the would-be practitioner. Little wonder, then, that Aristotle is not Hollywood's favourite story theorist. That honour goes to Joseph Campbell, an American professor of world mythologies, and one influenced by Freud and, particularly, Jung. Campbell's big idea was that human myths often had the same underlying structure. That structure, in effect, was a universal story. Campbell's ideas could have passed largely unnoticed by the wider world, except that George Lucas seized upon Campbell's *The Hero with a Thousand Faces* to redraft his original script for *Star Wars*. Lucas was generous in honouring that influence. Campbell was alert in making the most of it. And when *Star Wars* went on to make a fortune at the box office, Hollywood had a new hero.

Campbell's template for the hero's journey involved seventeen different stages. Few myths involved all seventeen, but these were the ingredients from which myth were brewed. A somewhat simplified Campbell-esque structure would be as follows. (I've used 'hero' and 'him', because most of Campbell's myths featured male heroes. There's no reason why female-centred stories shouldn't follow the same model, however.)

- *The call to adventure.* The hero is living an ordinary life when something happens that calls him away on an adventure into the unknown.
- *The refusal.* Not always, but often, the hero refuses that calls.
- *Meeting with the mentor.* The hero meets with someone (a wise woman, a seasoned traveller, a god) who gives him advice. The hero now feels able to accept the challenge.
- *The road of trials.* This is the middle act of a screenplay, where the hero struggles to achieve the goal. The road of trials is likely to be equipped with *tests, allies and enemies.* It

may involve a withdrawal to the *inmost cave*, a place where the hero and his allies prepare in secret for a final confrontation. It will almost certainly involve a test or *ordeal* of some sort, in which the hero has to prove his worthiness.

- *Achieving the goal* (or 'boon' in Campbell's terminology). After struggle, the hero achieves his goal.
- *Return to the ordinary.* The hero returns to the world he came from.
- *Application of the boon.* The world that the hero returns to is altered by his having achieved his quest.

When Lucas read *The Hero with a Thousand Faces*, he was looking for a way to recreate large-scale myth for a modern audience. (The Western had once provided something similar but was in decline, even then.) You can certainly feel the flavour of Campbell in *Star Wars* and *Harry Potter*, and also in *The Lord of the Rings* and much other fantasy fiction. Those insights can feel so compelling that they make you want to agree with Campbell's admirers and say, 'Yes, this stuff is truly universal'.

But is it? Remember that the novel is the art form which *replaced* mythic approaches to storytelling. It took story from *Beowulf* and *Le Morte d'Arthur* to *Pride and Prejudice* and *Catch-22*. It's not at all clear that Campbell's 'monomyth' has much to say about stories such as these. If you find Campbell's ideas are of help to you in structuring your own story, that's terrific. Feel free to plunder them as much as you like; he'd be happy if you did. If Campbell doesn't work for you, however, you needn't worry. You're just writing a different kind of story.

Syd Field's paradigm

Another screenwriting theorist, Syd Field, took Aristotle's basic three-act structure and sought to develop it into something more fully specified; something that could actually be applied by those wanting to write a story. In Field's later work, the three-act paradigm acquired a whole new degree of articulation.

- *Opening image.* An image that in some ways summarises the tone of the film.

- *Catalyst.* The moment that initiates the story. This is the moment when boy meets girl, when Bond is asked to investigate something, when two strangers meet on a train.

- *Plot point 1* (approx. 30 minutes into a 120-minute screenplay). This is the transition from act 1 to act 2, the moment where the hero is required to make the irrevocable step into adventure. This is when boy hasn't merely met girl but asks her out on a date. It's when the little thing Bond has been asked to investigate suddenly stops looking like a little thing. It's when the outrageous idea suggested by one stranger on a train isn't rejected by the other.

- *Pinch 1* (approx. 45 mins). A moment when the central drama or conflict of the story flares into life. It's a reminder, in effect, of where the heart of the story lies. (Bond has a shootout, girl and boy have their first serious row.)

- *Midpoint* (approx. 60 mins). A major incident right in the middle of the story, typically involving a reversal of fortunes or perhaps a revelation of information which means that the situation suddenly takes on a very different aspect. (Girl suddenly discovers something massive about boy, or vice versa. Bond discovers the plot to blow up the world.) A core part of the notion of the 'midpoint' is that it gives the story something to drive towards in the course of that long middle act. In effect, act 2 splits into two halves, acts 2a and 2b, which hinge on a major turning point midway into the story.

- *Pinch point 2* (approx. 75 mins). The second pinch point acts in the same way as the first: a reminder of the story's central conflict, and a major plot event to keep the wheels of story turning in that long half-hour from the midpoint to the end of act 2.

- *Plot point 2* (approx. 90 mins). The moment when act 2 closes and the final showdown begins. (Bond jetskis off to Dr Evil's lair. Girl and boy race to meet on the Empire State Building, or meet up at a best friend's wedding, or something else that has an air of finality, now-or-never to it.)
- *Showdown.* It's win-or-lose time. Bond is face to face with Dr Evil. Boy and girl have The Conversation.
- *Resolution.* Bond wins or loses. The girl gets the guy or doesn't.
- *Epilogue, or 'tag'.* Any final loose ends are tied up.

Field's teasing out of Aristotle's basic model is either helpful or infuriating, depending on your viewpoint. Studio executives welcome the model, as it gives a set of tools by which non-creatives can assess or tinker with the work of creatives. Equally, there's no doubt that those concepts of midpoints and pinch points may now and again help writers overcome blockages in their own forward flow. Plenty of novelists may find something in his paradigm that eases them over a particular plotting hurdle. (Oh, and personally I find Field quite annoying to read. If you want the same thing, but offered with a good bit more fun, I'd suggest Blake Snyder's *Save the Cat.*)

On the other hand, I'm profoundly sceptical myself that Syd Field's ideas accurately describe even the screenplays he uses as models. One of his favourite films is *Chinatown*, an early Jack Nicholson picture and one that boasts a very good screenplay indeed. Yet if one reads (or watches) the film, one doesn't experience plot points, pinches, midpoints and so on in the way he describes. The story feels *continuously* compelling, *continuously* dynamic in the way it creates its drama. Perhaps if you squint, you can see things Field's way. But why squint?

Chapter Summary

- A lot of theorising about story has been driven directly or indirectly by Hollywood.
- By all means, read the screenwriting literature to supplement your understanding of story, but do remember that prose narrative plays by different rules.
- Joseph Campbell may offer inspiration, especially if you are writing mythic or fantasy fiction.
- Syd Field may seem overly mechanical, but his 'how to' specifics may help you over a particular plot problem.
- Or just read Aristotle.

Diagnosing Your Plot Problems

The wonderful chick-lit author, Katie Fforde, told me once that her first novel emerged in wonderful shape for a debut effort, all things considered. The writing was good, the characters were zingy, there was warmth and humour and sex. But no plot. Everything was working, except that there wasn't really a story. Since readers, darn them, seem to have a thing about stories, Katie had to engineer one into the book. Since a plot is a rather large structural element, to put it mildly, the challenge facing her was a little bit like the builders in Gulliver's Travels who tried to build a house from the roof downwards. Maybe the thing could be done, but it couldn't be done easily. She managed to do so, however, and her career flourished from that point on. She's never quite tried to do things that way again, though. Once was enough.

If you've even partly followed the advice in this book, you won't find yourself in quite that predicament, but you will almost certainly find that you have plot problems nevertheless. Mostly, that's just life. Writing is hard. Novels are hard. Story is hard. If you want to make a career at this game, you'd better just accept that difficulties are part of the territory and learn to live with that. Nevertheless, there are techniques which can help you minimise those problems, and there are trouble-shooting recipes which, whilst they are not quite infallible, will provide you with a pretty good toolkit for sorting yourself out. First, a couple of techniques.

The one-third pause

The first technique – a crucial one – is the pause. Untellably large numbers of writers charge off into their novel, delighted to find how easy it is, how sweetly the story flows. Then, about twenty or thirty thousand words into their book, they somehow feel as though they've lost their mojo. The plot seems to be treading water. If they try to notch up the tension (throw in a murder, a war, a lover, a vampire), the book starts to seem cluttered rather than tense. The entire project seems to be on the point of failure.

The predicament is a common one. Writers often either abandon the project or struggle on through, hating their story a little bit more each time they come back to it. Or perhaps they have enough craft and talent to make something more or less workable, albeit something that misses that frisson of excitement which once seemed to be there.

The problem, almost always, is that the set-up phase of a book is often relatively easy to write. That's probably the part you had plotted out in your head before you started. It's also the part where you're launching your surprises, tipping your hero or heroine into a torrent of action and challenge, getting your secondary characters introduced and active. After that, things just get tougher. The decisions become knottier, the weight of narrative simply greater.

And that's OK. That's just the way stories are. When you reach that one-third stage, you simply need to be alert to your own feelings about your book. Is it going well or are you struggling? If the latter, stop. Don't write any further. Write a chapter-by-chapter plan which summarises the material you have so far (or rather, the material you're confident of. Don't tie yourself to chapters that feel wrong.) Then simply spend time thinking. Gary Gibson, a successful sci-fi author and a colleague of mine at Jericho Writers, did exactly that with his third book, *Stealing Light*. His two previous books had been well-received, but hadn't sold in huge numbers, and he'd felt all along that there was a problem in the plotting. With *Stealing Light*, he was determined to overcome that problem. He wrote a long (6,000-word) plan of the book before starting, in the confident belief that enough pre-planning would iron everything out. His publisher liked the synopsis. So did his agent. Thus bolstered, he launched off into the book ... only to find that, once he'd reached the approximate one-third point, that familiar nagging sense of something missing was there anyway.

So he stopped completely. He took four weeks off from writing his book in order to plan it. That 6,000-word synopsis became a 24,000-word one. In the course of developing that super-synopsis, he changed some key details about his leading characters and saw that he needed to tweak some of the plotting in the novel so far. But mostly, the value of that four-week period was that it gave him an opportunity to think about the book when it had already developed enough for him to have a good sense of roughly where it was heading. *Stealing Light* became Gary's breakout book, the one that confirmed him in his career, and he has followed approximately the same recipe ever since.

I do the same. I don't write a 24,000-word synopsis, or anything like it, because I hate and loathe synopses as a way to plan my work. I personally get by on a few pages of badly-written bullet points which would make pretty much no sense to an outside observer and would strike any publisher as a few scant millimetres from drivel. All the same, though our working habits *look* different, the fundamentals are the same. I get my book to a point where I can see it's starting to get away from me, then I stop and carve out enough of a signpost that I can see the way clear to my destination.

I find, and I think most authors find, that planning is the most arduous, the most exhausting and the least fun part of writing. You can spend day after day scratching around with a monster synopsis (in Gary's case) or a few pages of meagre jottings (in mine) and have no clear sense that you've made progress. It's not like the business of actually writing, where you get to check your word count, finish a chapter, turn the page. When it comes to planning, none of those things count for so much as a string bean. All that matters is that your book – your plot – *feels* right. That you understand it enough. That you have the right character in the right situation facing the right challenges. That you know how those things play out. There's no objective benchmark of that rightness apart from your feelings (and perhaps also a quick review of the major points in this chapter). It's tough work, but it may yet be the most important time you ever spend with your book.

The skeleton

If the pause is one killer-app of plotting, the skeleton is the other. One of the reasons plot is so hard to work with is because it's so huge. It's as though you're a painter working on a canvas intended to fill a palace wall. You have to work up close, brushstroke after brushstroke, but the only way you can actually see your work is to cross to the other side of the courtyard and look back. With plot, it's not only that the scale is so large, it's also that every part of it is so intricate. Writers always find themselves arguing things like, 'But I can't delete that Charlotte scene because otherwise how would Jonah know that she wasn't really working for Adrian, and Jonah has to know that Adrian is playing a double game, because if he didn't then Arkadia wouldn't come to think that Adrian might be the suspect'. Those twisting little tracks of logic keep flipping you out of the big view into the small one and the small view makes it impossible for you to nail the one thing you really need to pin down.

That's where the skeleton comes in. It's simply this: keep a note of what you're doing, chapter by chapter. I'd say that if your chapters are a standard 2 to 3,000 words or so, you should probably be boiling them down to no more than five sentences. If you can reduce them to one or two sentences, so much the better. Naturally, you'll be leaving out huge amounts of crucial detail, but that's the point. That's what you're trying to achieve. You should certainly create the skeleton for as much of the book as you've already written. If you feel half-confident of doing the same thing for the next bit of the book, or even all of it, then you should go ahead and do that too.

Once you have your skeleton, you need to test it for soundness. Your crucial strength-detector is the simple question, 'How does this chapter alter my protagonist's relationship to his/her goal?'. If that question has a clear and decisive answer, the chapter is fine. If not, it isn't. The beauty of the skeleton as a tool is that it makes bullshit all but impossible. You don't end up getting sucked into those twisting little logic tracks, because the entire exercise operates at a different level from that. Naturally, once you've dismantled any rotten parts of your plotting, you'll have to start re-mantling again – at which point you can't avoid those questions of logic – but at least your eyes will be firmly on the goal.

Oh, and both the skeleton and the pause work better if you have a clear sense of your book's shape. If you need a refresher there, just refer back to the chapter 'What is Your Plot?'.

Clutter

Turning now to diagnosing problems in your plot, one of the commonest problems is that of excess clutter. The problem can manifest in a host of different ways. Too many protagonists. Too many POV characters. Too many subplots. Too many goals. Too many logic-twists and secondary characters. The issue, almost always, is that the writer has worried that the story might not be strong enough, so they've found themselves adding in more. And more. It's as though you're trying to make a speedboat go faster by lashing on ever more outboard motors to the back end. You can almost feel the panic underlying the storytelling, the compulsion to add.

If you think this might apply to you, the recipe is delightfully simple. You ditch the surplus motors, scrape down the hull, chuck out some ballast, and emphasise streamlining over brute power. In less metaphorical terms, you need to figure out who your protagonist is (or who they are), figure out their Big Question, then delete pretty much everything that doesn't directly relate. What's more, if you've added a plot layer which does, sort of, propel the Big Question but which could be deleted or compacted without much harm, your book will almost certainly benefit from the tidying.

Even professional editors can get thrown by problems of this sort. I've several times seen publishers advise, in relation either to one of my books or to one of my clients' books, that new elements needed to be introduced or existing ones amplified. I can't say with any authority that such advice is always wrong; I do, however, believe that it mostly is. Your book will be excellent if you stick like glue to one question of profound importance to your protagonist, yourself and the reader. If you start hurling in additional ingredients, you're likely to end with a messy kitchen and an inedible stew.

For much the same reason, if you find that you've written a very long book – and anyone who writes a book of more than 140,000 words is in this category – you need to suspect yourself of excess verbiage, excess characters, excess matter. If your book is over 200,000 words, you are almost certainly guilty of these things.

You can't always judge these things by word count, however. It's quite common for people to write a perfectly well-formed novella, but to disguise it as a novel. So although the word count might look normal or even short (let's say, in the 70 to 100,000 word bracket), the book might have only enough plot for a 30 to 40,000 word novella. There's nothing wrong with the novella as an art form – I like them – but they're horribly hard to sell, at least until you've won your first Pulitzer or Booker. The disguised novella is perhaps particularly common with Creative Writing MA/MFA students – because the short story tends to be emphasised much more than it is in the world of publishing – but anyone can suffer.

Bareness

The inverse problem of clutter is bareness. Perhaps you've written a 70,000-word book. You've paused at the one-third point, you've written your skeleton, you've checked for soundness against your protagonist's Big Question – and all the same, the book feels bare and uninvolving.

Here, the problem often feels like it has to do with plot, because stories are what grab people, but the solution almost always lies elsewhere. Books that feel too bare are usually ones where the author has not yet succeeded in creating a sense of real life and real characters. Certainly, novels need to transport their readers, but first they need to persuade readers to step inside the vehicle: to suspend disbelief, to feel that the places you describe are real, that the characters you're talking about are living, breathing people.

Where bareness is the problem, you need to forget about plotting for the time being and focus on everything else. Check your characters. How much inner life do they have? How much passion? Check your settings. Do you create atmosphere, or does your action seem to take place on a blank stage in a white room? And how alive is your prose? Is it merely efficient or does it vibrate with something more? If the plot seems strong but the book seems dead, it's an easy bet that the problem lurks in one of these other areas. Find it. Address it. And you're done.

Who cares?

The third big plot failing is probably the rarest of the three. Sometimes the plot passes the skeleton test. The writing passes the tests of prose and character just mentioned. Yet somehow the book doesn't work. The work feels professional but strangely pointless, a book you're not quite sure anyone would want to read.

In a way, that's the scariest problem of all because the answer may be lethal. I once dealt with a client who was a very good writer. His prose wasn't showy, but it was very deft, observant, witty and with a nice edge of occasional malice. His character convinced from the opening pages. Any reader or agent picking up his work would have been eager to read on. What's more, the book dealt with an apparently strong subject: a parent dying of cancer in a nursing home, a crotchety relationship between father and son being slowly ironed out in the process. Almost all of us will lose a parent. Nearly everyone who does will find the experience one of the more significant of their lives. From a publisher's point of view, what's not to like?

From a purely literary point of view, perhaps the answer is nothing at all – as I say, this was a very capable writer. On the other hand, books have to be *marketed*, and this one didn't have a hook, didn't have an angle. If you imagine yourself browsing in a bookshop or on Amazon, this novel would give you almost no reason to buy it. It has no stand-out quality which would force it from the shelf and into your hand. In the end, the basic concept was not quite right. The book was simply too quiet to sell.

That's one kind of problem, which is more or less unfixable except by quite profound surgery. A variant of the same thing arises where the protagonist herself is not terribly affected by the events of the book. Suppose that Jane Austen's Lizzy had not cared all that much for marriage and was not all that into Mr Darcy. Suppose that her father's estate had not been entailed to someone else and that the five daughters would have lived perfectly comfortably no matter whether they married well or not at all. That book would move no one, resonate not at all. If this is your problem, the answer couldn't be simpler. You need to jack up the odds, increase the stakes. The protagonist has to care about the outcome of her story and to care with a passion. If the basic matter at stake is not vastly consequential, toss something else into the mix to make it so.

Above all, perhaps, you yourself need to have the right view of your book. You cannot allow yourself to think that you only want a small-scale publication by a small (but very refined) publisher. Such publishers barely exist these days, and to the extent that they do, they're looking for work which announces itself with a swagger. The reality of marketing doesn't allow for anything different. Nor should you allow yourself to blame philistine marketers for the failure of your work. The best books are ambitious. If you are deliberately timid, your book is simply missing a dimension that it needs to have. Ambitious doesn't have to mean shouty. It doesn't have to mean edgy, or gory, or epic, or surreal, or promise a belly-laugh on every page – but it has to mean *something*. You have to take some aspect of your voice or imagination and push it to the limits. It's at those limits that any real magic will take place. That's where agents and publishers and, above all, readers are willing you to be.

Did You Get That Help?

A few chapters back, I offered you a plotting worksheet. If you failed to grab it with both paws back then, here's a second chance to rectify your error. The aim of the worksheet is to help you systematise your thinking about your plot structure and vastly shorten the time it takes you to locate and eliminate problems. To get the worksheet, just scoot over here and do what needs to be done:

jerichowriters.com/how-to-write-a-novel-free-resources

Chapter Summary

- A very useful plotting tool is the one-third pause: taking stock roughly 20 or 30,000 words into your novel and reviewing your general plan for the book.
- If you care to, you can develop a substantial, closely-drafted synopsis at that point. If you don't, a few pages of bullet points may suffice. Either way, the one-third pause provides you with an opportunity to rethink where you're heading.
- A second useful tool is the skeleton plot – an outline so bare as to force you to concentrate on the main lineaments of story, so that you can check them for soundness. The detailed working out of your plot needs to happen too, but it needs to be subordinate to the demands of getting the overall shape right.
- The commonest plot problem is one of excess: too many plot strands, too many characters, too much incident. The solution

is simple. Figure out what the heart of your story is, then trim anything not directly relevant.

- The inverse problem is one of bareness – an inability to persuade the reader to engage properly with your story. In these cases, the plot is unlikely to be the main issue. You need to focus on the other main aspects of your work: prose, settings and character.

- Finally, if there's a kind of *who cares?* quality to your tale, you need to check that the concept is sound and that your character is seized with the importance of the events that are unfolding. If the things you're writing about aren't life-or-death to the character, they won't be to a reader.

- Be ambitious. Timidity doesn't sell.

Part Six

Scenes and Chapters

Of all forms of art realism is the easiest to practice, because of all forms of mind the dull mind is commonest. The most unimaginative or uneducated person in the world can describe a dull scene dully, as the worst builder can produce an ugly house. To those that say that there are artists, called realists, who produce work which is neither ugly nor dull nor painful, any man who has walked down a commonplace city street at twilight, just as the lamps are lit, can reply that such artists are not realists, but the most courageous of idealists, for they exalt the sordid to a vision of magic, and create pure beauty out of plaster and vile dust.

– Raymond Chandler

Dramatise, dramatise, dramatise.

– Henry James

THE SCENE

So far, we've ticked off most of the big issues that dominate writing technique. Prose style? Check. Characterisation? Check. Viewpoints? Check. Story? Check. So, what else remains?

Well, one of the things that remain is the delicate business of actually *writing*. Taking all those elements and stirring them up into a broth that tastes just right, where the balance of elements (description, dialogue, action, reflection) feels spot-on to the reader. And because a book is just a sequence of chapters, and because chapters are really just receptacles for scenes, the business of writing comes down to this: writing a succession of wonderful scenes. Those scenes have to cohere into a story. They have to be well-written and be populated by strong characters. But still, the essential unit of effective writing is the scene, and if you can write a strong scene, the chances are you can write a strong book.

Bringing it all together

The challenges in writing good scenes, however, are manifold – or, perhaps more accurately, all those manifold problems come down to a matter of balance. You know you need to keep the action moving, but there are times when you need to pause for explanation. Or you need to describe a setting. Or describe a new character. Or set the action in its broader context. Or you may have a number of other essential missions to fulfil, any of which threaten to slow the action, or even kill it.

In general, the right policy is a kind of authorial sneakiness. You need to filter in the relevant bits of information without the reader ever feeling lectured at. Indeed, if you judge things right, the reader will have almost the opposite feeling. Your paragraph of description will come at a point when the reader wants to know exactly what a room or person looks like. Your dive back into a fragment of memory, or your zooming out to get a wide-angle view of a particular moment, will be perfectly judged to complete an emotional need.

These things are hard to talk about in the abstract, so we'll plunge straight in with an example. The scene we're going to look at in detail is taken from *West End Girls* by Barbara Tate. Set in London in 1948–49, the book recounts a friendship between two women, one of whom is a prostitute, the other of whom – the narrator – comes to work as the prostitute's maid. It's a delightfully-told story, brimming with warmth, humour and period feel.

It's also a true story, a memoir. I've said repeatedly that the techniques of novel-writing and narrative non-fiction are essentially identical, and this chapter will prove my case. In the extract below, the regular text is a scene taken directly from the book. (It's a pivotal scene: one where Tate, the author, first meets Mae, the prostitute.) The italicised, indented comments are mine.

You may well want to read the entire scene through once before turning to my comments. I don't think there's any way to tell from the writing alone whether or not the scene is an extract from a novel or a memoir. For present purposes, it doesn't matter. All that matters is that this is a wonderful story, told with poise and judgement.

I should also acknowledge a personal connection with this book. Barbara Tate wrote her memoir in the 1970s, but didn't make any strenuous efforts to seek publication until, as an 83-year-old, she decided to give it a go. We at Jericho Writers had the good fortune to edit the manuscript for publication and we were delighted to see it become a bestseller in hardback and paperback. Barbara was a wonderful writer and a delightful client, and she deserved every bit of her success.

West End Girls, by **Barbara Tate**

One Saturday night, my shift had just begun and I was keeping my fingers crossed that the evening would be free of the scuffles that invariably happened at weekends. I was not to know that this particular evening was going to mark a change in my life I would never forget.

> *'One Saturday night': Notice the easy, fast, precise way with which time has been established. We know straight away that Barbara has been working here for a while. She hasn't said how long exactly, and that's because we don't care. On the whole, authors get more fussed about these time tags than readers do. The usual answer is to keep it sweet, easy and simple, just as Barbara did.*
>
> *'my shift had just begun': Here we go from a general time indicator ('one Saturday night') to a very specific one. The author is getting as specific as she can, as fast as she can. That's good practice. Scenes are alive when they are in the moment. Being 'in the moment' means three things. It means (i) being at a specific place, (ii) at a specific time, and (iii) allowing action to unfold more or less real time on the page.*
>
> *'I was not to know ... I would never forget': This sentence works because this is a memoir, narrated many years after the events described. The sentence promises forthcoming drama – and the drama won't disappoint. This kind of foreshadowing, however, tends to work badly in a novel, when there is a risk of losing immediacy. That's not to say the technique can't work, only that you need to use it with care.*

In the lull before the rush, Jim and Ronnie had gone over to *Benito's* for a meal. From there, they could keep an eye on who went into the club and judge when I would begin to need help. They'd worked all through the afternoon trade and had left a pile of glassware for me to wash, fresh ice to break for the lager bucket and four already-settled customers to look after.

'Jim and Ronnie had gone over ...': Having established where we are in time ('my shift had just begun'), Barbara then jumps backwards to set the scene. That scene-setting feels alive because we know that we are positioned in a particular place and time, with something about to happen. (No competently-told story positions the reader in a particular time and place unless something is about to happen.) Because of that knowledge, these details about Jim and Ronnie become interesting in a way that wouldn't have been the case if it had come by way of general introduction.

A burly, smiling man entered, wearing the look of slight desperation that I had come to recognise on all our male customers. He needed urgently to get within ordering distance of a bar. Whilst waiting, his anxious expression remained firmly in place as though he feared everything might be sold out at any moment. Only when I had taken his order could he relax and burst into bloom, acknowledging me with a 'How's tricks?' This was Syd: a staunch regular, along with all his pals, fellow meat porters at Smithfield Market.

'A burly, smiling man entered': We're 120 words into the scene, and we reach action for the first time. That's fine; it's good pacing. The reader is looking for action the whole time and if you let your scene runs for as much as 300 words before hitting any action (even something apparently minor like a man entering) you are liable to have an impatient reader. Do note, however, that the action involved can be fairly minimal. Readers know that an author wouldn't mention a particular man entering unless it was to initiate some important piece of action. The early clues can therefore be fairly minimal.

I rushed back to the washing up; I could see that, as usual, he was settling down for a chat but I wanted to get the work done first or I'd never catch up. I'd been caught like that by him once before.

'I rushed back ...': *The previous para hovered between this specific occasion (Syd entering) and things that generally happened. High time then to re-fix the story back in the present moment, which is just what happens here.*

The jukebox was on automatic, as it always was when there were too few people in to feed it with coins. I surveyed the room while I polished glasses. It was strange to see how nice it could look with the lights dim, knowing how tatty it really was when the bright overhead lighting was switched on for cleaning.

'I surveyed the room ...': *This is a pure descriptive para in the sense that it has no purpose other than to set the scene. On the other hand, because the description is so firmly anchored in what Barbara herself saw at a particular moment, it has almost the quality of action. Certainly, no reader will feel that the action is pausing. On the contrary, they'll feel (correctly) that something significant is about to be divulged.*

The other four customers consisted of a young couple huddled over a table in a dim, far corner of the room – who, under cover of the music, were engaged in deep and private conversation – and two women who were sitting together on stools at the end of the bar furthest from Syd. One of them was a young and spectacular blonde, while her companion was a stout, frowsy woman in her fifties. Neither spoke to the other and, although the blonde occasionally ordered gin and bitters, she had barely touched her own first one. The stout woman grimaced whenever she caught my eye, communicating her silent dislike of her partner.

'... a young and spectacular blonde': *This too is a descriptive para, but the tension in the scene has ratcheted up another couple of notches nevertheless. No capable storyteller would draw such specific attention to two individuals unless they were about to become highly relevant to the story. Readers understand these conventions, and their antennae will now be on high alert.*

'communicating her silent dislike …': Notice too how mobile this description is. There's clearly an argument simmering here, but there's a mystery about what that argument is. Two powerful reasons to read on. That books have Big Questions is something we've discussed enough while talking about plot. But scenes are propelled by Big Questions of their own. At this point, the Big Question is: 'Who is the blonde, and what's going on between her and her companion?'. Notice how early in the scene that question has been launched.

My chores done, I noticed Syd waving his glass again. As I refilled it, he gave a mock scowl.

'Talk about a bluebottle!' he complained, 'You never stand still, do you?'

'I'm standing still, now,' I said, plonking my elbows on the counter.

He started talking about work. Meat was still on ration after the war, and his work as a porter meant he was full of stories.

'Talk about a bluebottle!': Two paragraphs of description are nevertheless enough. Tate has promised action, and it's time to deliver. It's no accident that this is the first bit of the scene where dialogue appears. Dialogue is the most immediate sort of writing, because it's so specific to a particular moment. When Syd says, 'Talk about a bluebottle!', time elapses as he speaks the words. Earlier phrases such as 'I surveyed the room while I polished glasses' are specific to a time and place, but not as specific. Dialogue pins you to the particular instant more closely than anything else. The action that began with 'a burly, smiling man' has now got immediate and pressing. And notice that we've arrived in that happy position (i) quickly (we're still only 400 words or so into the excerpt), (ii) with the scene nicely set, (iii) with our characters established, and (iv) with a Big Question established. Nothing in the scene so far feels like astoundingly deft writing – but that's precisely because it is so deft. Most of the time, good writing is unnoticeable.

'What an interesting job you've got,' I remarked.

'Not half as interesting as hers, I shouldn't think,' he said, lowering his voice and giving a sort of jerk of his head in the direction of the two women.

'Which one, the young one?'

'Naturally!'

'Why, what does she do?' I asked, getting interested.

'She's on the game!'

'She's on the game!': Pow! 550 words into the scene and Barbara has delivered on all her implicit promises to the reader. She's been promising to tell us something powerful and significant and she's done so. Syd's revelation doesn't discharge tension from the scene, however; it adds to it. The Big Question is still there, but it's been transmuted: Who is the other woman? Why were they arguing? And why is all this going to be so significant for Tate, the narrator?

'I asked, getting interested': It's also worth noticing that Tate takes care to note her own reactions to Syd's revelations. Remember that nothing much matters to the reader unless we know it matters to the protagonist as well. Here, Tate reveals her own (carefully graduated) interest. As things develop, her interest will turn into something much more intense.

'What game?' I asked innocently.

Looking back, I find it hard to credit that I was ever so naïve. Syd obviously did as well because he gazed at me incredulously for a while, wondering if I were trying to tease him. Having decided that I wasn't, he leaned forward with a slightly reddened face and whispered hoarsely, 'She's one of the ladies, and that's her maid!'

I stole a quick glance at them but couldn't quite picture the girl as someone with a title, and the maid looked more like a bodyguard. Syd seemed nearly floored when I looked at him blankly again. He scratched his head and seemed to be searching for words. Then, leaning forward once more and studying my face for signs of comprehension, he said, with suitable pauses:

'She's a business girl … One of the birds … A tart … A prostitute!'

> *'What game?': Much of writing is about meeting your reader's legitimate expectations, but much else is about thwarting them – taking a different turning from the expected one. Tate does that here by revealing that her own reactions are quite different from those that Syd (and the reader) expected. It's the unexpected quality of this passage that gives it its vibrancy.*
>
> *'gazed at me incredulously …': Do also notice how much of this passage is taken up with noting thoughts and emotions – to such an extent that more of the writing is concerned with those emotions than with actually reporting who said what. The passage doesn't feel slowed down, however. Those emotions are critical to the way the reader feels the passage. The drama of the passage lies in this emotional movement.*

It was only his last word that I understood. He leaned back with relief when I blushed and gasped, 'Oh!'

I felt embarrassed. Syd was holding his glass out for another beer and, while I was filling it, I was relieved to see a couple of his friends arriving. I opened two more bottles so all three glasses were lined up when they turned to the bar after greeting Syd.

I left them and wandered back along the bar where the dumpy woman was now ready for another gin. I was able to study the blonde at closer range.

> *'I blushed and gasped': Barbara completes the sequence by noting her own reaction – an essential part of the mix, as the reader is interested in her. Syd isn't a material part of the story.*
>
> *'I opened two more bottles …': The fact that the story has largely dispensed with Syd is made clear in the swift paragraph which deals with the arrival of his friends.*

'I left them ... at closer range': It's been clear all along that the blonde and her grumpy assistant are where the real mystery and excitement lie so, having used Syd by way of intro, Barbara wastes no time in zooming back to the centre of her story. Do note, though, that Syd's appearance hasn't slowed anything down. Instead, rather like the skilful use of a prologue to a book, Barbara has used Syd to establish (i) that the blonde is a prostitute, and (ii) that she (Barbara) is amazingly naïve. Like any skilfully told prologue, Barbara has used Syd to alter the story question involved in this scene. The Big Question is now something like: what will happen when naïve Barbara talks to this glamorous prostitute? And the question about the role of that prostitute's maid is still hanging.

I was utterly intrigued but anxious not to make it obvious. I had never knowingly seen a prostitute before and I was filled with curiosity. Apart from her voice – which had a slight northern accent that she had clearly taken pains to disguise – the most noticeable thing about her was her hair, which was long and gleaming. In defiance of the 'upswept' fashion of the time, it was a mass of loose waves and curls. She was pretty; but more than that, she was provocative and reckless-looking. She wore quite a lot of make-up, especially around her eyes, and I was struck by her resemblance to a bust I'd seen of an Egyptian queen, Nefertiti. Her sweater was simple but looked expensive: turquoise silk with a V-neck showing her cleavage. She had pushed the sleeves up to just below her elbows. As I watched, she lightly swung her feet to the floor and walked with easy assurance to the jukebox. Marilyn Monroe could have learned something from that walk. Her skirt was grey, tight and straight, with a slit at the hem; the waist was cinched tight with a wide, black, patent-leather belt, and her extremely high-heeled shoes were of the same material. It was obvious her flair for clothes lay not so much in the things she chose to wear but in the careless negligence with which she wore them. I somehow knew that she would look good even in a sack. She had all the qualities I lacked: glamour, boldness and a flair for fashion. In spite of all these assets though, she was evidently unhappy.

> 'I was utterly intrigued ...': Syd has aroused our interest in the prostitute, but if our interest is to be maintained, we need to know that Barbara shares it. And she does. Barbara's writing isn't full of over-the-top emotional expressions, but here she tells us she was <u>utterly</u> intrigued. (Not just somewhat, quite, or rather intrigued.) So we are too.

> 'the most noticeable thing about her ...': There's a popular idea that descriptions slow down a book. That's rubbish! Bad or poorly timed descriptions slow a book. Good descriptions give it juice. This passage involves a longish description, but it's telling us something we really want to know by this point. If Barbara had skimped on the description, we'd have felt cheated.

> '... provocative ... reckless-looking ... Nefertiti ... Marilyn Monroe ... extremely high-heeled shoes ...': And what a description it is! Without seeming to push too hard, the passage compares the blonde with an Egyptian queen and an international film star. The other descriptors used (reckless-looking, expensive, careless negligence) convey qualities of danger and glamour, which is a heady mixture for any observer, still more so one as naïve and obviously fascinated as Barbara.

> '... all the qualities I lacked': The description also works because it ties back to the narrator. Barbara's candid revelation of the qualities she felt lacking in her means that the Big Question has now got an added dimension: what happens when Barbara (naïve, unglamorous, timid) meets this prostitute (her opposite)?

> '... evidently unhappy': The final masterstroke. We now see that this scene is going to be about a collision between two characters, each of whom are missing something (boldness and glamour in Barbara's case; happiness in the prostitute's case). This long paragraph has indeed been descriptive, but the Big Question has bounded forward in interest and complexity because of it.

Her companion caught my eye. She was dressed in a food-splattered, red Moroccan frock and a black, straw hat, decorated with bunches of artificial cherries nestling amongst crumpled leaves. Somewhere at her feet was the disgusting, matted fur wrap that I later found out was the reason for her nickname. Fumbling in her handbag, she produced a compact and smirked at her own reflection for a while.

> '... *food-splattered frock* ...': *Another essentially descriptive paragraph, but again one that adds a layer of story intrigue to the scene. Whereas the adjectives used to describe the prostitute were rich, bold and flattering, those connected with the maid (food-splattered, artificial, crumpled, disgusting, matted) are absolutely the opposite. The mystery has just deepened ... and it's deepened because of two paragraphs of description.*

Then, leering across at me with what she obviously believed to be a winsome smile, she spoke:

'It comes to something, don't it, when the maid's better looking than the mistress!'

> '*Then* ... *she spoke*': *Time, though, to slip back to dramatic action. The best way to do that is often through dialogue, and so it is here. We're back in the moment now, witnessing the scene unfold.*

I was saved from having to comment because Syd and his friends had run dry again.

A strange feeling came over me: everything seemed unreal. What on earth was I doing here amongst all these peculiar people, in this sleazy little basement club? I thought of my grandmother and blanched.

> '... *this sleazy little basement club*': *An unexpected but well-timed moment of zooming out of the close-up and specific to the removed and the general. It's as though Barbara is now hovering over the club, viewing it as a whole ('these peculiar people, in this*

sleazy little basement club'). The emotional space alters too, so that her (stern, unloving) grandmother is briefly invoked. This paragraph might seem like an interruption, except that it adds force to the strangeness and importance of what's going on. In particular, it nudges the reader to recall how disapprovingly Barbara's grandmother would view the unfolding scene. So again, what might seem like a stoppage in the forward flow of the scene is actually a skilfully placed enhancement of it, something to give it an additional edge.

The blonde returned to her seat and there she sat looking stiff and aloof; I felt sorry for her. Then, to my horror, the maid lumbered down off her stool and came towards me with one elbow slithering along the counter. As she reached where I was standing, she treated me to another of her ghastly smiles and hissed in a stage whisper:

'She's muck – and she knows it!'

Then she pushed herself away from the bar to pass Syd and his friends. She went through the archway that led to the toilets in the vaults below the pavement. I didn't know whether the blonde had heard but, when I looked, she was staring hard into her drink.

Just then, the jukebox got stuck and I went over to give it a remedial kick. Returning, I saw the woman reappear from the vaults, wearing a triumphant expression. She walked purposefully to where she had been sitting and, after delivering a few seemingly strong words to the girl, picked up her handbag and stomped out of the club.

'The blonde returned …': Although the scene has been building force and interest, any further stoppages would risk making it too static. So we now get moving with a series of essentially action-orientated paragraphs. The blonde returns. The maid adds further to the intrigue about what is going on between the pair of them. She leaves, comes back, says something obnoxious, then leaves again. The language here is brisk and to the point. It's driving forward the action as though to compensate for the previous mo-

ments of stasis. In effect, the author is saying to the reader, 'Yes, I know we've moved slowly for a while, but don't worry, I know we need to keep motoring.'

'... a remedial kick': We're now 1,300 words into the scene, and so far Tate herself has been present purely as an observer. It's therefore essential that she is soon thrust into the centre of the action. That's on the point of happening, but in the meantime the phrase 'remedial kick' usefully reminds us that Tate herself is perfectly capable of forceful direct action when needed.

I had just got back from serving the two at the corner table and was dropping the used glasses into the sink, when I was suddenly electrified by the sound of the blonde's voice, full of pent-up fury and exploding in venom.

'... exploding in venom': Another 'bingo!' moment. The scene has been brimming for a while, but it needs something to bring matters to a head. This outburst is more forceful than anything the reader was expecting, so it strikes with particular force. The energy of the moment also promises to break what has been a kind of deadlock thus far.

Alarmed, I spun round, thinking for one, awful moment that the girl was addressing me but she was sitting there with clenched hands, glaring belligerently into the remainder of her gin.

I was watching her with a growing sympathy as I swilled the dirty glasses in the sink. She looked up and caught my gaze. A grin spread across her face as she realised I'd heard her. It was surprising how impishly different she looked when she smiled.

'... how impishly different ...': These paras move Tate from observer to actor. This is the first person-to-person connection we've seen between Tate and the prostitute. And the distancing 'Nefertiti'-type language here becomes intimate and personal: 'impish', 'grin', 'growing sympathy'. Again, notice how much of the action of this scene is played out through changing emotional dynamics.

'... swilled the dirty glasses ...': A nice little example of how a lot of descriptive material doesn't have to feel descriptive. That phrase about swilling the dirty glasses helps build our picture of the scene: it rounds out our vision of the club and Tate's role there. On the other hand, (i) the phrase is so brief, and (ii) it stands in the middle of an emotional interaction, which is what dominates our attention. The result is that Tate has sneaked in a little descriptive touch without anyone noticing. The world Tate describes feels more real because it's full of those touches, but no reader will feel that the book is being slowed as a result of them.

'Sorry love,' she apologised. 'But I'm so bloody mad I could burst!'

'Well, I hope you won't, I replied, 'cos I have to mop up at the end of the evening.' My remark actually produced something akin to a giggle. She pushed the gin away from her, with an expression of distaste.

'I don't think you like that stuff any more than I do,' I said. 'Feel like joining me in lemonade?'

'Yeah, let's be devils!'

I poured us each a large glass and, not wanting to intrude too much, carried on working.

'... let's be devils!': What we see here is a bond of friendship being formed, first with a joke ('I have to mop up'), then with a shared drink. The dialogue anchors the scene in the immediate moment. The language and observation is intimate and personal. It's also plain and straightforward. Language doesn't have to be flowery or attention-seeking to do its job. Here, it simply allows a story to unfold, accurately, intimately and plainly. And we, the readers, are hooked.

'What a life!' she sighed, making it obvious she wanted someone to talk to. I moved towards her.

'Had a bad day?' I asked.

'Actually ...' she said, lifting herself from the slump she had fallen into, 'Actually, I've had a bloody good day. It's just that cow, Rabbits, who gets on my wick. That's my maid: the one who just went out. I wish she'd just drop dead and do everyone a favour!'

She seemed to take it for granted that I knew what her trade was.

> *'I moved towards her': Just as the reader moves in for more, so too does Barbara. Her physical movement here echoes an emotional one – and one that we share.*
>
> *'... that cow, Rabbits': Dialogue can be a terrific way to convey information to the reader in a livelier way than straightforward narration, but you can quickly kill a character by shoving words into their mouth that seem stilted or artificial. Here, it seems perfectly natural that the prostitute should name her companion, so one of the pieces of information the reader has been searching for is neatly and appropriately conveyed.*
>
> *'She seemed to take it for granted': One of the skills of a good writer is to anticipate the questions raised in a reader's mind. Here, a reader may well want to know why the prostitute hasn't felt the need to explain to this unknown person why she needs a maid. Not all readers will have that question, but some will. Where the question is important and complex, it needs a full and appropriate answer. But most questions aren't like that, they're just niggly things that, left unattended to, will slow down a reader's easy forward motion through a book. In such cases, the best solution is normally the simplest one: a short, clear sentence giving the necessary explanation, then moving on again without a glance back. Those readers who needed the explanation go away happy because they've got it. Those readers who didn't need it are scarcely interrupted.*

'What's Rabbits done, then?' I asked, now full of curiosity.

'Nothing – as usual – and that's the whole damn trouble! Absolutely bloody nothing! She sits on her fat arse all day and, if I even want a cup of tea, I have to get it myself. She's filthy dirty and never bothers to clean the place or do a bloody hand's turn. It makes me sick!'

She sipped at her lemonade gloomily and went on:

'I could just about put up with all that, but it doesn't stop there; she thinks she's the boss: always trying to order me about. Talks about me behind my back, too. She takes the piss and pulls all sorts of faces she doesn't think I notice.'

> *'… full of curiosity': Another marker reminding us how fully Barbara is engaged in this conversation. Because she's engaged, we are too.*

> *'… a bloody hand's turn': It's obvious enough that a prostitute is likely to have a coarse turn of speech, but the prostitute's language is full of more subtle markers of her individuality – such as the phrase 'hand's turn', which wouldn't feel ordinary today. The dialogue also beautifully conveys period, without straining too hard to achieve the desired effect.*

> *'… thinks she's the boss': A near-approach to answering one of the Big Questions of the scene: what is the argument between the maid and the prostitute? This is our biggest clue yet, and those Big Questions feel very much alive.*

She learned towards me, gradually getting angrier.

'Do you know, she's even stopped me having friends up to the flat because she reckons it wastes time – wants me to flog myself to death so she can get more tips. Tonight was the last straw though; she's gone a bit too far this time!' She sat back, her eyes wrathful with the recollection.

'What happened?' I asked.

'Well …' she replied, settling herself more comfortably, with the air of one preparing to tell all. 'It's what she just said that really choked me and I don't think I can stand the sight of her much more!' She paused again, leaving me positively burning with curiosity.

'What did she say?' I asked breathlessly.

She took a deep breath and her nostrils flared slightly. 'She only called my bed a meatstand!' Her eyes filled with angry tears as she went on: 'And I'm not taking that from anyone!'

'Oh!' I gasped, relieved to know, at last, the cause of the friction, although puzzled as to why its effect had been so devastating. Her annoyance was sufficiently infectious for me to add, with feeling, 'She didn't!'

> *'Tonight was the last straw …': The scene is building up to one of its climaxes (resolving the Big Question about argument between the maid and the prostitute). The 'last straw'-type language is effectively a drum roll to signify that a Big Answer is about to be vouchsafed. Because these things don't matter to us unless they matter to the narrator, it's no coincidence that Barbara tells us that she was 'positively burning with curiosity'. That word 'burning' is the strongest word Barbara has yet used in relation to herself, so the inner emotional climax is in sync with the impending outer one.*

> *'She only called my bed a meatstand!': You can't answer the Big Question of a novel with a moment of comic anti-climax, but it's fine to do so now and again in a scene. And here, the argument between maid and prostitute does seem ridiculous. After all, we, like Barbara, rather think that if you're a prostitute, you're unlikely to have delicate feelings about how people think of your bed. Do note, though, that even though there is an anti-climactic denouement to this Big Question, there's another still more important one looming, namely: what is going to happen between Tate and the prostitute. The anti-climax of the maid-related question only goes to enhance the importance of the other, as Tate is now effectively lying (in a nice way) to secure the prostitute's friendship. So the deflation of one question adds interest and importance to the other.*

'She bloody did!' she said, vehemently, though her temper was abating now she had someone to share her annoyance with.

'But why do you have to put up with all this?' I asked.

She sighed. 'In our business, love, maids sometimes go with the flat. I could find another place but I'd have to find another lot of key money. Besides, I like the flat I'm in – it's in a good spot – but that old sod's driving me potty!'

She was chewing her lips with the frustration of it all and I was searching around in my mind for some possible solution to her problem.

> *'In our business, love': Another good example of essential information being conveyed plausibly and naturally through dialogue. It would have interrupted the intimacy of the moment had Tate been obliged to deliver a short lecture (in her capacity as narrator) to the reader about the way these things worked.*

> *'She was chewing her lips ...': Do notice too how the scene started out by circling round the present moment and has ended up completely absorbed by it. So early on, there were paragraphs of description, prologues from Syd, thoughts of her grandmother which all held back from total intimacy in the present moment. Right now, however, the present moment is all there is. Structures of this sort are characteristic of good scenes (though they're not essential; there are many ways to tell your story).*

> *'... I was searching around in my mind ...': Additionally, notice how close Tate has come to the prostitute – so much so that the latter's problems are now her problems. The Big Question about Tate and the prostitute is now shivering on the verge of a solution – and we already know (to our delight) that the outcome is going to be one of intimacy between the two of them.*

While the girl and I had been talking, I'd noticed two more of Syd's friends came in. Syd was taking an interest in my conversation with the blonde. He told his friends he'd join them later and ordered another beer. In doing so, he stationed himself on a stool much closer to us.

'What about asking the agent if he could get Rabbits a job with someone else?' I asked. 'Tell him you can't work with her properly and soon won't be able to pay your rent. He can supply you with another maid and so he won't be any worse off, will he?'

'It's an idea,' she agreed. 'It's not as though the greedy cow's grateful for anything. I get good tips for her and I'm never out long before I bring someone back. Some maids have to wait for hours! And, do you know ...' she leaned closer to me across the bar '... Do you know, I've been up and down those bloody stairs twenty-four times today, already!'

> *'Syd was taking an interest ...': Although we're at a peak of our interest with Tate and the prostitute, there's a risk that the scene could become too closed, too claustrophobically close. So re-enter Syd to open out the focus again.*

> *'What about asking the agent ...?': For the first time, Tate truly drives the action. Her question now propels the range of possible solutions down a whole new road: why doesn't the prostitute get a new maid? Although Tate doesn't do anything vigorous – she doesn't hit anyone, launch rockets, chase people across rooftops – action isn't about Hollywood-style chases; it's about taking steps that alter the dynamic of a scene. Tate's simple question does that very effectively. We're now trembling on the brink of a solution to the prostitute's problems: she should get a new maid.*

'Oh!' I cried, caught between sympathy and surprise. 'Oh, your poor feet!'

Her jaw dropped open in amazement and she stared at me for an instant, then threw back her head and let out peal after peal of helpless laughter.

'My feet?' she choked. She tried to prevent more laughter and to regain her breath. 'Oh, you'll be the death of me – look, you've made my mascara run!'

> *'Oh, your poor feet!': This is a beautiful line. It captures Barbara's simple, affectionate naiveté and the prostitute's worldliness and warmth. We know now that these two women are to become the closest of friends ... and everything is now in place for what*

follows: the prostitute (Mae) persuading Tate to become her maid. When Tate says yes, there's clearly a significant external change in her circumstances. Yet this scene has already indicated that there'll be a significant internal change too. The relationship between Mae and Tate won't simply be that of employer and employee – it'll be one of two friends negotiating a colourful and turbulent life together.

The classic scene structure

There are many ways to write a scene – there's more scope for variety than there is when it comes to story structure more broadly – but you will find that many scenes share a number of characteristics.

- *The focus moves from broad to narrow.* If you look at the scene above, the opening sections contained a lot of information of a fairly general nature (what the club looked like, what Barbara's duties involved, who the customers were, and so on). All this information feels necessary when it's given to us – we wouldn't want to do without it – but at the same time, as the core business of the scene gets underway, the general information-giving is shoved aside and the focus falls relentlessly on the scene's central subject, in this case the Barbara–Mae encounter.

- *Time moves from general to specific.* Early in the scene, time has a rather floating quality to it. The scene starts with the phrase 'One Saturday night, my shift had just begun', but then almost immediately jumps backwards with a statement about how her two bosses *had gone* out for a meal before the rush. There are also a number of other touches early on ('The other four customers consisted of ...') which make statements that were generally true for the period in question – as though a routine half-hour were being described – the half-hour before seven o'clock, say, rather than a specific moment, 6.26 pm. As the scene moves into full flow (and becomes more dialogue-driven), time becomes more specific. So when Barbara notes that Mae's eyes 'filled with angry tears', we know that they filled with tears immediately after she reported the 'meatstand' comment made by Rabbits.

- *Description moves from full to partial.* There isn't, as it happens, much description of the bar itself in this scene, but what there is, we are given early on. The most important descriptive element in the scene deals with Mae's appearance. Not just her looks, but her manner, her excitingly reckless stylishness. These descriptive paragraphs, however, belong firmly in the early part of the scene. Thereafter, Tate restricts herself to little nudges, reminders in effect of where we are and who we're dealing with. Those nudges tend to take earlier elements of the description and either amplify or amend them. Thus the jukebox has already rated a mention in the scene when Barbara comes to give it a remedial kick. Mae has already been fully described when Barbara notes that she can also look impish. The nudges keep reminding us of the longer earlier description, so you get a continuing sense of the physicality of what is being described … but without continuing long stretches of descriptive prose.

- *Action rises to a climax.* Although there's plenty of movement and interest early in the scene, that movement rises into a satisfying climax: the 'your poor feet' comment which effectively seals this friendship. Most well-told scenes will have a similar feeling of a rise in intensity and some kind of pay-off in their closing passages. Because this is only a scene, not an entire novel, those climaxes don't need to be huge. 'Your poor feet' serves as a perfectly good ending for a scene. Clearly, however, it would hardly work as a way to end an entire book.

Although, as I say, there is plenty of variety in the way scenes are structured and told, the single biggest alternative model to the one above is, in effect, a fake version of the exact same thing. Scenes in action-driven commercial fiction often start out in the immediate, specific present. This sort of thing: "What the hell is that?' snapped the captain, jabbing his finger at the radar screen'. That immediate, specific present may be continued for a few sentences or even a few paragraphs. But it can't usually continue for long before the reader wants to know the setting for all this action – where are we? who's the captain? what is the situation? – and the scene will skip back to deliver more general information (descriptions, explanations, and so on) before running on again into the specific. There's nothing wrong with this technique and there are no rules for when it should or should not be used. You just need to use your judgement. (And of course, to the extent that your scene is unfolding in a known place with known characters, the need for description and explanation tends to fall away anyway.)

Movement, lovely movement

When we spoke about plotting, we saw how movement lies at the very heart of story. If a story becomes static, it dies and can do so alarmingly fast. The same thing, in essence, is true of scenes. The Big Questions that propel a particular scene will, of course, tend to be narrower than those raised by the book itself, but readers still expect to see constant motion in the way those questions are answered. Tate's scene is a perfect example of how those questions are raised, amended, part-answered, sabotaged and then fully answered ... and answered in a way that raises delightful new Big Questions for the book to address. The scene in this chapter started with the question 'What happens when Barbara meets the glamorous blonde?' and ended with a whole different set of questions planted in the reader's mind – roughly, 'Will Barbara becomes the prostitute's maid, and what on earth will happen if she does?'. It would be well worth re-reading the scene above, together with my notes, and studying the way that Big

Question is in continual motion. Literally not a page goes by without the Big Question having been altered in some way.

And just as plotting involves an internal journey as well as an external one, so too does the business of scene construction. Consider for a moment how empty the scene above would have been had there been no emotional language involved: if Mae had not been so expressive, if Barbara had not been so clearly intrigued by Mae (early on) and so attracted to her warmth and impulsiveness (later on). It's perfectly true that the scene in question is taken from a book about a friendship between two women. If the book had been a novel about a terrorist attack on Chicago, clearly emotions would have played a smaller role. But not much smaller. In the end, however, we read books because we like the way they make us feel, and even in action-adventure novels, we need to know that the hero is desperate to avoid the threatened attack, that he's at his wit's end, that he's exhausted but driven … and so on. We need to know about his inner journey in order to construct a full one of our own.

Chapter Summary

- The best way to understand scene construction is to engage in a blow-by-blow analysis of a specific scene – which we've done in this chapter.
- In general, scenes will be propelled by Big Questions of their own.
- The scene will be as full of movement (in relation to *its* Big Question) as a novel is (in relation to the overarching Big Question of the book). Movement is key!
- Description and other kinds of information should ideally be story-driven: the information should feel required by the story; it shouldn't feel like a data-dump from the author.
- Dialogue lends immediacy like almost nothing else.
- Many scenes will move from broad to narrow in focus, from general to specific.
- The action will tend to rise to a climax.
- It's fine if sometimes the action rises to an anti-climax, or a moment of comedy rather than drama.
- Remember that the reader is only interested in the action if the protagonist is interested.

THE SCENE THAT ISN'T

The previous chapter, and much of this book, has revolved around the principle of 'show, don't tell'. Barbara Tate's scene was a lovely illustration of that principle in action. She didn't blandly tell us, 'Then, in Soho, I met a prostitute called Mae and agreed to work as her maid.' Instead, she showed us that event unfolding in glorious moment-by-moment detail. Naturally, any scene involves snippets of 'telling'. To take one tiny example, Tate tells us, 'Meat was still on ration after the war, and [Syd's] work as a [meat] porter meant he was full of stories.' She doesn't writhe around in contortions trying to *show* us that meat was rationed. That fact isn't dramatically significant, so doesn't need to be dramatised. She just tells us the fact we need and moves swiftly on. Such snippets, however, are the exceptions. The scene, the classic scene, the scene that is the basic unit of the novel, is all about dramatising the moment; it's about *showing*. And to read some advice to writers, you'd think that was all there was to it.

A minor lake near Grand Rapids

Alas for writers, and fortunately for literature, the subject is a little more complex than that. In various types of fiction, but most prominently in literary fiction and some types of non-fiction, the business of *telling* occupies far more page space than you might think.

There's a good recent example of what I mean. In Jonathan Franzen's much-praised *Freedom*, the story itself – the actual moment-by-moment story; the one that is shown and not told – doesn't kick off until page 35:

> *As far as actual sex goes, Patty's first experience of it was being raped at a party when she was seventeen by a boarding-school senior named Ethan Post.*

That's a promising intro and the promise is kept. In less than a page, the story zooms in on a specific place at a specific time:

> *To avoid waking her little sister, she went and cried in the shower. This was, without exaggeration, the most wretched hour of her life.*

From then on, the story runs as you expect a story to run. Scenes unfold at specific places, at specific times, with a close causal connection between them. If this is a film, then we're through the ads and the trailers and the title sequence. This is the start of the story proper.

But a puzzle stays with us all the same. It took Franzen thirty-five pages to get properly started. In the course of those pages, he traces the entire course of a marriage. His two protagonists, Walter and Patty Berglund start, newly married, as the 'young pioneers of Ramsey Hill', a district of St Paul, Minnesota. The prologue ends more than twenty years later. Their son has gone off to college. Their marriage seems to be strained or breaking up. They're selling the house that they've spent so much of their lives investing in. Two lives, thirty pages.

During this lengthy prologue, he in effect reverses the traditional wisdom on telling and showing. For the most part, he chooses to *tell* the reader things. For example:

> *Neighbours who were closer to the Berglunds than the Paulsens reported that Miss Bianca had left her little mouse house, on a minor lake near Grand Rapids, exclusively to Walter and not to his two brothers. There was said to be disagreement between Walter and Patty about how to handle this, Walter wanting to sell the house and share the proceeds with his brothers, Patty insisting that he honour his mother's wish to reward him for being the good son.*

You couldn't ask for a clearer example of telling. Franzen doesn't tell us what those 'neighbours who were closer to the Berglunds than the Paulsens' said. There are no fragments of dialogue, no mini-scenes located in time and space. Indeed, Franzen doesn't even bother to tell us who those neighbours were. If Franzen had been operating in 'showing' mode, he'd have shown the whole thing unfolding: 'One day in spring, Mrs Briggs, wearing an astonishing flowered dress and non-matching purple boots, told us, "You know that Miss Bianca, right, down near Grand Rapids? Yes, well, you'll never guess what …"'. But he does no such thing. The advantage is that his storytelling is swift. (There would in fact be no other way to cover two lives in so little time.) The disadvantage is that it feels removed, abstract and distant.

Now, of course, Franzen is no fool. His novel was praised as 'a masterpiece' in *The New York Times* and as 'a Great American Novel' in *The Daily Telegraph* in the UK. You don't have to agree with the emphatic nature of those assessments to believe that he knows how to tell a tale, and if he chooses to 'tell' rather than 'show', it probably isn't because he hasn't figured out the difference. So what's going on? And when is it OK to tell rather than show?

A spattered wool shirt

The first point to make is that even Franzen's telling includes lots of showing. So just as Barbara Tate's scene *showed* a drama unfolding, it also incorporated little fragments of *telling*, as shorthand ways of imparting facts. The telling was there to service the showing, to keep the story moving, to keep the reader's attention firmly on the matter at hand.

Franzen's prologue does something similar, but in reverse. Franzen wants to *tell*, in order to relay a lot of facts swiftly, but he knows that he'll lose the reader if he sticks only in telling mode, so he drops in lots of snippets of showing. Those snippets are longer than Tate's single line about meat-rationing, but that's inevitable: it takes much more time to show something happening than simply to tell us that it's happened. What we have is a long narrative – an external view of a marriage – dotted with little moments of colour, fragments of dialogue, significant incidents, personal detail. Those things never really cohere into scenes, or at least they never get beyond the shortest and most limited of scenes. Nevertheless, they provide that vital colour, the splash and texture of human life:

> *For a long time, there was always Patty, down on her knees among her vegetables or up on a ladder in a spattered wool shirt, attending to the Sisyphean task of Victorian paint maintenance. If Connie couldn't be near Joey she could at least be useful to him by keeping his mother company in his absence. 'What's the homework situation?' Patty would ask her from the ladder. 'Do you want some help?'*
>
> *'My Mom's going to help when she gets home.'*
>
> *'She's going to be tired, it's going to be late. You could surprise her and get it done right now. You want to do that?'*
>
> *'No I'll wait.'*
>
> *When exactly Connie and Joey started fucking wasn't known …*

Franzen's technique in this section is delightfully duplicitous. This 'scene' does not take place at any specific place or time. Quite the opposite. The language makes it clear that we're being given examples of a commonplace exchange: 'There was *always* Patty …', 'Patty *would* ask …'. At the same time, the trickery of language half-allows us to visualise the scene. We half-see Patty bustling about the garden or up a ladder. The scene feels as though it is a specific, elapsing moment, even though in truth it's an amalgam of dozens of different such moments, each of which would have run a bit differently from this composite version. It's a delicious way to combine the economy of telling with the colour of showing.

And this, therefore, provides us with an important lesson: if you do choose to tell extensively, *à la* Franzen, you still need numerous splashes of colour, countless snippets that show (or pretend to show) the unfolding moment. You need to drop those splashes in the way Franzen does in the passage above. Unobtrusive, constant, specific and, if need be, duplicitous.

Yet that can't be the whole story. Franzen spends thirty-odd pages avoiding his main story, then plunges straight in – with scenes, with specifics, with close-up detailed action – as though he were the most by-the-book storyteller in the world. What's going on?

When telling works

The answer, in Franzen's case, is that his long prologue is there to set a mystery. It's providing us with a corpse (that of a marriage). Understanding how that corpse came to be there, and what finally becomes of it, will be the task of the book. His long prologue assembles the crime scene for our inspection, and his technique is factual, swift and above all *external*. We see Patty and Walter from outside, not from within. We're given the external, social outcome of their marriage, but we're not given the interior insight that allowed that situation to come into being. When we actually get to the story itself, we get there with the sense that the puzzle has now been set; it's up to us to solve it.

This is by no means the only reason why you may want to 'tell' at length in your novel. In the kind of novels where story takes something of a back seat – *Netherland* and *On Chesil Beach* are the most obvious examples discussed thus far – authors may well want the discursive depth that can only come from telling; the ability to discuss, analyse and reflect; the ability to transmit facts and then turn them over, pondering their significance. In *On Chesil Beach*, for example, there are plenty of clues early on that this wedding night is going to go horribly wrong. Those clues shift the nature of the question asked by the book from 'What is going to happen on this young couple's wedding night?' to 'Why is everything going to go horribly wrong?' The long chunks of telling are there to service that story question. They're like bits of evidence presented towards the solution of a mystery. The heart of *On Chesil Beach* – and every other novel under the sun – is still about the drama of the unfolding moment, but it is willing to make relatively long digressions into 'telling', because those digressions serve to increase the drama when it comes.

There is no simple rule of thumb to tell you what will or won't work. Or rather, there *is* such a rule, but you need to be a good writer to use it. And the rule is simple. When you find yourself writing a lengthy section that is told rather than shown, you ask yourself: 'Does this feel right? Is the story still a compelling one? Am I increasing dramatic tension or losing it?'. If the answers to those questions are affirmative, you're probably doing all right. If they're not, then be very careful. In particular, if your answers sound like excuses – 'I've got to tell the reader about Gloria's backstory, because that's going to become incredibly important in part three' – you have to reject them. In the end, the whole telling versus showing issue is something of a red herring. It doesn't matter whether you tell or show. What matters is that you create, build and sustain a drama. If your passages of telling support that goal, you're doing fine. If not, rethink. And if in doubt, always go with showing not telling. Or in Henry James's language: dramatise, dramatise, dramatise.

Chapter Summary

- Plenty of good books and good authors will use extensive passages of 'telling' rather than 'showing'.

- The habit is more prevalent in literary fiction and certain sorts of non-fiction. If you are writing plot-driven commercial fiction, you should strictly limit the amount of 'telling' that goes on.

- If you do find yourself 'telling' at length, then you need a strong story-led reason for doing so. The telling needs to enhance, not detract from, the dramatic question at the heart of the book.

- You also need to include plenty of snippets of showing – tangible, specific splashes of dramatised human colour – in the passages of telling.

DIALOGUE

Never use an adverb to modify the verb "said" . . . he admonished gravely. To use an adverb this way (or almost any way) is a mortal sin. The writer is now exposing himself in earnest, using a word that distracts and can interrupt the rhythm of the exchange. I have a character in one of my books tell how she used to write historical romances "full of rape and adverbs."

– Elmore Leonard

Novels are all about faking it – making up worlds, making up people, making up events, and making all these things seem as real as day. The same goes for dialogue. Your mission is *not* to write dialogue as people actually speak it, but to write dialogue that *feels* natural and energetic. The distinction, as we'll see, is important.

Expletive deleted

When the Watergate scandal broke over President Nixon's head, it emerged that he had ordered the covert taping of countless conversations at the White House, some of which bore directly on the Watergate break-ins. The tapes were subpoenaed and transcripts were released. Those transcripts shocked the world. Partly because they demonstrated that the President of the US was at the heart of the illegal activity. Partly because the transcripts were littered with the phrase 'expletive deleted', revealing that the US President wasn't merely a crook, but a crook who swore. And partly, because it made people think, 'Gosh, do we really talk like that?'

Here, for example, is a snippet from the 'smoking gun' tape – the one that finally connected Nixon to the blossoming scandal.

Nixon's interlocutor here, Bob Haldeman, was a political aide who was later sentenced to eighteen months in jail.

> HALDEMAN: *So I guess, so it's things like that that are gonna, that are filtering in. Mitchell came up with yesterday, and John Dean analyzed very carefully last night and concludes, concurs now with Mitchell's recommendation that the only way to solve this, and we're set up beautifully to do it, ah, in that and that ... the only network that paid any attention to it last night was NBC ... they did a massive story on the Cuban ...*
>
> PRESIDENT: *That's right.*
>
> HALDEMAN: *... thing.*
>
> PRESIDENT: *Right.*
>
> HALDEMAN: *That the way to handle this now is for us to have Walters call Pat Gray and just say, 'Stay the hell out of this ... this is ah, business here we don't want you to go any further on it.' That's not an unusual development ...*
>
> PRESIDENT: *Um huh.*
>
> HALDEMAN: *... and, uh, that would take care of it.*

This, amazingly enough, is how we speak. You and me. Nixon and Haldeman. Our speech is full of interruptions, hesitations, repetitions, vagueness and imprecision. You'd think that it would be impossible to communicate effectively in this way, yet Nixon and Haldeman between them managed to run a country and plot a burglary. At the same time, it's fairly obvious that if you tried writing dialogue like this, your reader would be baffled and your lovely sentences would disappear in a haze of, uh, that's right, a haze of, um huh, haziness.

Expletive retained

At the same time, modern readers expect dialogue to feel natural rather than staged. It needs to have the contemporary, broken, oblique feel of the Haldeman-Nixon dialogue, while being carefully managed to convey exactly the meanings that you want to get over. Here, for example, is a lovely bit of dialogue from Philip Roth's *Indignation*. The two speakers are the protagonist (Marcus) and a fellow student (Olivia) who recently gave him – much to his surprise – a blowjob. He has been avoiding her, until they meet at the student bookstore.

> '*Hello, Marc,*' *she said.*
> '*Oh, yes, hi,*' *I said.*
> '*I did that because I liked you so much.*'
> '*Pardon?*'
> *She pulled off her hat and shook out her hair – thick and long and not cut short with a little crimp of curls over the fore-head, as was the hairdo worn by most every other coed on the campus.*
> '*I said I did that because I liked you,*' *she told me.* '*I know you can't figure it out. I know that's why I haven't heard from you and why you ignore me in class. So I'm figuring it out for you.*' *Her lips parted in a smile, and I thought, With those lips, she, without my urging, completely voluntarily ... And yet I was the one who felt shy!* '*Any other mysteries?*' *she asked.*
> '*Oh, no, that's okay.*'
> '*It's* not,' *she said, and now she was frowning, and every time her expression changed her beauty changed with it. She wasn't one beautiful girl, she was twenty-five different beautiful girls.* '*You're a hundred miles away from me. No, it's not okay with you,*' *she said.* '*I liked your seriousness. I liked your ma-turity at dinner – or what I took to be maturity. I made a joke about it, but I liked your intensity. I've never met anyone so intense before. I liked your looks, Marcus. I still do.*'
> '*Did you ever do that with someone else?*'
> '*I did,*' *she said without hesitation.* '*Has no one ever done it with you?*'
> '*No one's come close.*'
> '*So you think I'm a slut,*' *she said, frowning again.*

This is a lovely bit of dialogue, because it retains all the naturalness of the Nixon conversation while being scrupulously marshalled and controlled all the while. Take the opening exchange. She says, 'Hello, Marc,' – as straightforward a greeting as you could ask for. He answers her with, 'Oh, yes, hi,' – and the 'Oh' and the 'yes' are both awkward and unnecessary if this dialogue were strictly about a transfer of meanings. It's as if the 'oh' is shorthand for 'oh gosh, it's *you*', and the 'yes' is shorthand for something like, 'Yes, well, this moment had to come and now here it is, so I'd better just get on with it and reciprocate that greeting'. Roth doesn't labour those points. He doesn't need to. The tiny glitch in the narrator's response to Olivia is all that's required.

The next moment is equally deft. 'I did that because I liked you so much.' Olivia doesn't say *what* she did and doesn't need to, because the *what* is ringing in Marcus's (and the reader's) mind. Equally, she doesn't bother to prepare the question at all. She doesn't say, 'Look, I know you're wondering why I did that. I did it because ...'. Again, that introduction is unnecessary. She knows what the issue is. Marcus knows. The reader knows. So she just gets on and says what's on her mind. The speech reads with a natural jumpy brokenness (because of that missing introduction), but it remains perfectly intelligible, perfectly in tune with the emotional dynamic of the moment.

Marcus's 'Pardon?' isn't, I don't think, because he hasn't understood her. It's because he still hasn't caught up with her directness. She then gives a long speech – long by the standards of this section, but still only forty-two words – to explain herself. In effect, she's now jumping backwards to explain the thing she led off with; she's giving Marcus time to catch up ... but he doesn't catch up. When she asks him if there's anything else he wants explained ('Any other mysteries?'), his answer is 'Oh, no, that's okay'. Now we know perfectly well what he means here, or what he intends to mean. He's trying to say, 'No, Olivia, your explanation has filled me in on everything I might possibly have wanted to know, and now I feel replete with the knowledge. I thank you, indeed'. Only his actual answer sabotages his intent. First of all, there's that unnecessary 'oh'. Secondly, he says 'that's okay', which isn't really an answer to the question he's been asked. Again, Roth doesn't make a big hoo-hah about this; the narrator's four-word answer – 'Oh, no, that's okay' – indicates everything we need to know: Marcus is still reeling with the memory of *that* moment. He can't move beyond it.

So Olivia tries again to explain herself. This is the longest speech of the whole passage – still only fifty-eight words – and she's as clear as she can be. She does, as it happens, repeats herself. ('It's *not* … No, it's not okay with you'.) She also uses sentences ('You're a hundred miles away from me.') that make sense in context, but which wouldn't be entirely clear out of context. All the same, in this short passage, we get as close as we ever get to formal, direct, eloquent conversation – the sort of conversation you might find in Jane Austen, for example.

And Marcus doesn't answer her. Except that he does. He says the thing that's been on his mind non-stop: 'Did you ever do that with someone else?' We know that's what's been on his mind, because it isn't, even remotely, the expected answer to Olivia's speech. She's just told him, in effect, that she likes him very much, that there's a romance waiting to bloom, if only he wants to reciprocate … and all he can think is, 'Does she do this all the time?'.

Marcus's direct question breaks the tension, and for the first time in the conversation an absolutely straight question is met with an absolutely straight answer. If conversation is meant to be like a game of tennis, then this is the first time that a conversational shot has been returned over the net, at full speed, without hesitation, and without any curious change of direction.

Needless to say, that brief moment of biff-bam tennis doesn't last very long. Marcus doesn't simply say 'no' to Olivia's question, he says 'no' a bit too forcefully: 'No one's come close'. That doesn't have to be an insult. It wasn't *meant* as an insult: Marcus is still just brimming over with the weird amazingness of what Olivia freely chose to do – but Olivia is only human, and she responds not to the literal sense of his words, but to the emotional overlay. 'Gosh, well, if you're saying no one has even come close, and you're saying that in that forceful way, you must be implying that I'm a slut.' So she frowns ... but we also know that Marcus *doesn't* think she's a slut. He's just decided that she isn't merely one beautiful girl, she's twenty-five of them. That's halfway to being in love, and all his hesitations indicate that he can't quite get his head round the amazingness of what he's being presented with.

The passage is so good, because so much is conveyed. Partly at a literal level, but much more at an implicit, emotional level. Not a word is wasted. The dialogue *feels* natural, but *is* carefully stage-managed. The dialogue forces the plot forward, altering a relationship as we watch.

Writing perfect dialogue

This passage from Roth suggests most of the techniques needed to write strong, convincing, emotionally nuanced dialogue. Prime among those techniques are:

- *Keep speeches short.* The longest speech in the passage above was less than sixty words, and when it came it felt like quite a long, full speech. Many first-time writers (especially perhaps of traditional fantasy) end up inadvertently using much longer speeches, so that everyone sounds as though they're declaiming rather than talking. Keeping speeches short – and often *very* short – is the simplest, best way to keep your dialogue fluid and dynamic. (Having said that, there may be points at which a character *is* making a speech, in which case it's fine to let him or her get on with it. But not too long, or too often, please.)

- *Prefer the oblique to the direct.* In the passage above, there was only one biff-bam moment of conversational tennis (the point where he asks if she ever gave anyone else a blow-job, and she says that she did, then comes right back at him with a similar question). In that one exchange, there was no indirectness at all. No swerve off-topic. No hesitation or fudging or delay. But that moment was an exception. Everywhere else, there's a small but definite gap between question and response. She says 'hello'; he says (in effect) 'oh my goodness, it's *you!*' She explains why she likes him and hints that she's like to explore a relationship, and he just says (again, in effect), 'Do you give blowjobs to all the guys?'. Those obliquenesses, those swerves off-course, are what give this dialogue its suppleness and movement. The reader is constantly kept on tenterhooks, unsure of which way the conversation is going to go next, alert to every emotional clue, no matter how small. If the conversation were ever allowed to be simple, direct and literal, it would lose almost all its energy, its lovely shimmer of possibility.

- *Use hesitations and interruptions, etc.* The multiple small confusions and hesitations that marked the Nixon-Haldeman passage made it hard to read, and its meaning unclear. The (many fewer) hesitations that stud the Roth dialogue are what opens out its meaning: like Marcus's 'Oh, yes, hi'. It's fine to use colloquial speech, contractions, and sentence fragments. It's fine to have characters interrupt each other or themselves. Feel free to use all those techniques to add a layer of effectively non-verbal meaning to the literal, verbal meaning of the words themselves.

- *But don't overdo it!* One of the commonest issues with dialogue written by new writers is that they tend to overuse the ellipsis ('...'). It's perfectly true that in real life speech, we do trail off frequently, but even in Roth's naturalistic dialogue, there's no trailing off, no ellipses. Nor is there even any formal interruption, even though there is a jerkiness in the speech itself. That's not to say you should never use ellipses or interruptions – both things are perfectly valid, and you should feel free to use them as appropriate – but watch yourself to make sure you're not overdoing things. (Just to be clear, if you want a character's speech to trail off into silence, you use the ellipsis: 'Blah, blah, blah ...' If you want a character to be interrupted, you use the dash: 'Yadda, yadda, yadda –').

- *Make sure your dialogue serves the emotional need of the moment.* Nowhere in Roth's passage is the dialogue broken or hesitant or oblique just for the sake of it. On the contrary, every such indirectness is there in order to mark some emotion that the characters are feeling, but not formally expressing. In effect, Roth gives us two bits of dialogue, one overlaid on the other. The first is the formal, literal meaning of the words. The second is the non-verbal, emotional, implied meaning in the hesitations and avoidances. And, naturally, that also means there'll be times when dialogue runs in a fairly straightforward way. If a detective is talking to her superior, for example, they may well have a rapid, effective, professional conversation, which conveys meaning concisely and clearly, and which doesn't have a huge overlay of anything else.

- *Prefer 'said' to more colourful verbs.* Roth uses just two different verbs of speech in the passage above: *said* and *told*. You don't need much else. (*Asked* and *answered* are also fine.) You don't, on the whole, need to set your characters murmuring, whispering, roaring, declaiming, exhorting, threatening, piping up ... or indeed, almost anything else you care to think of. All those verbs tend to distract from the dialogue itself, which is the only genuinely important bit. And besides, if your dialogue doesn't already convey that someone is threatening, exhorting or murmuring, you should rewrite the dialogue. You can't thrust an effect in simply by telling the reader what effect is meant to have been conveyed.

- *Don't get in a state over your 'he said's and 'she said's.* A lot of first-time writers end up worrying a lot over how often you need to mark who the speaker is. Some writers go to one extreme and mark the speaker for every single sentence. Others go to the opposite extreme and tell you who the two speakers are at the outset of a passage, then let the reader figure it out for themselves. Neither extreme makes much sense. Just pop a marker in when you feel it's needed, then forget about it. Readers don't actually notice those 'he said's anyway. They regard them (correctly) as equivalent to punctuation. They don't get in the way. They don't slow down a passage. They're just helpful little assistants to flow and meaning.

- *Avoid cliché.* Nowhere in Roth's dialogue does either character use an obvious cliché, despite the fact that the substance of the scene – featuring youthful awkwardness around sexuality – is hardly unknown in the annals of fiction. Although people do use hackneyed phrases in real life, that doesn't mean it's OK for an author to use them in dialogue. Although there'll be times where it's essential to use a cliché – you're probably emphasising something about the character who's speaking when you do it – you also need to remember that clichés tend to bore and distance the reader. That boring and distancing may only happen at a micro-level, well below the reach of consciousness, but even tiny increases in boredom are to be avoided. The moral: use clichés in dialogue if you truly have to, but take care and never overdo it.

- *Make use of action and narration in the midst of your dialogue.* There are a number of writers (often screen-influenced) who have developed a very pared-down style, in which dialogue is often presented with very little narratorial interjection, by which I mean the non-dialogue part of the writing. In Roth's passage, that would include things like the paragraph starting, 'She pulled off her hat ...', or the bit starting 'Her lips parted in a smile ...' When this very pared-down presentation is done well – Elmore Leonard is one of its most capable exponents – it can work very well indeed, but the style is not typical of most contemporary authors, whether literary or commercial. Much more normal would be Roth's technique above, which interrupts the dialogue with (i) short action sentences, (ii) brief descriptions, (iii) thoughts and feelings. Those additions have two functions. First of all, they give a context, physical and emotional, to the dialogue. The conversation itself resonates differently because the reader is aware of how beautiful Marcus finds Olivia. When she says, 'you think I'm a slut', we know that he's thinking nothing of the sort: he's thinking that she's twenty-five different beautiful girls. Secondly, they allow the author to determine the conversational rhythm without using the somewhat clunkier tools of ellipses, pauses, and so on. Thus, for example, when Olivia says, 'it's *not*', Roth breaks the dialogue with a couple of sentences about what she looks like and what Marcus thinks about what she looks like. When she then continues, 'You're a hundred miles away from me', Roth has, in effect, created a pause in her speech, without having to say directly, 'then she paused and waited half a second before continuing'. Simple, neat and easy.

That, more or less, is that. Decent dialogue is actually quite easy to write. Certainly, there are plenty of first-time writers who get the process pretty much right, pretty much straight away. It's not something that most people will need to spend a lot of time worrying about. The truth is that if you stay closely in touch with your characters and remain true to them and their emotional situation, you're not likely to go far wrong.

Regular human beings

Having said all the above, there are a couple of ways in which you might find yourself going off track, and a couple of genres where novelists struggle more often.

The first way of going wrong arises from an overly prescriptive injunction in some creative writing texts, which often tell you that each character should speak in a completely distinctive way. I just don't think that's either true or helpful. In Roth's dialogue, both characters are of the same age, same class, same race, same country, same education. Neither has odd, repetitive speech mannerisms. They just sound like regular human beings of the type you might expect to find knocking around an American university campus. That's not to say that he sounds like her and vice versa. In this dialogue, they certainly don't – but that's because their emotional position is different. A couple of pages later, the narrator's emotional position has shifted to one where he's more than capable of simple, assertive direct speech. (He says 'Oh, fuck you,' to his roommate, who responds by punching him.) Yes, the narrator sounds like himself all the time – that is, he never sounds like anyone else – but if you work too hard to make him sound like him-and-nobody-else all the time, you're almost certain to end up with dialogue that feels strained and contrived. Just let your characters speak in the way that is natural to them and the moment, and let it be.

Secondly, some writers read screenplays as a way of learning about dialogue in the raw. Screenplays *are* a good education in dialogue in many ways. They're swift and economical and (often) vibrant with strong one-liners. But they're screenplays, and any kind of writing for the screen ends up being far more pared back, far leaner than writing for the page. That's not because screenwriters are better at writing dialogue. It's because they're writing in a different format and for a different purpose. By all means, read screenplays. You'll certainly learn something. Just don't think that you can simply transfer screen techniques to the page. You can't.

The other Boleyn babe

One area that needs special care is any genre in which people aren't speaking ordinary modern English, notably historical fiction, fantasy and sci-fi. In either context, the use of ordinary contemporary English risks seeming too *specifically* contemporary. So, presumably, Roman teenagers did say the Latin equivalent of, 'That chariot looks well wicked'. No doubt space captains ploughing the interstellar highway between here and Alpha Centauri will have equivalent slang of their own. Yet if you have your Roman teenagers or space captains or orc commanders speaking in this way, your work will inevitably feel strained – if it doesn't simply feel plain weird.

The solution is not to go to the opposite extreme. It works no better to have your Latin teenagers saying, 'Great heavens, Lucius, methinks the lines of yon chariot betoken a conveyance of no small swiftness'. For the same reason, fantasy novels in which all the characters speak a kind of mock-medieval dialogue also feel lifeless and insipid.

The solution, nearly always, is to use ordinary contemporary language – the language of this book, say, or of any normal speech, that isn't keenly of the moment – and then flavour it. The flavouring can be relatively modest. The occasional exclamation, the odd untranslated foreign word, un-contemporary similes, expressions or turns of phrase. If you want a feel of historical language that doesn't sound archaic, using a somewhat formal version of ordinary English generally sounds about right. The idea is to flavour your language without overburdening it, allowing the reader to focus on the sense of what is being said more than on the business of saying it. If in doubt about how to do it for your particular genre, then simply study the work of published authors in your area. Do it like that.

Dialogue of the dead

When it comes to writing non-fiction, many writers are hesitant to use any dialogue at all. In certain contexts, that makes eminent sense. If you don't know what Cleopatra said to Antony before he went off to battle, you can't just make it up. You can and should use any letters or other personal material, but that's as much as you can do.

Some non-fiction authors, however, have more they can play with. Bryan Burrough and John Helyar included plenty of dialogue in their non-fiction epic, *Barbarians at the Gate*. Many of the conversations they reported were not recorded at the time, so the authors could have had no precise record of what *exactly* was said. On the other hand, they had been hugely thorough in their research and interviews. They never reported a conversation without having discussed that conversation with at least one of its participants. They were relentless in pursuing the little detail: who was wearing what, where the meeting took place, what X thought when he heard Y say Z. Armed with such meticulous research, they simply went ahead and silently invented the few little details they couldn't know for sure, such as the precise pattern of words used, the precise sequence of the interchange. In addition, they created a way of writing dialogue *outside* inverted commas, as for example here, in the book's opening (which I've edited slightly for length):

Johnson was clad casually in slacks and a light blue golf shirt adorned with RJR Nabisco's corporate logo. His silvery hair was worn unstylishly long. A gold bracelet dangled from his left wrist. Goldstone knew Johnson was pondering a move that would change his life – maybe all their lives – forever.

[...] So far his arguments hadn't swayed his client. Goldstone knew he had to press harder. 'You could lose everything,' he repeated. The planes. The Manhattan apartment. The Palm Beach compound. The villa in Castle Pines. The lawyer paused to let it sink in.

Don't you understand? You could lose everything?

That doesn't change the merits of the transaction, Johnson answered simply. It doesn't change the basic situation. 'I really have no choice,' he said.

The details about Johnson's clothing both satisfy the reader's desire to picture the scene and – by offering clear, precise fact – confirming to the reader that the scene has been thoroughly researched. What follows is a beautiful piece of the non-fiction writer's craft. Only four words are directly attributed to Goldstone ('you could lose everything') and only five words are directly attributed to Johnson ('I really have no choice.') Nevertheless, the last three paragraphs of the snippet above read like almost pure dialogue. And why not? We can trust Burrough and Helyar to have done their research properly. The actual phrases they are attributing to their two characters are so neutral, so bare, that it doesn't really matter whether the two individuals used those actual words or not. And as for the rest of it, the authors have captured the essence of the dialogue in a way which seems both fair, lifelike and readable. It's a compelling little scene.

And if it's OK for Burrough and Helyar to invent dialogue for scenes where neither man was present, it's OK for you to invent dialogue for scenes where you yourself *were* present. Some memoir writers are afflicted by an excessive desire for truthfulness. Because they can't remember the precise words someone said to them twenty years ago, they feel they have to report the whole scene without dialogue. And that's nonsense, of course. A recipe for an unreadably dull memoir. You need to be scrupulous about the big facts. You need to be careful with emotional truth, period verisimilitude and so forth. But as for the micro-details – the words someone used, the colour of someone's jacket, the smell in the room – you simply have to trust your own imaginative powers of reconstruction. Naturally that means you will get some small details wrong, but nobody cares. Think of yourself as writing one of those 'dramatic reconstructions' shown on TV. You need to get the big stuff right. For everything else: make it up.

Chapter Summary

- Don't try to write as people *actually* speak. People speak with innumerable hesitations, repetition and unclarities.
- Nevertheless, you do want to mimic real speech. You want to aim at a kind of broken, oblique, natural effect.
- Keep speeches short.
- Prefer the oblique to the direct.
- Use hesitations and interruptions (without overdoing it).
- Make sure the dialogue serves the emotional purpose of the scene.
- Prefer 'said' to fancier verbs of speech. Avoid adverbs. Use 'he said' or 'she said' wherever it seems natural to do so.
- Avoid clichés.
- Break up dialogue with action and narration.
- Historical or speculative fiction should mostly be written in ordinary contemporary English that's flavoured with period words or phrases.
- Non-fiction writers (especially memoir writers) should use dialogue, even if they can't precisely reconstruct the detail of who said what.

THE CHAPTER

Two chapters back, we analysed the scene: a continuous piece of writing that centres on the same place, time and group of characters. Some scenes may be long – the one in the previous chapter was 2,400 words. (Indeed, the same scene continued with various further adventures for a total of 4,800 words.) Other scenes may be very short, perhaps just two or three scant paragraphs which describe a particular encounter before moving on.

The evasive chapter

Chapters, too, are highly variable things. Modern commercial fiction tends towards relatively short chapters, each of which may well contain just one substantial scene. On the other hand, plenty of other authors – including some commercial ones – prefer longer chapters that contain a number of connected scenes. There are no rules for these things. My own chapters run, on average, to just over 2,000 words. A fast and furious commercial author might have an average chapter length of somewhere close to 1,500 words, or even less. Other authors might prefer chapter lengths running to more like 10,000 words. Those longer chapters won't necessarily make use of scenes that run on for longer, it's just that each chapter will connect more scenes together before taking a break.

And, of course, you don't actually *need* any chapters at all. Although most authors still use them – and I personally like them – you could do without them altogether. The only thing that really marks a chapter out is a page break, with the text resuming on a new page. That new page will sometimes have a numerical heading ('24', for example), sometimes a verbal one

('The Cornstubble Wars'). It doesn't necessarily need a heading at all, as you can perfectly well denote a new chapter typographically: a large initial capital letter for example.

On the other hand, pretty much all books benefit from pauses. Those pauses are usually denoted by a line break (at the least) and a page break (if we're talking about conventional chapters). If you like the idea of sometimes having section breaks within chapters, feel free to use them. If you hate the idea, then don't. Authors get more obsessive over these matters than any reader ever will. The simple truth is that no one but you cares all that much.

The structural chapter

Assuming, however, that you do have chapters, the way you arrange them matters in two respects. The first is that if there is any kind of structural complexity in the book – two different time periods, for example, or multiple protagonists – you need to be clear and consistent from the start in how you are going to divide things up. Will it be one protagonist per chapter? Or will you give each protagonist their own section within each chapter and use the chapters themselves to denote particular time periods or units of action? If you have multiple protagonists, are you going to alternate strictly between them, or will there be times when one of the group 'owns' a succession of sections or chapters?

There's no right or wrong answer here. All that matters is that your decision is clear and you carry it through consistently. Whether or not a reader ever consciously notices the scheme you've adopted isn't the point. Almost certainly, they'll use the structure you lay down as a kind of internal reference point, a guide to navigating your text. You need to make sure you don't confuse them by switching pattern halfway through.

Haggard cliffs, of every ugly altitude

The term 'cliffhanger' is thought to originate from the publication, in serial form, of Thomas Hardy's (truly bad) novel *A Pair of Blue Eyes*. The term, in this case, is literal. One of Hardy's chapters ends with the hero hanging by his arms from a cliff, apparently doomed. He's with a woman, who is willing to run for help, but such help will take forty-five minutes to arrive and, as the hero calmly remarks, 'That won't do; my hands will not hold out ten minutes'. With that message ringing in our ears – and after a minute or two's mute reflection by both parties – the heroine springs away to seek a miracle … while the hero is left contemplating his probable death. There the chapter ends. While a modern reader can simply turn the page (to discover one of the least plausible or exciting cliff-hanging episodes in literary history), a Victorian reader would have been left waiting for the next monthly instalment.

Hardy's execution may have been poor, but the idea itself was excellent. A reader is more likely to put a book down at a natural break point, such as the end of a chapter. And if the writer's job is to force the reader to read on, then why not try to craft the chapter ending in such a way as to force the reader to keep reading?

There's a problem, however. Readers like to be kept in suspense, but they won't take kindly to being tricked. Most perilous situations into which you might wish to plunge your characters are ones that don't lend themselves to a natural break. If Hardy's own cliff-hanging episode had been more vigorously and naturally rendered, the process in question – slipping off the cliff, hanging there, being rescued – would form a natural unity of action, an event that couldn't satisfactorily be chopped in half.

Modern novelists – particularly those working in the more story-driven genres – have grown adept at handling this balance. They want to leave the story in a place where the reader is anxious to know what happens next, but at the same time, they play by the rules by not breaking the story at a point where it feels unnatural. That also means that it's relatively rare for *every* chapter to end with a cliffhanger. More normal is the method adopted by, for example, Tess Gerritsen in *The Mephisto Club*. In that book, her opening sequence of chapter endings runs as follows:

One: *Amy Saul had no idea what they were about to bring home with them.*

Two: *He was still waving as she drove away.*

Three: *Jane looked at him. 'Joyce O'Donnell,' she said, 'is a vampire.'*

Four: *'I wouldn't put anything past her.' Jane let out the brake and pulled away from the curb. 'Anything.'*

Five: *'I don't know.' She sank back against the seat. 'But sooner or later, we'll hear all about it.'*

There are three clear 'cliffhanger' endings in this sequence (chapters one, three and four), but there's also a somewhat concealed one in chapter 2. The protagonist, Maura Isles, goes to church in order to see a priest with whom she has a not-quite-but-almost relationship. Just as they're getting into potentially committing emotional territory, she gets a phone call summoning her away to view a homicide scene. In that context, the sentence, 'He was still waving as she drove away,' is a way of suspending one drama (the emotional-romantic one) and promising the start of a new one (an investigative one). It too is a cliffhanger of a sort.

It's also, however, worth noticing that even in Gerritsen's story-driven fiction, not all chapters contain a cliffhanger. The ending of chapter 5 is an *ending*, a resting place, almost an invitation to the reader to the put the book down, turn the lights off and snuggle down for the night. Such natural pauses will occur in almost any novel, and you don't need to fight too hard to avoid them. By the time Gerritsen has got her reader to the end of chapter 5, she's introduced her crime, her characters and enough sinister detail to have the reader hooked. If simple realism demands that the protagonist be given a break and a time to rest, it's fine to permit that rest without a forced attempt to lever in more tension. Gerritsen knows that her reader will start again in the morning.

Chapter Summary

- You don't need to use chapters, but if you do ...

- ... any length is fine. Anywhere between 1,500 words and 10,000 words is perfectly normal.

- If you use your chapters structurally (eg: a new POV character per chapter), then be consistent.

- Don't break chapters in the middle of any scene that has a natural unity of action.

- Even action-fiction doesn't have to have cliffhangers in every chapter, but feel free to use some where it makes sense.

Part Seven

Towards Perfection

Style is knowing who you are, what you want to say and not giving a damn.

– Gore Vidal

I've learned that people will forget what you said, people will forget what you did, but people will never forget how you made them feel.

– Maya Angelou

No man was ever yet a great poet, without being at the same time a profound philosopher.

– Samuel Taylor Coleridge

THEMES

The first fictional heroine I fell in love with was Becky Sharp in Thackeray's *Vanity Fair*. I loved her green eyes and her wickedness and the sheer outrageous scale of her ambition. I can't now remember anything much about the plot, except that it's one of those ramshackle Victorian constructions, full of wills and bankruptcies and seductions and secret marriages, but the intricacies of how it all hangs together now passes me by. Likewise, I don't really remember any of the other characters. There's a decent, honourable soldier called Dobbin, somebody called Amelia – but it was a long time ago and I've forgotten the detail. It's only Becky – the beautiful green-eyed Becky – that made the book endure in my memory.

Character is one way in which a book can live long after first reading. The intense Captain Ahab, the intellectual Holmes, the crazy-sane Captain Yossarian, the hapless Bridget Jones. You'll always remember these individuals more than the stories they're involved with.

One of the other great ways is theme. The theme is the soul of a book. It's what a book is *about*. Quite likely, you've read *To Kill a Mockingbird*: some thirty million people have. If a few years have passed since you've read the book, your more specific memories may have vanished. Perhaps you remember the name of the lawyer father, Atticus Finch, and the narrator-protagonist, Scout. You'll probably remember that Atticus has to defend a black man falsely accused of raping a white woman, but many of the details will have blurred over time. But one thing, I predict, hasn't blurred: namely, your memory of the book's unswerving condemnation of Southern racism. The book doesn't simply have a point to make; it blazes with anger. A fierce, distilled rage that shocks you long after you set the book aside.

All great books have themes. F. Scott Fitzgerald's *The Great Gatsby* is, at one level, concerned with a thwarted romance between Jay Gatsby and Daisy Buchanan, but if the book had only been about that, it would never have endured. Instead, the book uses that romance to explore other, bigger themes: the corruption of the American Dream, the transition from the heroism and sacrifice of the First World War to the greed and corruption of the Roaring Twenties. John le Carré's *The Spy Who Came In from the Cold* is a well-told spy story, a nailed-on genre bestseller. But it's more than that. It's one of the very greatest works of post-war fiction, because le Carré used his spy-plot to deliver a great theme about love and betrayal. Cold War politics became a bleak metaphor for human interaction: cold, deceitful, and lethal.

Better yet, if you fumble your way to the magical chemistry of thematic greatness, many a fault becomes forgivable; invisible, almost. *The Great Gatsby* is, if truth be told, often overwritten. Its prose can smell like a bowl of tropical fruit left too long in the sun. *The Spy Who Came In from the Cold* is also not a perfect book. At times it feels rushed (which it was). The narrative voice can sometimes seem detached, dated and contemptuous. But a book doesn't have to be perfect to be great. Both *Gatsby* and *The Spy Who Came In from the Cold* so fully inhabit the worlds they describe, so perfectly locate some intersection between character, story and moment, that they overleap their faults, overleap them into greatness.

If your book is any good, it will have its theme too. Perhaps several. In *The Great Gatsby*, you'll find multiple themes looming through the text: the effect of money, the cruelty of the old upper classes, the vacuousness of the new ones, the decay of heroism, the loss of old values. You may not know precisely what your themes are before you sit down to write the book. Indeed, you may not know *afterwards*: perhaps on re-reading something, you'll see new pre-occupations loom into view that had previously passed you by. If so, you don't need to worry. Elusiveness tends to be a good thing when it comes to theme. It's why book groups exist, why English Literature courses exist. A wonderful book sets off a vibration that may take any amount of discussion and analysis to track down to its source. People find different things, even contradictory things, in the same book. They may all be right.

Luminous ichor

In that elusiveness lies a lesson for you, the author. Only seldom can a novel get away with stridency (Harper Lee's *Mockingbird* being one of the rare exceptions). On the whole, themes bubble up. They bubble through. They emerge from story and character. As you hone your book, work on character, nudge your story into shape, you'll find that your themes, like shadows clotting into solidity, take form as you work. If you approach these things too directly, they vanish, or at least become useless cut-outs of the thing you'd been hoping for. Just imagine if you came across writing like this in a Cold War spy novel:

> *Cassidy realised that he had been betrayed. His political masters had betrayed him just as he had been forced to betray those who had loved him. Was there no trust left in this world? It was as though the distrust and betrayals of his professional life had infected his personal life too. The simmering Cold War rivalry between two nuclear armed superpowers was like a metaphor for his own experience of love – perhaps the universal experience of human-kind.*

Do you feel how icky that is? It's icky, because the author has started lecturing the reader, and the character and story start to fracture as a result. As a novelist, you *have to* give primacy to your characters and your story. By giving them primacy, you let their own concerns, their own moral universes, fill the pages of your novel. You reach your reader through story, the only way a novelist should proceed.

Even wonderful novelists sometimes get this wrong. John Updike was a great novelist, one of the great writers of his generation. But in his late work *Terrorist*, he wrote the following paragraphs (slightly edited for length):

> *The deaths of insects and worms, their bodies so quickly absorbed by earth and weeds and road tar, devilishly try to tell Ahmad that his own death will be just as small and final. Walking to school, he has noticed a sign, a spiral traced on the pavement in luminous ichor, angelic slime from the body of some low creature, a worm or snail of which only this trace remains [...]*
>
> *So where did that body fly to? Perhaps it was snatched up by God and taken straight to Heaven. Ahmad's teacher, Shaikh Rashid, the imam at the mosque upstairs at 278½ West Main Street, tells him that according to the sacred traditions of the Hadith such things happen: the Messenger, riding the winged white horse Buraq, was guided through the seven heavens by the angel Gabriel to a certain place, where he prayed with Jesus, Moses and Abraham before returning to Earth, to become the last of the prophets, the ultimate one. His adventures that day are proved by the hoofprint, sharp and clear, that Buraq left on the Rock beneath the sacred Dome in the centre of Al-Quds, called Jerusalem by the infidels and Zionists, whose torments in the furnaces of Jahannan are well described in the seventh and eleventh and fiftieth suras of the Book of Books.*

This is terrible writing. There are things that Updike wants to tell us about life and death, the Muslim conception of heaven, the difference that faith makes. But to tell us these things he has to trample all over his central character. Ahmad is an eighteen-year-old boy who goes to a crappy public school in New Jersey, yet this kid sees a squashed worm and considers it 'a sign, a spiral traced on the pavement in luminous ichor'. I'd be willing to bet that you're better-educated and better-read than Ahmad is, but do you know what ichor is? I doubt it. (It's the ethereal fluid that the Greek Gods had instead of blood.) Straight from this piece of abstruse meditation, Ahmad hurtles into a short lecture on Mohammed's trip to heaven, Buraq's hoofprint, the wickedness of

Zionism and the scriptural references where all this can be looked up.

Seen as a riff by a Great Author, the material is all right. But we're reading a *novel*, for Pete's sake! We're meant to be getting into the mind of a confused Muslim kid in New Jersey, and all we get is Updike being Updike. Take the phrase 'whose torments ... are well described in the seventh and eleventh and fiftieth suras'. '*Well described*'? Do we really think that when Ahmad sees a squashed worm, he's going to start pondering the literary quality of various Koranic suras? That he's going to start listing the particular suras he has in mind? The truth is that we feel Updike's presence very strongly and Ahmad's presence hardly at all. The character who is supposedly leading the story simply has to stand aside while Updike spreads out his thematic wares. Meantime the story itself has just dwindled and died in a curl of luminous ichor.

The blue Pacific

That's the strange thing about themes. The closer you approach them, the cruder and less compelling they become.

In 1982, a popular author – Stephen King – wrote a collection of four novellas, titled *Different Seasons*. In the first of those, a jailed murderer, Red, reflected on his life in jail and on the successful jailbreak made by Andy Dufresne, a friend of his. Red doesn't know that Dufresne is planning to escape and only finds out after the break has been successfully made. He then starts to figure out how it was done, putting together the various elements of Dufresne's plan. One thing that puzzles Red is what took his buddy quite so long. He muses (slightly edited for length) as follows:

> *I think that maybe Andy got scared.*
> *I've told you as well as I can how it is to be an institutional man. At first you can't stand those four walls, then you get so you can abide them, then you get so you accept them ... and then, as your body and your mind and your spirit adjust to life*

on an HO scale, you get to love them. You are told when to eat,
when you can write letters, when you can smoke. [...]

I think Andy may have been wrestling with that tiger – that
institutional syndrome and also with the bulking fears that all of
it might have been for nothing.

How many nights must he have lain awake under his poster,
thinking about that sewer line, knowing that the one chance was
all he'd ever get?

Nothing in this passage pulls you away from the character or
the story. On the contrary, the passage pulls you into the story,
makes it vibrant. You think, 'Blimey, *yes*, what must it be like to
know you have one and only one chance of escape? What the
heck does imprisonment do to a person's sense of themselves?'
When you start looking for King's thematic concerns, you'll find
these issues popping up all over the place, but never idly, never
inappropriately. They pop up because the story puts them there,
because the characters do.

At the end of the novella, Red has finally served his sentence
and is let out on parole. Various clues lead him to the realisation
that Dufresne probably headed for Mexico and is inviting Red to
follow him. The novella ends:

I find that I am excited, so excited I can hardly hold the pencil in
my trembling hand. I think it is the excitement that only a free
man can feel, a free man starting a long journey whose conclusion
is uncertain.

I hope Andy is down there.
I hope I can make it across the border.
I hope to see my friend and shake his hand.
I hope the Pacific is as blue as it has been in my dreams.
I hope.

This is the moment when Red too is de-institutionalised. When
he feels excitement. When he realises that his outcomes are
uncertain. When he knows what it is to hope. The book is about

all these things: prison and freedom and courage and friendship and hope. It's about these things and it never once needs to tell you that it's about them. The story is what it is. The characters are what they are. The themes emerge as natural and inevitable as yolk from an egg.

I've chosen to illustrate this point with a Stephen King novella for a couple of reasons. The first is to remind you that you don't need to be a fancy writer to worry about themes. You don't have to be a John Updike for your work to have substance. You simply have to have a powerful story, tell it well, and let the magic of storytelling do the rest.

Secondly, you don't have to worry that thematic depth and commercial appeal are in contradiction. They aren't. Stephen King's novella was titled *Rita Hayworth and Shawshank Redemption*. In 1994, the novella was made into a film, *The Shawshank Redemption*, starring Tim Robbins and Morgan Freeman. The film's public release was poorly timed, and it was beaten up at the box office by *Forrest Gump*, *Pulp Fiction* and other work. Despite positive critical reviews (and seven Academy Award nominations), the film seemed, in commercial terms, to have flopped. Yet the film was, in its unflashy way, inspirational. It developed a cult following, and that cult following turned into a mass audience on video and DVD. The film came to have one of the most successful post-cinema lives of any film ever, and is regularly cited as one of the greatest films of all time.

If it's great, that's in part because of a good script, good acting, solid editing and all the rest of it. But those things aren't where its greatness lies. Its greatness lies in the power of its themes, and in the way they're allowed to emerge. Through character. Through story. If you are meticulous in taking care of those things, they'll take care of the rest – and the result will be a book that echoes in the memory, long after the specifics have been forgotten.

Chapter Summary

- Themes are the soul of a book – its deeper meaning and resonance.
- If you handle themes well, you may write a great book and a commercially successful one.
- But don't get didactic or too obvious – those things will kill your book.
- Instead, seek to ensure that your themes emerge naturally from your story and characters. If you do that, you won't have to force those deeper meanings to show themselves: they'll bubble up of their own accord.

Editing Your Manuscript

Interviewer: How much rewriting do you do?

Hemingway: It depends. I rewrote the ending of *Farewell to Arms*, the last page of it, thirty-nine times before I was satisfied.

Interviewer: Was there some technical problem there? What was it that had stumped you?

Hemingway: Getting the words right.

[**The Art of Fiction**, *The Paris Review* Interview, 1956]

Writing a book is a challenging business, to put it mildly, but you've already proved yourself a wise and discerning individual. After all, you've already purchased this book and read all the way to here. That's an exceedingly wise start, if I may say so. You now have two options:

- Absorb everything in this book. Complete your manuscript. Read it through once or twice, check it for typos, then send it to some agents. Or bung it up on Amazon. Either way, success awaits.

- Absorb as much as you can from this book. Finish writing and rewriting your work to the best of your ability. Put it to one side, come back to it cold, and set about another round of revisions (or two or five). Then, if you feel the need, get some professional editorial help. Use that help to drive your manuscript on to the next level. Go on working at your manuscript until it's as strong as you can possibly manage … then get it out to some agents or bung it up on Amazon.

I hope I don't need to tell you that the first of these options is not very likely to succeed. I know a good many authors, but I don't know a single one whose debut novel arrived more or less fully formed from the very first draft. I don't, if it comes to that, know many authors whose second, fifth or tenth book arrived with that much ease, either.

Alas, though, the second option isn't very likely to succeed either. Agents look at a thousand manuscripts for every one that they take on. Editors look at a fair number of manuscripts sent to them by agents for each one they take on. Self-publishers will look at the number of books on the Kindle store (well over seven million right now) and wonder about their chances of ever making it.

Readers and agents and publishers are right to be selective. The plain fact is that we live in an age when a lot of people take it into their heads to write a book. Many of those writers are undisciplined, careless, unlikely to succeed, but there will be many others, like yourself, who have talent, a good idea, and a willingness to work hard. At the same time, a narrowing retail climate means that publishers have been shrinking their lists, the editorial department has been losing acquisition authority to the sales and marketing teams, and an atmosphere of caution – based, in fairness, on harsh economic times – has militated against creative risk-taking. The digital revolution is exciting in one way, but also increases the uncertainties surrounding this most elderly of industries.

If you are to succeed against these unfavourable odds, in this unfavourable climate, your book needs to be excellent. It needs to dazzle. It needs to take a wonderful and necessary story, and to tell it in a wonderful and compelling way. If you aim even a fraction short of that target, you are unlikely to succeed. Even if you aim squarely at that target – even if you determine to be perfectionist right down to the last dot and comma, even if you are willing to rewrite and re-engineer your book until it is perfect – you will fall short. You'll fall short because perfection is not to be achieved in this world. Because even when you do all you can, your agent will see things that have passed you by and your publisher will call attention to a whole lot more. Never mind. The important point is that you cannot do too much. You cannot aim too high.

Ctrl-A, delete

The lesson here, then, is simple and tough. It's this: once you've reached the final full stop in your manuscript, you are only about halfway towards properly completing it. Perhaps a little more. More likely a darn sight less. Some writers talk about 'editing' their work in a way that suggests they think they've done the hard work, and what remains is just a question of chopping some excess verbiage and checking the commas. Such people will never be published. If they self-publish, they'd better be very productive and very committed marketers, because their work will never really excel.

At the same time, you'll find other people arguing that it makes no sense to chop and change a manuscript too much, since a publisher will demand changes of their own in any event. And indeed publishers will demand changes of their own – but they'll never do so from writers who think that way, because those writers will never be published, nor ever get close. You'll find other people willing to work tremendously hard at almost every aspect of their work, but who cannot give up on some central aspect of it which, for whatever reason, isn't suited to today's market or today's reader. Such writers may sweat away for years over multiple drafts, multiple revisions, multiple submissions to multiple agents. And they too will never be published.

The only mindset to adopt is one of radical openness to change. Every sentence, every paragraph, every scene and every chapter needs to be tested for soundness. Every character needs to be probed and inspected. The huge, unwieldy machinery of plot needs to be repeatedly checked for smooth function, pace, and credibility. The central conception of the novel itself – the very thing that first brought you to writing – needs to come under harsh review. Perhaps that conception is partly flawed. Perhaps you will have to give up on some of the things that led you here in the first place.

These are rules that all authors have to live by. My own first novel was a monster 180,000-words. By the time I'd finished it (with extensive editing en route), I had become a better writer than I was at the start. When I re-read the book, I realised that the first third of the book wasn't up to the standard of the rest, so I selected the first 60,000 words – that is, an amount equal to a short novel – and deleted them. Then I rewrote them. Then I edited the whole thing repeatedly until I was happy. Once, when I worried that I was overusing commas, I went through the entire manuscript, all 180,000 words of it, and removed half my commas. I wasn't peeved by having to do that. I was pleased when the novel read better.

And that first novel was a breeze. The second one was tough. I completed my second manuscript, a thriller of 120,000 words, in perhaps nine months of hard work. I'd found it tough and struggled to make the new book work, but thought I'd done enough. When I sent the work in to my publisher, they told me (in a very nice way) that the book was rubbish. Which it was. So I scrapped the whole thing and started again. The new version of that second book was still not my best novel, by any means, but it was infinitely better than the version before. When I got detailed (and relieved) editorial notes from my publisher, I was puzzled. My editor had made a load of useful but specific points about different aspects of the book, but there were some bigger issues I'd expected her to address that she hadn't mentioned. When I asked her directly if she felt that the middle third of the book was a tad weak, she said yes, it was. So I rewrote that middle section again and again, until I was happy with it. Then I got to grips with everything else that needed doing.

I'm happy to say that after that second book, my editorial disasters have been rather smaller in scale, my editing challenges fewer. On the other hand, I haven't turned into some superhuman novel-writing machine. I still edit carefully. My uncorrected drafts would still look like a very poor basis for a novel. But they don't matter. Jane Smiley once said, 'All first drafts are perfect, because all a first draft has to do is exist'.

She's right. Get a draft down. Use the tools you've acquired so far from this book to make sure that first draft is dodgy rather than terrible. Then start editing.

Your mother is a liar

There are no easy rules to guide you through this process. Logic would suggest that you stress-test the structural stuff first, then check character and voice, then get down to the nitty-gritty of pace, and scene, and prose – working from the large structural elements all the way down to sentences, words and commas. The trouble, however, is that creativity isn't a logical business. If you get a flash of insight about plot when working on your words-and-commas edit, you have to respond to that flash, no matter what your workflow plan happens to say. Likewise, it's often only the patient business of micro-editing that will reveal the structural disorders of plot that are afflicting the entire novel. If you're the sort of person who likes to set out with a plan, by all means fold one into your coat pocket before you set off. Just be prepared to ditch it at a moment's notice.

Nevertheless, in this land without rules, some guidelines do exist. Not all of them will work for every writer, but many of them will be useful to most. They are:

- *Give yourself time.* Once you've finished your manuscript – and after every major round of editing – give yourself a proper break from it. Two or three weeks as a minimum. Two or three months, ideally. In those off-periods, try not to think about your book. Go on holiday, learn a language, have an affair, climb some mountains. Do whatever it takes to give yourself as much distance from the manuscript as possible. You needed to create it with a warm eye. You should edit it with a cold one.

- *Try reading out loud.* This is a technique that doesn't work for me and I feel like an idiot if ever I try it. But some writers swear by it, and you may be one of them. So: stand in an empty room, a long way away from mirrors, tape recorders or loved ones and read your book aloud. If it sounds glitchy or awkward, your prose may need correcting. If it sounds fluid and smooth, you are a creative genius who got things right first go. (A friend who teaches writing says she recommends this exercise a lot and about a third of her students say they really benefit. So do give it a go.)

- *Find your editing rhythm.* Some professional authors like to slap a first draft down on paper as fast as they can, in order to have something to work with. They know that a massive amount of reworking awaits them, but they'd rather be reworking *something* than be grappling to create the thing in the first place. I, and probably a majority of authors, take the opposite approach. I re-edit fairly extensively as I write, because re-editing is my way of thinking myself into the book. It's what provides me with the creative depth to nudge the story forwards in broadly the right direction. That doesn't release me from the burden of editing after completing the book, but it leaves me with a better first draft than I'd otherwise have.

- *Do edits for specific issues.* If you know there is a particular problem in your book that you need to address – a pacing issue, let's say, or some aspect of characterisation – then be prepared to go through the manuscript looking for that issue, and that issue alone. If you simply embark on a succession of general-purpose edits, you'll find yourself repetitively addressing and re-addressing whichever issues are uppermost in your mind and ignoring other, possibly more relevant, ones.

- *Don't trust your mother.* Your mother loves you. She will love your manuscript. So let her read it by all means. Listen to what she has to say about it. But that glow of loving adoration doesn't mean you're Tolstoy. It means she's your mother.

- *Re-read this book.* If you first encountered this book as you were starting to put your own manuscript together, you should re-read it once you're done. Issues that didn't register large with you the first time round may resonate differently a second time. If you have other 'how to write' work on your shelves, re-read that too. Argue with it. Grapple with those rules and suggestions in the context of your now-completed manuscript. If a suggestion doesn't seem to make sense – and if you're certain that's not your stubbornness or resistance to the market speaking – it's fine to ignore it. Even the process of argument will clarify things.

- *Read lots of fiction.* The more you write, the more wisely and insightfully you will read. You'll start to notice how some good writers break certain rules and appear to get away with it. You'll notice how other writers break the same rules and write lousy books. Start to read like a writer and your work will improve. It can't not.

Getting the words right

The editing road can be long and hard. At times, it can seem endless and unrewarded. There's not much comfort I can offer, except to say that we've all had to walk it. I've had to. Hemingway had to. You'll have to. And whether it's rewarding or not depends a little on what you mean by reward. Hemingway won a Nobel Prize, which may be a little outside my grasp and yours, but he wasn't thinking of Oslo when he tore that thirty-ninth sheet of paper victorious from his typewriter. He was thinking of his *words*, that sense of achievement when he – finally, finally! – found a form of expression that precisely and economically said what he meant. That kind of satisfaction is in my grasp, and in yours. It's why we do what we do.

Need More Help?

I love editing. I love having the real meat of a novel down on the page and having the opportunity to tweak it and pluck it into beautiful order. But the process (especially for less experienced writers) can be overwhelming. So we created a tool that helps you organise your editing process into layers. Follow the tool – create a beautiful book. Easy, right? You get the tool (and its sisters) right here:

jerichowriters.com/how-to-write-a-novel-free-resources

Chapter Summary

- Editing your first draft manuscript is not about cutting some excess verbiage and checking for typos. It's about everything: plot, character, prose style, subplot – everything.
- Unless you have a radical willingness to make alterations in your work – including, where necessary, elements that you've always considered to be central – your work won't succeed.
- Edit and edit and edit and edit.
- Then edit some more.

GETTING HELP

Novelists need help. Professional novelists need help the least, but they get the most. They have their agent and their editor and, quite likely, some professional novel-writing friends on hand to assist. What's more, they have a history of engagement with the industry and the craft. When talent and inspiration prove insufficient, pro authors have experience and technique and confidence of past success to fall back on. Even with such things to help, many a good novelist writes many a bad novel. It's not an easy game and inspiration is an uncertain mistress. With a little luck, though, a pro author won't have their career derailed by a single dodgy book. Both publishers and readers are wise enough to forgive the odd mistake.

The amateur writer is in a worse position in every respect. You are likely to need more help than those grizzled old pros. You do not have an agent or an editor on your team. You do not have the experience of successful authorship to get you through those sticky patches. And you cannot afford for your first novel to be anything less than dazzling. If you are writing espionage fiction, then your novel will be competing head-to-head with John le Carré. If you're writing romance, you're going right up against Nora Roberts. Their books will have far more retail prominence than yours; more (and probably better) reviews; more investment by the publisher; a loyal readership; infinitely more brand recognition – and, e-books aside, they will be priced the same as yours. It's an appalling commercial position to find yourself in. Your only possible option is to ensure that your product – your book – is stunning. Nothing else will do.

Some new writers scrabble to that happy position without external help. That's partly the good fortune of inspiration. Most writers come to writing because they're struck by the necessity to tell a particular story in a particular way. If that inspiration is a good one, it may bear the writer safely over any number of technical challenges. When I wrote my first novel, I was a less good writer than I am today, but I had a cracking idea for a story and that idea was enough to carry the book, despite my technical deficiencies. My learning on the job since then has been an apprenticeship carried out under battlefield conditions; a daft way to learn a trade.

And I've been lucky. Plenty of authors have experienced a much rougher entry into the profession. I know one internationally bestselling, prize-winning, critically acclaimed author who has more unpublished novels in his bottom drawer than he has published novels on the shelves above – and he's published a fair few books. I know other, less famous, authors of whom the same is true.

One moral to draw from these ruminations is that persistence counts for a lot – and it does, it truly does. But you can play it dumb or you can play it smart. Persistence isn't only about trying the same thing again and again until, by some mysterious chemistry, you happen to get it right. Persistence can be – should be – about two things: learning the craft and improving your book. The two things are different, and you need to do both.

Learning the craft

This book has offered a disciplined walk-through of a massive and elusive subject. It's hardly the last word on the subject, however, and I hope you feel inspired to read other 'how to' books that come at the same topics with a different emphasis. Let the books you read argue with each other. Argue back at them. When you read fiction, read it with a new eye, a technician's eye, and let every book you read join in the argument. You won't find unanimity, or anything like it, but you will, by sorting through the disagreements, come to know your own views. You'll learn what works for you, understand the areas where your work is weakest, start to assemble tools and techniques for dealing with them.

Courses offer something similar. If you've already started to write your novel, and if you've made decent use of this book, you're probably already beyond most elementary 'how to write' courses, but that doesn't mean there aren't courses that could help. If you're the sort of person who likes courses, you should be looking for two things. First, you need a course leader with a credible track record. For my money, that means that you should avoid the kind of creative writing tutor whose publication record consists of poetry, short stories, specialist non-fiction, or literary novels produced by marginal publishers. I don't have anything against any of those things. T.S. Eliot never wrote a novel, but I believe his poetry is considered quite good. Alice Munro has never written a novel, but her short stories are thought to be all right. Nevertheless, you are writing a novel (or book of narrative non-fiction) and you are hoping to sell it to the kind of publisher that actually does some of the things publishers are meant to do: pay advances, secure retail space, invest in marketing, and so on.

You *may* be able to learn the necessary skills from someone who has never achieved that goal themselves, but personally I wouldn't count on it. If you want to make a chair, learn from someone who makes chairs for a living. If you want to write a book, learn from someone who has written books that have been bought for proper money by proper publishers. Nothing else makes sense.

Secondly, you need to make sure that the course comes with a proper amount of one-to-one feedback. It needs to be a course where you write stuff and get told, personally, what is and isn't working in the piece you've written. If you don't get that personalised feedback, if what you get is essentially just a set of course notes and assignments, you may as well not bother with the course and simply read a good book about writing technique – this one, for example. It'll cost you less, take less time, and you can do it in the bath.

You should also studiously ignore qualifications and certificates. There are people who have MAs and MFAs and PhDs in Creative Writing. They've achieved Distinctions and Magna Cum Laudes – and they've never published a book. They've written a load of pretty sentences and they can talk better than I can about the post-Barthesian reader and the Flaubertian flâneur, but *they've never published a book*. If you want a certificate to decorate your wall, then commission something grand from your local printer. Make yourself a Knight Commander of the Holy Roman Empire, for all I care. In the meantime, if you want to get published, focus only on doing what it takes to write and sell something marvellous. An MA or MFA *may* be part of that process. It may well be right for you (and it'll probably enrich your life in numerous important ways). But do remember that the qualification itself is, in publishing terms, an irrelevance.

If a full-length course is too much for your wallet, your life, or your patience, then there are some very good, short residential courses available. These are often fun, often inspirational. Again, though, do check what you're going to get from them. Plenty of courses aim at making you *feel* like a writer. They aim to give you the heady rush of creating a lovely metaphor or a group-written short story. But writers don't necessarily feel like writers; they just *are* writers. I don't get all pink and gigglesome when a nice metaphor pops onto my page. I have never experienced the rush of a group-written short story and I most likely never will. A good residential course is led by a grizzled pro novelist and allows plenty of time for that grizzled pro novelist to tell you, personally and precisely, why your work is no bloody good. That kind of learning isn't always fun, but your writing will stride forwards.

I should also say that Jericho Writers offers a number of courses. We're not as comprehensive in what we offer as some other providers, but we are keenly, keenly aware of what works for students. If a course works, we try to expand it. If a course doesn't really sizzle, we'll quietly fold it away. Because we're run by writers for writers, the thing that matters most to us is whether our clients benefit from what we sell. Making money is, and has always been, secondary to that goal. (For that reason, we have never once employed a salesperson. I suspect we never will.)

Improving your book

Much though they offer, books and workshops and courses have one limitation. Of necessity, they teach the craft of writing. They're about how to write *in general*; they're not about *your* book. And in the end, it doesn't really matter if you don't understand multi-protagonist plotting in a dual-time-strand story. If that doesn't apply to you, you can be as cack-handed with time-travelling multiple protagonists as you care to be. You don't have to know the rules in any formal academic sense, because you will never be tested on them. All that ultimately matters – to you, your putative agent and your putative publisher – is this: *Is your manuscript any good?* If the answer to that question is 'No, not yet, not enough', then crouching in the shadows next to it is the million-dollar follow-up: *What must you do to get your manuscript into shape?*

There is now a gold-standard way of approaching that most terrifying of questions. You hire a professional editor to read through your manuscript, cover to cover. You pay that editor to tell you the unvarnished truth. Is your book good enough? If not, why not? And what do you need to do to fix it? You will get a long editorial report on your work and (if it's a decent consultancy) the opportunity to grill your editor.

Obviously, my own consultancy – Jericho Writers – offers precisely that service. We are, I think, very good and we're good in part because most of us are authors ourselves. We're foot soldiers, like you. Dirty boots and rifles that jam. That common experience means we've shared your problems and have had to grope our way, ourselves, to solutions. It's that experience we get to share with you.

The editorial process won't give you a systematic introduction to writing technique – that's not its purpose – but it will tell you exactly what your issues are and offer some kind of road map for solving them. If you have a decent editor, you're likely to find the experience in equal parts shocking and inspiring. It's shocking, because of the appalling clarity with which a good pro editor can see the issues in your work. It's inspiring for exactly the same reason. If you're a genuine writer, with a proper degree of commitment to your project, then coming to understand its deficiencies will produce a sense of relief. (Not straight away, necessarily. It's perfectly normal to spend a day or two drinking, crying, or kicking the cat.) The relief comes from knowing what to do, from finding your vague and elusive anxieties about your manuscript given concrete and specific expression. Going on to fix those issues is a whole new challenge, of course – but you're a writer, so you're up for a challenge. At least you know what you need to do and have been given a good idea of how to go about doing it.

Now, of course, I do have an interest to declare. Jericho Writers offers these exact services, so it's hardly a surprise that I think these services are useful. On the other hand, if editorial feedback weren't helpful, publishing houses wouldn't employ editors. Agencies such as mine are simply making the same services available to those who don't yet have a publisher. It's a bold author who thinks they are beyond editing altogether.

If you want to know what I think, it's that expert third-party feedback still represents the gold-standard method for improving a book. Nothing else comes close. Yes: courses build skills and they're great. Yes: writers' conferences are a brilliant way to understand the industry and pitch direct to agents. But if I could only pick one service? The one I'd pick every time is that one-on-one editorial interaction. It's like an authorial equivalent of Douglas Adams's Pan Galactic Gargle Blaster, like 'having your brains smashed in by a slice of lemon wrapped around a large gold brick'. The experience is intimidating and shocking and exhilarating and liberating. All those things, in one.

Finally, let me be clear about what 'editing' means. Editors almost never *edit* a book. Their job is to provide advice and suggestions, but it remains the author's job to integrate that advice into the final manuscript. Editing is, almost always, an advisory function and if you seek third-party editorial help, you should expect to receive advice rather than hands-on editing. The distinction is crucial. There are any number of editors who will offer to do a hands-on edit of your work, for a fee often running into the thousands of dollars. (The service is usually called developmental editing, but it goes by various names.) To a new writer, the proposition can look very tempting. A pro author is offering to fix your manuscript? Sounds great! What's a few thousand bucks, if publication is the prize?

Alas, the deal sounds far better than it is. The trouble is that the vast majority of manuscripts by first-time authors have significant structural issues. Those things can only be fixed by heavy-duty structural work, of the sort that could easily take months to carry out. The fee you pay for hands-on editing won't cover that amount of work, so what you'll end up with is a manuscript that's been spruced up – excess adjectives cut, sentences tightened, commas all in the right place – but still fundamentally flawed. In effect, you'll have paid to wallpaper a room that hasn't yet been plastered. You'll have a clean and tidy version of what is, fundamentally, still an unsaleable manuscript.

When it comes to fiction, I've almost never come across a novel that was basically saleable but just needed a heavy-duty copyedit. After fifteen years of running Jericho Writers – and literally thousands of novels later – I can think of only a tiny handful of exceptions, and those were mostly cases where the author was a non-native speaker of English. With non-fiction, things are a little different. If you have an amazing story to tell, but aren't a fluent storyteller, it may well be worth getting a hands-on edit from a pro author. But take care. It's easy to spend a lot of money for little reward. If in doubt, go with the cheaper option – taking editorial advice from a reputable source – then seeing what your editor soberly recommends. In some cases, it will make sense for you to revise the manuscript yourself. In other cases, self-publication is the logical option. In a small minority of cases, it may be worth spending the money needed for a proper hands-on edit.

Getting support

Everything we've discussed so far in this chapter sounds terribly sensible. Books to read, courses to go on, advice to seek. And while sense matters, it's not the only thing. Writing is a famously lonely business, and there are times when any writer needs support: times when your mother's unshakeable belief that you're Leo Tolstoy feels comforting rather than delusional. By all means, grab whatever support you can. Cups of tea and slices of cake and mildly delusional talk about great Russian writers are, in my experience, all indispensable. But once you've wiped your mouth and pushed your chair back, there may be other things to think about too.

- *Online writing communities.* These vary a lot in quality. The worst ones are overwhelmed by suspicious amateurs spreading conspiracy theories about the literary industry and trying to promote their own unreadable e-books. The best ones have a good sprinkling of pro authors on board and are mostly populated by serious amateur writers seeking a supportive but not uncritical environment. Jericho Writers hosts just such a community and I think it's very good indeed. But is it right for you? I have no idea. You simply need to browse a variety of sites, understand their different flavours, and set up camp wherever you feel most at home. The more you put in, the more you'll get out.

- *Writers' circles.* These too vary a lot in quality. The best are excellent (and will often contain at least a couple of published writers). The worst are bitchy, depressing and counter-productive. There's no way to tell in advance whether a given group is going to help you or not. The answer is simply to try it and see. You'll soon know whether it's going to work out or not.

- *The blogo-tweeto-sphere.* If you like the whole blogging, tweeting, Facebook thing, you are probably already doing it. If you're not, you probably wouldn't enjoy it if you did. But if you do have an active online presence, and if you haven't yet hooked up with other passionate writers, you should nose around on the web to find people who share your passions. Because writers care about how they present themselves in words, the quality of blogs tends to be high, tweets tend to be witty, and messages of support tend to be genuine.

- *Workshops and courses.* Finally, I spoke about workshops and courses in the previous section purely as a means of learning, in a disciplined fashion, about writing technique. But courses (especially residential ones) are also about bonding and community. If writing alone is getting you down, a well-run course may well give you the shot of energy you need to keep you going. Nor do those courses any longer have to be held in intimidatingly rundown facilities with terrible plumbing. There are now plenty of creative writing holidays that combine prose tutorials in the morning and hot beaches in the afternoon. There's no reason why your writing vacation shouldn't be a proper vacation as well as teaching you something about writing.

Making contacts

I used to think that making contacts didn't matter. I used to be of the view that the only thing that really mattered was writing a wonderful book, presenting it to agents in a suitably professional manner, and letting the logic of the industry take care of the rest. I still mostly think that.

But there are exceptions. Jericho Writers runs the biggest writers' conference in the UK. It's a place where writers can come to attend workshops, talks and courses. Numerous agents and publishers are also present, and a key feature of any decent conference is the availability of one-to-one sessions where agents and editors give writers direct feedback on their work. To begin with, I had some private reservations about the value of all this. Sure, I could understand the benefit of workshops on writing technique, and the like, but I couldn't really see that those one-to-one sessions added anything at all. If a writer wants proper feedback on their work, why not get a full-length editorial report? If a writer wants to submit work to an agent, why not simply send a few emails?

Those reservations have been proved wrong. For one thing, there's the value of direct feedback from an agent. Instead of a pre-printed rejection slip, the writer will get a candid opinion. 'I couldn't sell this manuscript because your prose style is sloppy.' 'This manuscript seems well-written, but your pitch was unclear and I felt uncertain how such a book could be marketed.' 'Actually, this project intrigues me. I don't think the quality of execution is yet strong enough, but I'd love to see a rewrite if you're doing one.' Such comments can be hugely valuable, especially because you have the opportunity to explore what lies behind them, and to do that face to face with your chosen agent. A full-length editorial report from someone who has read the entire manuscript is still the gold-standard form of feedback, but the brief snippets you can get from an agent add something different, and valuable, to your store of knowledge.

Secondly, there *is* something depressing in the slush pile. No agent, no matter how generous-hearted, is immune to the sinking feeling inspired by a tottering pile of unread paper. If you meet that agent, your manuscript is no longer faceless. And if you remember to smile plenty, say your pleases and thank yous, avoid spilling coffee down the agent's new Christian Lacroix number, and generally make yourself agreeable, the agent in question may even remember you with fondness. A little thing, perhaps, but little things can make a difference.

Then too, there's the synchronicity of it all. You might go to a workshop on plotting in the morning, get feedback from an agent in the afternoon, glean insights from fellow writers over tea, then share a drink with a publisher over dinner. The sheer wealth and simultaneity of insights can vastly accelerate your learning process. The buzz and inspiration can turbo-charge your enthusiasm for the various steps that face you next. There's no particular logic in this; it's just that the human animal isn't a particularly logical creature.

And finally, all good books start with buzz. Usually that buzz starts when an agent gets a wonderful manuscript out to publishers, but it can start very much sooner. At the very first festival we ran, we held a competition which involved a small group of first-time writers reading their work out loud to the festival audience. The competition was judged by popular vote and threw up a clear winner. By the end of that evening, the writer in question had been approached by two agents. By the end of the weekend, by six. Not long after that, the book was sold for an excellent price at a widely contested auction. Clearly that kind of outcome isn't the normal result of going to a festival, but it couldn't have happened quite like that any other way.

If the idea of going to a conference appeals to you, there are a few things to look for. First, as ever, make sure that those leading talks and workshops have a proper depth of experience. Secondly, do make sure that you'll have the opportunity to sit down one-to-one with an agent or two and – ideally – that your work will have been read by that person well in advance of your session. Thirdly, and crucially in my view, it's important that the conference offers overnight accommodation. Many of the most important encounters at these events are informal ones: sharing lunch with a publisher, buying a drink for an agent. If the publishers and agents are simply dropping in to deliver their gig, then rushing off again, the opportunities for those informal meetings will be drastically reduced. While it's easiest for conference organisers to locate their events close to the publishing world's key hubs in London and New York, you may well get more value from events held out of town. If in doubt, ask the organisers. Don't just pitch up and hope for the best.

It's also important to prepare. Make a list of the agents and publishers attending a particular event. Write short notes on who they are and what they handle. Mark the names of your key targets, those who you are keenest to meet, and also identify the people you don't want to waste your time with. Carry that information with you at the event and refer to it as you need. That doesn't mean you should be crass or pushy with agents when you do meet them – nothing will put them off faster – but it does mean that you will make the most of the opportunities that come your way. Additionally, it's just dumb to turn up to one of these things with an undercooked manuscript. There's no point in an agent remembering how charming you were if they also remember how bad your manuscript was. Work hard on your manuscript before the event, and if necessary get third-party editorial advice on it well in advance. Even if your manuscript isn't yet the finished article, agents will remember work of real promise and will be anxious to see it again.

Knowing when to stop

Self-editing, rewriting, persistence, self-belief. These have been the watchwords of this chapter and the previous one. They are the watchwords of any decent writer's search for publication.

At the same time, it's important to know when to stop. Not when to stop writing, but when to ditch your current project. Most writers come to writing because they're struck by a bolt of inspiration so compelling, so urgent in its insistence, that they have to obey its call. Good. Obey it. But perhaps this project isn't the one that is going to be your breakthrough. Perhaps that original conception becomes a dead weight which prevents you from moving on to new, different, stronger ideas.

Writers get better by writing. A prose style shot through with hackneyed or cumbersome expressions becomes cleaned up into something swift and efficient. A plot overburdened with events becomes slick and well-engineered. But slick efficiency isn't, these days, normally enough to sell a book. You need more. You need dazzle. You need a voice that sounds like you and no one else.

That voice will come, more than anything else, from practice. Rewriting an existing manuscript is one sort of practice. Writing a whole damn novel from scratch is quite another. You may need to do both. If your first novel doesn't get taken on, your second might. If your second doesn't, your fifth might. Just practice, get better, improve.

There's one exception to this rule. Everything in this chapter applies to the writer of non-fiction, except for what I've just said in this very last section. If you are writing some form of memoir, quite likely you can't simply drop one tale and pick up another. Few lives have *any* books in them; it's darn rare that a life has more than one. If you write your story, and edit it to the highest possible standard, and pitch it as professionally as you can, and still get nowhere, then you have a tough decision to make, whose primary choices are:

(A) give up, pleased nevertheless to have given it a go;

(B) self-publish the book, so that your loved ones have a secure, permanent record;

(C) explore whether your story is strong enough that it makes sense to employ a ghostwriter.

I'd hope that few writers chose option (A). It's easy enough to self-publish these days, that it seems crazy to me to write your life story and then not get it properly printed and bound. The costs aren't extravagant, and the result may be something that your great-grandchildren will treasure a century down the line.

The third option, ghostwriting, will not work for most people. Most life stories simply aren't so dazzling that a ghostwriter is all that stands between them and publication. But there are exceptions. If you care to explore whether your story could be one of those exceptions, do remember that the people you talk to will generally have a significant financial incentive to sell you their services – and ghostwriting (if it's competent) doesn't come cheap. You therefore need to deal with reputable providers and to use your own commercial nous. If you're a thrice-decorated helicopter gunship pilot with battle scars from four different conflicts, then, my friend, I know a publisher who wants your story. If you have enjoyed some entertaining caravanning holidays with your wife, the only likely publisher is you. Both stories are worthwhile, as mementoes of a life. But commercial publishers aren't interested in lives – they're only interested, poor saps, in the money.

Chapter Summary

- Professional writers have agents and editors to help them over difficulties. You don't need to be shy about calling for help too.

- Courses and workshops can be a good way to review the essentials of the writing craft.

- If you want specific feedback on your manuscript, getting editorial advice from a properly qualified editorial consultant can be a vastly helpful step to take.

- Most writers will not, however, want to pay an editor to 'edit' the manuscript directly: this is almost always a waste of money.

- If you want support, ask your mum.

- If you want more support, try writers' groups, online or offline.

- Writers' festivals and conferences can be a brilliant way to meet agents and get feedback direct from market practitioners. It's best to come to such things well-prepared, and with your manuscript in decent shape.

- At a certain point, give up. Not all writers will succeed with their first manuscript. Plenty of pro authors have been in the same position.

- If you've written a memoir and haven't been able to secure a publisher despite your most diligent efforts, then for Pete's sake, self-publish, so you have some bound copies to preserve your work. You owe it to yourself and to your family in equal measure.

CONCLUSION

Der Worte sind genug gewechselt,

lasst mich auch endlich Taten sehn!

[Enough words have been exchanged;

now at last let me see some deeds!]

– Goethe

Enough. This has been a theoretical book about a practical subject. You need to know the theory of metalworking before it makes sense to let you loose on a lathe, but it's only when the first bit of swarf starts curling from the tip of your cutting tool that you'll really start to learn the subject in the way that matters. In your fingertips, with a workman's eye.

So get stuck in. Write. Write a bad manuscript, because that's typically the essential first step to writing a good one.

Read plenty. Read books in your area. Read books in other areas. Re-read this book and let yourself disagree with it.

Pound your manuscript hard. Write it, edit it, then rewrite it and re-edit it. Nothing is too much. You and Hemingway both: the golden thirty-ninth.

Get help. Get tough, challenging, professional help, and make the very most of the insights that such help can provide. Don't let anyone boss you, though. It's your book, your decisions. Do as you think is right, don't do as you're told.

Meet writers. Engage with them and with agents and the industry. Don't look down on the commercial aspects of your craft. You're creating a product for market, so understand the market. That's not selling out, it's selling.

Above all, enjoy it. Writing is a mug's game. It's insanely competitive, appallingly paid, and the only good news about the terrible pay is that the job is so woefully insecure you probably won't have to endure it for long. No one goes into an industry like this to advance a career or pay a heating bill. You go into it for the joy of it, the creative joy. Don't lose that. It's the precious metal from which all else is beaten.

Now nothing remains but to get started. Good luck.

GET MORE HELP

As I mentioned throughout the book, we've designed specific tools to help support you in your writing journey. Here they are in all their glory:

The Idea Generator –
Exactly what it sounds like. You'll think it can't work, but it really does.

The Ultimate Character Builder –
Designed to help you build detailed, richly imagined character profiles

Plotting Worksheets –
Want to get a grip of your plot? These beauties will help you do just that.

Self-editing Pyramid –
A tool that helps you organise your editing process.

The simplest way to get your paws on them is to go here and have us send them to you:

jerichowriters.com/how-to-write-a-novel-free-resources

These tools are completely free, and they're there to help!

ABOUT JERICHO WRITERS

If you've read this far, you'll already have gathered something about what we at Jericho Writers have to offer. But, just so you have everything in one place, we offer:

- **A membership service.** We have a whole ton of video courses, masterclasses, agent search tools, and more. Basically, once you pay your (fairly modest) membership fee, you get a whole all-you-can-eat-buffet of writerly goodness. If you want to know more, go to jerichowriters.com and hit Join Us. That'll tell you everything you need to know. Our aim is to offer more resources for less money than anyone else and to achieve that aim by a country mile.

- **An editorial service.** I've already told you all you need about that. Basically: we get one of our brilliant editors to read your manuscript, cover to cover, and tell you exactly where it's falling down and how to fix it. That's an awesome service, but don't go rushing out to buy it yet. You'll only get good value from the service if you've written your book, worked damn hard on editing it into shape, and are then looking for help with the final stages. That's where we'll be most helpful, most value-added.

- **Courses.** And mentoring. And pretty much anything else you might require. The purpose behind all these things is to help you write better and achieve your goals for publication.

- **Events.** This is where you get to meet authors and agents and publishers and self-publishing experts and everyone else you need to make sense of your career. The best event of all is our annual Festival of Writing (held in York,

England) which is inspirational, exhausting, amazing – and a reliable creator of terrific book deals.

That's the business side of what we do, but we're here for everyone, not just those with cash to spend. We also:

- Run an online writers' community. It's free. It's intelligent. It's superbly well-informed. And it's extremely welcoming of people like you – that is to say, of all writers. You can find our community here: community. jerichowriters.com

- Send out regular advice emails. About writing technique, publishing issues, self-publishing techniques and the market for books. These emails aren't salesy. They're there to help you solve the problems that you encounter now and in your future career. We have tens of thousands of readers and we get a ton of feedback telling us that people appreciate the help. You can sign up to that email list here: jerichowriters.com/sign-up-news-updates

Oh, and if you want to talk to me, you can. Readers often reply to my weekly advice email and I try to answer everyone who writes in.

Finally, don't think that this book is all there is. The first of the Jericho Writers Guides, and a sister book to *How to Write a Novel, Getting Published: how to hook an agent, get a deal and build a career you love* is available to purchase now. As is my *52 Letters* series, a years' worth of advice on writing, editing, book marketing, writing from the heart, and so much more. We'll be bringing out further titles pretty soon. They're all stuffed full of good things, and your life won't be complete until you have 'em all.

Thanks for reading – and enjoy your writing.

Harry
Oxfordshire, 2020

Printed in Great Britain
by Amazon

23427119R00264